Regulating Credit Rating Agencies

ELGAR FINANCIAL LAW

Series editor: Takis Tridimas, *Queen Mary, University of London, UK*

This important series comprises high-quality monographs on a wide range of topics in the field of financial law, hosting work by established authors of international reputation, alongside younger and more emerging authors. The series is synonymous with original thinking and new, challenging research. The subjects under consideration range from financial services law, through securities regulation, to banking law and from financial fraud, through legal aspects of European Monetary Union and the single currency, to the legal workings of international financial institutions.

Titles in the series include:

Law and Corporate Finance
Frank B. Cross and Robert A. Prentice

Secured Transactions Reform and Access to Credit
Edited by Frederique Dahan and John Simpson

Financial Regulation in Crisis?
The Role of the Law and the Failure of Northern Rock
Edited by Joanna Gray and Orkun Akseli

Law Reform and Financial Markets
Edited by Kern Alexander and Niamh Moloney

Regulating Credit Rating Agencies
Aline Darbellay

Regulating Credit Rating Agencies

Aline Darbellay

University of Zurich, Switzerland and University of San Diego, USA

ELGAR FINANCIAL LAW

Edward Elgar

Cheltenham, UK • Northampton, MA, USA

Published by
Edward Elgar Publishing Limited
The Lypiatts
15 Lansdown Road
Cheltenham
Glos GL50 2JA
UK

Edward Elgar Publishing, Inc.
William Pratt House
9 Dewey Court
Northampton
Massachusetts 01060
USA

A catalogue record for this book
is available from the British Library

Library of Congress Control Number: 2013936173

This book is available electronically in the ElgarOnline.com Law Subject Collection, E-ISBN 978 0 85793 936 4

MIX
Paper from responsible sources
FSC® C013056

ISBN 978 0 85793 935 7

Typeset by Columns Design XML Ltd, Reading
Printed and bound in Great Britain by T.J. International Ltd, Padstow

To my husband Alfusainey

Contents

Foreword viii
Acknowledgements x
List of abbreviations xi
Table of cases xiii
Table of legislation and statutory instruments xiv

PART 1: PRELUDE TO THE CREDIT RATING INDUSTRY

1. Introduction 3
2. History of credit rating agencies 13
3. Description of the credit rating industry 29

PART 2: REGULATORY STRUCTURE

4. Rating-based regulations 45
5. Regulatory treatment of credit rating agencies 64
6. Regulatory trends 85

PART 3: USES AND ABUSES OF CREDIT RATINGS IN STRUCTURED FINANCE

7. Growth of the structured finance segment 93
8. Wrong incentives in the credit rating industry 120
9. Regulatory response to the problems of structured finance ratings 144

PART 4: SYSTEM-WIDE EFFECTS OF CREDIT RATING DOWNGRADES

10. System-relevance of credit ratings 155
11. Market reactions to credit rating downgrades and their consequences 179
12. Regulatory response to the systemic issue 197

PART 5: TRENDS AND OUTLOOK

13. Restoring competition in the credit rating industry 207
14. Concluding remarks 236

Bibliography 238
Index 255

Foreword

Credit rating agencies have become the first port of call for corporate issuers, investors and financial institutions in assessing credit risk and for determining compliance with regulatory requirements. The multitude of regulations that require credit ratings to be used for assessing credit risks and that only a few designated rating agencies are allowed to issue official ratings has had the effect of limiting competition in the ratings industry and contributing to market failures. As a result, rating agencies have acquired immense influence and power, particularly in financial markets. The failure of the ratings industry to provide accurate risk assessments was demonstrated with the collapse of Enron and the bursting of the Dotcom bubble in the early 2000s and later with the collapse of the US residential mortgage market and structured finance and securitization markets in 2007 and 2008. These market and regulatory failures led to calls for fundamental reform of the regulation of the ratings industry. Although there have been numerous studies examining how poor governance and conflicts of interest at rating agencies created the moral hazard that led to grossly optimistic assessments of risk in the mortgage and wholesale debt markets, few have systematically analyzed how credit ratings have come to influence the development of financial markets over the past century and how regulation of the ratings industry and the use of credit ratings in regulatory requirements have played a key role in substantially limiting competition in the credit ratings industry and how regulatory reforms in Europe and the US continue to fail to address the regulatory and financial risks posed by the ratings industry.

Aline Darbellay's *Regulating Credit Rating Agencies* is an important work that addresses these issues. The book shows how the ratings industry developed and came to play such an important role in influencing not only investor behavior, but also the structure of financial markets. In doing so, the book traces the historical development of the ratings industry in the United States in the late nineteenth and early twentieth centuries and how the US regulatory reforms of the 1930s led to a move away from the investor-pays model to the issuer-pays model of credit ratings and how ratings began to be embedded in US financial regulation. The book discusses the conflicts of interest and moral hazard that can be attributed to the issuer-pays model to the extent that rating agencies may award higher ratings in order not to jeopardize business relationships with their client issuers. This was especially the case with rating agencies that awarded AAA ratings to structured finance products that were arranged by investment banks – such as, for example, Barclays Capital, Merrill Lynch, UBS, Lehman Brothers and Goldman Sachs – in the period before the global financial crisis began in 2007. The weaknesses in this model contributed to a financial crisis from which the global economy has not yet recovered and has led to regulatory reforms, such as the US Dodd-Frank Act of 2010, that seek to expunge ratings from all financial regulatory requirements.

The book details how the evolving regulatory framework governing the ratings industry and the regulation of institutional investors and prudential bank regulation provided the main impetus for the systemic role that rating agencies play in today's global financial markets. Other important parts of the book detail how the regulation of rating agencies and the issuance of credit ratings of financial instruments became important drivers of financial innovation and growth in the equity, wholesale debt and structured finance markets. The book's outstanding contribution to the literature will be to show how financial regulation itself has led to an uncompetitive oligopolistic structure in the ratings industry and how this has impaired the quality of ratings, particularly in assessing investment risks for regulated institutional investors and in determining the level of regulatory capital for banks and other financial institutions and the implications for financial stability and the efficient operation of financial markets.

Kern Alexander, Cambridge, England

Acknowledgements

I would like to thank Professor Rolf H Weber to whom I am greatly indebted for his academic support. A lot of credit goes to him for his time, input and guidance throughout my research activities. A special thank you goes to Professor Frank Partnoy for his precious advice and invaluable suggestions. He has been a significant source of inspiration for this academic work. I acknowledge Professor Kern Alexander for his helpful observations and his involvement in this study.

I am very grateful to the University of Zurich and to the University of San Diego School of Law for making this research possible and, moreover, acknowledge that this academic work would not have been possible without the generous financial support of the Swiss National Science Foundation (Fellowship for Prospective Researchers) and the support of Professor Thomas Gächter in this context.

I am grateful to Professor George Mundstock, Professor Daniel J Mogin, Sean Egan, Dr David Vasella, Aneesh Pande and David Rosario for their insightful comments and stimulating discussions. My particular thanks go to Professor Christine Kaufmann for her encouragement. I also wish to express my very sincere thanks to Dr Alison Wiebalck for her contribution with respect to the language.

I thank Professor Lars Gorton and Professor Jan Kleineman for having me as a speaker at the Stockholm University Conference on Credit Rating Agencies; Professor Laurence Claus for giving me the opportunity to present my results at the University of San Diego School of Law; Professor Stephen K Halpert, Professor Robert E Rosen and Professor Richard L Williamson for allowing me to present my results at the University of Miami School of Law; Professor Jesper Lau Hansen and Anna Simonova for inviting me to give a lecture on my research project at the University of Copenhagen; Nicholas Lerche-Gredal for the opportunity of explaining my academic work at the Danish law firm Gorrissen Federspiel; and Professor Rolf H Weber, Professor Douglas W Arner and Professor Kern Alexander for letting me present my research at the University of Zurich. Their constructive feedback significantly enhanced my study.

All errors remain my sole responsibility.

Abbreviations

ABCP	Asset-Backed Commercial Papers
ABS	Asset-Backed Security
ADBI	Asian Development Bank Institute
AIG	American International Group
AMF	Autorité des Marchés Financiers
BCBS	Basel Committee on Banking Supervision
BIS	Bank for International Settlements
CDO	Collateral Debt Obligation
CDS	Credit Default Swap
CESR	Committee of European Securities Regulators
CFR	Code of Federal Regulations
CGFS	Committee on the Global Financial System
Circ	Circular
CMBS	Commercial Mortgage-Backed Security
CRA	Credit Rating Agency
CRMPG	Counterparty Risk Management Policy Group
CRT	Credit Risk Transfer
DNB	De Nederlandsche Bank
EC	European Community
ECAI	External Credit Assessment Institution
ECB	European Central Bank
ESMA	European Securities and Markets Authority
ESRB	European Systemic Risk Board
EU	European Union
FCIC	Financial Crisis Inquiry Commission
Fed Reg	Federal Register
Fed	US Federal Reserve
FICO	Fair Isaac Corporation
FINMA	Financial Market Supervisory Authority
FSB	Financial Stability Board
FSF	Financial Stability Forum
HEL	Home Equity Loan
IMF	International Monetary Fund

IOSCO	International Organization of Securities Commissions
IRB	Internal Ratings-Based
ISIN	International Securities Identifying Number
MBS	Mortgage-Backed Security
NBER	National Bureau of Economic Research
NRSRO	Nationally Recognized Statistical Rating Organization
NYU	New York University
NZZ	Neue Zürcher Zeitung
OCR	Office of Credit Ratings
OTH	Other Structured Finance Instruments
RMBS	Residential Mortgage-Backed Security
SEC	Securities and Exchange Commission
SIV	Structured Investment Vehicle
SNB	Swiss National Bank
SPE	Special Purpose Entity
SPV	Special Purpose Vehicle
TALF	Term Auction Lending Facility
TARP	Troubled Asset Relief Program
TBTF	Too Big To Fail
UCITS	Undertakings for Collective Investment in Transferable Securities
UK FSA	United Kingdom Financial Services Authority
UNU/WIDER	United Nations University World Institute for Development Economics Research
US	United States

Table of cases

Central Hudson Gas & Electric Corp v *Public Service Commission* [1980] 447 US 557,.....77.
Compuware Corp v *Moody's Investors Services, Inc* [2004] 324 F Supp 2d 860 (ED Mich 2004).....78.
In re Fitch [2003] 330 F 2d 104, 111 (2d Cir 2003).....78.
Newby v *Enron Corp* [2005] US Dist LEXIS 4494 (SD Tex, 16 February 2005) ...78.

Table of legislation and statutory instruments

EUROPEAN UNION

Directive 2006/49/EC of 14 June 2006 on the Capital Adequacy of Investment Firms and Credit Institutions [2006] OJ L177/201 (Capital Requirement Directive) ....49.

EU Commission Delegated Regulation (EU) No 448/2012 of 21 March 2012 supplementing Regulation (EC) No 1060/2009 with regard to regulatory technical standards for the presentation of the information that credit rating agencies shall make available in a central repository established by the European Securities and Markets Authority [2012] OJ L140/17, ...146.

EU Commission Delegated Regulation (EU) No 449/2012 of 21 March 2012 supplementing Regulation (EC) No 1060/2009 with regard to regulatory technical standards on information for registration and certification of credit rating agencies [2012] OJ L140/32, ...146.

Regulation (EC) No 1060/2009 of 16 September 2009 on credit rating agencies [2009] OJ L302/1 (CRA Regulation), ...4, 72–75, 93, 144, 146–148, 150–151.

Regulation (EU) No 513/2011 of 11 May 2011 amending Regulation (EC) No 1060/2009 on credit rating agencies [1011] OJ L145/30 (CRA II Regulation), ...73, 151.

FRANCE

Loi française No 2010-1249 du 22 octobre 2010 de régulation bancaire et financière (codified in Code monétaire et financier), ...80–82.

SWITZERLAND

Federal Ordinance of 29 September 2006 concerning Capital Adequacy and Risk Diversification for Banks and Securities Traders [2006] SR 952.03 (Capital Adequacy Ordinance),.......................11, 235.

FINMA Circular on Recognition of Rating Agencies for the Assessment of Capital Adequacy Requirements, FINMA-Circ 08/26 (20 November 2008)...........47, 49.

UNITED STATES

Credit Rating Agency Reform Act of 2006, S 3850, 109th Congress (2006) ..29, 68, 166, 198, 208, 214.

Dodd-Frank Wall Street Reform and Consumer Protection Act of 2010, HR 4173, 111th Congress, 2nd Session (2010) (Dodd-Frank Act) ......4, 9, 11, 61, 64, 69–71, 79, 86, 89, 93, 144–145, 148–150, 155, 197, 225–226, 231, 233.
SEC, Rating Agencies and the Use of Credit Ratings under the Federal Securities Laws, 68 Fed Reg 35,258 (June 12, 2003) ....23.
– Oversight of Credit Rating Agencies Registered as Nationally Recognized Statistical Rating Organizations, 72 Fed Reg 33,564 (June 18, 2007) ....69.
– Amendments to Rules for Nationally Recognized Statistical Rating Organizations, 74 Fed Reg 6,456 (February 9, 2009) ....69.
– References to Ratings of Nationally Recognized Statistical Rating Organizations, 74 Fed Reg 52,358 (October 9, 2009) ....60.
– Amendments to Rules for Nationally Recognized Statistical Rating Organizations, 74 Fed Reg 63,832 (December 4, 2009) ....69.
– Release No 68703, Order Making Findings and Imposing Remedial Sanctions and Cease-and-Desist Orders Pursuant to Sections 15E(d) and 21C of the Securities Exchange Act of 1934 against Egan-Jones Ratings Company and Sean Egan (January 22, 2013) ....150–151.
Securities Act of 1933, 15 USC § 77a et seq (as amended through PL 112-106, approved April 5, 2012) ....78.
Securities Exchange Act of 1934, 15 USC § 78a et seq (as amended through PL 112-158, approved August 10, 2012) ....71, 145, 147–150.

PART 1

Prelude to the credit rating industry

1. Introduction

1.1 BACKGROUND

> These errors make us look either incompetent at credit analysis or like we sold our soul to the devil for revenue, or a little bit of both.[1]

The leading credit rating agencies (CRAs) Moody's, Standard & Poor's and Fitch gained prominence in the financial markets.[2] Since the global financial crisis hit the world economy in 2007, significant concern has been raised about the role of CRAs and the use of their credit ratings. Recent events have attracted the attention of regulators, lawmakers, market participants and academic researchers to the dubious rating practices of the leading CRAs. First and foremost, the leading CRAs bear a part of the responsibility for causing the subprime mortgage meltdown.[3] They gave their highest ratings to novel mortgage-related securities that turned out to perform very poorly.[4] In addition, the leading CRAs are accused of exacerbating the euro debt crisis by downgrading Greek bonds

---

[1] Gretchen Morgenson, 'Debt Watchdogs: Tamed or Caught Napping?' *The New York Times*, December 7, 2008 (quoting a Managing Director, Moody's, responding anonymously to an internal management survey in September 2007).

[2] For convenience, this academic work refers to Moody's, Standard & Poor's and Fitch collectively as the "leading CRAs."

[3] See, eg, Jérôme Mathis, James McAndrews and Jean-Charles Rochet, 'Rating the Raters: Are Reputation Concerns Powerful Enough to Discipline Rating Agencies?' (2009) 56 Journal of Monetary Economics 657. See also Lawrence J White, 'Financial Regulation and the Current Crisis: A Guide for the Antitrust Community' (2009) SSRN eLibrary, 29 ‹http:ssrn.com/abstract=1426188› accessed 10 January 2013 (also mentioning that without inflated ratings on poor quality mortgage-related securities, the housing boom would have ended sooner, and the subprime mortgage debacle would have been less severe).

[4] Edward I Altman, Sabri Oncu, Anjolein Schmeits and Lawrence J White, 'What Should Be Done about the Credit Rating Agencies?' *New York University (NYU) Stern Regulating Wall Street Blog*, April 6, 2010 ‹http://w4.stern.nyu.edu/blogs/regulatingwallstreet/2010/04/what-should-be-done-about-the.html#more› accessed 10 January 2013; Kathleen Casey and Frank Partnoy, 'Downgrade the

just as European officials were about to unveil a support plan.[5] The strong effect of rating announcements on the financial markets highlights the continuing reliance on leading CRAs despite their numerous shortcomings. Although the novel financial instruments that they were rating collapsed, the leading CRAs did not suffer much from the financial meltdown directly. Since their inception, CRAs have survived many financial crises regardless of their repeated rating inaccuracies. Surprisingly, they even become more powerful in the aftermath of financial debacles. From the perspective of the financial system, this gives rise to an unsustainable situation.

Given this context, financial regulatory reforms are the most important catalysts for change in the rating industry. CRA reforms have thus enjoyed a prominent place in regulatory efforts made in response to the 2007–2009 global financial crisis. Lawmakers and regulators around the world have concentrated on strengthening CRA oversight. In the United States (US), the Dodd-Frank Act of 2010 has acknowledged that CRAs should be regulated in the same way as other gatekeepers such as securities analysts and auditors.[6] This US agency reform comprises the most sweeping regulatory intervention in the rating industry since its creation at the beginning of the twentieth century. In Europe, the absence of CRA regulation prior to the subprime mortgage crisis, and the general outcry with respect to their role in the financial crisis, put immense pressure on the European Union (EU) to adopt mandatory and enforceable rules in this field immediately.[7] The EU CRA Regulation of 2009 has strived to respond to these concerns.[8] In November 2010 the EU public consultation on CRAs was launched with a view to taking the

---

Ratings Agencies' *The New York Times*, June 4, 2010 (stating that CRAs helped create the financial crisis by giving inflated ratings).

[5] 'The Other Vampires, Pressure Mounts on an Oligopoly' *The Economist*, May 15, 2010, 83–84 (emphasizing that European politicians were livid at Greece's downgrades by Standard & Poor's and Fitch); John Ryan, 'The Negative Impact of Credit Rating Agencies and Proposals for Better Regulation' (2012) SWP Working Paper FG 1, 2012/No 1, 11–12 ‹http://www.swp-berlin.org/fileadmin/contents/products/arbeitspapiere/The_Negative_Impact_of_Credit_Rating_Agencies_KS.pdf› accessed 10 January 2013.

[6] Dodd-Frank Wall Street Reform and Consumer Protection Act of 2010, HR 4173, 111th Congress, 2nd Session (2010) (Dodd-Frank Act) Sec 931(2).

[7] EU Commission, 'Staff Working Document, Impact Assessment, Accompanying Document to the Proposal for a Regulation amending Regulation (EC) No 1060/2009 on credit rating agencies' COM (2010) 289 final, 7.

[8] Regulation (EC) No 1060/2009 of 16 September 2009 on credit rating agencies [2009] OJ L302/1 (CRA Regulation).

second step toward regulating CRAs.[9] Accordingly, the need to regulate the rating industry has increasingly been recognized worldwide.

The CRA reforms referred to above will partly address the problems in the credit rating industry. At any rate, a new era has begun in which lawmakers and regulators are aware of the importance of ratings in modern financial markets. They may aim to reduce the market dominance of the leading CRAs, yet have realized that they must take CRAs into account in their regulatory frameworks. CRAs are a part of the international financial architecture.[10] The road ahead will provide challenges in regulating the rating industry and simultaneously decrease market over-reliance on the leading CRAs. As soon as the trend toward the decreasing use of ratings in regulations is successfully implemented in the financial markets, the role of CRAs will have to be newly defined. Not all problems can be solved instantly through financial regulatory reforms.

As a consequence, the CRA topic presents an interesting agenda for research. Before the global 2007–2009 financial crisis, insufficient academic attention was paid to CRAs despite their crucial place in the financial markets. Little academic research has been carried out in assessing the CRA regulatory framework and its impact on competition among CRAs. Scholars have repeatedly pointed out the need to remove rating-based regulations, yet little research has demonstrated the repercussions of such measures on the rating industry. Scholars have already written about the lack of supervision of CRAs, yet little research has shown how the rating industry will evolve in the aftermath of regulatory intervention. The ongoing period represents without doubt a time of significant change in the rating industry. There is extreme uncertainty with respect to the future development of CRAs. This academic research focuses on the interaction between regulatory intervention and competitive incentives among leading CRAs. Although CRAs are required to abandon their quasi-regulatory function, no academic consensus exists with respect to the necessity of competitive incentives in the rating industry.

---

9 EU Commission, 'Public consultation on credit rating agencies' (November 5, 2010).

10 Rawi Abdelal, *Capital Rules, The Construction of Global Finance* (Harvard University Press 2007) 165.

1.2 EVOLVING ROLE OF CREDIT RATING AGENCIES IN MODERN FINANCIAL MARKETS

> Rating agencies profoundly impact the ordering of global financial markets.[11]

CRAs assess the creditworthiness of borrowers and debt instruments by attributing different grades to them. The three leading CRAs in the world – Moody's, Standard & Poor's and Fitch – are essentially based in the US, yet they operate worldwide through subsidiaries established in many countries and their credit ratings are widely used around the globe.[12] European lawmakers, regulators and market participants may wonder how it came about that this small number of American CRAs plays such a significant role in their affairs.[13] Among other things this study strives to analyze this phenomenon of modern financial markets.

Ratings are of interest to investors and financial institutions as well as regulators. Financial markets need institutions that facilitate information intermediation; CRAs traditionally perform this function. Ratings are generally considered to be opinions or judgments about the creditworthiness of borrowers or debt instruments, but are not untestable assertions in the sense that CRAs' performance can be measured *ex post*.[14] Further, CRAs measure only credit risk and leave the other components of risk in the hands of investors' own due diligence.[15]

The functions performed by the leading CRAs are assessed in the light of the use of their ratings in modern financial markets. As information intermediaries, CRAs help link borrowers and investors. They provide investors with useful information for decision-making. Over the last few decades, investors and issuers have increasingly attached importance to the ratings of the leading CRAs. The globalization of finance, the

---

[11] Steven L Schwarcz, 'Private Ordering of Public Markets: The Rating Agency Paradox' [2002] (Issue 2) University of Illinois Law Review 1, 2.

[12] EU Commission, 'Staff Working Document accompanying the Proposal for a Regulation on credit rating agencies, Impact Assessment' COM (2008) 704, 9–10 (stating that the three leading CRAs have their head office and main management, administrative and supervisory bodies in the US; nevertheless, they operate in the EU through subsidiaries).

[13] Abdelal, *Capital Rules* (n 10) 166 (taking into account Moody's and Standard & Poor's as the dominant CRAs; the author considers the chances of Fitch displacing the two biggest ones as slim).

[14] John Patrick Hunt, 'Credit Rating Agencies and the "Worldwide Credit Crisis": The Limits of Reputation, the Insufficiency of Reform, and a Proposal for Improvement' [2009] Columbia Business Law Review 109, 162–163.

[15] ibid 157.

increase of issuers and the complexity of new financial instruments imply an increasing role for CRAs given the lack of any alternative capital market overview.[16] In modern financial markets it is almost impossible to initiate public offerings without issues being rated by the leading CRAs.[17] The rating of novel financial instruments over the last four decades has resulted in the leading CRAs appearing to be more profitable than ever before.[18]

However, CRAs are considered to have been one of the culprits in recent financial debacles. It is surprising that CRAs became so powerful despite their shortcomings. The main argument against CRAs is their inaccurate ratings. For instance, the subprime mortgage crisis has shed light on troubles resulting from dealing inconsistently with asymmetric information in the financial markets. First, CRAs were hired by issuers to help enhance the liquidity and marketability of novel financial instruments such as residential Mortgage-Backed Securities (RMBS) and Collateral Debt Obligations (CDOs). The favorable ratings of the leading CRAs were crucial for investor acceptance of these complex financial instruments.[19] However, when the housing bubble burst in 2007, evidence showed that price discovery mechanisms failed to work and that the price of mortgage-related securities was not driven by the private market forces of supply and demand. Confidence shriveled up when investors realized that the ratings were inaccurate but that they were left with no other independent means of valuing the complex securities they were buying.[20] In a very short period of time the subprime mortgage market became illiquid and collapsed. In fact, buyers could not discern between good and

---

[16] SEC, 'Report on the Role and Function of Credit Rating Agencies in the Operation of the Securities Markets, As Required by Section 702(b) of the Sarbanes-Oxley Act of 2002' (January 2003) 5; Uwe Blaurock, 'Verantwortlichkeit von Ratingagenturen – Steuerung durch Privat- oder Aufsichtsrecht?' [2007] ZGR 603, 609.

[17] Claire A Hill, 'Regulating the Rating Agencies' (2004) 82 Washington University Law Quarterly 43, 47.

[18] See, eg, SEC, 'Report on the Role and Function of Credit Rating Agencies in the Operation of the Securities Markets' (n 16) 19, 27–29 (discussing the importance of ratings in modern financial markets).

[19] Hunt, 'Credit Rating Agencies' (n 14) 119.

[20] FSF, *Report of the Financial Stability Forum on Enhancing Market and Institutional Resilience* (April 2008) 37–38. See also IOSCO, *Report of the Task Force on the Subprime Crisis* (Final Report, May 2008) 23.

bad assets. As a consequence of confidence loss and uncertainty, no trade took place even at discount prices.[21]

Despite the massive dislocation associated with the recent financial crisis and the abysmal performance of CRAs, market participants have continued to rely on ratings.[22] This gives rise to concerns about the role of ratings and the reason for leading CRAs' success in the financial markets regardless of repeated scandals. Accordingly, scholars have written about the paradox of ratings.[23] Although CRAs were heavily criticized in the recent financial crises, hitherto little change has occurred with respect to their rating practices. CRAs have succeeded in imposing their presence and are considered to be indispensable entities to which many market participants refer when making decisions.

The best explanation of the paradox of ratings arises out of the significant use of ratings in financial market regulations.[24] CRAs became private-sector entities with a quasi-governmental function.[25] They could not have become as profitable solely by responding to the needs of the market for information. The rating market has gained in importance in modern financial markets for other reasons, especially regulatory concerns. Indeed, rating-based regulations have artificially increased the role of the leading CRAs in the financial markets. Issuers tend to hire CRAs

---

[21] See generally George A Akerlof, 'The Market for "Lemons": Quality Uncertainty and the Market Mechanism' (1970) 84 The Quarterly Journal of Economics 488, 490–491.

[22] Frank Partnoy, 'Overdependence on Credit Ratings was a Primary Cause of the Crisis' (2009) University of San Diego Legal Studies Research Paper Series No 09-015, 10. See also David Gillen, 'In Ratings Agencies, Investors Still Trust' *The New York Times*, June 5, 2009.

[23] Frank Partnoy, 'The Paradox of Credit Ratings' in Richard M Levich, Giovanni Majnoni and Carmen M Reinhart (eds), *Ratings, Rating Agencies and the Global Financial System* (Kluwer Academic Publishers 2002) 65–84; Schwarcz, 'Private Ordering of Public Markets' (n 11) 1–27.

[24] Frank Partnoy, 'The Siskel and Ebert of Financial Markets?: Two Thumbs Down for the Credit Rating Agencies' (1999) 77 Washington University Law Quarterly 619, 681–707 (already discussing the negative effects of rating-based regulations on the financial system in 1999; significantly, Professor Partnoy suggested removing regulatory references to ratings from regulations almost a decade before lawmakers and regulators began to take the problem seriously).

[25] 'Rating the Raters: Enron and the Credit Rating Agencies: Hearing Before the Senate Committee on Governmental Affairs' (2002) 107th Congress, S Hrg 107-471 (opening statement of Joseph I Lieberman, Chairman, Committee on Governmental Affairs) 1. See also Susan Emmenegger, 'Die Regulierung von Rating-Agenturen' [2006] Swiss Review of Business and Financial Market Law 32, 41.

followed the regulatory trend of establishing CRA oversight, preferring to leave the responsibility to the home regulators of the leading CRAs, ie mainly US regulators.[32] Moody's, Standard & Poor's and Fitch exert their Swiss business from their US headquarters or through their European subsidiaries in Frankfurt or London.[33] Nevertheless, the ratings of the three leading CRAs are crucial for Swiss regulators mainly because of the Basel framework.[34] The Swiss financial market authority may only influence the leading CRAs by assessing whether they meet the conditions so that Switzerland uses their ratings for regulatory purposes.[35] Therefore, this example illustrates the importance of US regulations on CRAs worldwide.

Broadly speaking, troubles in the rating industry arose out of the regulatory use of CRAs as private-sector entities. The Dodd-Frank Act of 2010 has implicitly recognized that rating-based regulations are inconsistent with the proper functioning of market forces in the rating industry. Without mentioning competition as an objective, the Dodd-Frank Act has acknowledged that the rating industry should be subject to private market forces; indeed, its CRA reform removes references to ratings from financial market regulations.[36] Therefore, this study proceeds on the assumption that the market for ratings should become more competitive in the future.

1.4 OUTLINE

This academic work proceeds as follows:

Part 1 provides a description of the credit rating industry. An historical overview of CRAs illustrates how these entities became profitable and how their role has evolved since their inception. Further, CRAs are defined in terms of their core activities, the rating process and the main uses to which their ratings are put.

---

[32] Heinz Meier, 'Regulierung von Ratingagenturen, Auswirkungen auf die Schweiz' [2009] Der Schweizer Treuhänder 945, 948–949. See also 'Debatte um "Schuld" der Rating-Agenturen, Schweizer Zurückhaltung bei anstehender Regulierung' *NZZ*, September 4, 2010, 35.

[33] Emmenegger, 'Die Regulierung von Rating-Agenturen' (n 25) 33.

[34] Federal Ordinance of 29 September 2006 concerning Capital Adequacy and Risk Diversification for Banks and Securities Traders [2006] SR 952.03 (Capital Adequacy Ordinance) (implementing Basel II in Switzerland).

[35] Meier, 'Regulierung von Ratingagenturen' (n 32) 947.

[36] Dodd-Frank Act, Sec 939–939A.

Part 2 discusses the regulatory context of credit ratings. Here the focus is on the structural aspects that have an impact on the financial markets. The regulatory structure creates incentives and is responsible for the functioning of market forces. On the one hand, regulators have initiated a trend to move away from rating-based regulations. CRAs will have to abandon their quasi-governmental function, thereby contenting themselves with their position of private-sector entities. On the other hand, new regulations have improved the oversight of CRAs by enhancing the supervisory framework. Regulations have also increased CRAs' accountability by making them liable for their misconduct.

Part 3 focuses on structured finance ratings. This topic has gained prominence due to the subprime mortgage crisis. The leading CRAs have played a crucial role in the growth and design of novel financial products. Criticism has been raised about the creation of wrong incentives in the rating industry, thereby distorting competition. In particular, the structured finance ratings segment is subject to severe conflicts of interest that jeopardize the independence of the leading CRAs. This study presents the newly enacted regulatory provisions that aim to reform the structured finance segment.

Part 4 analyzes the systemic importance of credit ratings. Interest in this topic has increased in the light of the downgrades of sovereign ratings and the euro debt crisis. System-relevance emerges from market over-reliance on a concentrated rating industry, giving the leading CRAs excessive market power. As a consequence, financial markets are to some extent characterized by a homogenization of financial information and of market behavior. Market over-reliance on the leading CRAs results in a reluctance to downgrade ratings given the spillover effects of rating announcements. Accordingly, this situation jeopardizes the independence of the leading CRAs because they have to take the repercussions of their ratings into account prior to downgrading. This study analyzes the recent regulatory trends in order to explain how to move away from the systemic relevance of ratings.

Part 5 concludes the study. A number of regulatory amendments concentrate on restoring competition in the rating industry. This study favors sector-specific regulation as compared to antitrust intervention. The key to reforms consists of creating better incentives in the rating industry. In particular, investors should perform their own due diligence, regulators should enhance disclosure requirements and find substitutes to the use of ratings for regulatory purposes.

2. History of credit rating agencies

> Somebody, sooner or later, will bring out an industrial statistical manual and when it comes, it will be a gold mine.[1]

The historical context highlights the evolution of the credit rating industry and helps to explain the current position of CRAs in the financial markets. The rating industry is only about one century old. Originally, capital markets developed without CRAs. Over the last few decades CRAs have become key actors whose position has evolved along with the various uses of ratings by market participants and regulators.[2]

2.1 BEFORE 1907: FROM INFORMAL SOURCES OF INFORMATION TO MERCANTILE AGENCIES

2.1.1 Dominance of Informal Channels and Increasing Need for Credit Information

For almost three centuries, capital markets developed without the benefit of external ratings.[3] In fact, in the early decades of US history, business was inherently local and therefore transactions were between people who knew each other.[4] Early nineteenth-century American merchants could

---

[1] Lee MacDonald Wakeman, 'The Real Function of Bond Rating Agencies' in Michael C Jensen and Clifford W Smith, Jr (eds), *The Modern Theory of Corporate Finance* (McGraw-Hill 1984) (quoting John Moody, Wall Street Analyst and founder of Moody's) 392.

[2] Further, since financial crises intervene as motors of change in the financial markets, the various periods related to the evolution of the rating industry are closely linked to the major financial crises of the last few decades.

[3] Richard Sylla, 'An Historical Primer on the Business of Credit Rating' in Richard M Levich, Giovanni Majnoni and Carmen Reinhart (eds), *Ratings, Rating Agencies and the Global Financial System* (Kluwer Academic Publishers 2002) 21.

[4] Ibid 23.

rely for much of their credit information on personal ties.[5] This system worked well as long as trade was local or conducted by merchants who traveled and came into direct contact with suppliers and customers.

However, the nineteenth century heralded the era of industrialization. In this context, the expansion of capital markets was needed to foster the pooling of sufficient resources to modernize the industrial infrastructure. The scale and geographical scope of transactions increased. At the same time, credit information on suppliers about whom business merchants had no personal knowledge was needed as the US population and the volume of trade increased.[6] Informal channels were no longer sufficient to satisfy the rising need for information.

More particularly, the market area expanded as the construction of railroads required the allocation of significant resources. Railroad corporations were indeed America's first big businesses, in the sense of multi-divisional enterprises operating over large geographical distances and employing cadres of professional managers.[7] From a structural perspective, only large banking houses could afford to hire full-time credit agents or develop their own systems of reporting as it was too costly for other merchants.[8] Moreover, the need for knowledge about distant and unknown customers stimulated several larger business houses to develop more formal methods of acquiring credit information.[9] Reports of higher quality could be obtained from an agent with specific responsibility for credit reporting only. Hence structural changes in the capital markets called for innovative solutions.

---

[5] James H Madison, 'The Evolution of Commercial Credit Reporting Agencies in Nineteenth-Century America' (1974) 48 The Business History Review 164, 165 ("Country merchants from the West and South traveled to seacoast cities where year after year they purchased their goods from the same wholesalers. Even if the seller did not know a prospective buyer personally, he had available sources of information in the form of the experience and opinions of other merchants").

[6] Sylla, 'An Historical Primer on the Business of Credit Rating' (n 3) 22–23 ("The crying capital need of the United States during much of the nineteenth century was for funds to build railroads, to open up and knit together an economy of continental proportions").

[7] ibid 23.

[8] Madison, 'The Evolution of Commercial Credit Reporting Agencies in Nineteenth-Century America' (n 5) 166.

[9] ibid.

2.1.2 Creation of Mercantile Agencies

Mercantile agencies were the precursors of modern CRAs.[10] The most important immediate factor leading to their creation was the financial crisis of 1837.[11] The severity of the collapse of 1837 was due in part to the inadequacy of existing methods of gaining information. Information asymmetries were perceived as an obstacle to the reallocation of financial resources. Merchants began to realize that one cause of the crash was inherent in the conditions that governed the granting of credit.[12] Many merchants discovered that their trust in some of their customers had been ill founded.[13] Therefore, mercantile agencies came into existence in the aftermath of that financial crisis as a response to a need for improved scrutiny of credit risks.

The financial crisis of 1837 hit New York businessmen especially. Lewis Tappan was a New York merchant who suffered heavily from the crisis. When the house of Tappan failed in the crisis, the credit records which Tappan had wisely gathered were in great demand; Tappan decided to extend and elaborate his well-known records and sell them to the business world.[14] In 1841 he founded the Mercantile Agency.[15] The Agency sold information about the business standing and creditworthiness of US entities all over the US.

Broadly speaking, credit reporting agencies attempted to provide in a formal and institutional manner a service that had so far been almost exclusively a function of personal ties within the mercantile community.[16] Moreover, the business of credit reporting agencies was centered in New York. At the time mercantile agencies expanded their

---

[10] Timothy E Lynch, 'Deeply and Persistently Conflicted: Credit Rating Agencies in the Current Regulatory Environment' (2009) 59 Case Western Reserve Law Review 227, 236–237.

[11] Gilbert Harold, *Bond Ratings as an Investment Guide, An Appraisal of their Effectiveness* (The Ronald Press Company 1938) 7.

[12] Theodore N Beckman, *Credits and Collections in Theory and Practice* (McGraw-Hill 1930) 135.

[13] Madison, 'The Evolution of Commercial Credit Reporting Agencies in Nineteenth-Century America' (n 5) 166.

[14] Harold, *Bond Ratings as an Investment Guide* (n 11) 7.

[15] Sylla, 'An Historical Primer on the Business of Credit Rating' (n 3) 23.

[16] Madison, 'The Evolution of Commercial Credit Reporting Agencies in Nineteenth-Century America' (n 5) 167 (also explaining that Tappan recruited correspondents across the country who submitted reports to the firm's New York office twice a year; clerks copied them into large ledgers and read the reports aloud for subscribers who called at the Mercantile Agency's office).

coverage there were high expectations about their eventual merits based on the belief that reliable reports would reduce losses by bad debts to a minimum.[17]

Credit reporting agencies continuously faced criticism and had to improve their practices in order to satisfy subscribers' needs. The primary charge leveled against them was the inaccuracy of their ratings. The source of the problem can be traced back to the very beginning of the credit information process, ie with the correspondents who gathered the data.[18] During the first half-century of their existence mercantile agencies made gradual but significant improvements in two major areas of credit reporting. First, they modified their procedures for the acquisition of information.[19] Second, they also modified their procedures for the transformation of data to subscribers.[20] The major new service was the rating or reference book: the first reference book was published by Bradstreet in 1857.[21] Later, in 1868, Henry Varnum Poor started to publish his annual report on the creditworthiness of the railroads.[22]

Severe criticism tended to destabilize the credit reporting agencies. First, legal threats came from rated businessmen who were outraged by their commercial credit ratings.[23] However, the credit reporting agencies defended them well against these legal suits. The courts held that if the agencies exercised reasonable diligence they could not be held liable even if their reports were inaccurate.[24] Second, there were attempts to pass regulatory legislation. This failed partly due to strong resistance from the Dun Agency. Third, the entry of new competitors challenged the Bradstreet and Dun agencies. After attacking the established agencies, these new agencies promised better service at lower rates.[25] "In order

---

[17] Peter R Earling, *Whom to Trust: A Practical Treatise on Mercantile Credits* (Rand, McNally & Co 1890) 31–32.

[18] Madison, 'The Evolution of Commercial Credit Reporting Agencies in Nineteenth-Century America' (n 5) 170.

[19] ibid.

[20] ibid 170–171 (adding that the major weakness in the mercantile agencies' system was their low-paid, part-time correspondents).

[21] ibid 173 (stating that the agencies first published annual volumes; by the early 1870s, they published quarterly editions).

[22] Alfred D Chandler, *Henry Varnum Poor: Business Editor, Analyst and Reformer* (Harvard University Press 1956); Rawi Abdelal, *Capital Rules, The Construction of Global Finance* (Harvard University Press 2007) 167.

[23] Madison, 'The Evolution of Commercial Credit Reporting Agencies in Nineteenth-Century America' (n 5) 177.

[24] ibid 179.

[25] ibid 182.

to offer lower subscription rates, the cheap agencies cut the costs of gathering credit data, largely by reducing the number of middlemen."[26] However, such competition did not last long due to the fact that investors preferred to pay well for reliable reports.[27] Unreliable reports were considered useless even at discount prices. Quality counted above everything else. Although mercantile agencies thrived in the late 1800s, their reports contained complex information and very detailed data that would eventually deserve to be distilled into more simple rankings.

2.2 1909–1930S: ORIGINS OF THE CREDIT RATING INDUSTRY

2.2.1 Emergence of the First Credit Rating Agencies

> You young pipe dreamer, why throw away your ten years' experience of learning the rules of the game? Why give the public all the facts regarding the corporations for the price of a book? You will be showing them how to play safe and get rich, while you will make nothing yourself. Anyway, if you begin to flaunt too many facts, there won't be much inside knowledge left to work on; you will be spoiling our game. Use your information yourself; don't be a philanthropist. There's no money in it![28]

Security ratings were inaugurated at the beginning of the twentieth century in the light of the experience of commercial credit ratings.[29] Security ratings were first published by Moody's in 1909.[30] Compared with mercantile agencies, Moody's idea was to synthesize the complex

---

[26] ibid 183–184 (mentioning further that some new agencies even subscribed to an established credit reporting service and simply resold the credit information to their own subscribers).

[27] ibid 184 (adding that one type of agency that was created in the 1870s provided more legitimate competition to the older agencies: this was the local or specialty agency, which concentrated on a small geographical area or on one line of trade).

[28] Frank Partnoy, 'The Siskel and Ebert of Financial Markets?: Two Thumbs Down for the Credit Rating Agencies' (1999) 77 Washington University Law Quarterly 619, 638 (quoting an "old Wall Street buccaneer" who was warning John Moody before he published his first rating book).

[29] Harold, *Bond Ratings as an Investment Guide* (n 11) 9.

[30] ibid 12. See also Arturo Estrella and others, 'Credit Ratings and Complementary Sources of Credit Quality Information' (2000) BCBS Working Papers No 3, 97 ‹http://www.bis.org/publ/bcbs_wp3.pdf› accessed 10 November 2012.

data in the reports into a single rating symbol for each security.[31] The credit ratings applied to both stocks and bonds. The second agency to go into the business was Poor's Publishing Company.[32] Further, in the 1920s and 1930s, Moody's and Poor's Publishing Company faced competition from a third CRA, the Standard Statistics Company.[33] This CRA began to interpret the collected data, condensing their language into a symbol or rating.[34] At the fourth place in the field of security ratings appeared the Fitch Publishing Company.[35]

2.2.2 Attitude of Investors to Credit Ratings

In general, the security ratings were warmly received, especially by commercial banks and many individual investors. However, some traders – especially those who were capable of intelligent analysis themselves – greeted their arrival coldly. They probably regarded the application of the ratings as a factor limiting the probable market fluctuation of the rated bonds. According to them, security ratings acted as a brake on their own speculative profits.[36]

Since their inauguration as concise judgments on investment quality, bond ratings had been used widely by commercial banks and individual investors. Financial institutions relied on ratings to varying degrees. The general rule seemed to be that the larger New York City institutions used the ratings merely as a check on their own findings, while the smaller and the outside banks depended on the ratings almost exclusively as authoritative guides.[37] Furthermore, with respect to investment houses, the manuals of one or more CRAs were freely displayed in the reading rooms of practically all brokerage offices or other places where customers used to congregate.[38] Insurance companies too, as well as other types of institutional investors, were daily consultants of the ratings.[39]

---

[31] Partnoy, 'The Siskel and Ebert of Financial Markets?' (n 28) 638.

[32] Harold, *Bond Ratings as an Investment Guide* (n 11) 12.

[33] Richard R West, 'Bond Ratings, Bond Yields and Financial Regulation: Some Findings' (1973) 16 Journal of Law and Economics 159, 160; Abdelal, *Capital Rules* (n 22) 167 (also mentioning that in 1941 Poor's Publishing Company merged with Standard Statistics Company to form Standard & Poor's).

[34] Harold, *Bond Ratings as an Investment Guide* (n 11) 13.

[35] ibid.

[36] ibid 14.

[37] ibid 20.

[38] ibid 21.

[39] ibid 22.

One important factor in the growing use of credit ratings appeared to be a saving in the costs of investigation. Large institutional investors, even though they employed investment staff, did not have to employ such large departments or so many analysts as would be required if ratings were not available.[40] Among the large institutional investors the process of individual analysis – though not eliminated – was reduced by the availability of ratings; among the smaller institutions, the tendency to rely on ratings was more pronounced.[41] The greater change brought by the CRAs was that even individual investors could take part in the capital markets. Direct access to the capital markets seemed to improve the position of the ordinary investor. However, during this period, the chief deterrent to individual investors to become subscribers to the ratings was apparently the cost because rating manuals were very expensive.[42]

The investing community as a whole, however, was willing to pay for the ratings given the valuable information that CRAs provided. The success of the ratings confirmed the belief that investors did not want detailed analyses but positive statements of the relative value of investment securities.[43] Even though large institutions relied on their own findings and own analysts, they consulted ratings to compare their results.[44] Smaller institutions bought rating manuals because they were dependent on ratings as an exclusive source of information.[45] The books were too expensive for individual investors but they could consult them in investment houses.

2.2.3 Building Reputational Capital

During the first phase of their existence, CRAs had to provide the investing community with credit ratings of good quality in order to build reputational capital. CRAs continued to accumulate reputational capital during the 1920s while being able to gather and synthesize valuable information.[46] In a competitive market for financial information, CRAs would issue inaccurate ratings at their peril given the low barriers to

---

40 ibid 38.
41 ibid 39.
42 ibid 25.
43 ibid 35.
44 Partnoy, 'The Siskel and Ebert of Financial Markets?' (n 28) 644.
45 Harold, *Bond Ratings as an Investment Guide* (n 11) 20.
46 Partnoy, 'The Siskel and Ebert of Financial Markets?' (n 28) 640.

entry.[47] A CRA's name, integrity and credibility were subject to inspection and critique by the entire investment community.[48] Therefore, reputational considerations were the most important driver of CRA behavior in order to gain market share. The market for ratings was a competitive market.

By the end of the 1920s the rating systems and scales were well established.[49] Ratings were divided into different categories based on the credit quality of the rated financial instrument.[50] Even though a diversity of rating symbols was used, by 1930 it was possible in practice to match CRAs' rating symbols with each other.[51]

2.3 1930S–1970S: DECREASING INTEREST IN THE CREDIT RATING AGENCIES

> We obviously cannot ask payment for rating a bond. [...] To do so would attach a price to the process, and we could not escape the charge, which would undoubtedly come, that our ratings are for sale.[52]

2.3.1 First Uses of Credit Ratings in Regulation

The first use of credit ratings as a regulatory tool dates back to the mid-1930s.[53] Initially, regulators used ratings to distinguish investment-grade from speculative-grade securities.[54] The direction toward tying financial regulation to bond ratings was mainly given following the adoption of the US Banking Act of 1936.[55] On the heels of a sharp decline in credit quality in 1931, the Office of the Comptroller of the Currency stated that bank holdings of publicly rated bonds had to be

---

47 ibid.

48 ibid.

49 ibid 641.

50 ibid.

51 Harold, *Bond Ratings as an Investment Guide* (n 11) 75; Partnoy, 'The Siskel and Ebert of Financial Markets?' (n 28) 642.

52 Gretchen Morgenson, 'Debt Watchdogs: Tamed or Caught Napping?' *The New York Times*, December 7, 2008 (quoting Edmund Vogelius, former vice-president, Moody's, explaining the company's business model in a 1957 article).

53 West, 'Bond Ratings, Bond Yields and Financial Regulation' (n 33) 161.

54 See, eg, Lawrence J White, 'Financial Regulation and the Current Crisis: A Guide for the Antitrust Community' (2009) SSRN eLibrary, 30 ‹http:ssrn.com/abstract=1426188› accessed 12 November 2012.

55 West, 'Bond Ratings, Bond Yields and Financial Regulation' (n 33) 161.

rated at least triple-B to be carried at book value; otherwise the bonds were to be written down to market value and 50 percent of the resulting book losses were to be charged against capital.[56] If a bond was not rated above a certain level, its short-term price action would have an impact on the adequacy of bank capital, regardless of whether a loss was realized.[57] Further, in 1936, the Office of the Comptroller and the Federal Reserve (Fed) took a crucial step by prohibiting banks altogether from holding bonds not rated at least triple-B by two CRAs.[58]

Since 1938, developments have tended to widen the use of ratings as tools of financial regulation.[59] Nevertheless, until the 1970s, rating-based regulations evolved at a slow pace only. They were not considered to be an inherent part of the financial system.

At any rate, the most important development of the 1930s was the threshold investment grade. Since the 1930s, ratings have divided securities into investment-grade and speculative-grade securities as a result of legislation permitting fiduciaries such as pension funds and insurance companies from only investing in bonds above a level deemed prudent.[60]

2.3.2 Doubts over Credit Rating Accuracy and Decline of Investor Confidence

> By the late 1960s the rating agencies were unexceptional firms with only modest revenues derived from selling their reports to subscribers, the same business model that John Moody had conceived in 1909. Few businesses were as uninteresting, uneventful, and unimportant.[61]

Particularly from the 1930s to the 1970s, the importance of CRAs ebbed and flowed.[62] The large number of rating changes and rating lags were

[56] Richard *Cantor* and Frank Packer, 'The Credit Rating Industry' [1994] FRBNY Quarterly Review 1, 6.

[57] West, 'Bond Ratings, Bond Yields and Financial Regulation' (n 33) 162.

[58] Cantor and Packer, 'The Credit Rating Industry' (n 56) 6.

[59] West,'Bond Ratings, Bond Yields and Financial Regulation' (n 33) 162.

[60] Timothy J Sinclair, *The New Masters of Capital, American Bond Rating Agencies and the Politics of Creditworthiness* (Cornell University Press 2005) 35.

[61] Abdelal, *Capital Rules* (n 22) 167.

[62] Claire A Hill, 'Regulating the Rating Agencies' (2004) 82 Washington University Law Quarterly 43, 47; John Flood, 'Rating, Dating, and the Informal Regulation and the Formal Ordering of Financial Transactions: Securitisations and Credit Rating Agencies' in Michael B Likosky (ed), *Privatising Development: Transnational Law, Infrastructure and Human Rights* (Martinus Nijhoff Publishers 2005) 161.

interpreted as a decline in the accuracy of ratings. Doubt was increasingly raised over CRAs' ability to generate valuable information. In the aftermath of the 1929 stock market crash, investor confidence in the CRAs began to decline. Investors were no longer very interested in purchasing ratings given the CRAs' poor track record in anticipating the financial crisis.[63]

Nevertheless, the business depression of the early 1930s appeared to be a factor in increasing the reliance placed upon bond ratings by commercial bankers, who emerged as the largest single group of rating adherents.[64] This fact cannot be interpreted as evidence of the increasing confidence of commercial bankers in ratings. Rather, the situation may best be explained by the regulatory use of ratings in determining the adequacy of bank capital. While other investors were reducing their use of ratings, commercial bankers increasingly started to purchase ratings following the newly adopted rating-based regulations.

Overall, the period from the 1930s to the 1970s is characterized by a declining interest in ratings. Many studies raised doubts about the accuracy of ratings. Especially as far as rating changes were concerned, CRAs were alleged to have generated information of little or no value.[65] Studies found that the changes merely reflected information already incorporated into stock market prices. Evidence showed that CRAs were slower than the markets in reacting to the changing financial and operating conditions of firms.[66] Ratings were considered as a lagging indicator of market fluctuations.

At the same time, CRAs were driven by reputational constraints. CRAs calculated most of their ratings only after bond issues had been distributed.[67] Investors did not purchase ratings if they did not trust the CRAs. Hence any loss of reputational capital directly generated a waning use of ratings. While CRAs were losing their reputation, fewer investors were interested in purchasing ratings. The importance of ratings was logically

---

[63] Frank Partnoy, 'How and Why Credit Rating Agencies Are Not Like Other Gatekeepers' (2006) University of San Diego Legal Studies Research Paper Series No 07-46, 63.

[64] Harold, *Bond Ratings as an Investment Guide* (n 11) 20.

[65] Partnoy, 'How and Why Credit Rating Agencies Are Not Like Other Gatekeepers' (n 63) 63.

[66] George E Pinches and J Clay Singleton, 'The Adjustment of Stock Prices to Bond Rating Changes' (1978) 33 The Journal of Finance 29, 41.

[67] Partnoy, 'The Siskel and Ebert of Financial Markets?' (n 28) 643.

decreasing. Even though the rating business was already dominated by few CRAs only, competition and market forces were playing a disciplinary role.

2.4 SINCE THE 1970S: ENHANCED PROFITABILITY OF THE CREDIT RATING BUSINESS

From the mid-1970s to today, credit rating agencies have exploded in size.[68]

2.4.1 Expanding Use of Credit Ratings in Regulation

Since the 1970s CRAs have been more influential and profitable than ever before in their history, even though they have not changed their rating system in any substantial way since the 1930s.[69] Relating to the context, private companies in the US and abroad began to tap international capital markets in the early 1970s.[70] CRAs benefited from greater capital mobility and from financial disintermediation.[71]

Financial turmoil in the early 1970s led the Securities and Exchange Commission (SEC) to implement the Nationally Recognized Statistical Rating Organization (NRSRO) concept, thereby conferring a privileged status on a few select CRAs.[72] The introduction of the NRSRO designation in 1975 was about to influence the rating industry decisively.[73]

Over the last four decades, regulators have increasingly used ratings to assess the risk of investments held by regulatory entities and to provide an appropriate disclosure framework for securities of differing risks.[74] As additional regulations increasingly depended on NRSRO ratings, ratings

---

[68] ibid 648.

[69] ibid.

[70] Abdelal, *Capital Rules* (n 22) 168.

[71] ibid (stating that the collapse of the Bretton Woods system in the early 1970s was accompanied – at least in the US – by the loosening of US capital controls in 1974, thereby resulting in the enhanced mobility of capital. Moreover, financial disintermediation implied that capital could flow directly from investors to issuers of securities, as opposed to going through banks).

[72] Andrew Fight, *The Ratings Game* (John Wiley & Sons Ltd 2001) 7.

[73] Abdelal, *Capital Rules* (n 22) 168. See also White, 'Financial Regulation and the Current Crisis' (n 54) 30.

[74] SEC, Rating Agencies and the Use of Credit Ratings under the Federal Securities Laws, 68 Fed Reg 35,258 (June 12, 2003) 35,258.

of those certified CRAs became more important and more valuable.[75] In this regard, the phenomenal growth of CRAs began in the 1970s.

2.4.2 Shift from Subscribers' Fees to Issuers' Fees

During the 1970 recession, investors began to question the financial condition of many companies. The default of Penn Central on 82 million US dollars of commercial paper – which had been rated as investment grade – in 1970 was a catalyst in the transition to charging issuers.[76] Facing a liquidity crisis, many companies defaulted and issuers began to actively seek ratings in order to reassure nervous investors.[77] Issuers turned to CRAs in order to calm the market.[78] Therefore, one reason explaining why issuers started to pay for the ratings was to restore investor confidence in the capital markets.

From a structural perspective, it is interesting to point out why CRAs shifted from an investor-pays to an issuer-pays business model. On the one hand, investors ceased paying for ratings due to the free-rider problem.[79] Before the 1970s investors typically paid for the ratings but this system was subject to abuse as ratings were easy to transmit; investors could often rely on free ratings so that some issues were eventually never rated.[80] This phenomenon became acute in the 1970s due to the low-cost photocopying revolution.[81] On the other hand, the increasing regulatory use of ratings incentivized issuers to pay for ratings. Rating-based regulations indeed played a decisive role. Issuers started to pay for the ratings because of the regulatory privileges they

---

75 Partnoy, 'How and Why Credit Rating Agencies Are Not Like Other Gatekeepers' (n 63) 64.

76 Cantor and Packer, 'The Credit Rating Industry' (n 56) 4.

77 ibid.

78 Arthur R Pinto, 'Control and Responsibility of Credit Rating Agencies in the United States' (2008) Brooklyn Law School Legal Studies Research Papers No 119, 8.

79 Partnoy, 'The Siskel and Ebert of Financial Markets?' (n 28) 653.

80 House of Lords, Select Committee on Economic Affairs, *Banking Supervision and Regulation* (June 2009) 40.

81 SEC, 'Report on the Role and Function of Credit Rating Agencies in the Operation of the Securities Markets, As Required by Section 702(b) of the Sarbanes-Oxley Act of 2002' (January 2003) 41; Lawrence J White, 'A New Law for the Bond Rating Industry' [2007] Regulation 48, 49.

could get. As a consequence, in modern financial markets, one reason for CRAs' profitability is the issuers' strong demand for ratings.[82]

2.4.3 Rating Novel Financial Instruments

As the US economy evolved and increasingly complex financial instruments were developed, the CRAs branched out into the rating of novel financial products.[83] Rating complex financial instruments became a profitable source of revenue for CRAs. CRAs were incentivized by promising business opportunities arising from a new market segment. Issuers took advantage of hiring CRAs to rate innovative financial products because they could enhance the marketability of their products. The favorable ratings of the leading CRAs were crucial for investor acceptance of the new financial instruments.[84]

Until the mid-1990s CRAs derived most of their revenues from corporate or sovereign ratings; however, with the growth of structured markets, they increasingly engaged in the highly lucrative activity of rating structured finance instruments.[85] Today the leading CRAs derive the major part of their revenues from the structured finance segment.[86]

Market reliance on ratings increased while investors often had no other independent means to assess credit risk. In fact, investors depended on CRAs' assessments of the risks of securitized products due to their complexity and because the contents of the underlying asset pools were

---

[82] Urs Birchler and Monika Bütler, *Information Economics* (Routledge 2007) 106–107 (also stating, however, that the rating industry's profits are less impressive when compared to the aggregate value of rated bonds).

[83] Fight, *The Ratings Game* (n 72) 6.

[84] John Patrick Hunt, 'Credit Rating Agencies and the "Worldwide Credit Crisis": The Limits of Reputation, the Insufficiency of Reform, and a Proposal for Improvement' [2009] Columbia Business Law Review 109, 119.

[85] EU Commission, 'Staff Working Document accompanying the Proposal for a Regulation on credit rating agencies, Impact Assessment' COM (2008) 704, 10.

[86] Joshua D Coval, Jakob Jurek and Erik Stafford, 'The Economics of Structured Finance' (2008) Harvard Business School Finance Working Paper No 09-060, 4 (reporting that 44 percent of Moody's' revenues in 2006 came from rating structured finance products, surpassing the 32 percent of its revenues from rating corporate bonds).

frequently not revealed.[87] Therefore, the leading CRAs may have acted as gatekeepers in the development of the structured finance market.[88]

2.5 ANALYZING THE EVOLUTION OF THE CREDIT RATING INDUSTRY

> No policymakers planned to put the rating agencies at the center of the international financial architecture, and yet, both formally and informally, that is where they are.[89]

The three leading CRAs – Moody's, Standard & Poor's and Fitch – have dominated the rating industry since their inception at the beginning of the twentieth century.[90] The rating industry has then evolved tremendously and eventually skyrocketed in profitability. Surprisingly, most of the financial crises of the twentieth century have contributed to increasing the importance of CRAs and their ratings. Moody's and Standard & Poor's have become so powerful in modern financial markets that it is almost impossible to do public offerings without getting ratings from one and often both; even private offerings are frequently rated by the leading CRAs.[91]

In a nutshell, this trend was initiated in the 1970s given, in particular, the following three factors: the growth of internationalized capital markets, the use of ratings in financial market regulations and the rating of complex financial products. The rating industry first emerged in the US from the market-based system, ie the phenomenon of bank disintermediation.[92] Although CRAs should be less relevant in a bank-based system, over the last few decades CRAs have also gained importance in Europe.

---

[87] House of Lords, *Banking Supervision and Regulation Report* (n 80) 40 (referring to the subprime mortgage crisis that hit the financial markets in 2007).

[88] Hunt, 'Credit Rating Agencies and the "Worldwide Credit Crisis"' (n 84) 176.

[89] Abdelal, *Capital Rules* (n 22) 165.

[90] Indeed, the first CRAs were chronologically Moody's, Poor's Publishing Company, Standard Statistics Company and Fitch Publishing Company. See, eg, West, 'Bond Ratings, Bond Yields and Financial Regulation' (n 33) 161 (reporting that in 1941 Standard Statistics was merged with Poor's to form Standard & Poor's).

[91] Hill, 'Regulating the Rating Agencies' (n 62) 47.

[92] See further Heinz Zimmermann and Wolfgang Hafner, 'Trotz Kritik kein Verzicht auf Rating-Agenturen, Ungebrochene Nachfrage nach Bonitätsbewertungen in unsicheren Zeiten' *NZZ*, August 19, 2010, 26 (giving an additional

Only private market forces were present at the origins of the rating industry. At the beginning of their existence CRAs responded to investors' needs for additional information. Competition played a disciplinary role. However, in modern financial markets the leading CRAs keep their high market shares regardless of the quality of their ratings. Above all, rating-based regulations had a substantial effect on the rating industry. The core function of CRAs shifted from informational intermediaries to providers of "regulatory licenses."[93] The historical evolution of the rating industry indicates that genuine demand fueled by market forces was displaced by artificial demand fueled by regulatory requirements.[94]

Further, the shift from the investor-pays to the issuer-pays business model distorted competitive incentives in the rating industry. Since the 1970s, investors have increasingly had access to financial information for free, yet they ended up paying high prices while being misled by inaccurate ratings. The lesson is that financial information has a price. The history of the mercantile agencies – or reporting agencies – shows that, in a competitive market, information of bad quality is worthless, even at a discounted price. Therefore, financial information has a value and it may well be worth paying for additional information.

From another perspective, ratings have economic effects on individual investors and their private freedom of contracting and trading. Initially, access to financial markets was limited to businessmen and bankers. Individual investors were not able to directly intervene in the capital markets. CRAs were created to provide individual investors with relevant information on investing in capital markets. This service responded to an informational need so that investors were able to engage freely in market transactions.

In modern financial markets, individual and unsophisticated investors have direct access to capital markets. Credit ratings provide a source of easily treatable information, accessible to a wide range of investors.[95] However, the world of finance has become increasingly complex especially over the last four decades. Even though investors are able to buy structured products, they sometimes lack the necessary knowledge or

---

reason for the importance of ratings in the US: under the American approach companies are considered to be a "nexus of contracts." It is therefore possible to split companies' debts into independent parts and rate them separately).

93 Partnoy, 'The Siskel and Ebert of Financial Markets?' (n 28) 623.

94 Jonathan R Macey, *Corporate Governance: Promises kept, Promises Broken* (Princeton University Press 2008) 114.

95 Sinclair, *The New Masters of Capital* (n 60) 3.

information to understand complex financial instruments.[96] If they are left with ratings to assess the products, they have no other option but to rely on them. Yet ratings should not be the sole information at the disposal of investors to assess the quality of financial products. Therefore, although ratings helped investors in the first place, in modern financial markets they have misled investors while being wrongly considered as a sufficient source of information to assess complex financial instruments. Limits on the private freedom to access capital markets must focus on investor protection. Unsophisticated investors in particular need to be protected. This objective is sometimes achieved by investment restrictions, yet such regulations are tricky to implement.

From another perspective, CRAs' main task was – at the inception of the industry at the beginning of the twentieth century – to collect sufficient amounts of information. Gathering relevant information was the most important issue in the financial markets at the time as it was not easy to obtain. If CRAs were created to provide investors with information, nowadays access to information is no longer the most significant problem. Increasingly, since the 1930s many of the CRAs' assessments are from publicly available news.[97] Information is easily accessible.[98] Nevertheless, market participants face new challenges in modern financial markets due to the quantity of information at their disposal. CRAs are used to screen valuable information and distill the complexity of the financial world into simple rankings. Therefore, selecting, analyzing and summarizing information play the most crucial role in the modern world. Available information must be assessed with respect to relevance and reliability. Yet the question arises as to whether simple rankings still have any value when assessing complex structured products.

[96] Even if there are substantive disclosure requirements and information has become easily available to investors, financial innovation and investment instruments have become so complex that they have become arcane to the average investor.

[97] Partnoy, 'The Siskel and Ebert of Financial Markets?' (n 28) 644.

[98] Technology makes information easily available on a large scale.

3. Description of the credit rating industry

3.1 CORE ACTIVITIES OF THE CREDIT RATING AGENCIES

CRAs are business institutions dealing with information relevant to the financial markets. The three leading CRAs worldwide are Moody's, Standard & Poor's and Fitch and they are commonly called the Big Three. Broadly speaking, their business activities concentrate on two key aspects. First and foremost, CRAs typically provide investors with external credit ratings, ie, they help them make investment decisions. Second, they may also engage in offering ancillary services to issuers.

3.1.1 Providing Investors with External Credit Ratings

> Ratings are a fact of life in modern society where non-specialists want complex information distilled by experts into easy-to-use symbols and rankings.[1]

3.1.1.1 Definition of a credit rating

The traditional CRA activity consists of selling external credit ratings. Through their ratings CRAs assess the creditworthiness of borrowers and debt instruments.[2] This activity allows for the transfer of information from borrowers to investors. Ratings reflect a CRA's opinion of how likely it is that an issuer will repay a particular debt or financial obligation, or its debts generally.[3] Two elements are at the core of every rating decision. First, the credit information is based on the probability of

---

1 John C Coffee Jr, *Gatekeepers: The Professions and Corporate Governance* (Oxford University Press 2006) 283.

2 Credit Rating Agency Reform Act of 2006, S 3850, 109th Congress (2006) Sec 3(a) (codified as amended in the Securities Exchange Act of 1934) (describing a rating as an assessment of the creditworthiness of an obligor as an entity or with respect to specific securities or money market instruments).

3 IOSCO, *Report on the Activities of Credit Rating Agencies* (September 2003) 1.

default of a borrower or a debt instrument. Second, CRAs assess the expected recovery in the event of default. Besides, for investments with multiple assets, CRAs also determine the correlation of defaults.[4] The resulting ratings give a single ranking that accounts for these relevant assumptions.

The rating scale developed by Standard & Poor's is the best known and the most widely used by CRAs: AAA; AA; A; BBB; BB; B, and so on.[5] The triple-A rating is the highest rating. Rating scales make an important distinction between investment-grade and speculative-grade ratings.[6] On Standard & Poor's scale the investment-grade rating comprises BBB- or above.[7]

Further, there is a distinction between external and internal credit ratings. On the one hand, external ratings are the ratings provided by independent private entities such as CRAs. On the other hand, internal ratings are generated directly by debt issuers and investment entities of financial institutions such as banks.[8]

Finally, CRAs have always insisted that their ratings merely provide the markets with their own opinions without actually recommending any rated product.[9] However, although CRAs deliver mere opinions about the creditworthiness of borrowers or debt securities, ratings are not untestable assertions given that rating performance can be measured *ex post*.[10]

---

[4] CGFS, *Ratings in Structured Finance: What Went Wrong and What Can Be Done to Address Shortcomings* (BIS, CGFS Paper No 32, July 2008) 13.

[5] See, eg, BCBS, *International Convergence of Capital Measurement and Capital Standards, A Revised Framework (Basel II)* (BIS, June 2004) para 50 and accompanying note (stating that the notations of the Basel II framework follow the methodology of Standard & Poor's as a reference). See also Lawrence J White, 'Financial Regulation and the Current Crisis: A Guide for the Antitrust Community' (2009) SSRN eLibrary, 29 ‹http:ssrn.com/abstract=1426188› accessed 10 January 2013.

[6] Timothy J Sinclair, *The New Masters of Capital, American Bond Rating Agencies and the Politics of Creditworthiness* (Cornell University Press 2005) 35; Uwe Blaurock, 'Verantwortlichkeit von Ratingagenturen – Steuerung durch Privat- oder Aufsichtsrecht?' [2007] ZGR 603, 604.

[7] See, eg, White, 'Financial Regulation and the Current Crisis' (n 5) 30.

[8] Blaurock, 'Verantwortlichkeit von Ratingagenturen' (n 6) 604.

[9] See, eg, 'Credit Rating Agencies and the Financial Crisis: Hearing Before the House Committee on Oversight and Government Reform' (2008) 110th Congress 2nd Session, HR Serial No 110-155, 117 (statement of Raymond W McDaniel, Chairman and Chief Executive Officer, Moody's).

[10] John Patrick Hunt, 'Credit Rating Agencies and the "Worldwide Credit Crisis": The Limits of Reputation, the Insufficiency of Reform, and a Proposal for Improvement' [2009] Columbia Business Law Review 109, 165–166.

Moreover, the trend toward the establishment of a liability regime for CRAs acknowledges the fact that ratings are more than opinions protected by the constitutional freedom of speech. CRAs provide commercial speech and need to be accountable.[11] Therefore, CRAs are judged by the investing community in regard to rating accuracy and can be judged by the courts in regard to potential securities fraud.

3.1.1.2 Financial information embedded in credit ratings

Broadly speaking, CRAs assess the creditworthiness of borrowers and debt instruments. Ratings are traditionally assigned to the credit risk of long-term corporate bonds, and additionally to the credit risk of Asset-Backed Securities (ABS), bank certificates of deposit, commercial paper and medium-term note programs, sovereign bonds, municipal bonds, preferred stock, private placements and shelf registrations.[12] Either the debt-issuing entity or the debt instrument is rated. Over the last four decades CRAs have entered the business of rating innovative financial instruments. New business opportunities have led them to rate increasingly complex products.

CRAs gather and select relevant information, eventually issuing ratings. Through this process, a vast amount of qualitative and quantitative information on credit quality is distilled into a simple ordinal ranking.[13] In fact, CRAs only assess credit risk.[14] Generally speaking they do not evaluate the other risk components which must be assessed by investors themselves.

Credit ratings can be classified into three main categories: corporate ratings, structured finance ratings and sovereign ratings.

(i) Corporate ratings Corporate ratings are assigned to all kinds of companies in the private sector. For instance, rated entities can be financial institutions such as banks, securities firms, insurance, real estate and non-bank finance companies. CRAs are active in debt markets.

(ii) Structured finance ratings Structured finance ratings comprise the assessment of novel instruments by CRAs. Indeed, CRAs started to

---

11 Text to n 87 in ch 5.

12 Arturo Estrella and others, 'Credit Ratings and Complementary Sources of Credit Quality Information' (2000) BCBS Working Papers No 3, 97 ‹http://www.bis.org/publ/bcbs_wp3.pdf› accessed 10 November 2012.

13 ibid 126.

14 Hunt, 'Credit Rating Agencies and the "Worldwide Credit Crisis"' (n 10) 157.

operate in the structured finance segment in the mid-1970s.[15] The central assumptions at the core of CRA models in structured finance are default rates, recovery rates and correlations.[16] Leading CRAs argued that their ratings were consistent between traditional and novel instruments, but this statement was refuted in the aftermath of recent financial debacles.[17]

(iii) Sovereign ratings CRAs rate government debts. Sovereign ratings are attributed to entities in the public sector. The art of forecasting the likelihood that a government will default on its debt is particularly challenging due to the fact that the central issue in sovereign borrowing is not the ability to pay but rather the willingness to pay.[18] This requires interpretive work on the part of the CRAs. At any rate, sovereign ratings affect every other bond rating in the private sector because of sovereign ceilings. Sovereign ceilings mean that CRAs do not generally rate domestic firms' foreign-currency debt higher than that of their government.[19]

3.1.2 Counseling Issuers in Doing Ancillary Business

In addition to issuing ratings, some CRAs also offer ancillary business services. Although this activity is not regarded as the typical agency product, it has gained momentum over the past decades. Accordingly, ancillary business grew at an extraordinary pace until generating substantial profits for CRAs. The significance of these new activities eventually

---

15 IOSCO, *Report of the Task Force on the Subprime Crisis* (Final Report, May 2008) 20 (stating that the leading CRAs first issued ratings for Mortgage-Backed Securities (MBS) in the mid-1970s).

16 CGFS, *Ratings in Structured Finance* (n 4) 13.

17 Hunt, 'Credit Rating Agencies and the "Worldwide Credit Crisis"' (n 10) 161. In structured finance ratings, the estimate of recovery rates plays a crucial role in contradistinction to its lesser importance in corporate ratings (in corporate ratings, default rates play the most significant role; in structured finance ratings, the highest tranche of a CDO – for instance – may have a relatively low default rate but a very low recovery rate so that investors lose almost everything in the event of default). Estimating the correlation of defaults plays a crucial role in structured finance ratings but is less relevant in corporate ratings.

18 Rawi Abdelal, *Capital Rules, The Construction of Global Finance* (Harvard University Press 2007) 162 (explaining that no third party can enforce a sovereign debt contract; moreover, sovereign governments never really run out of assets to cover their obligations although they may fall short of foreign exchange or choose to repay one debt instead of another).

19 ibid.

raised concerns about CRAs' corporate governance. Confusion has especially arisen during the 2007–2009 financial crisis.

For instance, ancillary services include rating assessment services whereby issuers present hypothetical scenarios to the CRA to determine how their rating might be affected by a proposed business activity; other services may include risk management and consulting services to help financial institutions manage credit and operational risk.[20] CRAs provide this service in exchange for a fee.

The practical importance of CRAs' ancillary services is mainly linked to structured products. In fact, CRAs advise arrangers about the rating consequences of proposed structures. Before issuing the financial product, the arranger can change its structure according to the feedback of the CRA. Ancillary services give the issuers the opportunity to work with CRAs on the composition of structured products.[21] This process allows issuers to get higher ratings than they would have had they not implicated CRAs in the structuring process.

Concerns have especially been raised about ancillary business services with respect to the financial crisis triggered in 2007. In the subprime mortgage market in particular, issuers did not purchase these ancillary services to get professional advice but rather to know how to take advantage of the rating process.[22] Doing ancillary business may generate conflicts of interest.[23] The purchase of ancillary services remains closely connected with the issuance of ratings. The question therefore arises as to whether the formulation of ratings should be completely separate from the ancillary services offered to issuers on the engineering of complex financial products.[24]

---

20 IOSCO, *Report on the Activities of Credit Rating Agencies* (n 3) 4.

21 Gretchen Morgenson and Louise Story, 'Rating Agency Data Aided Wall Street in Deals' *The New York Times*, April 23, 2010.

22 IOSCO, *Report on the Activities of Credit Rating Agencies* (n 3) 11 (also mentioning that issuers may hope to get higher ratings if they purchase ancillary services or may conversely fear that their failure to do so could negatively impact their ratings).

23 See, eg, Claire A Hill, 'Regulating the Rating Agencies' (2004) 82 Washington University Law Quarterly 43, 51. See also Frank Partnoy, 'How and Why Credit Rating Agencies Are Not Like Other Gatekeepers' (2006) University of San Diego Legal Studies Research Paper Series No 07-46, 68.

24 The High-Level Group on Financial Supervision in the EU, 'De Larosière Report' (2009) 19 ‹http://ec.europa.eu/internal_market/finances/docs/de_larosiere_report_en.pdf› accessed 10 January 2013.

3.2 RATING PROCESS

Credit ratings are attributed to borrowers or debt instruments after the completion of a rating process. CRAs deal with the information at their disposal in a systematic way. They strive to provide the financial actors with timely ratings. On the one hand, they issue initial ratings as soon as the rating process is performed. On the other hand, they keep monitoring their ratings and change them according to market fluctuations. CRAs generally receive separate revenue streams for initial ratings and ongoing monitoring.[25]

A rating committee lies at the core of the rating process used by the leading CRAs.[26] In general, rating decisions are made by a simple majority vote of the rating committee.[27] The rating committee is competent to provide initial ratings or rating updates. This central organ of a CRA is typically composed of a lead analyst, managing directors or supervisors, and junior analytical staff.[28]

3.2.1 Providing Initial Credit Ratings

In general, the rating process starts when a subscriber or an issuer requires a rating, giving rise to the issuance of a solicited rating.[29] The demand comes from subscribers in the investor-pays business model and from issuers in the issuer-pays business model. CRAs provide the rating service in exchange for a fee. Initial rating fees are typically calculated as a percentage of the total value of the deal.[30] CRAs sometimes get involved in assessing borrowers or debt instruments without request, thereby providing unsolicited ratings.[31] In any case, CRAs take several specific steps prior to issuing their ratings.

First, CRAs' analysts gather relevant information with a view to rating borrowers or debt instruments. Relevant information includes quantitative and qualitative data, and depends most notably on whether a financial

---

[25] Joshua Rosner, 'Toward an Understanding: NRSRO Failings in Structured Ratings and Discreet Recommendations to Address Agency Conflicts' (2009) 14 (Issue 4) Journal of Structured Finance 7, 14.

[26] IOSCO, *Report on the Activities of Credit Rating Agencies* (n 3) 5.

[27] ibid.

[28] ibid.

[29] Blaurock, 'Verantwortlichkeit von Ratingagenturen' (n 6) 604.

[30] Rosner, 'Toward an Understanding' (n 25) 14 (adding that initial rating fees can often reach into the hundreds of thousands of US dollars).

[31] Blaurock, 'Verantwortlichkeit von Ratingagenturen' (n 6) 605–606.

entity or a debt instrument is rated.[32] CRAs' analysts also request information from borrowers or issuers and research other available sources for information.[33] Rating decisions are not only based on publicly available information but also on information acquired from private sources. For instance, issuers or borrowers provide to the CRAs qualitative information about their policy choices and strategic plans; the major CRAs gather qualitative information about borrowers' or issuers' business environment, for instance their economic and political environment.[34] Since existing information is voluminous, the primary task of the CRAs consists of selecting relevant data.

Second, CRAs analyze the collected data. CRAs assemble analytical teams that undertake research, if applicable meet with issuers, and prepare a report containing a rating recommendation and explaining the rationale.[35] CRAs mix quantitative and qualitative data in their rating decision, thereby suggesting that they produce a subjective judgment about the borrower or debt instrument. However, they are aware of the fact that public views tend to revolve around the numbers, referring to a technical rather than judgmental rating process.[36] With respect to structured finance ratings, CRAs typically use mathematical models, such as the Monte Carlo simulation. The Monte Carlo simulation is the mathematical benchmark most widely used by professionals for comparison purposes.[37]

Third, the rating process requires a rating determination. After the teams of analysts present their view to a rating committee of senior CRA officials, the rating committee votes on the final determination.[38] Ratings are established according to rating scales. CRAs reduce the relevant information to a letter symbol.

---

[32] Estrella and others, 'Credit Ratings and Complementary Sources of Credit Quality Information' (n 12) 111 (explaining that three basic types of information are relevant to estimate the probability of default, namely the financial statements, the market prices of a firm's debt and equity, and subjective appraisals of the firm's prospects and risks).

[33] IOSCO, *Report on the Activities of Credit Rating Agencies* (n 3) 5.

[34] Sinclair, *The New Masters of Capital* (n 6) 33.

[35] ibid 33.

[36] ibid 35.

[37] John M Griffin and Dragon Yongjun Tang, 'Did Subjectivity Play a Role in CDO Credit Ratings?' (2010) McCombs Research Paper Series No FIN-04-10, 23.

[38] Sinclair, *The New Masters of Capital* (n 6) 33.

Fourth, the last step is the disclosure of the rating. CRAs disseminate ratings as soon as practicable.[39] Ratings are typically disclosed to the public in the issuer-pays business model, yet only to subscribers in the investor-pays business model. In the issuer-pays business model, the disclosure decision is generally subject to appeal by the issuer.[40] Therefore, there is a possibility that the rating is never published if the issuer is not satisfied with the outcome. Such a rating practice is common in the structured finance segment. The issuer can accept the rating determination and have the trust issue the securities with the proposed capital structure.[41] The issuer may adjust the structure to provide the requisite credit enhancement in order to obtain the desired rating and then accept disclosure of the rating.[42] Alternatively, the issuer can choose to not hire the CRA and – depending on the engagement contract – pay the CRA a "break-up fee."[43] In this case, the issuer may hire another CRA to rate the structured product and may finally be able to obtain the desired rating.

3.2.2 Reviewing Credit Ratings

> Surveillance should be thought of as the continuation and extension of the links between issuers, raters, and investors.[44]

The rating business is a continual process. In addition to giving initial ratings, the CRAs monitor their ratings on an ongoing basis, upgrading and downgrading as they deem appropriate, or putting ratings on "credit watch" if a change may occur soon.[45] Surveillance fees are typically assessed annually at a fixed price and often range from 2,000 US dollars to an atypically high 30,000 US dollars depending on the size and complexity of the deal.[46]

Reviewing ratings is a very important stage in the rating process since market participants will react to rating changes and to rating outlooks as

---

[39] IOSCO, *Report on the Activities of Credit Rating Agencies* (n 3) 9.

[40] Sinclair, *The New Masters of Capital* (n 6) 33.

[41] IOSCO, *Report of the Task Force on the Subprime Crisis* (n 15) 21.

[42] ibid (explaining, for instance with respect to CDOs, that the issuer may provide the requisite credit enhancement for the highest tranche to get the triple-A rating).

[43] ibid 21.

[44] Sinclair, *The New Masters of Capital* (n 6) 41.

[45] Hill, 'Regulating the Rating Agencies' (n 23) 48–49.

[46] Rosner, 'Toward an Understanding' (n 25) 14.

well. CRAs place great emphasis on the ongoing monitoring of issuers since new events can have an effect on the quality of any rating.[47]

Leading CRAs have surveillance teams that monitor ratings.[48] The reason is that timeliness is an important objective of the rating business. As far as procedural aspects are concerned, prior to revising the attributed rating, CRAs typically have rating outlooks and rating reviews, such as watchlists.[49] Especially with respect to rating downgrades, CRAs typically warn issuers or borrowers before disclosing the lower rating. Issuers or borrowers are thus given a chance to improve their creditworthiness and avoid an undesired downgrade. This proceeding implies interactions between the rated entity and CRAs that may result in conflicts of interest.

3.3 MAIN USES OF CREDIT RATINGS IN MODERN FINANCIAL MARKETS

Credit ratings are widely used around the globe. CRAs effectively have an immense impact on the availability and cost of credit. It is worth describing the main uses of ratings in order to understand their importance in modern financial markets. First, CRAs traditionally provide investors with financial information. Second, over the past decades regulators have increasingly incorporated ratings in all kinds of financial market regulations. Third, ratings are also widely used in contracting regardless of any regulatory mandates.

3.3.1 Credit Ratings as Providing Financial Information

CRAs traditionally act as information intermediaries.[50] They are important producers and disseminators of financial market information.[51] Their role primarily consists of addressing information asymmetries in the

---

47 Sinclair, *The New Masters of Capital* (n 6) 41.

48 Blaurock, 'Verantwortlichkeit von Ratingagenturen' (n 6) 605.

49 Christian Hirsch and Christina Bannier, 'The Economic Function of Credit Rating Agencies – What Does the Watchlist Tell Us?' (2009) SSRN eLibrary, 1 ‹http:ssrn.com/abstract=1343421› accessed 10 January 2013.

50 Steven L Schwarcz, 'Private Ordering of Public Markets: The Rating Agency Paradox' [2002] (Issue 2) University of Illinois Law Review 1, 12. See also William H Beaver, Catherine Shakespeare and Mark T Soliman, 'Differential Properties in the Ratings of Certified Versus Non-certified Bond-rating Agencies' (2006) 42 Journal of Accounting and Economics 303, 306.

51 Urs Birchler and Monika Bütler, *Information Economics* (Routledge 2007) 105.

financial markets.[52] First, CRAs provide investors with relevant information for decision-making. Prospective borrowers always know more than their potential lenders about their own creditworthiness.[53] The existence of independent sources of information such as ratings prevents borrowers and issuers from disclosing information selectively in order to bias outsiders' opinion. The presence of information intermediaries is deemed to increase transparency in the financial markets. If no means existed for transmitting relevant information, worthy investment projects would fail to be financed, thereby implying a market failure.[54]

Second, borrowers and issuers also benefit from reducing information asymmetries since this fact has a positive impact on the availability and cost of credit.[55] Indeed, companies with a bad rating or no rating are forced to accept a risk premium to borrow capital.[56] High ratings give access to cheaper credits. Borrowers and issuers are therefore interested in being highly rated with a view to reducing their cost of borrowing.[57] Moreover, the effectiveness of ratings in communication leads to their use in marketing and advertising.[58] Borrowers and issuers frequently refer to the ratings that they have obtained to convince investors of their creditworthiness.

Third, investors save costly research and time.[59] In fact, CRAs can assess the creditworthiness of borrowers or debt securities on behalf of many individual investors, thereby achieving an economy of scale.[60] This service is especially valuable if the costs of a credit analysis are too high compared with the investment.[61] In particular, small and unsophisticated

---

52 Blaurock, 'Verantwortlichkeit von Ratingagenturen' (n 6) 608; Nelson Camanho, Pragyan Deb and Zijun Liu, 'Credit Rating and Competition' (2012) SSRN eLibrary, 2 ‹http:ssrn.com/abstract=1573035› accessed 10 January 2013 (referring to the pivotal impacts of ratings due to asymmetric information between issuers and investors).

53 Estrella and others, 'Credit Ratings and Complementary Sources of Credit Quality Information' (n 12) 11.

54 ibid.

55 See, eg, Ulrich Ackermann and Joachim Jäckle, 'Ratingverfahren aus Emittentensicht' (2006) 61 Betriebs-Berater 868, 878–879.

56 Blaurock, 'Verantwortlichkeit von Ratingagenturen' (n 6) 609.

57 House of Lords, Select Committee on Economic Affairs, *Banking Supervision and Regulation* (June 2009) 40.

58 Sinclair, *The New Masters of Capital* (n 6) 40.

59 Blaurock, 'Verantwortlichkeit von Ratingagenturen' (n 6) 608.

60 Schwarcz, 'Private Ordering of Public Markets' (n 50) 12.

61 ibid; Beaver, Shakespeare and Soliman, 'Differential Properties in the Ratings of Certified Versus Non-certified Bond-rating Agencies' (n 50) 306–307.

investors cannot always afford the cost of undertaking their own credit assessments.

In this way, CRAs gain in prominence in a market-based system. When financing is provided directly by a large number of small lenders, it is unlikely that any single lender has enough at stake to be sufficiently incentivized to make an adequate information-gathering effort.[62] In contrast, CRAs typically do not have a crucial place in a bank-based system. This is because substantial evaluation and monitoring costs might only be worth bearing for a bank fully exposed to potential borrower default.[63]

3.3.2 Credit Ratings as Regulatory Tools

The use of credit ratings in regulations stems from the 1930s and has increased tremendously since the 1970s. As a consequence, CRAs wield quasi-governmental power.[64] Their ratings are not only used by investors but also by regulators. In this respect, CRAs have ventured far beyond their traditional role as information intermediaries. Rating-based regulations have encouraged CRAs to sell "regulatory licenses" in modern financial markets.[65] Obtaining favorable regulatory treatment is another reason to purchase ratings. In some cases, credit ratings are not in demand for their informational value but only for their regulatory value.

Ratings are primarily used in regulations for the purpose of determining capital requirements and identifying eligible assets or permitted asset concentrations.[66] With respect to bank capital requirements, the Basel II framework has fostered the use of ratings in order to measure regulatory capital on the global scale.[67] The revised Basel III framework

---

62 Estrella and others, 'Credit Ratings and Complementary Sources of Credit Quality Information' (n 12) 11.

63 ibid.

64 'Rating the Raters: Enron and the Credit Rating Agencies: Hearing Before the Senate Committee on Governmental Affairs' (2002) 107th Congress, S Hrg 107-471 (opening statement of Joseph I Lieberman, Chairman, Committee on Governmental Affairs) 1.

65 Frank Partnoy, 'The Siskel and Ebert of Financial Markets?: Two Thumbs Down for the Credit Rating Agencies' (1999) 77 Washington University Law Quarterly 619, 623.

66 See further The Joint Forum, *Stocktaking on the Use of Credit Ratings* (BIS, June 2009) 3–4.

67 See, eg, Kern Alexander and others, 'Crisis Management, Burden Sharing and Solidarity Mechanisms in the EU' (2010) European Parliament, Policy Department, Economic and Scientific Policy, 12 ‹http://www.europarl.europa.eu/

maintains a great extent of reliance on ratings in capital requirement regulations.[68] With respect to investment restrictions, regulators have widely used ratings in the pension funds and insurance sectors in the US. Accordingly, financial market regulators effectively outsourced their safety judgments to third-party CRAs.[69]

However, concern has been raised about the negative effects of rating-based regulations in the financial markets.[70] Especially in the US, lawmakers and regulators have already initiated a trend toward the complete withdrawal of regulatory references to ratings.[71]

3.3.3 Credit Ratings as Contracting Tools

> Ratings are currently used more as benchmarks for market participants than as a source of information for investors.[72]

Ratings have also been widely used for contracting purposes. In modern financial markets, investors increasingly turn to ratings. Credit ratings can be used in agreements – such as merger or loan agreements – by sophisticated and unsophisticated investors.

In particular, "rating triggers" can cause payment obligations to accelerate or require the posting of collateral based upon rating downgrades. Concern has increasingly been raised about the fact that "rating triggers" enhance the effects of rating changes, thereby increasing market volatility and amplifying financial shocks.[73]

Further, rating downgrades below a certain level can result in companies violating their debt covenants, thereby possibly triggering a

committees/en/cris/studiesdownload.html?languageDocument=EN&file=31711› accessed 10 January 2013.

[68] BCBS, *Basel III: A Global Regulatory Framework for More Resilient Banks and Banking Systems* (BIS, December 2010) 52–53.

[69] White, 'Financial Regulation and the Current Crisis' (n 5) 30.

[70] See, eg, Partnoy, 'The Siskel and Ebert of Financial Markets?' (n 65) 681–707.

[71] Text to n 94 in ch 4.

[72] Staff of Senate Committee on Governmental Affairs, 'Financial Oversight of Enron: The SEC and Private-Sector Watchdogs' (2002) 107th Congress, 2nd Session, S Prt 107-75, 78.

[73] Blaurock, 'Verantwortlichkeit von Ratingagenturen' (n 6) 611.

default on their debt obligations.[74] In the worst-case-scenario, rating downgrades may even throw companies into default.[75]

Finally, rating updates – upgrades and downgrades – are often used as contractual signals of borrowers' creditworthiness: above all, downgrades can lead to demands for more collateral, higher interest rates on loans or bonds, or even immediate debt repayments.[76] The consequence of rating downgrades depends on contractual clauses; for instance, downgrades below a certain level may be enough to trigger the foreseen effects.[77] By being used to determine contractually acceptable collateral, CRAs play a significant role in the financial markets. For instance, investors can require investment-grade securities as collateral. CRAs effectively decide what assets can be used as guarantees.

3.3.4 Credit Ratings as Monitoring Tools

> Their role has moved from being purveyor of information to being monitor of financial probity.[78]

CRAs screen possible investments and monitor borrowers or debt instruments. As a consequence of market reliance on ratings, CRAs eventually select which loans are viable or not. Traditionally, banks fulfill this function and scrutinize borrowers. In a market-based system, investors tend to rely on CRAs to a great extent. CRAs play a role in monitoring borrowers as private-sector watchdogs.[79] In fact, by monitoring borrowers and directly influencing investor investment decisions, CRAs literally take a function that banks generally perform.

---

74 Beaver, Shakespeare and Soliman, 'Differential Properties in the Ratings of Certified Versus Non-certified Bond-rating Agencies' (n 50) 307.

75 'Rating the Raters' (n 64) (testimony of Jonathan R Macey, J DuPratt White Professor of Law, Cornell Law School) 44.

76 'Exclusion Zone, Regulators Promise a Belated Review of the Ratings Oligopoly' *The Economist*, February 8, 2003, 65–66.

77 IOSCO, *Report on the Activities of Credit Rating Agencies* (n 3) 8.

78 John Flood, 'Rating, Dating, and the Informal Regulation and the Formal Ordering of Financial Transactions: Securitisations and Credit Rating Agencies' in Michael B Likosky (ed), *Privatising Development: Transnational Law, Infrastructure and Human Rights* (Martinus Nijhoff Publishers 2005) 167.

79 Staff of Senate Committee on Governmental Affairs, 'Financial Oversight of Enron' (n 72) 1–2, 5.

Under some circumstances, CRAs even exercise an active monitoring function.[80] In particular, watchlists have developed into active monitoring devices allowing CRAs to exert real pressure on the reviewed companies.[81] The threat to downgrade puts rated entities under pressure. CRAs will monitor borrowers and update their ratings whenever circumstances change. Discipline may take the form of a rating update or a listing on Moody's "Watchlist" or Standard & Poor's "CreditWatch," thereby signaling positive rating trends or, more usually, negative rating concerns prior to a rating downgrade.[82]

However, the subprime mortgage crisis highlighted the weaknesses of the model. CRAs performed poorly and a great number of their ratings of mortgage-related securities went wrong. Excessive outsourcing of credit risk assessment to CRAs was rapidly recognized as an extremely risky practice. Accordingly, one main lesson from the subprime mortgage meltdown is that CRAs cannot successfully act as monitors of borrowers and debt instruments.

---

80 Flood, 'Rating, Dating, and the Informal Regulation and the Formal Ordering of Financial Transactions' (n 78) 167 ("Their role has moved from being purveyor of information to being monitor of financial probity").

81 Hirsch and Bannier, 'The Economic Function of Credit Rating Agencies' (n 49) 23.

82 Sinclair, *The New Masters of Capital* (n 6) 41.

PART 2

Regulatory structure

4. Rating-based regulations

The regulatory context highlights why CRAs have become so central to the capital markets even though credit ratings are not the only source of financial information. Favorable regulatory treatment has given a significant privilege to CRAs – especially to leading and certified CRAs such as Moody's, Standard & Poor's and Fitch.[1] Indeed, rating-based regulations enhance the importance of ratings in the financial system. CRAs are less subject to private market forces if market participants are – for regulatory purposes – forced to rely on their ratings regardless of their performance. Rating-based regulations also give a regulatory privilege to certified CRAs as opposed to non-certified CRAs.

The first use of credit ratings in financial market regulations stems from the 1930s in the US. Especially since the 1970s ratings have been increasingly used in all kinds of regulations. As additional regulations came to depend more on ratings, these ratings became more important and more valuable; however, the value of the information they generate did not increase.[2] In fact, the regulatory use of ratings has had a detrimental impact on competition in the rating industry and has been heavily criticized by many scholars.[3] Rating-based regulations are purported to create wrong incentives in the rating industry, thereby jeopardizing the quality of the ratings. Major problems arise insofar as CRAs are private-sector entities with quasi-regulatory power.[4] Concern has been

---

1 CRAs enjoy a regulatory advantage as opposed to other gatekeepers, and certified CRAs enjoy a regulatory advantage as opposed to non-certified CRAs.

2 Frank Partnoy, 'How and Why Credit Rating Agencies Are Not Like Other Gatekeepers' (2006) University of San Diego Legal Studies Research Paper Series No 07-46, 64.

3 See, eg, Frank Partnoy, 'Do Away with Rating-based Rules', *The Financial Times*, July 8, 2008. See also Edward I Altman, Sabri Oncu, Anjolein Schmeits and Lawrence J White, 'What Should Be Done about the Credit Rating Agencies?' *New York University (NYU) Stern Regulating Wall Street Blog*, April 6, 2010 ‹http://w4.stern.nyu.edu/blogs/regulatingwallstreet/2010/04/what-should-be-done-about-the.html#more› accessed 10 January 2013.

4 See, eg, Susan Emmenegger, 'Die Regulierung von Rating-Agenturen' [2006] Swiss Review of Business and Financial Market Law 32, 41.

raised among scholars about the fact that regulators should completely withdraw rating-based regulations and find an alternative to ratings. For instance, many researchers plead for the use of market-based information as a substitute for ratings.[5]

4.1 REGULATIONS DEPENDING ON CERTIFIED CREDIT RATINGS

Credit ratings are used for regulatory purposes both at the international and national level.[6] The use of ratings in financial market regulations depends on the authorities that establish the regulatory and supervisory frameworks. The most significant uses of ratings in regulations stem from US financial market regulations and, on the global scale, from the Basel II Accord. To some extent, they persist in the Basel III framework.[7]

CRAs that issue the credit ratings used for regulatory purposes are commonly called certified CRAs. Their ratings are labeled certified credit ratings. The specific terminology attributed to this concept depends on the regulators using ratings in their financial market regulations. US regulators use the NRSRO concept.[8] The US framework has historically known the most elaborate use of ratings for regulatory purposes. Certified CRAs are called NRSROs. Their ratings are labeled NRSRO ratings. On the global scale, the Basel Committee on Banking Supervision (BCBS)

---

[5] Frank Partnoy, 'The Siskel and Ebert of Financial Markets?: Two Thumbs Down for the Credit Rating Agencies' (1999) 77 Washington University Law Quarterly 619, 705 (proposing the use of market-based information as an alternative to external ratings; in this early paper, Professor Partnoy promotes the use of credit spreads instead of ratings for regulatory purposes); Frank Partnoy, 'Overdependence on Credit Ratings was a Primary Cause of the Crisis' (2009) University of San Diego Legal Studies Research Paper Series No 09-015, 15 (suggesting that regulators could alternatively use credit spreads or credit default swap prices in their financial market regulations); Mark J Flannery, Joel F Houston and Frank Partnoy, 'Credit Default Swap Spreads As Viable Substitutes for Credit Ratings' (2010) 158 University of Pennsylvania Law Review 2085.

[6] FSF, *Report of the Financial Stability Forum on Enhancing Market and Institutional Resilience* (April 2008) 38.

[7] Kern Alexander, 'Bank Capital Regulation and the Role of External Ratings: Unresolved Issues' in Jan Kleineman and Lars Gorton (eds), *Credit Rating Agencies* (Stockholm Centre for Commercial Law, forthcoming 2013).

[8] Rawi Abdelal, *Capital Rules, The Construction of Global Finance* (Harvard University Press 2007) 168. See also Lawrence J White, 'Financial Regulation and the Current Crisis: A Guide for the Antitrust Community' (2009) SSRN eLibrary, 30 ‹http:ssrn.com/abstract=1426188› accessed 10 January 2013.

defines certified CRAs as External Credit Assessment Institutions (ECAIs) in the Basel II and III frameworks.[9] National regulators are free to decide whether to implement the Basel II Accord or the newly revised Basel III framework, and use the ECAI terminology in their own financial laws.[10] For instance, the Financial Market Supervisory Authority (FINMA) is in charge of recognizing CRAs used in Switzerland for regulatory purposes.[11] This supervisory authority publishes a list of certified CRAs and monitors the agencies on its list regularly.[12]

As long as the application of financial market regulations turns on ratings, there is no doubt that a regulatory approval of CRAs is needed.[13] A variety of recognition criteria determine the regulatory decisions as to which CRAs deserve to be labeled certified CRAs.[14] The most significant criterion relates to CRAs' credibility with international or domestic market participants.[15]

Credit ratings are generally used by regulators for two main purposes: determining risk-sensitive capital requirements and defining investment restrictions.[16]

---

[9] BCBS, *International Convergence of Capital Measurement and Capital Standards, A Revised Framework (Basel II)* (BIS, June 2004) para 90; BCBS, *Basel III: A Global Regulatory Framework for More Resilient Banks and Banking Systems* (BIS, December 2010) 52–53.

[10] IOSCO, *Report of the Task Force on the Subprime Crisis* (Final Report, May 2008) 23; EU Regulation (EC) No 060/2009 of the European Parliament and of the Council on Credit Rating Agencies, art 2, para 3 (referring to the ECAI terminology).

[11] See, eg, Carlo Lombardini, *Droit bancaire suisse* (2nd edn, Schulthess 2008) 146.

[12] FINMA Circular on Recognition of Rating Agencies for the Assessment of Capital Adequacy Requirements, FINMA-Circ 08/26 (20 November 2008) para 39. See also Heinz Meier, 'Regulierung von Ratingagenturen, Auswirkungen auf die Schweiz' [2009] Der Schweizer Treuhänder 945, 946.

[13] Steven L Schwarcz, 'The Role of Rating Agencies in Global Market Regulation' in Eilís Ferran and Charles AE Goodhart (eds), *Regulating Financial Services and Markets in the 21st Century* (Hart Publishing 2001) 307.

[14] IOSCO, *Report on the Activities of Credit Rating Agencies* (September 2003) 8.

[15] ibid.

[16] The Joint Forum, *Stocktaking on the Use of Credit Ratings* (BIS, June 2009) 3–4.

4.1.1 Bank Capital Requirement Regulations

Bank capital requirement regulations are especially used in the banking and securities sectors.[17]

First, capital requirement regulations consist of the most elaborate incorporation of credit ratings in financial market regulations. On the global scale, the BCBS enacted the Basel II framework in 2004, providing a solution to determine the riskiness of assets based on CRAs' assessments.[18] The BCBS proposed to use ratings in risk-sensitive bank capital requirements because ratings provide a relatively standardized, harmonized and easy-to-understand measure of credit risk.[19] The Basel II framework was heavily criticized in the financial crisis that hit the financial markets in 2007 because of its failure to establish adequate measures to supervise the banking system. Post-crisis reforms were needed. Basel III is considered to be the core regulatory response to problems revealed by the recent financial crisis.[20] Basel III consists of a compilation of reform measures to strengthen the regulation, supervision and risk management of the banking sector. Although reducing reliance on ratings is portrayed as an area of focus, at this stage Basel III reforms still rely extensively on ratings to assess bank capital requirements.[21] The BCBS has not yet been able to propose any suitable alternative to

---

[17] See further ibid 4–8.

[18] *Basel II* (n 9) para 50. The BCBS is an international body that establishes international standards relevant for national regulators and financial institutions such as banks. See, eg, Rolf H Weber and Aline Darbellay, 'The Regulatory Use of Credit Ratings in Bank Capital Requirement Regulations' (2008) 10 Journal of Banking Regulation 1, 4; Kern Alexander and others, 'Crisis Management, Burden Sharing and Solidarity Mechanisms in the EU' (2010) European Parliament, Policy Department, Economic and Scientific Policy, 12 ‹http://www.europarl.europa.eu/committees/en/cris/studiesdownload.html?languageDocument=EN&file=31711› accessed 10 January 2013; Kern Alexander, 'Bank Capital Management and Macro-Prudential Regulation – A Law and Finance Perspective' [2012] Journal of Banking Law and Banking 331, 335.

[19] BCBS, *Consultative Document, Strengthening the Resilience of the Banking Sector* (BIS, December 2009) 55.

[20] Nout Wellink, 'The New Framework for Banking Supervision' *Basel Committee Speeches, Remarks at the FSI High Level Meeting on 'The Emerging Framework to Strengthen Banking Regulation and Financial Stability' for Africa* (Cape Town, 27 January 2011) 4 ‹http://www.bis.org/speeches/sp110127.pdf› accessed 10 January 2013.

[21] ibid; Alexander, 'Bank Capital Regulation and the Role of External Ratings: Unresolved Issues' (n 7).

external ratings, thus ratings continue to play an important role in bank capital requirement regulations.

National regulators implement the Basel II Accord, and subsequently the Basel III framework, on a voluntary basis. In the EU, the Capital Requirement Directive of 2006 outlined necessary measures with respect to the establishment of capital adequacy requirements applying to investment firms and credit institutions; the Directive implemented Basel II at the EU level.[22] In Switzerland, the Federal Council enacted the Capital Adequacy Ordinance of 2006 with a view to partly incorporating the Basel II Accord into Swiss legislation.[23] Based on the Ordinance, the FINMA published a circular to define the criteria used in Switzerland to recognize CRAs for regulatory purposes.[24] The EU and Switzerland have assessed proposals to implement Basel III reforms in their financial laws.[25] Overall, focus is put on addressing the "too big to fail" problem.[26] In addition, the EU is currently planning to reduce over-reliance on credit ratings by removing regulatory references to ratings.[27]

4.1.2 Regulatory Investment Restrictions

Investment limitations are especially used to supervise institutional investors. Credit ratings may be used for regulatory purposes in the insurance and pension funds sectors. Above all, investment restrictions

---

22 Directive 2006/49/EC of 14 June 2006 on the Capital Adequacy of Investment Firms and Credit Institutions [2006] OJ L177/201 (Capital Requirement Directive) preamble (5). See also Piero Cinquegrana, 'The Reform of the Credit Rating Agencies: A Comparative Perspective' (2009) ECMI Policy Brief No 12, 5–6.

23 Meier, 'Regulierung von Ratingagenturen' (n 12) 946; Peter Nobel, *Schweizerisches Finanzmarktrecht und internationale Standards* (3rd edn, Stämpfli 2010) 205.

24 FINMA-Circ 08/26.

25 See, eg, 'Final Report of the Commission of Experts for Limiting the Economic Risks Posed by Large Companies' (Swiss TBTF Report) (30 September 2010) 4 (adding that the proposed requirements are more rigorous than the minimum standards of Basel III).

26 Christine Kaufmann and Rolf H Weber, 'The Role of Transparency in Financial Regulation' (2010) 13 Journal of International Economic Law 779, 785.

27 EU Commission, 'Public consultation on credit rating agencies' (5 November 2010) 5; European Parliament, 'Resolution of 8 June 2011 on credit rating agencies: future perspectives' (2010/2302(INI)).

were used in the US for institutional investors.[28] In the US, many state insurance laws described permitted investments or concentration limits in terms of ratings.[29] In the EU, insurance and reinsurance directives have not contained any provisions that placed excessive reliance on CRAs.[30]

Broadly speaking, ratings used for investment restrictions serve to identify or classify eligible assets, or to define permitted asset concentrations. In this regard, the rule that has the most significant effect on the financial system relates to threshold investment-grade rating. Investment-grade rating is the opposite of speculative-grade rating. Constrained investors may be forced to hold assets rated above a certain level deemed prudent. As a consequence, they may have to sell assets if their assets are downgraded below the investment-grade level. Therefore, it is not surprising that there is a large yield discontinuity between investment-grade and below-investment-grade ratings.[31] Rating-based regulations in effect influence the availability and cost of capital.

In the banking and securities sectors, investment limitations may be imposed on specific entities. Investment limitations refer to asset identification, including – for instance – the designation of permitted investments for mutual funds as well as the establishment of investment concentration limits for particular types of assets.[32] Moreover, a significant number of jurisdictions have used ratings for regulatory purposes in the fields of securitizations and covered bond offerings.[33] Some regulations may require that issuance has to be rated by one or more CRAs prior to being offered to investors. The breadth of the regulatory use of ratings can vary, some regulations covering all securitizations and some

---

28 See further The Joint Forum, *Stocktaking on the Use of Credit Ratings* (n 16) 7 (explaining that – with respect to the designation of permitted investments – many jurisdictions reported that ratings were used both in the banking and securities sector; the United Kingdom Financial Services Authority (UK FSA), however, noted that ratings were not used for asset identification in any of its three financial sectors).

29 ibid.

30 ibid 5.

31 Partnoy, 'Overdependence on Credit Ratings was a Primary Cause of the Crisis' (n 5) 4.

32 The Joint Forum, *Stocktaking on the Use of Credit Ratings* (n 16) 7.

33 ibid 8 (also describing securitizations as the process of pooling assets and issuing securities representing interests in that pool of assets, and describing covered bond offerings as debt securities issued by banks and other credit institutions, repayment being secured by a pool of assets backing the bond).

others covering only certain identified types of securitizations.[34] Nevertheless, the financial reforms post-crisis have initiated a trend to move away from these uses of ratings for regulatory purposes.

4.2 DISTORTIONS OF COMPETITION WITH RESPECT TO RATING-BASED REGULATIONS

Rating-based regulations provide the most insightful example of regulatory failure. Broadly speaking, the regulatory use of credit ratings distorts CRAs' incentives to provide valuable information, thereby jeopardizing competition in the rating industry. It creates artificial demand for the services of certified CRAs regardless of their usefulness to investors.[35] Indeed, regulations guarantee a fixed stable demand for CRAs' services.[36]

Rating-based regulations create incentives for market participants to pay for regulatory entitlements stemming from the CRAs' ratings instead of paying for the content of the ratings.[37] In short, regulatory reliance on ratings has encouraged CRAs to shift from the business of providing valuable credit information to the far more lucrative business of selling "regulatory licenses."[38]

4.2.1 Regulatory Barrier to Entering the Credit Rating Industry

> Whatever the cause of the entry barriers, standard economic theory would suggest that their existence, especially in an industry with very few players, would lead to less vigorous competition than would be the case if there were fewer entry barriers and more players.[39]

---

[34] ibid (explaining that, for instance in Italy, ratings are required by regulation only when securities are sold to non-professional investors).

[35] Jonathan R Macey, *Corporate Governance: Promises Kept, Promises Broken* (Princeton University Press 2008) 115.

[36] 'Rating the Raters: Enron and the Credit Rating Agencies: Hearing Before the Senate Committee on Governmental Affairs' (2002) 107th Congress, S Hrg 107-471 (testimony of Jonathan R Macey, J DuPratt White Professor of Law, Cornell Law School) 44.

[37] Partnoy, 'The Siskel and Ebert of Financial Markets?' (n 5) 624.

[38] ibid 623.

[39] Claire A Hill, 'Regulating the Rating Agencies' (2004) 82 Washington University Law Quarterly 43, 63.

Barriers to entry can undermine competition.[40] An essential feature of a competitive market structure is to keep barriers to entry as low as possible.[41] Certain types of barriers to entry are inherent to the industry due to distinctive market components in the targeted market. Other types of barriers to entry are artificially created and may at least be partially addressed in view of enhancing competition. The rating industry is characterized by relatively high barriers to entry as follows.

CRAs face historical, natural, institutional and regulatory barriers to entry.[42] On the one hand, historical and natural barriers to entry are inherent in the rating industry and cannot be avoided. The historical barrier to entry results from trust based on the reputational capital that the leading CRAs have built up over many years.[43] Issuers tend to hire CRAs that are widely recognized among investors; yet new entrants – ie potential competitors – cannot present historic track records.[44] The natural barrier to entry is derived from the fact that the rating market may not be able to accommodate many general-purpose CRAs.[45]

On the other hand, the regulatory barrier to entry is created by regulators and does not exist "per se." Rating-based regulations raise a regulatory barrier to entry.[46] In particular, the regulatory recognition of

---

[40] Reducing barriers to entry is an objective of general competition law, for instance with respect to preventing abuse of dominant position; it can also be part of sector-specific regulation, in particular when general competition law is not able to solve the problems caused by regulatory barriers to entry.

[41] Jeffrey Manns, 'Rating Risk After the Subprime Mortgage Crisis: A User Fee Approach for Rating Agency Accountability' (2009) 87 North Carolina Law Review 1012, 1017–1018.

[42] Hill, 'Regulating the Rating Agencies' (n 39) 84, 91.

[43] John Flood, 'Rating, Dating, and the Informal Regulation and the Formal Ordering of Financial Transactions: Securitisations and Credit Rating Agencies' in Michael B Likosky (ed), *Privatising Development: Transnational Law, Infrastructure and Human Rights* (Martinus Nijhoff Publishers 2005) 160.

[44] Uwe Blaurock, 'Verantwortlichkeit von Ratingagenturen – Steuerung durch Privat- oder Aufsichtsrecht?' [2007] ZGR 603, 607.

[45] Hill, 'Regulating the Rating Agencies' (n 39) 62 (adding that pre-NRSRO history provides some support for this argument).

[46] Michel G Crouhy, Robert A Jarrow and Stuart M Turnbull, 'The Subprime Credit Crisis of 07' (2008) SSRN eLibrary, 9 ‹http:ssrn.com/abstract=1112467› accessed 10 January 2013; FSF, *Report of the Financial Stability Forum on Enhancing Market and Institutional Resilience* (n 6) 38; Weber and Darbellay, 'The Regulatory Use of Credit Ratings in Bank Capital Requirement Regulations' (n 18) 6.

CRAs can potentially act as a barrier to entry for potential competitors.[47] Therefore, the certification process reduces competition in the rating industry by limiting new entrants.[48]

The question arises as to what barriers to entry best explain the high concentration of leading CRAs in the credit rating industry. The combination of historical with regulatory barriers to entry ensured that the dominance of the leading CRAs would become widespread.[49] Above all, regulatory barriers to entry have been created through regulatory intervention.[50] It is worth mentioning that highly regulated markets typically have high regulatory barriers to entry.[51] Regulations automatically have an effect on competition. With respect to the rating industry, the regulatory barrier to entry contributes to privileging certified CRAs as opposed to non-certified CRAs. As long as ratings are used in financial market regulations, CRA certification and qualification processes are needed.[52] Therefore, the regulatory barrier to entry is inevitable if ratings are used for regulatory purposes.

As a consequence, it is recommended to keep the regulatory barrier to entry as low as possible in order to enhance competition among CRAs. As soon as rating-based regulations are removed from legal frameworks, a certification process for CRAs will no longer be needed. Such an amendment would reduce the regulatory barriers to entering the rating market. Instead of a certification process, a mere registration process

---

47 FSF, *Report of the Financial Stability Forum on Enhancing Market and Institutional Resilience* (n 6) 38. But see IOSCO, *Report on the Activities of Credit Rating Agencies* (n 14) 9; IOSCO, *Report of the Task Force on the Subprime Crisis* (n 10) 27 (noting that the nature of the rating market makes it difficult for new entrants to succeed regardless of any regulatory barriers to entry; moreover, regulatory recognition criteria are based on how extensively ratings are used by market participants, ie the reputation of CRAs in the market; nevertheless, market participants prefer to use ratings that regulators also use, implying that the cycle of discrimination is perpetual).

48 Arthur R Pinto, 'Control and Responsibility of Credit Rating Agencies in the United States' (2008) Brooklyn Law School Legal Studies Research Papers No 119, 9 (referring to the NRSRO status in the US).

49 Abdelal, *Capital Rules* (n 8) 173.

50 See, eg, White, 'Financial Regulation and the Current Crisis' (n 8) 30.

51 Highly regulated entities can take advantage of regulatory barriers to entry if these barriers enable established companies to charge higher prices such as quasi-monopoly prices. It is not surprising that regulated entities tend to be very prosperous. Typical examples are the banking sector, the insurance sector, the pharmaceutical industry, the audit industry and telecommunications services.

52 Schwarcz, 'The Role of Rating Agencies in Global Market Regulation' (n 13) 307.

could still exist so that regulators are able to maintain an oversight of the rating industry.

4.2.2 Market Over-reliance on Credit Ratings

> [Rating-based regulations have] created an oligopoly that lulls users of their ratings into a false sense of security and spreads moral hazard: investors tend to rely on the ratings rather than making credit judgments of their own.[53]

Regulatory mandates that require market participants to obtain or use credit ratings artificially increase market reliance on leading CRAs.[54] The two main types of rating-based regulations have an impact on the position of CRAs in the financial system.

First, risk-sensitive measures of regulatory capital increase the importance of certified CRAs in the sense that their ratings are widely used to attribute the various risk weights to assets in the financial markets. The Basel II Accord encouraged the global implementation of risk-sensitive bank capital requirements.[55] Its wide acceptance increased the importance of ratings.[56] The result of the Standardized Approach of the Basel II framework was that CRAs received a substantial regulatory enhancement of the usage of their products and increased market confidence therein.[57] Before the subprime mortgage crisis, banks were able to report relatively high risk-weighted capital ratios.[58] Basically, banks were taking advantage of risk-sensitive capital requirements. They were holding triple-A

---

53 'Negative Outlook, Europe Misfires in its Attack on the Rating Agencies' *The Economist*, November 15, 2008, 91.

54 See, eg, FSF, *Report of the Financial Stability Forum on Enhancing Market and Institutional Resilience* (n 6) 38 (stating that the regulatory use of ratings encourages market over-reliance on certified CRAs).

55 The use of external ratings in order determine the appropriate risk weights is described under Basel II's Standardized Approach: *Basel II* (n 9) para 50.

56 Kern Alexander and others, 'Financial Supervision and Crisis Management in the EU' (2007) European Parliament, Policy Department, Economic and Scientific Policy, 20 ‹http://www.europarl.europa.eu/document/activities/cont/201108/20110818ATT25070/20110818ATT25070EN.pdf› accessed 10 January 2013.

57 Douglas W Arner, 'The Global Credit Crisis of 2008: Causes and Consequences' (2009) Asian Institute of International Financial Law Working Paper No 3, 26.

58 Alexander and others, 'Financial Supervision and Crisis Management in the EU' (n 56) 20 (arguing that at the end of 2006, the ratio of regulatory capital to risk-weighted assets was 13 percent in the US, 12.9 percent in the UK, 12.2

assets on their balance sheets. As long as these assets were highly rated, banks could extend their balance sheets and enjoy high leverage ratios with the consent of regulators. However, cracks became visible along with massive rating downgrades in July 2007. As soon as certified CRAs revised their ratings for CDOs downwards, banks were required to adjust their risk-weighted capital requirements upwards.[59] The wide repercussion of these sudden rating downgrades on bank capital ratios highlights the excessive reliance on ratings due to bank capital requirement regulations. The source of the problem was primarily the rating-based approach described in the Basel II Accord.[60] As a consequence, the BCBS acknowledges the necessity of reducing reliance on CRAs in capital requirement regulations, but the Basel III framework has not yet fully overhauled its regulatory use of external ratings.[61]

Second, regulations create and maintain dependence on certified CRAs insofar as investment limitations imposed on charter-constrained investors depend on credit ratings. Financial market regulations designing permitted investments were developed primarily in the US for` the pension funds and insurance sectors. The fact that regulated market participants are subject to portfolio restrictions contributes to increasing the importance attributed to the ratings of certified CRAs. With respect to the subprime crisis, these constrained investors had to sell their mortgage-related assets as soon as certified CRAs downgraded them to junk status, ie below investment grade.[62] They had to sell at the worst moment since the repricing of credit risk implied a repricing of asset price at lower levels. Therefore, regulations forcing market participants to rely on ratings imply an over-reliance on certified CRAs.

Accordingly, market over-reliance on certified credit ratings is at least partly a consequence of the regulatory use of ratings. Official recognition of credit ratings in regulatory and supervisory policies may have encouraged investors' over-reliance on ratings by discouraging some investors

---

percent in Germany, 10.7 percent in Italy, significantly above the 8 percent minimum).

59 The High-Level Group on Financial Supervision in the EU, 'De Larosière Report' (2009) 12 ‹http://ec.europa.eu/internal_market/finances/docs/de_larosiere_report_en.pdf› accessed 10 January 2013.

60 BCBS, *Strengthening the Resilience of the Banking Sector* (n 19) 55 (discussing how the rating-based approach of Basel II incentivized banks to rely heavily on ratings, thereby neglecting their own independent internal assessment).

61 Wellink, 'The New Framework for Banking Supervision' (n 20) 4.

62 See, eg, Kathleen Casey and Frank Partnoy, 'Downgrade the Ratings Agencies' *The New York Times*, June 4, 2010.

from paying close attention to what the ratings actually meant.[63] To some extent, investors relied on ratings instead of performing their own due diligence.[64] Moreover, if higher-rated assets attract lower capital requirements, market participants who are subject to capital regulation would even welcome rating inflation.[65] They would rely on ratings even when ratings lack informational value. Issuers became interested in ratings as well. In a competitive market, if investors were to suspect rating inflation, they would cease to trust their assessments, and issuers would no longer be prepared to pay for the ratings.[66] Yet the regulatory use of credit ratings implies another kind of issuers' interest in obtaining high ratings. Issuers get regulatory privileges if they obtain high ratings. Therefore, they are incentivized to hire the certified CRAs that attribute the higher grade to their financial instruments.

Nevertheless, rating-based regulations alone do not cause over-reliance on credit ratings. Investors and issuers also prefer CRAs that have accumulated a certain reputational capital. Investors respect CRAs with a reputation for rating accuracy and timeliness; in addition, issuers desire to obtain ratings from CRAs respected by investors.[67]

To make matters worse, regulatory and market-based over-reliance are interconnected. On the one hand, regulatory recognition criteria for CRAs are based on how extensively credit ratings are used by issuers and investors.[68] Regulators tried to come up with objective criteria in order to decide which CRAs could be used for regulatory purposes. The most important criterion refers to national recognition, ie, only well-established CRAs can meet such a requirement.[69] On the other hand, market-based reliance on ratings is influenced by regulatory recognition in the sense that investors and issuers prefer to obtain and use CRAs that

---

[63] FSF, *Report of the Financial Stability Forum on Enhancing Market and Institutional Resilience* (n 6) 38.

[64] See, eg, ibid 39; BCBS, *Strengthening the Resilience of the Banking Sector* (n 19) 55.

[65] House of Lords, Select Committee on Economic Affairs, *Banking Supervision and Regulation* (June 2009) 42.

[66] Ibid 40.

[67] IOSCO, *Report on the Activities of Credit Rating Agencies* (n 14) 9; IOSCO, *Report of the Task Force on the Subprime Crisis* (n 10) 27.

[68] IOSCO, *Report on the Activities of Credit Rating Agencies* (n 14) 9; IOSCO, *Report of the Task Force on the Subprime Crisis* (n 10) 27.

[69] See, eg, *Basel II* (n 9) para 91 (referring to validation based on historical experience owing to the objectivity criterion).

government regulators also use.[70] Therefore, both regulatory recognition of CRAs and market-based recognition of ratings influence each other significantly. This results in excessive market over-reliance on leading CRAs.

4.2.3 Rating-driven Market Behavior

Rating-based regulations create incentives for market participants to behave in a way that merely responds to rating-driven concerns. Various types of rating-driven market behavior include rating-driven transactions, regulatory arbitrage and "rating shopping."

First, issuers are so interested in obtaining the highest credit ratings that they may engage in transactions that make no economic sense but ensure a better grade. Especially from 2002 to 2007 in the subprime mortgage market, some securities were developed precisely to have high ratings.[71] Rating-based regulations create incentives for issuers to seek high ratings regardless of product quality.[72] The presence of rating-driven transactions may be a consequence of market over-reliance on credit ratings. It is worth recalling that market over-reliance on ratings is not only derived from regulatory reliance but also from behavioral reliance. In addition, rating-driven transactions do not only impair the proper functioning of the rating industry but can affect the financial markets as a whole. Market forces cannot work adequately if market participants structure deals in order to get high ratings instead of improving the quality of their financial products.

Second, high credit ratings may help financial institutions such as banks to get involved in regulatory arbitrage. Rating-based regulations allow for banks to reduce their capital requirements with the consent of the regulators. Above all, the risk-based approach under Basel II allowed banks to build up excessive leverage by reducing their risk-weighted

---

[70] IOSCO, *Report on the Activities of Credit Rating Agencies* (n 14) 9; IOSCO, *Report of the Task Force on the Subprime Crisis* (n 10) 27.

[71] Claire A Hill, 'Why Did Rating Agencies Do Such a Bad Job Rating Subprime Securities?' (2010) 71 University of Pittsburgh Law Review 1, 4.

[72] See, eg, Richard Cantor and Frank Packer, 'The Credit Rating Industry' [1994] FRBNY Quarterly Review 1, 7 (stating that the regulatory advantages of obtaining high ratings may consist of reaching a broader range of investors, reducing capital requirements or diminishing the amount of disclosure that is needed).

capital requirements.[73] Low risk weights imply banks can expand their balance sheets and still report strong capital ratios. As a result, rating-based regulations create incentives for investors and issuers to engage in regulatory arbitrage and other rating-driven activities. Regulatory arbitrage reflects a distortion of competitive incentives. Under such circumstances market forces do not function properly. At any rate, market participants will always attempt to circumvent regulations, making the design of incentive-based regulations necessary. Appropriate regulations would create better incentives in the financial markets. Although Basel III has not fully revised its use of ratings in its risk-sensitive approach, it has already taken measures able to reduce the possibilities for banks to build up excessive leverage. Above all, the establishment of a leverage ratio as a backstop to the risk-weighted ratio consists of a significant improvement because it will reduce banks' ability to over-extend their balance sheets in good times.[74]

Third, inappropriate competition among certified CRAs may result in "rating shopping" and rating inflation. In the years preceding the subprime mortgage crisis, if a CRA said no to a transaction, investment bankers would be able to engage in "rating shopping", ie taking their business to another CRA to obtain the desired triple-A rating.[75] Increased competition among CRAs worsens the problem of "rating shopping" as long as credit ratings are used for regulatory purposes.[76] The withdrawal of rating-based regulations is thus the only viable solution to the problem. Moreover, rating-based regulations create incentives for certified CRAs to produce inflated ratings instead of accurate assessments.[77]

---

73 Adrian Blundell-Wignall and Paul Atkinson, 'Thinking Beyond Basel III: Necessary Solutions for Capital and Liquidity' [2010] (Issue 1) OECD Journal: Financial Market Trends 1, 12–13 ‹http://www.oecd.org/finance/financialmarkets/45314422.pdf› accessed 10 January 2013 (illustrating this phenomenon in the light of an example).

74 ibid 9; Wellink, 'The New Framework for Banking Supervision' (n 20) 2.

75 'Credibility of Credit Ratings, the Investment Decisions Made Based on those Ratings, and the Financial Crisis, Hearings & Testimony Before the FCIC' (June 2, 2010) (testimony of Eric Kolchinsky, former Managing Director, Moody's) 3.

76 Jérôme Mathis, James McAndrews and Jean-Charles Rochet, 'Rating the Raters: Are Reputation Concerns Powerful Enough to Discipline Rating Agencies?' (2009) 56 Journal of Monetary Economics 657, 659.

77 BCBS, *Strengthening the Resilience of the Banking Sector* (n 19) 55 (emphasizing that issuers and investors are interested in high ratings which attract lower capital requirements and expand the range of products eligible for investments or credit protection). See also Christian C Opp, Marcus M Opp and

For instance, the Credit Rating Agency Reform Act of 2006 created inappropriate incentives in the financial markets. Increasing the number of NRSROs may have actually resulted in increased competitive pressures to inflate ratings.[78] The Act may well have caused a "race to the bottom" whereby issuers hired the certified CRA that was the most malleable and the most liberal with its investment-grade rating.[79]

4.3 WITHDRAWAL OF RATING-BASED REGULATIONS

4.3.1 Trend to Reduce Regulatory Dependence on Credit Ratings

> It is important to ensure that the use of ratings by authorities does not contribute to the lack of competition in the CRA industry.[80]

Eliminating regulatory dependence on credit ratings is the best way to foster a competitive environment for the rating industry. Some scholars contend that regulators should have already withdrawn rating-based regulations.[81] In fact, one of the main lessons from the recent financial crisis is that regulators should cease incorporating ratings into their rules.[82]

Milton Harris, 'Rating Agencies in the Face of Regulation' (2012) SSRN eLibrary, 3–4 ‹http:ssrn.com/abstract=1540099› accessed 10 January 2013 (showing empirical evidence that rating-based regulations create incentives for CRAs to inflate their ratings).

[78] Joshua Rosner, 'Toward an Understanding: NRSRO Failings in Structured Ratings and Discreet Recommendations to Address Agency Conflicts' (2009) 14 (Issue 4) Journal of Structured Finance 7, 11.

[79] Macey, *Corporate Governance* (n 35) 116–117.

[80] FSF, *Report of the Financial Stability Forum on Enhancing Market and Institutional Resilience* (n 6) 38.

[81] Partnoy, 'The Siskel and Ebert of Financial Markets?' (n 5) 681–707 (already in 1999 discussing the negative effects of rating-based regulations on the financial system; in fact, Professor Partnoy suggested that regulatory references to ratings should be removed from regulations almost a decade before lawmakers and regulators began to take the problem seriously). See also Lawrence J White, 'A New Law for the Bond Rating Industry' [2007] Regulation 48, 50 (stating that the SEC should have already abandoned the NRSRO framework after the Enron scandal at the beginning of the 2000s).

[82] Casey and Partnoy, 'Downgrade the Ratings Agencies' (n 62).

In October 2009 the SEC initiated a trend toward a decreasing reliance on NRSROs.[83] The SEC eliminated certain references to ratings in its regulations, thereby recognizing the detrimental effects of rating-based regulations on the financial markets.[84] The efforts made by the SEC to reduce the significant number of rating-based regulations have contributed to reducing a non-quality-dependent source of demand for ratings.[85]

However, at the beginning of 2010, there were still approximately 2,000 references to credit ratings in the US Federal Register.[86] Even regulatory measures to deal with the financial crisis depended to a great extent on ratings. For instance, in the US the Fed's 1 trillion US dollars Term Auction Lending Facility (TALF) plan – a colossal program to encourage lending – mandated that only securities rated by at least two major certified CRAs were eligible for aid.[87] Nevertheless, in the long run lawmakers and regulators are aware that they have to dismantle rating-based regulations.

On the global scale, the Basel III framework is expected to reduce reliance on certified ratings. Although Basel III has not fully withdrawn its use of certified ratings, the BCBS has already mentioned that reducing the use of ratings is an important area of focus.[88] The BCBS has acknowledged the negative effects of the regulatory use of ratings.[89] Two extreme alternative approaches can for instance be envisaged in removing external ratings from the Basel II framework: to return to a Basel I-type approach or to use internal credit risk models.[90] A Basel I-type approach involves abandoning the risk-sensitive measurement of bank capital requirements. The shortcoming of this approach is that it creates another

---

83 Partnoy, 'Overdependence on Credit Ratings was a Primary Cause of the Crisis' (n 5) 10.

84 SEC, References to Ratings of Nationally Recognized Statistical Rating Organizations, 74 Fed Reg 52,358 (October 9, 2009) 52,359.

85 John Patrick Hunt, 'Credit Rating Agencies and the "Worldwide Credit Crisis": The Limits of Reputation, the Insufficiency of Reform, and a Proposal for Improvement' [2009] Columbia Business Law Review 109, 151.

86 Casey and Partnoy, 'Downgrade the Ratings Agencies' (n 62) (adding that in 2010 the SEC endorsed ratings in regulations governing money market funds, even after removing references to ratings in other rules).

87 Aline Darbellay and Frank Partnoy, 'Credit Rating Agencies and Regulatory Reform' in Claire A Hill and Brett H McDonnell (eds), *Research Handbook on the Economics of Corporate Law* (Edward Elgar 2012) 278.

88 Wellink, 'The New Framework for Banking Supervision' (n 20) 4.

89 BCBS, *Strengthening the Resilience of the Banking Sector* (n 19) 55–56.

90 ibid 55.

type of incentive for banks to engage in risky activities.[91] Banks would hold risky assets in order to make more profit. Alternatively, the use of internal credit risk models implies further implementation of the Internal Ratings-Based (IRB) Approach of Basel II.[92] The Basel II framework did not permit the use of full credit models given the uncertainty and lack of data with respect to asset correlations, thereby forcing banks to use supervisory established correlations.[93]

4.3.2 Dodd-Frank Act of 2010

The most significant step to move away from over-reliance on credit ratings was taken when President Obama signed the Dodd-Frank Act of 2010 on July 21. Indeed, the agency reform embedded in the Dodd-Frank Act seeks to eliminate regulatory reliance on ratings. The NRSRO status should lose its importance in the long term. In fact, the agency reform has expressly removed statutory references to ratings.[94] Moreover, every Federal agency has one year to remove regulatory reliance on ratings.[95] References to ratings thus have to be removed from all types of government rules. Further, although CRA reform has not directly required the private sector to get rid of references to credit ratings, it should be interpreted as an important message from Congress.[96] It is recommended that market participants do not refer to ratings in investment guidelines or other internal rules. In other words, the government has taken the lead and the private sector should follow. As a consequence, investment culture is expected to change with respect to references to ratings.

The withdrawal of rating-based regulations is considered an important piece of the reform puzzle.[97] It will remove many of the incentives that led banks and CRAs to create an enormous market for mortgage-related securities.[98] The simple requirement to remove the regulatory use of

---

91 Dimitris N Chorafas, *Economic Capital Allocation with Basel II, Cost, Benefit and Implementation Procedures* (Elsevier Butterworth-Heinemann 2004) 43.

92 *Basel II* (n 9) para 211.

93 BCBS, *Strengthening the Resilience of the Banking Sector* (n 19) 55–56.

94 Dodd-Frank Wall Street Reform and Consumer Protection Act of 2010, HR 4173, 111th Congress, 2nd Session (2010) (Dodd-Frank Act) Sec 939(a–f).

95 ibid Sec 939A.

96 Darbellay and Partnoy, 'Credit Rating Agencies and Regulatory Reform' (n 87) 292.

97 Casey and Partnoy, 'Downgrade the Ratings Agencies' (n 62).

98 ibid.

ratings will force regulators and investors to find substitutes.[99] It remains a very challenging aspect of the financial reform and will take time for regulators and market participants to fully implement. This has proved to be more difficult than expected and US regulators delayed the implementation deadline.[100] Scholars have raised concern due to the fact that there is no ready alternative.[101] In sum, this part of the reform was easy to phrase but hard to do. At any rate, it is worth mentioning that the CRA reform does not entirely ban the use of ratings, just does not require it by law.[102]

4.3.3 EU Proposals

The EU is also planning to move away from regulatory reliance on credit ratings. The EU public consultation of November 2010 suggested that reducing the regulatory use of ratings is a crucial aspect of future reform.[103] In June 2011 the EU Parliament issued a non-legislative resolution in which it acknowledged that the regulatory system's key problem comes from over-reliance on ratings.[104]

In November 2011 the EU published a proposal for an amendment of the CRA Regulation, recognizing that the existing Regulation has not sufficiently addressed the problem of over-reliance on ratings.[105] This proposal includes a provision requiring certain financial institutions to perform their own due diligence. They shall make their own credit risk assessment and supervisors shall monitor that they do not over-rely on ratings.[106] Moreover, EU regulators such as ESMA shall not refer to

---

[99] ibid. Text to n 136 in ch 13.

[100] Kern Alexander, 'Bank Capital Regulation and the Role of External Ratings: Unresolved Issues' in Jan Kleineman and Lars Gorton (eds), *Credit Rating Agencies* (Stockholm Centre for Commercial Law, forthcoming 2013).

[101] Claire A Hill, 'Limits of Dodd-Frank's Rating Agency Reform' (2011) 15 Chapman Law Review 133, 144.

[102] Casey and Partnoy, 'Downgrade the Ratings Agencies' (n 62) (adding that using ratings should be an option not a mandate to follow a government-enshrined oligopoly).

[103] EU Commission, 'Public consultation on credit rating agencies' (n 27).

[104] EU Parliament 'Resolution of 8 June 2011 on credit rating agencies' (n 27) preamble (H).

[105] EU Commission, 'Proposal for a Regulation amending Regulation (EC) No 1060/2009 on credit rating agencies' COM (2011) 747 final ('Proposal for a CRA III') explanatory memorandum.

[106] ibid art 5a.

credit ratings for regulatory purposes if such references would trigger mechanistic reliance on ratings.[107]

In addition, the principle of avoiding over-reliance is also integrated in the proposal for a Directive amending the Directive relating to the Undertakings for Collective Investment in Transferable Securities (UCITS) and the Directive on Alternative Investment Funds Managers (AIFMs).[108] Here regulatory focus is put on the risk management process. UCITS and AIFMs shall not solely or mechanistically rely on credit ratings for assessing the creditworthiness of assets.[109] Nevertheless, ratings may be used as one factor among others.

With respect to bank capital requirements, the EU is willing to shift from the widespread use of the Standardized Approach to another approach that would not use ratings. In particular, the EU Parliament supports the increasing use of the IRB approach.[110] The EU is now expecting the BCBS to suggest other alternatives in the Basel framework. In this area, the EU is not ready to withdraw the regulatory use of credit ratings without ensuring that suitable alternatives are available.

---

107 ibid art 5b.

108 EU Commission, 'Proposal for a Directive amending Directive 2009/65/EC on the coordination of laws, regulations and administrative provisions relating to undertakings of collective investment in transferable securities (UCITS) and Directive 2011/61/EU on alternative investment funds managers in respect of the excessive reliance on credit ratings' COM (2011) 746 final.

109 ibid arts 1–2.

110 EU Parliament 'Resolution of 8 June 2011 on credit rating agencies' (n 27) para 4.

5. Regulatory treatment of credit rating agencies

> Credit rating agencies [...] play a critical "gatekeeper" role in the debt market that is functionally similar to that of securities analysts, who evaluate the quality of securities in the equity market, and auditors, who review the financial statements of firms. Such role justifies a similar level of public oversight and accountability.[1]

5.1 OVERSIGHT OF THE CREDIT RATING INDUSTRY

5.1.1 From Self-regulation to the Creation of Regulatory Frameworks for Credit Rating Agencies

5.1.1.1 Self-regulation in the credit rating industry

Self-regulation has so far played a crucial role in establishing standards of conduct with respect to CRAs.[2] Self-regulation refers to voluntary codes aiming at influencing industry practice. The most important body that sets up self-regulatory frameworks for CRAs is the International Organization of Securities Commissions (IOSCO). Its most relevant reference document is the IOSCO Code of Conduct.[3]

Adhesion to the IOSCO Code of Conduct is not compulsory so that its rules are based on voluntary compliance. Nevertheless, the IOSCO Code of Conduct has been widely recognized as the global benchmark for business standards to which CRAs are expected to adhere.[4] CRAs' compliance with the self-regulatory framework is interpreted among the investing community as a sign of good governance.

---

[1] Dodd-Frank Wall Street Reform and Consumer Protection Act of 2010, HR 4173, 111th Congress, 2nd Session (2010) (Dodd-Frank Act) Sec 931(2).

[2] See, eg, Susan Emmenegger, 'Die Regulierung von Rating-Agenturen' [2006] Swiss Review of Business and Financial Market Law 32, 37.

[3] IOSCO, *Code of Conduct Fundamentals for Credit Rating Agencies* (Revised May 2008).

[4] CESR, *Report on Compliance of EU Based Credit Rating Agencies with the 2008 IOSCO Code of Conduct* (May 2009) 10.

One of its core principles is the "comply or explain" principle,[5] ie CRAs can deviate from the IOSCO Code of Conduct if their own codes or practices are adequate. The IOSCO Code of Conduct provides no enforcement mechanism and merely uses the "comply or explain" approach.[6] Moreover, not all the IOSCO provisions are applicable to CRAs that provide credit ratings on a subscriber basis, ie the investor-paid CRAs.[7]

The IOSCO principles address (i) the quality and integrity of the rating process, (ii) CRAs' independence and the avoidance of conflicts of interest, and (iii) CRAs' responsibilities to investors and issuers.[8] Furthermore, the three leading CRAs' own Codes of Conduct contain only a few significant but well-documented variations from the IOSCO Code of Conduct.[9]

5.1.1.2 Merits and weaknesses of self-regulation

> Self-regulation does not take place effectively where the pressure of reputation as a controlling power only exists to a certain, limited degree due to a lack of existing competition.[10]

The credit rating industry has a long tradition of being subjected to international self-regulation. As the main advantage, self-regulation is considered to be sufficiently flexible to accommodate changing market circumstances.[11] Moreover, the needs of individual CRAs may be more

---

[5] Niamh Moloney, *EC Securities Regulation* (2nd edn, Oxford University Press 2008) 695.

[6] EU Commission, 'Proposal for a Regulation on credit rating agencies' COM (2008) 704 final, explanatory memorandum.

[7] CESR, *Report on Compliance of EU Based Credit Rating Agencies with the 2008 IOSCO Code of Conduct* (n 4) 11.

[8] Moloney, *EC Securities Regulation* (n 5) 695–696.

[9] ibid 698.

[10] Uwe Blaurock, 'Control and Responsibility of Credit Rating Agencies' (2007) 11 Electronic Journal of Comparative Law 1, 30. See also Siegfried Utzig, 'The Financial Crisis and the Regulation of Credit Rating Agencies: A European Banking Perspective' (2010) ADBI Working Paper No 188, 6 ‹http://www.adbi.org/working-paper/2010/01/26/3446.credit.rating.agencies.european.banking› accessed November 15, 2012; Jakob De Haan and Fabian Amtenbrink, 'Credit Rating Agencies' (2011) De Nederlandsche Bank (DNB) Working Paper No 278, 9.

[11] Harry McVea, 'Credit Rating Agencies, the Subprime Mortgage Debacle and Global Governance: the EU Strikes Back' (2010) 59 International and Comparative Law Quarterly 701, 717; Rolf H Weber, 'Mapping and Structuring

readily accommodated thanks to "comply or explain", instead of more prescriptive rules.[12] Accordingly, the danger of prescriptive rules would be to increase barriers to entry as smaller CRAs would encounter more difficulties in implementing stringent regulatory rules.

However, the 2007–2009 financial crisis shows that the absence of legally binding rules is a shortcoming rather than a benefit from the perspective of the financial markets as a whole. Market forces do not play their disciplinary role in the rating industry given the lack of competition; as a consequence, CRAs are not incentivized to implement international standards satisfactorily on a voluntary basis. In the years preceding the crisis, regulators experienced difficulties policing the IOSCO Code of Conduct, and in ensuring that CRAs claiming to comply with international standards were effectively doing so.[13] More precisely, the financial crisis that hit the world in 2007 exposed the weaknesses inherent in the IOSCO Code of Conduct when it came to identifying and addressing the risks posed by structured finance.[14] Further, the IOSCO Code of Conduct lacks enforcement mechanisms.[15]

5.1.1.3 Toward the regulation and supervision of credit rating agencies

The rating industry evolved over a period of a hundred years without being regulated.[16] Until recently the rating industry has almost exclusively relied on self-regulation.[17] However, the introduction of a governmental oversight regime is inevitable because schemes for self-regulation have not been robust or stringent enough to cope with problems of the industry.[18] The 2007–2009 financial crisis has indeed shed light on the

---

International Financial Regulation – A Theoretical Approach' (2009) 20 European Business Law Review 651, 657.

[12] ibid.

[13] ibid 718.

[14] Moloney, *EC Securities Regulation* (n 5) 699.

[15] De Haan and Amtenbrink, 'Credit Rating Agencies' (n 10) 17. See generally Weber, 'Mapping and Structuring International Financial Regulation' (n 11) 658.

[16] Lars Gorton and Aron Verständig, 'General Background of the Conference' in Jan Kleineman and Lars Gorton (eds), *Credit Rating Agencies* (Stockholm Centre for Commercial Law, forthcoming 2013).

[17] See, eg, Amadou NR Sy, 'The Systemic Regulation of Credit Rating Agencies and Rated Markets' (2009) IMF Working Paper No 09/129, 3 ‹http://www.imf.org/external/pubs/ft/wp/2009/wp09129.pdf› accessed January 10, 2013.

[18] EU Commission, 'Proposal for a Regulation on credit rating agencies' (n 6) explanatory memorandum. See also Piero Cinquegrana, 'The Reform of the

limits of self-regulatory approaches.[19] Unlike in the US, in the EU CRAs had not been subjected to direct supervision because public authorities in the Member States were not entitled to sanction a CRA when it violated the IOSCO standards of integrity, quality and transparency.[20] At any rate, the new regulatory frameworks for CRAs may incorporate elements of the IOSCO Code of Conduct in order to make those elements fully operational.[21]

Especially over the last decade, pressure has increased toward establishing a regulatory framework for CRAs.[22] In the light of the recent rating scandals, strong consensus had emerged internationally that regulatory intervention was needed.[23] In the US and in the EU, regulatory concern has focused on providing for oversight of the rating industry. This industry has been subject to a major overhaul. CRA regulations have also emerged in many jurisdictions around the world such as Japan, Australia, Mexico, Hong Kong and Canada.[24]

Credit Rating Agencies: A Comparative Perspective' (2009) ECMI Policy Brief No 12, 6.

[19] See generally Weber, 'Mapping and Structuring International Financial Regulation' (n 11) 688 (discussing the establishment of a new regime with respect to international financial regulation).

[20] EU Commission, 'Staff Working Document accompanying the Proposal for a Regulation on credit rating agencies, Impact Assessment' COM (2008) 704, 14.

[21] EU Commission, 'Proposal for a Regulation on credit rating agencies' (n 6) explanatory memorandum.

[22] But see Steven L Schwarcz, 'Private Ordering of Public Markets: The Rating Agency Paradox' [2002] (Issue 2) University of Illinois Law Review 1, 13 (arguing that there is little reason to believe that an increased regulation of CRAs will improve the reliability of ratings).

[23] Stéphane Rousseau, 'Regulating Credit Rating Agencies after the Financial Crisis: The Long and Winding Road Toward Accountability' (2009) SSRN eLibrary, 27 ‹http:ssrn.com/abstract=1456708› accessed January 10, 2013; IOSCO, *Regulatory Implementation of the Statement of Principles Regarding the Activities of Credit Rating Agencies* (Consultation Report, May 2010) 10.

[24] ibid 11–12 (describing the establishment of regulatory frameworks for CRAs in Japan, Australia, Mexico and Hong Kong); Rousseau, 'Regulating Credit Rating Agencies after the Financial Crisis' (n 23) 28 (referring to regulatory initiatives for CRA oversight in Canada). But see 'Debatte um "Schuld" der Rating-Agenturen, Schweizer Zurückhaltung bei anstehender Regulierung' *NZZ*, September 4, 2010) 35 (stating that Switzerland has not followed this regulatory trend, preferring to leave the responsibility for CRA oversight to their home country).

5.1.2 Strengthening Credit Rating Agency Oversight

5.1.2.1 US model for agency regulation and supervision

(i) The Credit Rating Agency Reform Act of 2006 The US initiated the trend toward the creation of a supervisory framework for CRAs. The Credit Rating Agency Reform Act aimed to improve rating quality by fostering accountability, transparency and competition in the rating industry.[25]

The SEC was given statutory authority to oversee the rating industry, more particularly NRSROs.[26] Only NRSROs fall within the scope of the regulation, ie those certified CRAs that are used in financial market regulations. The purpose of the CRA Reform Act is to enhance competition among NRSROs so that smaller CRAs can compete with the likes of Moody's and Standard & Poor's.

Regulators proceeded on the assumption that competition would best be increased by opening up the process of designating NRSROs. US lawmakers and regulators believed that more NRSROs would enhance competition in the rating industry. Therefore, the framework introduced an NRSRO registration and qualification process.[27] The idea was to establish formal procedures for designating NRSROs and to monitor their activities.[28]

However, the Credit Rating Agency Reform Act of 2006 may have been counterproductive as far as competition is concerned. The Act may cause a "race to the bottom" in the sense that issuers may hire the certified CRA that is the most malleable and the most liberal with investment-grade rating.[29]

---

[25] Credit Rating Agency Reform Act of 2006, S 3850, 109th Congress (2006) preamble and Sec 2(5).

[26] ibid Sec 2(6).

[27] ibid Sec 4.

[28] See, eg, Richard Cantor and Frank Packer, 'The Credit Rating Industry' [1994] FRBNY Quarterly Review 1, 8 (explaining that serious criticism had been raised on the informality of the NRSRO designation process and the opacity of the criteria). See also Frank Partnoy, 'How and Why Credit Rating Agencies Are Not Like Other Gatekeepers' (2006) University of San Diego Legal Studies Research Paper Series No 07-46, 64 (mentioning that although the concept of NRSROs had been used since the 1970s, the SEC had not defined the term).

[29] Jonathan R Macey, *Corporate Governance: Promises kept, Promises Broken* (Princeton University Press 2008) 116–117.

Increasing the number of NRSROs may actually result in ill-conceived competition whereby CRAs are actually incentivized to inflate ratings.[30]

Further, it is worth mentioning how the SEC made use of the regulatory powers given by the CRA Reform Act in order to supervise the rating industry. In June 2007, just before the subprime mortgage crisis hit the financial markets, the SEC adopted final rules to implement provisions of the Act.[31] In February 2009 the SEC amended its rules to impose additional requirements on NRSROs as regards rating integrity.[32] In December 2009 the SEC amended its rules to impose additional disclosure requirements and measures to address conflicts of interest on NRSROs.[33] The SEC aimed at making it possible for more NRSROs to rate structured finance products.[34] The regulation permitted disclosure of material non-public information to an NRSRO regardless of whether the NRSRO makes its ratings publicly available.[35] Above all, the amendment intended to accommodate subscriber-based NRSROs that do not make their ratings available for free.[36]

(ii) Dodd-Frank Act of 2010 In the US, the Dodd-Frank Act of 2010 recently reformed the credit rating industry. This Act comprises the most sweeping changes to financial regulation since the reforms that followed the Great Depression. The financial regulatory reform bill is depicted as putting consumers first at the expense of the financial industry. It seeks to fix the "too big to fail" problem and to avoid further bailouts in the financial system.[37] With respect to CRAs, the US Congress acknowledged that the "gatekeeper" role of CRAs justifies the same level of public oversight and accountability as other gatekeepers such as securities analysts and auditors.[38] Concern had been raised about addressing

---

30 Joshua Rosner, 'Toward an Understanding: NRSRO Failings in Structured Ratings and Discreet Recommendations to Address Agency Conflicts' (2009) 14 (Issue 4) Journal of Structured Finance 7, 11.

31 SEC, Oversight of Credit Rating Agencies Registered as Nationally Recognized Statistical Rating Organizations, 72 Fed Reg 33,564 (June 18, 2007) 33,564.

32 SEC, Amendments to Rules for Nationally Recognized Statistical Rating Organizations, 74 Fed Reg 6,456 (February 9, 2009) 6,456.

33 SEC, Amendments to Rules for Nationally Recognized Statistical Rating Organizations, 74 Fed Reg 63,832 (December 4, 2009) 63,832.

34 ibid 63,844.

35 ibid 63,850.

36 ibid 63,850.

37 Dodd-Frank Act, preamble.

38 ibid Sec 931.

the contradiction with respect to the competitive environment in the rating industry: CRAs became private-sector entities with quasi-governmental power, yet there was weak oversight of their rating practices.[39]

If ambitious proposals were made to completely overhaul the rating industry, legislative efforts have resulted in a compromise. Nevertheless, there are very interesting amendments to the rating industry.

With respect to oversight, the Dodd-Frank Act of 2010 sets up a new regulatory structure for CRAs, increasing powers to supervise the rating industry. These regulatory and supervisory rules result from the appreciation that CRAs play a fundamentally commercial role, thereby implying that they have to be subject to similar standards in comparison to other gatekeepers such as auditors and securities analysts.[40] The agency reform creates a new authority within the SEC, the Office of Credit Ratings (OCR).[41] The SEC established the OCR in June 2012 with the appointment of Thomas Butler as its Director.[42]

The Dodd-Frank Act is characterized by numerous regulations with respect to NRSROs. Regulations have been improved and regulators enjoy greater powers to set standards in the rating industry. Emphasis is especially put on transparency, requiring from CRAs a significant amount of disclosure. The intent is to provide regulators and investors with more information about NRSRO ratings. NRSROs have to file reports to the SEC and these reports must be made available to the public as well.

The regulation of the NRSRO status is enhanced. The SEC has the ability to bar NRSROs. The SEC even has the ability to revoke the registration of an NRSRO with respect to a particular class of securities.[43]

There are new governance rules. NRSROs have to establish effective internal control structures. Internal controls strive to govern the implementation of the policies, procedures and methodologies for determining ratings.[44] A few governance rules require CRAs to monitor

---

39 See, eg, Emmenegger, 'Die Regulierung von Rating-Agenturen' (n 2) 41.

40 ibid, Sec 931.

41 ibid Sec 932(a)(8).

42 Staff of the SEC, '2012 Summary Report of Commission Staff's Examinations of Each Nationally Recognized Statistical Rating Organization, As Required by Section 15E(p)(3)(C) of the Securities Exchange Act of 1934' (November 2012) 8.

43 Dodd-Frank Act, Sec 932(a)(3)(I).

44 ibid Sec 932(a)(2)(B).

conflicts of interest. For instance, dealing with conflicts of interest counts as a duty of the board of directors of the NRSROs.[45]

The SEC requires that NRSROs disclose their rating performance.[46] These disclosure requirements aim at allowing users to evaluate the accuracy of ratings and to compare the performance of ratings by different NRSROs.[47]

With respect to rating symbols, NRSROs have to define the meaning of any symbol and apply any symbol consistently.[48] Concretely, NRSROs can use the same symbol across different categories of financial instruments if the symbol is used in a consistent manner. A triple-A rating in structured finance would have the same meaning as a triple-A rating in corporate or sovereign debt.[49] If the meaning of symbols is different across different categories of financial instruments, NRSROs have to use different symbols.

The Dodd-Frank Act establishes new regulation of rating methodologies.[50] With respect to rating procedures and methodologies the SEC prescribes rules for the protection of investors and in the public interest.[51]

The qualifications of the analysts also fall under regulatory scrutiny. There are requirements for standards governing CRAs' analysts.[52] A new training process is set up and supervised by the government. Hence, regulators now have a role to play with respect to who is hired by CRAs and whether analysts have sufficient skills.

The Dodd-Frank Act directs the SEC to implement its provisions. The SEC adopted final rules in certain areas and proposed new rules in others. In January 2011 the SEC adopted a final rule that requires NRSROs to include information regarding the representations, warranties and enforcement mechanisms available to investors in an Asset-Backed Securities (ABS) offering in any report accompanying a rating issued in connection with such offering, including a preliminary rating.[53] Many

---

45 ibid Sec 932(a)(8).

46 ibid.

47 ibid.

48 ibid Sec 938(a)(2–3). The requirements for universal rating symbols ended up being a bit different than people had conceived.

49 Aline Darbellay and Frank Partnoy, 'Credit Rating Agencies and Regulatory Reform' in Claire A Hill and Brett H McDonnell (eds), *Research Handbook on the Economics of Corporate Law* (Edward Elgar 2012) 285.

50 Congress succeeded in establishing new rules with respect to rating methodologies and procedures even though CRAs lobbied hard against them.

51 Dodd-Frank Act, Sec 932(a)(8).

52 ibid Sec 936.

53 Securities Exchange Act of 1934, 17 CFR 240.17g-7.

other SEC rules are at the stage of proposals, for instance the rule addressing conflicts of interest with respect to sales and marketing concerns.[54]

5.1.2.2 EU model for agency regulation and supervision

The idea of establishing a supervisory framework for CRAs was immediately put forward in the EU as a response to the subprime mortgage meltdown. The absence of regulation of CRAs and the general outcry with respect to their role in the 2007–2009 financial crisis put substantive pressure on the EU to adopt promptly mandatory and enforceable rules in this field.[55] Broadly speaking, the EU has focused on establishing a more efficient, integrated and sustainable European system of supervision.[56]

In order to reassure the financial markets during the financial crisis, the EU intended to come up with new regulations rapidly, although the withdrawal of rating-based regulations was not feasible in the short term.[57] As a consequence, the EU decided to create a stringent supervisory regime for CRAs. The EU interpreted the troubles in the rating industry as a failure of self-regulatory efforts. Therefore, the EU opted for tight rules in order to restore the confidence of the financial markets in CRAs.[58]

The main sources of inspiration for EU regulation of CRAs are twofold: the EU seeks convergence of its policies (i) with the US legal framework for CRAs and (ii) with the IOSCO Code of Conduct for CRAs. Apart from that, the two regulatory topics of most interest are probably (i) conflicts of interest and (ii) disclosure. First, CRAs have an obligation to ensure that credit ratings are not affected by conflicts of

---

[54] Marilyn Blumberg Cane, Adam Shamir and Thomas Jodar, 'Below Investment Grade and Above the Law: A Past, Present and Future Look at the Accountability of Credit Rating Agencies' (2012) 17 Fordham Journal of Corporate & Financial Law 1063, 1114.

[55] EU Commission, 'Staff Working Document, Impact Assessment, Accompanying document to the Proposal for a Regulation amending Regulation (EC) No 1060/2009 on credit rating agencies' COM (2010) 289 final, 7.

[56] EU Commission, 'Proposal for a Regulation on amending Regulation (EC) No 1060/2009 on credit rating agencies' COM (2010) 289 final ('Proposal for a CRA II Regulation') explanatory memorandum.

[57] As far as the EU is concerned, the most comprehensive use of ratings for regulatory purposes consists of bank capital requirement regulations stemming from the Basel framework.

[58] Regulation (EC) No 1060/2009 of 16 September 2009 on credit rating agencies [2009] OJ L302/1 (CRA Regulation) preamble (43).

interest.[59] Second, disclosure is a broad topic that includes the production of a transparency report by the registered CRAs,[60] and also the disclosure of methodologies, models and key rating assumptions.[61]

The CRA Regulation of 2009 introduced a framework for oversight of CRAs operating in the EU by means of a registration process for CRAs. Under the initial version of the CRA Regulation, the competent authority was the regulator designated by the Member State where the CRA is established. Because Moody's, Standard & Poor's and Fitch have subsidiaries in various EU countries, several EU regulators were responsible for their registration in the EU.

At a further stage, it became necessary to adapt the CRA Regulation to the new European supervisory architecture.[62] An amendment came into force in May 2011 so that CRAs fall within the scope of supervision by the European Securities and Markets Authority (ESMA). By this means the EU centralizes regulatory competence in the hands of a single authority.[63] The ESMA newly assumes general competence in matters relating to the registration and ongoing supervision of registered CRAs.[64]

EU legislation primarily targets CRAs whose ratings are used for regulatory purposes.[65] There are many explicit references to ratings in the sense of rating-based regulations. For instance, entities such as insurance undertakings and pension funds are only allowed to use ratings for regulatory purposes if they are issued by registered or certified CRAs.[66] However, the trend toward a decreasing use of ratings in financial market regulations has been initiated. The EU launched a public consultation in

---

[59] ibid art 6; McVea, 'Credit Rating Agencies, the Subprime Mortgage Debacle and Global Governance' (n 11) 724; Patrick Andrieu, *Ratingagenturen in der Krise, Über die Einführung von Qualitätsstandards für Ratings durch die Europäische Union* (Peter Lang 2010) 101–106.

[60] CRA Regulation, art 12; Andrieu, *Ratingagenturen in der Krise* (n 59) 101.

[61] CRA Regulation, art 8; McVea, 'Credit Rating Agencies, the Subprime Mortgage Debacle and Global Governance' (n 11) 726.

[62] EU Commission, 'Staff Working Document' (n 55) 4.

[63] Felix Flinterman, 'ESMA: The European Supervisor of Credit Rating Agencies' in Jan Kleineman and Lars Gorton (eds), *Credit Rating Agencies* (Stockholm Centre for Commercial Law, forthcoming 2013).

[64] Regulation (EU) No 513/2011 of 11 May 2011 amending Regulation (EC) No 1060/2009 on credit rating agencies [1011] OJ L145/30 (CRA II Regulation) preamble (6).

[65] CRA Regulation, art 2 paras 1, 3. See also Cinquegrana, 'The Reform of the Credit Rating Agencies' (n 18) 6.

[66] CRA Regulation, art 4 para 1.

November 2010 to analyze topics that were not addressed in the EU Regulation of 2009.[67] The proposal for an amendment of the CRA Regulation that was published in November 2011 strives to reduce over-reliance on ratings.[68]

With respect to the scope of application, the EU directly supervises CRAs that have their headquarters or subsidiaries in the EU. Registration in the EU is one of the premises for credit ratings to be used in the EU. By this means, the CRA Regulation encourages CRAs established in third countries to set up subsidiaries in the EU if they are willing to be used for regulatory purposes in the EU.[69]

Nevertheless, credit ratings issued outside the EU can possibly be used in the EU through two means, ie certification or endorsement.[70] On the one hand, certification based on an equivalence decision of the EU Commission is subject to certain conditions.[71] First, the ratings are issued by a CRA subject to supervision in that third country. Second, the EU Commission has formally adopted an equivalence decision that recognizes the third-country framework as equivalent to the EU requirements. In September 2010 the EU Commission adopted its first equivalence decision concerning the Japanese framework for CRAs. In October 2012 the EU Commission adopted equivalence decisions with respect to the US, Canadian and Australian frameworks. Since then, the question arises as to whether Moody's, Standard & Poor's and Fitch can be used in the EU based on an equivalence decision. It is also interesting to mention a further condition of the equivalence regime: this opportunity is solely at the disposal of CRAs that are not of systemic importance to the financial stability or integrity of the EU financial markets.[72] In this respect, there are grounds to believe that the Big Three would be regarded as systemically relevant to the EU and would therefore not benefit from the equivalence decision.

On the other hand, the endorsement regime allows CRAs registered in the EU to endorse credit ratings issued in third countries if such ratings comply with requirements that are at least as stringent as the EU

---

[67] EU Commission, 'Public consultation on credit rating agencies' (November 5, 2010) 1–28.

[68] Text to n 105 in ch 4.

[69] CRA Regulation, preamble (55).

[70] ESMA 'Guidelines on the Application of the Endorsement Regime under Article 4(3) of the Credit Rating Regulation 1060/2009, Consultation Paper' (March 18, 2011) 5.

[71] CRA Regulation, art 5.

[72] ibid art 5, para 1, let d; 'ESMA Guidelines' (n 70) 5.

requirements.[73] In this respect, third-country CRAs are required to set up subsidiaries in the EU to allow for the effective use of the EU endorsement regime.[74] This regime is likely to play a crucial role because the three leading CRAs – Moody's, Standard & Poor's and Fitch – are most likely considered to be of systemic importance and may not be able to count on the equivalence decision of the US regulation to use their ratings in the EU. In such a context, the Big Three have to be registered in the EU through their subsidiaries, which they are. In turn, they would be able to endorse ratings issued in third countries based on the endorsement regime. To comply with the EU Regulation, the Big Three would have to demonstrate to the EU regulator that their ratings issued outside the EU fulfill requirements that are at least as stringent as the requirements set out in the EU Regulation.[75]

In November 2011 the EU released a proposal for another amendment of the CRA Regulation. The proposal introduces further requirements related to conflicts of interest and disclosure requirements.[76] It also integrates a civil liability regime.[77] Besides that, the proposal includes detailed rules. For instance, a provision requires the use of two obligatory ratings under certain circumstances.[78] The idea is to obtain two different and competing assessments and the most conservative one would be used for regulatory purposes.[79] In my opinion, this provision is misguided in a context in which regulators are planning to move away from over-reliance on ratings. US regulators previously adopted this approach but they have already pulled back. One of the unintended consequences was to reinforce the Moody's and Standard & Poor's' duopoly. Therefore, I am skeptical about the benefits of this new provision. Nevertheless, overall the 2011 proposal for an amendment of the CRA Regulation remains a positive step toward regulating the aspects that were not addressed initially.

---

[73] CRA Regulation, art 4 para 3 and preamble (13).

[74] ibid preamble (55).

[75] ibid art 4 para 3.

[76] EU Commission, 'Proposal for a Regulation amending Regulation (EC) No 1060/2009 on credit rating agencies' COM (2011) 747 final ('Proposal for a CRA III Regulation'); Gorton and Verständig, 'General Background of the Conference' (n 16). Text to n 33 in ch 9.

[77] Text to n 119.

[78] 'Proposal for a CRA III Regulation' (n 76) art 8b.

[79] European Parliament, 'Resolution of 8 June 2011 on credit rating agencies: future perspectives' (2010/2302(INI)) para 31.

5.2 LIABILITY REGIMES FOR CREDIT RATING AGENCIES

5.2.1 Privileged Treatment of the Credit Rating Industry

CRAs historically benefit from a special treatment. In particular, CRAs differ from other gatekeepers because they have been largely immune to civil and criminal liability for malfeasance.[80] The special treatment for CRAs has without doubt had a negative impact on the level of competition in the rating industry. Such a situation empowers CRAs with a privileged position in comparison to other gatekeepers. In this regard, other gatekeepers are considered as potential competitors. The rating industry takes advantage of the special treatment that other financial industries do not have. These distinctive market features partly explain how CRAs have become so important in the financial system.

The level of competition in the rating industry varies to a certain extent depending on the existence of liability rules. The threat of liability can be an effective tool in encouraging gatekeeper accountability.[81] From a theoretical point of view, the competitive landscape changes significantly depending on whether or not courts recognize CRA liability. The threat of litigation costs would incentivize CRAs to provide more accurate ratings. In fact, the presence of competition refers to a situation where the price for ratings is directly connected to their informational value. While analyzing the competitive environment in the rating industry, liability rules must be considered since they tend to make sure that the cost of providing bad ratings exceeds the gains resulting from the fees collected. Moreover, the absence of successful lawsuits against CRAs gives them a privileged position in comparison to other gatekeepers. The CRAs enjoy a competitive advantage. From another perspective, liability rules may, however, reduce competition if they imply an over-reliance on CRAs by market participants. A competitive rating market exists only if market participants perform their own due diligence while deciding to follow the ratings of a specific CRA. Therefore, the effects of liability rules on competition must be analyzed by taking into account the pros and cons of litigation in the rating industry. Liability rules are adequately designed if they are able to discipline the rating industry.

---

[80] Partnoy, 'How and Why Credit Rating Agencies Are Not Like Other Gatekeepers' (n 28) 61.

[81] Darbellay and Partnoy, 'Credit Rating Agencies and Regulatory Reform' (n 49) 288.

5.2.2 US Liability Regime for Credit Rating Agencies

5.2.2.1 Historically privileged position of credit rating agencies

Historically, CRAs have been immune to civil and criminal liability. CRAs have successfully defended themselves against litigation by claiming that their credit ratings are opinions protected by the First Amendment of the US Constitution.[82] In other words, they have enjoyed free speech protection. It is thus not surprising that CRAs prefer to compare themselves to publishing companies than to gatekeepers such as securities analysts and auditors.[83] Several judges have accepted the argument that ratings are opinions protected by the First Amendment of the US Constitution.[84] Recently a court has also dismissed a case in which the underwriter liability of CRAs was questioned.[85]

Even though CRAs can invoke the First Amendment, free speech protection is not absolute and CRAs are not fully exempted from securities laws. "Free speech protection in the securities area is narrow."[86] Because ratings are considered to be "commercial speech," there is no heightened First Amendment protection. In this area, free speech protection goes less far than for other forms of speech.[87] For instance, the US Supreme Court has indicated that "commercial speech" can be regulated to the extent that it is false or misleading.[88] This reasoning was illustrated in the *Enron* case: the court stated that any First Amendment protection

---

[82] Partnoy, 'How and Why Credit Rating Agencies Are Not Like Other Gatekeepers' (n 28) 66 (explaining why CRAs have been immune to liability but disagreeing with the judges who accepted their argument); Cinquegrana, 'The Reform of the Credit Rating Agencies' (n 18) 2.

[83] See, eg, 'Credit Rating Agencies and the Financial Crisis: Hearing Before the House Committee on Oversight and Government Reform' (2008) 110th Congress 2nd Session, HR Serial No 110-155, 117 (statement of Raymond W McDaniel, Chairman and Chief Executive Officer, Moody's). But see Partnoy, 'How and Why Credit Rating Agencies Are Not Like Other Gatekeepers' (n 28) 61, 81 (stating that even though CRAs consider themselves similar to financial journalists, their ratings are far more valuable than even the most prominent and respected financial publishers).

[84] But see ibid 61 (disagreeing with the judges that exempted CRAs from liability because of the First Amendment).

[85] Andrew R Sorkin, 'A Hand in a House of Cards' *The New York Times DealBook*, February 16, 2010.

[86] Partnoy, 'How and Why Credit Rating Agencies Are Not Like Other Gatekeepers' (n 28) 95.

[87] ibid 85.

[88] *Central Hudson Gas & Electric Corp* v *Public Service Commission* [1980] 447 US 557.

for ratings was not absolute but qualified, ie ratings can be regulated the same as other "corporate speech."[89]

In the period prior to the Dodd-Frank Act of 2010, courts never held CRAs liable. There was even a rule in securities laws that expressly exempted CRAs from liability. CRAs were not subject to a strict liability regime because they were immune from prosecution under Section 11 of the Securities Act of 1933.[90] Even though courts did not hold CRAs liable for fraud, there was still room for CRA liability in future cases. There were other liability rules that could have applied had CRAs committed securities fraud. This area needed clarification due to disparate judicial decisions.[91] Some decisions tended to reject CRA liability more than others. Where CRAs only played the role of information gatherers, courts were more sympathetic to their free speech claims than where CRAs were involved in structuring the transaction.[92] Nevertheless, the Dodd-Frank Act has brought the necessary clarity with respect to CRA liability, which will help litigators sue CRAs.

5.2.2.2 Dodd-Frank Act of 2010

The Dodd-Frank Act of 2010 seeks to remove the special treatment for CRAs. With respect to CRA liability, the CRA reform introduces a liability regime in order to make CRAs more accountable for the quality of their ratings. CRA liability is particularly necessary in modern financial markets because of the different role of structured finance ratings as compared with corporate ratings.[93] The Dodd-Frank Act has clarified the situation thanks to two provisions of the securities laws. On the one hand, the Securities Exchange Act of 1934 was amended so that the state of mind in private actions offers an easier path to sue CRAs. In the future it will be sufficient to prove that CRAs knowingly or recklessly failed to conduct a reasonable investigation or to obtain reasonable

---

[89] *Newby* v *Enron Corp* [2005] US Dist LEXIS 4494 (SD Tex, February 16, 2005).

[90] Securities Act of 1933, 17 CFR 230.436(g)(1).

[91] Partnoy, 'How and Why Credit Rating Agencies Are Not Like Other Gatekeepers' (n 28) 88.

[92] Compare, eg, *Compuware Corp* v *Moody's Investors Services, Inc* [2004] 324 F Supp 2d 860 (ED Mich 2004) (in which Moody's was entitled to protection as a journalist) with, eg, *In re Fitch* [2003] 330 F 2d 104, 111 (2d Cir 2003) (in which Fitch played a significant role in structuring the transaction, that is, the CRA went beyond the activities of a journalist).

[93] Rosner, 'Toward an Understanding' (n 30) 15.

verification of factual elements relied upon by their methodology.[94] The new rule provides a mechanism to establish the civil liability of CRAs, thereby facilitating litigation against CRAs.[95]

On the other hand, CRAs will be subject to expert liability under Section 11 of the Securities Act of 1933 thanks to the repeal of Rule 436(g).[96] Rule 436(g) had shielded CRAs from liability with respect to the disclosure of ratings in registration statements. Pursuant to the Dodd-Frank Act, issuers have to seek CRAs' written consent if they want to include ratings in their registration statements. If CRAs deliver their consent, they are potentially liable as experts under Section 11 of the Securities Act of 1933. Nevertheless, this provision seems difficult to apply in practice due to the resistance of the leading CRAs. CRAs refused to consent to the inclusion of their ratings in transaction documents so that deals could unlikely take place.[97] In response, the SEC had to issue no-action letters to refrain from enforcement actions so long as the amendment could not be effectively implemented. In such a context, the provision that aimed to include expert liability may have reached an impasse.

5.2.3 EU Liability Regime for Credit Rating Agencies

5.2.3.1 National liability regimes

In the EU, there are as many liability regimes as there are EU countries. Nevertheless, the legal frameworks of EU countries have similarities among themselves with respect to civil liability rules.

There is debate at the EU level on the necessity of introducing a common EU level principle of civil liability for CRAs.[98] Many commentators suggest that the EU should harmonize national regimes throughout Europe.[99] This change may occur in the near future as the EU proposal

---

94 Dodd-Frank Act, Sec 933(b)(2).

95 Darbellay and Partnoy, 'Credit Rating Agencies and Regulatory Reform' (n 49) 292.

96 Dodd-Frank Act, Sec 939G.

97 Stacy-Marie Ishmael, 'What's the SEC to do about 436(g)? Call a time out' *FT Alphaville*, July 22, 2010.

98 EU Commission, 'Public consultation on credit rating agencies' (n 67) 24–25.

99 'AMF Response to the European Commission Consultation on Future Measures to be taken on Credit Rating Agencies' (6 January 2011) 6. But see 'The United Kingdom Authorities Response to the European Commission Internal Market and Services Consultation Document on Credit Rating Agencies' (31 January 2011) 2, 18 (contending that there is no need to introduce civil

for an amendment of the CRA Regulation includes a provision that would render CRAs liable under specific circumstances.[100] Unless this proposed civil liability rule comes into force, the rules will continue to be enshrined at the level of the Member States. Moreover, Member States will at any rate remain competent for any type of liability not covered by the EU Regulation.

As of January 2013, Member States determine whether or not their laws hold CRAs liable for their misconduct.[101] It is worth describing the main legal systems in the EU to analyze whether or not they include a liability regime for CRAs.

Broadly speaking, legislators have two options. The first implies including CRA liability in the general rules. In this respect, CRAs would receive the same legal treatment as other gatekeepers, market participants and individuals. It is the current situation in most legal frameworks, such as Germany. German policymakers have not deemed it necessary to introduce a special liability regime for CRAs. The second option consists of establishing CRA liability in a special law. This would be the case in the EU if the EU regulator adopted the special liability rule of the proposed Regulation concerning CRAs exclusively.

Hitherto France has offered the best example of a special liability regime for CRAs.[102] Indeed, in 2010 the French law of banking and financial regulation introduced a special provision establishing CRA liability.[103] The French legislator proceeded on the assumption that the general framework for civil, contractual and tort liability is not well designed to deal with the role of CRAs in financial markets.[104] By this means, France followed the path of the US Dodd-Frank Act of 2010 and

liability in the EU framework for CRAs, because it would be counterproductive to reducing the reliance on ratings, as well as risk weakening competition).

[100] 'Proposal for a CRA III Regulation' (n 76) art 35a.

[101] Ivan Tchotourian, 'Agences de notation: encadrement et responsabilité' [2011] Bulletin Joly Bourse 119, 119ff.

[102] But see Cécile Thépot, 'L'encadrement légal de l'activité des agences de notation par la loi de régulation bancaire et financière' (2010) 250 Petites Affiches 26, 26ff; Cécile Thépot, 'L'encadrement des agences de notation: "trop de loi tue la loi"' (2011) (on file with author) 6 (criticizing the new liability rule for CRAs).

[103] Loi française No 2010-1249 du 22 octobre 2010 de régulation bancaire et financière, art 10 (codified in Code monétaire et financier, art L 544-5) (Loi française de régulation bancaire et financière).

[104] Jérôme Chartier, 'Rapport fait au nom de la commission des finances, de l'économie générale et du contrôle budgétaire sur le projet de loi de régulation bancaire et financière (No 2165)' (Assemblée nationale, May 25, 2010) 72.

adopted a special liability rule in relation to CRAs. However, although the new liability regime offers an easier path to sue CRAs, the difficulties in proving CRA liability will make successful cases rare albeit not inexistent.[105]

In the various legal systems, the basis for civil liability may be contractual, quasi-contractual or tortious, depending on the relationship between the CRA and the market participant that sustained losses. If the two parties concluded an agreement, the ground for liability is contractual liability. Under the investor-pays business model, CRAs and investors are contractually bound, ie investors can sue CRAs based on their contractual relationship. Under the issuer-pays business model, the contractual relationship is between CRAs and issuers. Issuers can possibly sue issuer-paid CRAs on a contractual basis but investors are third parties.[106]

If the legal basis is contractual, the conditions for liability are typically breach of contract, damage, causality and fault.[107] The advantage of contractual liability is that there is – in most legal systems – a reversal of the burden of proof that can make it easier to prove fault.[108] From another perspective however, contractual liability is generally trumped by CRAs' standardized contractual clauses on limitations and exclusions from liability.[109] Nevertheless, legal systems generally do not allow unrestricted limitations of contractual liability. In France, the new liability rule states that contractual clauses including limitations of liability that are possibly total exclusions of liability are void.[110] In Germany, concern has been voiced – given the CRAs' position of trust – that even an exclusion of liability for slight negligence jeopardizes the purpose of the contract and is thus invalid.[111]

In many cases however, there is no contract between CRAs and damaged market participants. The typical case is when investors sustain

---

105 Philippe Marini 'Rapport No 703 (2009–2010) fait au nom de la commission des finances' (Sénat, September 14, 2010) 7.

106 Gorton and Verständig, 'General Background of the Conference' (n 16).

107 David Vasella, 'Die Haftung von Ratingagenturen, Ein Beitrag zur Expertenhaftung' in Kern Alexander and others (eds), *Zürcher Studien zum Privatrecht, Band 236* (Schulthess 2011) 291–292.

108 Blaurock, 'Control and Responsibility of Credit Rating Agencies' (n 10) 18–19.

109 ibid 19.

110 Loi française de régulation bancaire et financière, art 10 (codified in Code monétaire et financier, art L 544-6).

111 Blaurock, 'Control and Responsibility of Credit Rating Agencies' (n 10) 19 (with accompanying note).

losses due to their reliance on inaccurate credit ratings. If the issuer-pays business model prevails, investors cannot invoke contractual liability. This was the case relating to subprime mortgage ratings.

In the absence of a contract, the question arises as to the potential legal basis for liability. Clearly, tort liability is the most common possibility. In France, the new legislation on banking and financial regulation refers to tort law as a potential ground for liability.[112] Typically, the conditions that need to be met in order to prove liability are a tortious act, damage, causality and fault. The presence of a tortious act refers to the fact that CRAs acted unlawfully.

Other legal frameworks know original types of liability that can be qualified as quasi-contractual. Broadly speaking, the ground for liability is not based on a contract but on confidence. This is the case in Germany where the notion of "liability based on confidence" or "liability based on trust" was developed.[113] In this respect, there are two particular conditions to be met. First, the "special position of trust" requires the presence of a relationship equivalent to a contract.[114] Second, the notion of "disappointment of confidence" means that the CRA deceived the trusting party.[115] The idea of these two conditions relates to the fact that this type of liability protects the confidence of a party that has no contract but deserves special treatment. The other conditions are – as for other types of liability – damage, causality and fault.[116] As for contractual liability, there is a reversal of the burden of proof with respect to the condition of fault.

More particularly, there are types of liability that can count as a subset of "liability based on confidence," such as expert liability and prospectus liability.[117]

---

112 Loi française de régulation bancaire et financière, art 10 (codified in Code monétaire et financier, art L 544-5) (mentioning tort liability as "responsabilité délictuelle" et "quasi-délictuelle").

113 In German "Vertrauenshaftung"; the Latin expression liability for "culpa in contrahendo" is also commonly used.

114 In German "Sonderverbindung." See, eg, for Germany, Peter Korth, 'Dritthaftung von Ratingagenturen' in Gunther Teubner and others (eds), *Internationale Studien zur Privatrechtstheorie, Band 10* (Nomos 2009) 77–78 (with accompanying note).

115 In German "Vertrauensenttäuschung." See, eg, Vasella, 'Die Haftung von Ratingagenturen' (n 107) 306, 328–329.

116 ibid 306.

117 ibid 303. See also Susan Emmenegger, 'Rating und Haftung' in Wolfgang Wiegand (ed), *Basel II – die rechtlichen Konsequenzen* (Stämpfli Verlag 2006) 88 (with accompanying note).

Finally, it is worth mentioning that the UK is reluctant to recognize CRA liability.[118] The UK authorities have recently raised concern about the detrimental impact of CRA liability on the behavior of market participants. CRA liability may potentially reduce market participants' own incentives to exercise due diligence.

In a nutshell, it tends to be more difficult to prove CRA liability if the regime is based on general liability rules. The creation of special liability rules makes it easier for market participants to sue CRAs because it demonstrates the willingness of lawmakers to make CRAs more accountable.

5.2.3.2 EU special liability regime

The EU proposal for an amendment of the CRA Regulation introduces a special and centralized rule to govern the civil liability of CRAs. The proposed CRA Regulation would render a CRA liable under certain circumstances. When a CRA commits intentionally or with gross negligence any infringement of the CRA Regulation having an impact on a credit rating, any investor that relied on such rating may bring an action against the CRA for any damage caused to that investor.[119] There are five elements: (i) infringement of the CRA Regulation, (ii) damage, (iii) causality, (iv) intentional or gross negligence and (v) reliance.

In modern financial markets, investors and CRAs do mostly not have any contractual relationship. This special liability is in this respect a type of tortious liability. The elements of tortious liability are found in the proposed rule. As for the presence of a tortious act, the proposed Regulation refers to any infringement of the CRA Regulation. The notion of damage is there in terms of any damage caused to that investor. As for the causality element, the proposed article requires that the infringement has an impact on the credit rating. The aspect of fault is a high standard, which may be difficult to prove: the CRA is liable only for intentional acts and gross negligence, but not simple negligence. A CRA acts with gross negligence if it seriously neglects its duties imposed by the CRA Regulation.[120] Finally, the proposed Regulation adds the element of reliance in the sense that the investor may bring an action only if he or she relied on the rating in question.

In practice, these elements may be difficult to prove. To make it easier for investors to show an infringement of the CRA Regulation, the

---

118 'The United Kingdom Authorities Response' (n 99) 2, 18.

119 'Proposal for a CRA III Regulation' (n 76) art 35a.

120 ibid art 35a para 3.

proposed article shifts the burden of proof to the CRA if the investor is first able to establish the facts from which it may be inferred that a CRA has committed any infringement of the CRA Regulation.[121]

Apart from that, civil liability under the proposed Regulation shall not be excluded or limited in advance by agreement; such an agreement shall be deemed null and void.[122] This rule protects investors against attempts from CRAs to exclude their liability, for instance in subscription agreements to their websites.

[121] ibid art 35a para 4.
[122] ibid art 35a para 5.

6. Regulatory trends

6.1 PRACTICAL IMPORTANCE OF THE CREDIT RATING AGENCY REFORMS

In the aftermath of the financial crisis triggered in 2007, lawmakers and regulators have acknowledged that the credit rating industry needs structural change. The CRA Regulation in the EU and the Dodd-Frank Act of 2010 in the US represent the most significant regulatory overhaul since the creation of the industry.

Broadly speaking, the implementation of the CRA Regulation and the Dodd-Frank Act will mark a turning point relating the position of CRAs in modern financial markets.[1] In the US they will lose their privileged position and no longer benefit from regulatory reliance. Step two of the EU CRA Regulation will probably follow the US trend as suggested by the EU public consultation on CRAs and the November 2011 proposal for an amendment of the CRA Regulation. In general, over the last few decades there have been three significant periods with respect to the regulatory structure of the rating industry. First, at the beginning of the twentieth century through to the 1970s, CRAs were neither regulated nor significantly used in financial market regulations. Second, especially since the 1970s, CRAs were still not regulated, but increasingly used for regulatory purposes. Third, since the Dodd-Frank Act, a transition period has been initiated so that CRAs will no longer be used in financial market regulations, but will become as highly regulated as other gatekeepers such as auditors and securities analysts. The impact of the CRA reforms in the US and the EU remains – to some extent – uncertain, but one definitive point is that they will change the position of CRAs in modern financial markets.

With respect to the US, the Dodd-Frank Act of 2010 has substantial effects on the rating industry and the financial markets. The competition

[1] Aline Darbellay, 'Regulating Ratings, The Credit Rating Agency Oligopoly from a Regulatory Perspective' in Dieter Zobl, Mario Giovanoli and Rolf H Weber, *Schweizer Schriften zum Finanzmarktrecht, Band 102* (Schulthess 2011) 76.

level among leading CRAs will undoubtedly evolve pursuant to implementation of the CRA reform. Some of the new amendments may have positive effects on competition, while some others may be detrimental to competition in the rating industry.

First, the withdrawal of rating-based regulations enhances competition in the rating industry. In the long term, certified CRAs will cease to benefit from regulatory privilege if regulators overcome the difficulties they face in implementing the provision. CRAs should no longer sell "regulatory licenses" but merely provide investors with financial information. Competition will ideally be based on the quality of the rating services. However, how long the transition toward the complete withdrawal of rating-based regulations will last is uncertain, depending on how regulators find substitutes for ratings. The Dodd-Frank Act of 2010 expressly states that every Federal agency has one year to remove regulatory reliance on credit ratings,[2] but regulators had to delay this deadline. More time is needed so that governmental entities can implement revised regulations using alternatives to ratings. Rating-based regulations cannot be instantaneously unwoven since mandates to use ratings have become part of the fabric of financial markets. It will be very challenging for regulators and market participants to develop alternatives to ratings. Moreover, market over-reliance on certified ratings will not be easy to withdraw due to the fact that over the past decades behavioral reliance has added to regulatory reliance.[3]

Second, the regulatory oversight of CRAs generates diverging and controversial opinions with respect to its effects on competition. The Dodd-Frank Act of 2010 states that the critical gatekeeper role played by CRAs justifies the same enhanced level of regulation as that which applies to securities analysts and auditors.[4] According to this view, public oversight is necessary to discipline the rating industry. However, some scholars are skeptical of expanding CRA oversight to a great extent.[5] While alleviating some problems, regulators may introduce new ones.

---

[2] Dodd-Frank Wall Street Reform and Consumer Protection Act of 2010, HR 4173, 111th Congress, 2nd Session (2010) (Dodd-Frank Act) Sec 939A.

[3] Frank Partnoy, 'Overdependence on Credit Ratings was a Primary Cause of the Crisis' (2009) University of San Diego Legal Studies Research Paper Series No 09-015, 10.

[4] Dodd-Frank Act, Sec 931(2–3).

[5] See, eg, Timothy J Sinclair, *The New Masters of Capital, American Bond Rating Agencies and the Politics of Creditworthiness* (Cornell University Press 2005) 9 ("Indeed, tight regulation would potentially destroy the key thing agencies have to sell: their independent opinion on market matters").

The regulatory oversight of CRAs may heal the symptoms but not the causes of troubles in the rating industry. Concerns have been raised about the detrimental effects of public oversight on competition.[6] Regulating ratings might inadvertently result in empowering CRAs.[7] In general, critics contend that the path to more competition simply requires lawmakers to lower regulatory barriers to entry.[8] Yet regulating the rating industry may add further barriers to entry.[9] The key point is that regulatory compliance is onerous for new entrants. Therefore, although one regulatory barrier to entry may be addressed through the withdrawal of rating-based regulations, another regulatory barrier to entry may be created by the new regulatory oversight of CRAs.

Third, the special treatment for CRAs must without any doubt be eliminated in order to enhance competition in the rating industry. The effects of the new liability rules mainly have positive effects on competition. First, CRAs will be subject to the same treatment as other

---

[6] David Segal, 'Debt Raters Avoid Overhaul After Crisis' *New York Times*, December 8, 2009 (arguing that the reform bills are misguided and wrongheaded due to their ironic effect of making the incumbents even more important) (quoting Professor Lawrence J White, NYU Stern School of Business). See also Claire A Hill, 'Why Did Rating Agencies Do Such a Bad Job Rating Subprime Securities?' (2010) 71 University of Pittsburgh Law Review 1, 19 (arguing that if self-interested money managers failed to discipline CRAs, regulators would not be able to do a better job of detecting the bad rating quality); Edward I Altman, Sabri Oncu, Anjolein Schmeits and Lawrence J White, 'What Should Be Done about the Credit Rating Agencies?' *New York University (NYU) Stern Regulating Wall Street Blog*, April 6, 2010 ‹http://w4.stern.nyu.edu/blogs/regulatingwall street/2010/04/what-should-be-done-about-the.html#more› accessed January 10, 2013 (expressing concerns about the fact that too much oversight would undermine competition in the rating industry by raising regulatory barriers to entry).

[7] Sewell Chan, 'Documents Show Internal Qualms at Rating Agencies' *The New York Times*, 22 April 2010, (quoting Professor Lawrence J White, NYU Stern School of Business).

[8] See, eg, 'Assessing the Current Oversight and Operation of Credit Rating Agencies: Hearing Before the Senate Committee on Banking, Housing and Urban Affairs' (2006) 109th Congress, S Hrg 109-997 (statement of Glenn L Reynolds, Chief Executive Officer, CreditSights) 35 (already arguing that it is not efficient to remove one set of regulatory barriers to entry and replace it with another).

[9] 'Negative Outlook, Europe Misfires in its Attack on the Rating Agencies' *The Economist*, November 15, 2008, 91 (criticizing the European efforts to regulate the rating industry; tying CRAs even more tightly into the regulatory system is likely only to exacerbate the problem by raising barriers to new entrants and making the CRAs appear even less fallible).

gatekeepers such as other providers of financial information. Second, the new liability rules will partly enhance reputational constraints so that CRAs will face litigation costs if they issue reckless ratings. However, one negative aspect related to competition is that the liability regime for CRAs does not address market over-reliance on ratings. Investors are even more likely to rely on ratings given the creation of liability rules. Therefore, courts will have to define how to delimit the liability criteria so that investors do not expect too much from the new rules.

With respect to the EU framework for CRAs, the CRA Regulation of 2009 relates to CRA oversight. EU regulators proceeded on the assumption that the rating industry should be highly regulated. Their primary concern was to fill a gap in the EU regulatory structure as CRAs were unregulated prior to the 2007–2009 financial crisis. The CRA Regulation is regarded by scholars as a first step in the right direction as it marks the first attempt to regulate CRAs in the EU.[10] However, EU regulators were aware that they did not respond to every concern. Therefore, step two of the CRA Regulation addresses topics that were not included in the Regulation of 2009 but that deserve particular attention, ie over-reliance on credit ratings, sovereign ratings, lack of competition, CRA liability and proposals for a new revenue model.[11] The November 2011 proposal for an amendment of the CRA Regulation partly responds to these concerns. More regulatory amendments are thus expected in the EU.

Finally, both US and EU legislators refer to the problems arising from conflicts of interest, yet they were not able to adopt mandatory rules to solve the causes of such conflicts in the rating industry.[12] The US Dodd-Frank Act of 2010 merely acknowledges that CRAs face conflicts

---

[10] Thierry Granier, 'Éclairage. Le règlement communautaire sur les agences de notation: un début de régulation de l'activité?' [2010] Bulletin Joly Bourse 8.

[11] EU Commission, 'Public consultation on credit rating agencies' (5 November 2010) 1–28.

[12] With respect to the US, see Andrew R Sorkin, 'Congress Drops Changes for Credit-Rating Agencies' *The New York Times DealBook*, June 16, 2010, (explaining that Senator Al Franken had championed a proposal that would end the practice of issuers choosing CRAs; the Franken amendment would have created a board, overseen by the SEC, which would have assigned CRAs to provide ratings in order to eliminate conflicts of interest; however, the House of Representatives did not accept the proposed solution and Congress had to strip the Franken amendment out of the financial reform Bill). With respect to the EU, see EU Commission, 'Public consultation on credit rating agencies' (n 11) 26–28 (envisaging to set forth a new revenue model for CRAs in step two of the CRA Regulation).

of interest that need to be explicitly addressed in legislation.[13] Further, with respect to oversight, the new Office of Credit Ratings has to ensure that NRSRO ratings are not unduly influenced by conflicts of interest.[14] A few governance rules require CRAs to monitor conflicts of interest. For instance, in the US dealing with conflicts of interest counts as a duty of the board of directors of the NRSROs.[15] Similarly, the EU CRA Regulation of 2009 requires CRAs to mitigate conflicts of interest and avoid them if possible. Critics suggest that governance rules merely heal the symptoms but do not cure the causes of the problem. Conflicts of interest arise out of the issuer-pays business model. The most adequate solution would consist of moving back to subscriber-paid credit ratings. However, the current situation has proven tricky to change.

In the US, Congress was merely able to agree on the fact that the issuer-pays business model in its current form was not satisfactory, and called for the SEC to undertake studies analyzing how to address conflicts of interest in the rating industry. Two SEC studies may play a role in this regard: the SEC study on strengthening credit rating agency independence and the SEC study and rule-making on assigned credit ratings.[16] In December 2012 the Staff of the SEC published its report to Congress in which it assesses the idea of assigning credit ratings.[17] This study analyzes the current system, the proposal for an assignment system and also alternative means for compensating CRAs. In terms of the feasibility of assigning NRSROs to provide ratings, the study notes that commentators are skeptical about such a system due to operational and legal issues.[18] In the EU, the public consultation on CRAs asked commentators to come up with new suggestions regarding conflicts of interest embedded in the issuer-pays business model; the EU will probably move forward with a proposal for a new revenue model in the near future.[19] Therefore, although the recent CRA reforms are the most sweeping overhaul in the credit rating industry, there are still regulatory topics of interest for future research. Regulators will still have to amend

---

13 Dodd-Frank Act, Sec 931(4).

14 ibid Sec 932(a)(8).

15 ibid.

16 ibid Sec 939C and 939D.

17 Staff of the SEC, 'Report to Congress on Assigned Credit Ratings, As Required by Section 939F of the Dodd-Frank Wall Street Reform and Consumer Protection Act' (December 2012).

18 ibid 33–35, 45–48.

19 EU Commission, 'Public consultation on credit rating agencies' (n 11) 26–28.

the frameworks for CRAs and introduce new rules, in particular with respect to solving conflicts of interest in the rating industry.

6.2 PRELIMINARY CONCLUSION

CRA reforms have played an important role in the US and in the EU in the aftermath of the 2007–2009 financial crisis.

Three key aspects relate to the regulatory structure in the credit rating industry. First, the withdrawal of regulatory references to ratings is a positive trend. It enhances the level of competition in the rating industry. CRAs that are not recognized for regulatory purposes may be able to compete with the leading CRAs more easily. Looking for alternatives to ratings may also open the door to new entrants in the market for financial information.

Second, enhanced CRA oversight may have positive but also detrimental impacts on competition. Although public oversight is necessary to discipline CRAs, the establishment of a stringent regulatory framework may also raise additional barriers to entering the rating market. Policymakers may have overreacted in the wake of the recent financial crisis. Enhanced oversight may have the unintended consequence of keeping the three leading CRAs at the core of the financial architecture. Accordingly, designing CRA oversight should always be assessed as to its effects on competitive incentives.

Third, the financial reforms strive to modify the special treatment for CRAs. In the US, CRAs used to benefit from a privileged position given their immunity from lawsuits. The Dodd-Frank Act of 2010 amended the legal and regulatory framework so that CRAs will be treated the same as other financial gatekeepers such as securities analysts and auditors. The EU is also considering harmonizing CRA liability regimes throughout Europe to enhance accountability in the rating industry. The provision establishing an EU principle of CRA liability will likely come into force in the near future.

In sum, regulatory intervention has become one of the most important catalysts for change in the rating industry, in particular since CRAs have become increasingly regulated post-crisis.

PART 3

Uses and abuses of credit ratings in structured finance

7. Growth of the structured finance segment

The role of the leading CRAs in structured finance ratings has given rise to significant concern in modern financial markets. In the run-up to the subprime mortgage crisis, CRAs attributed inflated credit ratings to mortgage-related securities that ended up performing very poorly.[1] In the aftermath of the resulting rating scandals, lawmakers reformed the rating industry by means of a financial regulatory overhaul.[2]

7.1 CREDIT RATINGS AND STRUCTURED FINANCE

The rating of structured finance products has contributed to a major change in the rating business over the last four decades. If the structured finance segment has enhanced the profitability of CRAs, credit ratings

---

[1] John M Griffin and Dragon Yongjun Tang, 'Did Subjectivity Play a Role in CDO Credit Ratings?' (2010) McCombs Research Paper Series No FIN-04-10, 28–29 (finding empirical evidence that CRAs shockingly inflated ratings by issuing even higher ratings than implied by their own risk models); Edward I Altman, Sabri Oncu, Anjolein Schmeits and Lawrence J White, 'What Should Be Done about the Credit Rating Agencies?' *New York University (NYU) Stern Regulating Wall Street Blog*, April 6, 2010 ‹http://w4.stern.nyu.edu/blogs/regulatingwallstreet/2010/04/what-should-be-done-about-the.html#more› accessed January 10, 2013; Gretchen Morgenson and Louise Story, 'Rating Agency Data Aided Wall Street in Deals' *The New York Times*, April 23, 2010 (discussing how the leading CRAs collaborated with Wall Street banks to structure the deals); Kathleen Casey and Frank Partnoy, 'Downgrade the Ratings Agencies' *The New York Times*, June 4, 2010 (stating that CRAs helped create the financial crisis by giving inflated ratings); Aline Van Duyn, 'Reform of Rating Agencies Poses Dilemma' *The Financial Times*, June 10, 2010 (arguing that the great number of triple-A ratings fueled the demand for risky mortgage-related securities and generated substantial revenues for the leading CRAs).

[2] Dodd-Frank Wall Street Reform and Consumer Protection Act of 2010, HR 4173, 111th Congress, 2nd Session (2010) (Dodd-Frank Act); Regulation (EC) No 1060/2009 of 16 September 2009 on credit rating agencies [2009] OJ L302/1 (CRA Regulation).

have played an equally crucial role in the extraordinary expansion of structured products. Indeed, the key to the successful launch of novel instruments was their assessment by a supposedly independent third party. From an issuers' perspective, the leading CRAs appeared to be the ideal entities to provide this service. Moreover, from the 1970s to the 2000s regulators increasingly used ratings in their financial market regulations. Investors were, in turn, willing to buy securitized assets that received high ratings.[3]

In addition, courts considered ratings to be mere opinions protected by the First Amendment of the US Constitution. CRAs were exempted from liability even when their ratings proved to be inaccurate.[4] Accordingly, CRAs benefited from a privileged position in the financial markets. Issuers took advantage of hiring CRAs in order to rate mortgage-related securities. They were able to convince CRAs to give high ratings to complex financial instruments in exchange for a fee.

As the structured finance segment grew, CRAs faced new incentives. Rating complex financial instruments rapidly generated a significant source of revenue for CRAs.[5] From 2002 to 2007 in particular, the three leading CRAs doubled their revenues, from approximately 3 billion US dollars to 6 billion US dollars per annum.[6] The problem was that leading CRAs were not competing on rating quality in order to increase their market share. The leading CRAs were attracted by significant profits and were not deterred from rating complex financial instruments by reputational constraints. In the short term, they had little to lose when providing investors with inaccurate ratings. The leading CRAs were competing with

---

[3] Investor reliance on ratings was partly due to the regulatory use of ratings in financial market regulations.

[4] Text to n 82 in ch 5.

[5] Joshua D Coval, Jakob Jurek and Erik Stafford, 'The Economics of Structured Finance' (2008) Harvard Business School Finance Working Paper No 09-060, 4 (reporting that 44 percent of Moody's revenues in 2006 came from rating structured finance products, surpassing the 32 percent of its revenues from rating corporate bonds).

[6] 'Credit Rating Agencies and the Financial Crisis: Hearing Before the House Committee on Oversight and Government Reform' (2008) 110th Congress 2nd Session, HR Serial No 110-155, 211; 'Wall Street and the Financial Crisis: The Role of Credit Rating Agencies, Hearing Before the Permanent Subcommittee on Investigations of the Senate Committee on Homeland Security and Governmental Affairs' (April 23, 2010) (opening statement of Senator Carl Levin) 2. See also Roger Lowenstein, 'Triple-A Failure, The Ratings Game' *The New York Times*, April 27, 2008 (stating that Moody's' stock price increased sixfold and its earnings grew by 900 percent).

each other in order to attract more business. They were concerned about maintaining and increasing their market share. As a consequence, they had incentives to satisfy the interests of their principal clients who were the issuers of debt securities. If their rating models were too strict, issuers would hire another CRA that enjoyed the same regulatory and behavioral reliance but did not have such high rating standards.[7]

The structured finance segment highlights how the rating industry became very profitable without providing investors with valuable information. In competitive markets, CRAs that do not provide useful information should not be paid to rate financial products. In fact, CRAs were involved in rating financial instruments that were increasingly complex without having any incentive to allocate more resources to improve rating quality.[8] They did not have any incentives to refuse to rate financial instruments that they could not fully understand.[9] When large banks asked the leading CRAs to rate synthetic CDOs, they did not have adequate rating models at their disposal. Instead of refusing to rate excessively complex securities, CRAs accepted rating the novel products with the assistance of banks that provided their own models.[10] Given their links with CRAs, banks could easily figure out how to maximize the ratings of mortgage-related securities.

In competitive markets, investors would not blindly rely on credit ratings. Market participants should be able and willing to do their own

---

[7] 'Wall Street and the Financial Crisis' (n 6) Exhibits, 1–4 (reporting that the leading CRAs could not afford to use rigorous rating models if they wanted to maintain or gain market share).

[8] Claire A Hill, 'Regulating the Rating Agencies' (2004) 82 Washington University Law Quarterly 43, 81 (arguing that CRAs did probably not make a sufficient investment in order to keep pace with the increasingly complex securities that they were rating). See also Joshua Rosner, 'Toward an Understanding: NRSRO Failings in Structured Ratings and Discreet Recommendations to Address Agency Conflicts' (2009) 14 (Issue 4) Journal of Structured Finance 7, 8 (arguing that CRAs were not sufficiently well equipped to rate most structured securities).

[9] See further 'Credibility of Credit Ratings, the Investment Decisions Made Based on those Ratings, and the Financial Crisis, Hearings & Testimony Before the FCIC' (June 2, 2010) (testimony of Eric Kolchinsky, former Managing Director, Moody's) 3 (explaining that, to make matters worse, "rating shopping" prevented CRAs from saying no to a deal since issuers could merely hire another CRA that would give the desired triple-A rating).

[10] Michael Lewis, *The Big Short, Inside the Doomsday Machine* (WW Norton & Company 2010) 76 (quoting a former CDO trader, Goldman Sachs).

research and take informed investment decisions. Instead, investors ended up buying highly rated securities without sufficient knowledge of the underlying assets. CRAs – traditionally considered as information intermediaries – contributed to the creation of an opaque market for securitized assets. The lack of transparency that allowed the market to grow in the first place ensured that the entire market would collapse as soon as a crisis of confidence arose. Accordingly, the subprime mortgage crisis was triggered in 2007 by massive rating downgrades by the leading CRAs. Investors instantly lost confidence in CRAs with respect to their ability to rate structured products.

7.2 FINANCIAL MARKET CONTEXT

7.2.1 From a Bank-based to a Market-based Financial System

Banks traditionally act as an intermediary between investors and borrowers. Financial disintermediation has allowed capital to flow directly from investors to issuers of securities, and CRAs have benefited from this evolution.[11] Whereas banks always scrutinized the creditworthiness of potential borrowers on behalf of depositors, the increasingly widespread practice by holders of capital to bypass the bank and invest directly in securities strengthened the profile of CRAs which can accumulate and simplify information about the risks associated with a wide range of securities.[12] In a market-based financial system, CRAs are increasingly involved in rating debt instruments rather than the direct borrowers. If investors directly intervene in the financial markets, CRAs will focus more on rating the issued securities rather than the financial institutions that provide funding.

In fact, the process of disintermediation removes intermediaries – such as bank lenders – between the company and the ultimate source of funds, the capital markets.[13] The primary reason is that bank loans are expensive and corporations tend to seek means of funding that do not entail bank

[11] Rawi Abdelal, *Capital Rules, The Construction of Global Finance* (Harvard University Press 2007) 168.

[12] ibid.

[13] Steven L Schwarcz, 'Enron and the Use and Abuse of Special Purpose Entities in Corporate Structures' (2002) 70 University of Cincinnati Law Review 1309, 1315.

lending.[14] In modern financial markets, a large fraction of financial assets are sold directly by borrowers to investors, via stock and bond markets, thereby bypassing traditional banking.[15] For instance, big companies issue commercial papers to gain access to a cheaper source of funds than bank loans.

As market participants increasingly gained direct access to the financial markets, the financial system shifted from a bank-based to a market-based financial system. This shift has incentivized banks to engage in a more diverse range of activities. Banks have responded to increased competition by shifting their business models from reliance on traditional deposit-taking and lending to new business segments.[16] Banks have accommodated themselves to the system by intervening in the capital markets, for instance by acting as brokers and being paid a fee for their service. Under such a system they engage in lucrative activities while holding less risk on their balance sheets. In the market-based system financial innovation has gained prominence; hence banks have developed new financial instruments to capture a greater part of the profit opportunities. Even when they do not intervene as bank lenders, they play a key role in managing and structuring transactions.

The market-based financial system was initially praised because it dispersed risk among investors instead of being concentrated in the hands of financial institutions.[17] Many types of Credit Risk Transfer (CRT) instruments were subsequently created to promote credit risk as a separate asset class.[18]

---

[14] John Flood, 'Rating, Dating, and the Informal Regulation and the Formal Ordering of Financial Transactions: Securitisations and Credit Rating Agencies' in Michael B Likosky (ed), *Privatising Development: Transnational Law, Infrastructure and Human Rights* (Martinus Nijhoff Publishers 2005) 153.

[15] Darryll Hendricks, John Kambhu and Patricia Mosser, 'Systemic Risk and the Financial System, Background Paper' (2006) NAS-FRBNY (Federal Reserve Bank of New York) Conference on the New Directions in Understanding Systemic Risk, 7 ‹https://www.newyorkfed.org/registration/research/risk/background.pdf› accessed January 10, 2013.

[16] Stephen Lumpkin, 'Resolutions of Weak Institutions: Lessons Learned from Previous Crises' [2008] OECD Journal: Financial Market Trends 1, 18 ‹http://www.oecd.org/finance/financialmarkets/41942943.pdf› accessed January 10, 2013.

[17] Hendricks, Kambhu and Mosser, 'Systemic Risk and the Financial System' (n 15) 8.

[18] Claudio Borio, 'The Financial Turmoil of 2007–?: A Preliminary Assessment and Some Policy Considerations' (2008) BIS Working Papers No 251, 4 ‹http://www.bis.org/publ/work251.pdf› accessed January 10, 2013.

However, the subprime mortgage crisis showed that risk had not successfully moved outside the financial system. Concern has been raised, for instance, about the concentration of risk in a large number of investors acting homogeneously.[19] CRT instruments failed to spread risk. Accordingly, the danger in a market-based financial system results from the occurrence of a market-gridlock systemic crisis.[20] When financial turmoil erupts, financial institutions are not immune. They may suffer losses that can destabilize the financial system. When risk is supposedly spread, and market participants cannot locate the losses in the financial markets, they will pay increasing attention to counterparty risk while trading in the markets. In such a situation market participants tend to distrust their counterparty and move away from the markets.

In sum, the market-based system involves different risks compared with the bank-based system, and those types of risk should be increasingly taken into account in modern financial markets.

7.2.2 Expansion of Credit Risk Transfer Instruments

New financial instruments were created to disperse credit risk throughout the financial system. Modern financial markets are characterized by an extraordinary expansion of CRT instruments. Banks can trade credit risk in the capital markets instead of holding that risk until maturity. Banks have primarily been interested in the novel instruments for reasons of funding.[21] Two developments in modern financial markets for transferring credit risk have been credit derivatives and CDOs.[22] Credit derivatives allow CRT without the sale of the loan, and CDOs are an application of the securitization technology.[23]

In the subprime mortgage market, securitization was the primary tool used by financial institutions to transfer credit risk to a broad range of

---

[19] Kern Alexander and others, 'Financial Supervision and Crisis Management in the EU' (2007) European Parliament, Policy Department, Economic and Scientific Policy, 5 ‹http://www.europarl.europa.eu/document/activities/cont/201108/20110818ATT25070/20110818ATT25070EN.pdf› accessed January 10, 2013.

[20] Hendricks, Kambhu and Mosser, 'Systemic Risk and the Financial System' (n 15) 8.

[21] Christopher R Whalen, 'The Subprime Crisis, Cause, Effect and Consequences' (2008) Networks Financial Institute Policy Brief No 2008-PB-04, 5.

[22] Douglas J Lucas, Laurie S Goodman and Frank J Fabozzi, 'Collateralized Debt Obligations and Credit Risk Transfer' (2007) Yale ICF Working Paper No 07-06, 3.

[23] ibid.

investors. It is worth mentioning that asset securitization started in the mid-1980s and has expanded significantly over the last three decades.[24] Basically, securitization helps to raise funds and reduces the cost of credit.[25] Moreover, asset securitization is supposed to enhance liquidity in the market. As regards mortgage loans, a market for securitized assets can be created where traditional banking would have carried mortgages on bank balance sheets until maturity. Further, securitization allows the arranger to turn medium-quality debt into a mix of high- and low-quality debt, thereby changing debt quality.[26] Last but not least, securitization can allow banks to raise large amounts of money while shifting the resultant debt off the balance sheet.[27] Large banks have used and abused financial innovation to hide part of the risks they have been taking.

7.2.3 Increasing Leverage of Financial Institutions

The typical large bank balance sheet has become much more complex as a result of the shift from traditional lending to trading and market-making in various market segments.[28] The opportunity for financial institutions to dramatically increase their leverage consists of another feature of the modern financial markets. Financial institutions like leverage, yet regulators try to prevent them from excessively increasing it. As a consequence, financial institutions have a tendency to circumvent regulatory requirements in order to become more leveraged. As opposed to other types of businesses, the particularity of financial institutions is that their balance sheets do not reflect the size of their risk exposure.[29] The use of financial

---

[24] Michel G Crouhy, Robert A Jarrow and Stuart M Turnbull, 'The Subprime Credit Crisis of 07' (2008) SSRN eLibrary, 8 ‹http:ssrn.com/abstract=1112467› accessed January 10, 2013.

[25] Frank Partnoy, 'The Siskel and Ebert of Financial Markets?: Two Thumbs Down for the Credit Rating Agencies' (1999) 77 Washington University Law Quarterly 619, 666.

[26] John Patrick Hunt, 'Credit Rating Agencies and the "Worldwide Credit Crisis": The Limits of Reputation, the Insufficiency of Reform, and a Proposal for Improvement' [2009] Columbia Business Law Review 109, 177.

[27] Flood, 'Rating, Dating, and the Informal Regulation and the Formal Ordering of Financial Transactions' (n 14) 148–149.

[28] Lumpkin, 'Resolutions of Weak Institutions' (n 16) 18.

[29] Warren E Buffet, 'Berkshire Annual Report 2002' (2002) 15, ‹http://www.berkshirehathaway.com/2002ar/2002ar.pdf› accessed January 10, 2010 ("When Charlie and I finish reading the long footnotes detailing the derivatives activities of major banks, the only thing we understand is that we *don't* understand how much risk the institution is running"). See also Frank Partnoy

engineering makes banks appear better capitalized and less risky than they are in reality.[30]

Over the past decades banks increased their leverage in two ways that were supported by the regulators. First, banks engaged in off-balance-sheet activities. Regulators accepted the fact that certain banking activities did not need to be included in the financial statements. Hence banks took leveraged positions that were hidden from regulators and investors.[31] For instance, securitization helped many banks to free up their balance sheets while allowing them to put the resulting assets in off-balance-sheet vehicles.[32] Another way of increasing leverage in the financial market was to take advantage of the fact that derivatives markets were not sufficiently regulated. Financial institutions were in a position to engage in transactions that lacked capital or margin requirements. Therefore, a strategy of many financial institutions was to sell debt insurance – for instance in the form of Credit Default Swap (CDS) contracts – as a means of generating premiums and recording income from off-balance-sheet contracts.[33] Second, the shift to risk-sensitive bank capital requirements enabled banks to extend their balance sheets.[34] Banks took advantage of attributing low risk weights to their assets. Under the Standardized Approach in Basel II, which remains part of Basel III, banks were able to rely on credit ratings in order to measure their

---

and Jesse Eisinger, 'What's Inside America's Banks?' *The Atlantic*, January/February, 2013).

[30] Frank Partnoy and Lynn E Turner, 'Bring Transparency to Off-Balance Sheet Accounting' (2010) Roosevelt Institute, 14 ‹http://www.rooseveltinstitute.org/sites/all/files/Off-Balance%20Sheet%20Transactions.pdf› accessed January 10, 2013).

[31] ibid.

[32] Anna Katherine Barnett-Hart, 'The Story of the CDO Market Meltdown: An Empirical Analysis' (BA thesis, Harvard College 2009) 7 ‹http://www.hks.harvard.edu/m-rcbg/students/dunlop/2009-CDOmeltdown.pdf› accessed January 10, 2013. See also Alexander and others, 'Financial Supervision and Crisis Management in the EU' (n 19) 10–11 (arguing that Structured Investment Vehicles (SIVs) enable banks to finance long-term debt with short-term debt; by conducting business through capital markets SIVs escape the capital adequacy regulation to which banks are subject).

[33] Austin Murphy, 'An Analysis of the Financial Crisis of 2008: Causes and Solutions' (2008) SSRN eLibrary, 18 ‹http:ssrn.com/abstract=1295344› accessed January 10, 2013.

[34] Rolf H Weber and Aline Darbellay, 'The Regulatory Use of Credit Ratings in Bank Capital Requirement Regulations' (2008) 10 Journal of Banking Regulation 1, 8.

risk-weighted assets.[35] If banks carried highly rated assets on their balance sheets, they needed less regulatory capital than without the allocation of risk weights. The new capital adequacy rules significantly helped banks extend their balance sheets. As a consequence, bank balance sheets no longer reflected banks' actual risk exposure.

7.3 SUBPRIME MORTGAGE CRISIS

7.3.1 Events at the Core of the Meltdown

> When the music stops in terms of liquidity, things will get complicated. But as long as the music is playing, you have got to get up and dance. We are still dancing.[36]

The financial turmoil that had the US subprime mortgage market at its epicenter spread throughout the world and through other market segments. The resulting financial crisis resulted from a chain of events and from the involvement of various actors in the process. The term subprime mortgage crisis refers to the earlier stages of the financial crisis.[37] The factors that led to the collapse of the subprime mortgage market provide a striking example of wrongdoing in the rating industry. It is worth focusing on the structural causes and on the first stage of the 2007–2009 financial crisis.

Concern has been raised about determining the extent of the role of the various market participants implicated in the process, instead of pointing the finger of blame at one specific group over another. While those involved early in the chain did not bear the risk, those involved later in the chain did not know what and where the risk was.[38] The demand side was blinded by the appetite for securitized assets offering higher yields than equally rated corporate or municipal debt issues. The leading CRAs were involved in the subprime mortgage market as a part of the chain. Although they were supposed to enhance transparency relating to asset

---

[35] BCBS, *International Convergence of Capital Measurement and Capital Standards, A Revised Framework (Basel II)* (BIS, June 2004) para 50.

[36] Andrew Sorkin, 'Citi Chief on Buyouts: "We're Still Dancing"' *The New York Times*, July 10, 2007 (quoting Charles O Prince, former Chairman and Chief Executive Officer, Citigroup).

[37] Steven L Schwarcz, 'Keynote Address: Understanding the Subprime Financial Crisis' (2009) 60 South Carolina Law Review 549, 549.

[38] Alexander and others, 'Financial Supervision and Crisis Management in the EU' (n 19) 29.

valuation, they actually raised uncertainty due to their poor rating performance. Their credibility and the quality of their risk models were questioned as soon as they started to massively downgrade mortgage-related securities.

At a structural level in the financial system, the conditions prevailing before the financial crisis were ample liquidity and low interest rates.[39] The exceptional liquidity of the financial markets fostered higher leverage and greater risk-taking.[40] Low interest rates had driven up housing prices artificially.[41]

Moreover, asset securitization increased risk throughout the financial system. Financial innovation contributed to the dramatic growth of the subprime mortgage market segment. In particular, novel structured products could help meet investor demand for highly rated assets that had higher yields than corporate bonds.[42] This favorable context enabled CDO arrangers to get involved in a very lucrative business. They generated a positive net present value investment merely from repacking cash flows.[43] Instead of holding credits that they had originated, financial institutions would sell them off into the capital markets.[44] The process of pooling loans and selling them to investors through securitization is referred to as the "originate-and-distribute" model of financial intermediation.[45] This process, in turn, boosted the demand by CDOs for RMBS and created pressure to increase the supply of subprime mortgages.

This business model seemed to work brilliantly as long as the markets were very liquid. However, the financial crisis that hit the financial markets in 2007 dramatically confronted market participants, the investing community and regulators with the downsides of the model. After a prolonged phase of risk-taking and credit expansion, the subprime

---

39 The High-Level Group on Financial Supervision in the EU, 'De Larosière Report' (2009) 14 ‹http://ec.europa.eu/internal_market/finances/docs/de_larosiere_report_en.pdf› accessed 10 January 2013.

40 Crouhy, Jarrow and Turnbull, 'The Subprime Credit Crisis of 07' (n 24) 5.

41 Schwarcz, 'Keynote Address' (n 37) 551.

42 Crouhy, Jarrow and Turnbull, 'The Subprime Credit Crisis of 07' (n 24) 6, 7.

43 ibid 7.

44 Borio, 'The Financial Turmoil of 2007–?' (n 18) 4.

45 Harry McVea, 'Credit Rating Agencies, the Subprime Mortgage Debacle and Global Governance: the EU Strikes Back' (2010) 59 International and Comparative Law Quarterly 701, 709.

mortgage crisis represented a sharp repricing of credit risk.[46] The resulting financial instability turned into a liquidity crisis.

One underlying feature of the financial turmoil was that mortgage lenders had no incentive to ensure high lending standards given the fact that they were able to transfer credit risk through MBS or CDOs.[47] Moreover, financial disintermediation meant that banks did not monitor the borrowers as they would have done if they had kept the mortgages on their balance sheets. In this situation, financial markets needed a gatekeeper. Market participants would buy complex financial instruments only if they were rated by an independent and reputable third party.[48] Issuers hired the leading CRAs, which were attracted by significant fees to accomplish this service; issuers gained advantages in terms of the marketability of their products and regulatory privileges. The problem was that CRAs were not driven by any incentive to provide investors with valuable information. Conflicts of interest were particularly acute in the structured finance segment and reputational constraints did not play their disciplining role. CRAs ended up basing their ratings on inaccurate or outdated risk models. CRAs lacked sufficient historical data relating to the US subprime market, underestimated correlations in the defaults that would occur during a downturn, and failed to take into account the severe weakening of underwriting standards by certain originators.[49]

It was well known that subprime borrowers were typically not very creditworthy and that they were often offered mortgage products to finance 100 percent of their homes.[50] Market participants paid no attention to these troubles as long as the financial markets were very liquid and borrowers could refinance with rising housing prices.[51]

Distress among subprime mortgage lenders already became visible in 2006 when the Fed started to raise interest rates in the US, thereby raising the cost of borrowing and making it more expensive for people to meet the floating rate interest payments on their loans.[52] Another reason for the rise in mortgage defaults was the increase in teaser interest rates to market levels after the introductory period of, typically, five years had

---

46 Borio, 'The Financial Turmoil of 2007–?' (n 18) 9.

47 De Larosière Report (n 39) 9.

48 Alexander and others, 'Financial Supervision and Crisis Management in the EU' (n 19) 18.

49 De Larosière Report (n 39) 9.

50 Crouhy, Jarrow and Turnbull, 'The Subprime Credit Crisis of 07' (n 24) 6.

51 ibid 5.

52 ibid 11.

expired.[53] Overall, the resulting foreclosures brought an excess supply of homes onto the market, thereby causing residential real estate prices to fall.[54] The model failed for borrowers who were relying on refinancing for loan repayment.[55] Subprime lenders had to tighten their underwriting standards significantly and many originators completely stopped originating subprime mortgage loans.[56] New Century, a big subprime lender, filed for bankruptcy in early April 2007.

Under the circumstances outlined above, the subprime mortgage machine was ready to explode. It was merely waiting for an event to trigger the crisis. And the most immediate trigger of the financial crisis was the massive downgrading of securitized assets by the leading CRAs in July 2007.[57] During the second week of July 2007, Standard & Poor's downgraded 7.3 billion US dollars of securities, and a few weeks later Moody's slashed credit ratings on 691 securities originally worth 19.4 billion US dollars.[58]

If the financial markets expected the lowest CDO tranches to deteriorate in value, the biggest surprise came from the losses of "senior" tranches. The losses were the greatest for the highest-rated tranches because these tranches were the most overestimated.[59] Investors rapidly lost confidence in ratings, and fewer investors meant that the price of debt securities started falling.[60] The success of the originate-and-distribute model of intermediation depends to a great extent on the liquidity of the financial markets. The problem is that liquidity is a very elusive and slippery concept. Liquidity can rapidly dry up.

The subprime mortgage financial crisis highlighted the fact that novel financial instruments cannot successfully transfer credit risk outside the

53 Murphy, 'An Analysis of the Financial Crisis of 2008' (n 33) 13.

54 ibid.

55 Schwarcz, 'Keynote Address' (n 37) 550.

56 CGFS, *Ratings in Structured Finance: What Went Wrong and What Can Be Done to Address Shortcomings* (BIS, CGFS Paper No 32, July 2008) 24.

57 'Wall Street and the Financial Crisis' (n 6) (opening statement of Senator Carl Levin) 4.

58 Crouhy, Jarrow and Turnbull, 'The Subprime Credit Crisis of 07' (n 24) 9; Weber and Darbellay, 'The Regulatory Use of Credit Ratings in Bank Capital Requirement Regulations' (n 34) 11.

59 Philip R Wood QC, 'The Regulation of Credit Reference Agencies: A Wider View' in Jan Kleineman and Lars Gorton (eds), *Credit Rating Agencies* (Stockholm Centre for Commercial Law, forthcoming 2013).

60 Schwarcz, 'Keynote Address' (n 37) 552.

financial system.[61] For regulatory or reputational reasons, banks had to take risk back to their balance sheets or they failed to transfer risk because for some other reasons they also had kept more risk than expected on their balance sheets. When this reality became clear, financial markets raised concerns about counterparty risk, ie banks ceased to trust each other, which led to the collapse of the interbank market in particular.

7.3.2 Financial Instruments at the Heart of the Crisis

> Wall Street reaped huge profits from creating filet mignon AAAs out of BB manure.[62]

Financial innovation has given rise to much concern in modern financial markets. Attention is being paid to the financial instruments that played a role in generating the financial turmoil. Overall, financial innovation supported the originate-and-distribute model of intermediation and helped financial institutions build up more leverage in the financial system. Novel financial instruments have supported banks' off-balance-sheet activities as well as regulatory arbitrage with respect to bank capital requirements.

The subprime mortgage crisis has given rise to concerns about the securitization of lower-quality mortgage loans. Asset securitization has been a fact of modern financial markets since it started in the mid-1980s.[63] The securitization process implies that loans are originated, structured and then sold to investors.

The securitization process involves a financial institution that buys mortgage loans from the original lender. Any kind of loans can be securitized. The underlying loans at the core of the subprime mortgage crisis include subprime loans[64] and Alt-A loans.[65] In fact, the loans that have typically underperformed in recent years are subprime or Alt-A

---

[61] Laurent Clerc, 'A Primer on the Subprime Crisis' (2008) Banque de France, Occasional Paper No 4, 1, 3 ‹http://www.banque-france.fr/fileadmin/user_upload/banque_de_france/La_Banque_de_France/pdf/Economie_et_Statistiques/primer_subprime_crisis.pdf› accessed 10 January 2013.

[62] Barnett-Hart, 'The Story of the CDO Market Meltdown' (n 32) 14 (quoting Mike Blum, former CMBS surveillance expert, Goldman Sachs).

[63] Crouhy, Jarrow and Turnbull, 'The Subprime Credit Crisis of 07' (n 24) 8.

[64] Douglas J Lucas, Laurie S Goodman and Frank J Fabozzi, *Collateralized Debt Obligations, Structures & Analysis* (2nd edn, John Wiley & Sons, Inc 2006) 113 (explaining that subprime borrowers fail to satisfy the underwriting standards of mortgage lenders; their borrower characteristics include a compromised

adjustable-rate mortgages. One type of loan especially illustrates the deterioration of lending standards in the years preceding the subprime mortgage crisis: the interest-only, negative-amortizing, adjustable-rate, subprime mortgage.[66] This type of loan highlights how lenders were actually willing to extend credit without caring about the borrowers' ability to pay off the principal. Subprime lenders did not monitor borrowers and uncreditworthy borrowers would end up in increasing debt.

The financial institution then pools the purchased subprime mortgages into securities. Financial institutions designed securities labeled MBS, which are a special case of ABS. These securities can be transferred to buyers. Financial institutions are the initial buyers and they created CDO structures – an application of the securitization technology – in order to make the targeted assets marketable to a broader range of investors. A CDO is generally constructed by creating an entity that buys assets and issues bonds backed by the assets' cash flows.[67] The issuing entity is set up by the deal arranger – typically a bank – and acquires a pool of assets, namely MBS. The purchase of assets is financed by issuing bonds to investors.[68] Technically, the CDO arranger partitions the purchased assets into tranches of bonds in order to make them marketable. Each tranche has a different claim on the pooled assets.[69] In principle the tranches are called "junior," "mezzanine" and "senior."[70] Should the portfolio of assets experience any losses due to the failure of individual assets, these losses

---

credit history and a payment-to-income ratio that is too high. Subprime mortgages and home equity loans (HEL) are used interchangeably to designate these loans).

[65] Lucas, Goodman and Fabozzi, *Collateralized Debt Obligations* (n 64) 112–113 (explaining that – like prime A loans – Alt-A loans are meant to include creditworthy borrowers; but the Alt-A program offers flexibility in terms of necessary documentation and borrowers are willing to pay a premium for the privilege).

[66] Lewis, *The Big Short* (n 10) 28–29. See also Michael J Burry, 'I Saw the Crisis Coming. Why Didn't the Fed?' *The New York Times*, April 4, 2010 (referring to pay-option, adjustable-rate mortgages to characterize the types of loan in which the borrower does not need to pay off the principal).

[67] Barnett-Hart, 'The Story of the CDO Market Meltdown' (n 32) 5. The issuing entity is referred to as a Special Purpose Entity (SPE), Structured Investment Vehicle (SIV), Special Purpose Vehicle (SPV) or trust.

[68] Alexander and others, 'Financial Supervision and Crisis Management in the EU' (n 19) 12.

[69] ibid.

[70] ibid.

are first allocated to the "junior" tranche, then to the "mezzanine" tranche and eventually to the "senior" tranche.[71]

Credit enhancement is the amount of loss that can be absorbed before the targeted tranche sustains any loss.[72] In a CDO structure, credit enhancement comes from subordination, overcollateralization, excess spread or CDS. Subordination represents the maximum level of loss that could occur immediately without being allocated to the tranche in question.[73] Overcollateralization requires the CDO arranger to commit more assets to the securitization pool than there are liabilities.[74] Alternatively, the CDO arranger could rely on external credit enhancement through reliance on CDS typically sold by insurance companies such as American International Group, Inc (AIG).[75]

CRAs played a significant role as regards the composition of CDO structures. They closely participated in the design of the novel financial instruments.[76] They were in a position to perform such a function because investors relied on their ratings for many novel products.[77] Issuers were willing to make sure that their debt instruments would attain the required rating. CRAs, in turn, gained a new status in the financial markets. They were practically fixing the structuring criteria as regards CDOs. Issuers could exploit the importance of ratings while convincing CRAs to adjust their rating models.

Technically, CRAs were assessing how much credit enhancement was needed in order to issue a given rating. The rating process could be split into two steps: first the estimation of a loss distribution and second the simulation of the cash flows.[78] Then, with a loss distribution in hand, CRAs were able to measure the amount of credit enhancement necessary for a tranche to attain a given rating.[79]

---

71 ibid 13.

72 Adam B Ashcraft and Til Schuermann, 'Understanding the Securitization of Subprime Mortgage Credit' (2008) Federal Reserve Bank of New York Staff Reports, 40 ‹http://www.newyorkfed.org/research/staff_reports/sr318.pdf› accessed January 10, 2013.

73 ibid.

74 Lucas, Goodman and Fabozzi, *Collateralized Debt Obligations* (n 64).

75 Brian JM Quinn, 'The Failure of Private Ordering and the Financial Crisis of 2008' (2009) 5 NYU Journal of Law & Business 549, 579.

76 Crouhy, Jarrow and Turnbull, 'The Subprime Credit Crisis of 07' (n 24) 9.

77 ibid 8–9.

78 Ashcraft and Schuermann, 'Understanding the Securitization of Subprime Mortgage Credit' (n 72) 40.

79 ibid.

Relating to the CDO structures, the "senior" tranche often got a triple-A rating, the "mezzanine" tranche could range from double-A to single-B rating.[80] The "junior" tranche – not being investment grade – was normally not rated and was also called an equity tranche since it was generally not sold to investors. Depending on the underlying assets, the probability of receiving payment was so low that the equity tranche would have been associated with junk status.

Tranching could effectively raise the credit rating of some parts of the underlying assets. Being rapidly able to get around rating models, CDO arrangers could calculate how to build CDO structures that would generate a sum of tranches greater than the whole portfolio. This process amounted to the financial wizardry of CDO arrangers. They could earn a lot of money out of the packaging process.

"CDO squared" structures would allow CDO arrangers to exploit such profitable opportunities even further. A "CDO squared" consisted of repackaging the hard-to-sell "mezzanine" CDO tranches to create more triple-A bonds for institutional investors.[81] CDO arrangers were able to make money merely by repackaging triple-B CDOs. Due to the high ratings they were also able to sell off credit risk to investors where it would normally not have been possible. Notably, in the process CDO equity – which could normally not be sold to investors – was partly included into the squared structure.

This business became so lucrative that financial institutions sought more "mezzanine" tranches to repackage. At one point supply of "mezzanine" tranches was insufficient.[82] Finding enough "mezzanine" tranches became cumbersome. Accordingly, CDO arrangers found a more convenient way to fuel the CDO machine. In 1997 they started to get involved in building synthetic CDOs.[83] As opposed to cash CDOs, these debt instruments do not need to be sold to an issuing entity such as a Special Purpose Vehicle (SPV).[84] Thanks to the use of credit derivatives, CDO arrangers did not need to purchase the portfolio of assets on which the CDO would be structured. Instead, the transfer or credit risk was synthetic.[85] The synthetic CDO gained credit exposure to the subprime

---

80 Alexander and others, 'Financial Supervision and Crisis Management in the EU' (n 19) 13.

81 Barnett-Hart, 'The Story of the CDO Market Meltdown' (n 32) 12.

82 ibid 14; Lewis, *The Big Short* (n 10).

83 Alexander and others, 'Financial Supervision and Crisis Management in the EU' (n 19) 58.

84 ibid.

85 ibid.

mortgage market by selling credit protection via CDS.[86] Thus, banks took advantage of credit derivatives in the sense that CDS could replicate the payoff profile of cash bonds without requiring the upfront funding of buying a cash bond.[87]

From the perspective of the Wall Street banks that arranged the CDO structures, the use of CDS made it easy for them to construct enormous CDO transactions and to generate quick and high profits from building the synthetic CDO structures. To create a cash CDO composed of triple-B-rated subprime mortgage bonds in order to repackage took time and effort.[88] To create a synthetic CDO was quick and boundless. As a result, the subprime mortgage market experienced an explosion of synthetic ABS CDOs from 2006 through 2007. By the end of 2007, the CDS market was a 60 trillion US dollars market.[89] The use of credit derivatives helped the CDO machine to grow at an extraordinary pace. Synthetic CDOs accelerated the securitization process and allowed market participants to amplify their risk exposure to the subprime mortgage market. Wall Street banks used CDS to feed the CDO machine.

From the perspective of the market, CDS needed buyers and sellers. On the sell-side, sellers were typically insurance companies such as AIG or monoline insurers.[90] There were also investors with a risk appetite for highly rated instruments having a higher yield than other highly rated assets; these investors were typically pension funds. There were also financial institutions that perceived profitable opportunities without needing regulatory capital upfront while significantly increasing their exposure to the subprime mortgage market.

On the buy-side, Wall Street banks first experienced more difficulty in finding counterparties. Eventually, a handful of investors entered the CDS market to bet against the subprime mortgage market. In fact, shorting the subprime mortgage market directly was not practically feasible because

---

86 Lucas, Goodman and Fabozzi, 'Collateralized Debt Obligations and Credit Risk Transfer' (n 22) 9; Frank Partnoy, 'Overdependence on Credit Ratings was a Primary Cause of the Crisis' (2009) University of San Diego Legal Studies Research Paper Series No 09-015, 6.

87 Barnett-Hart, 'The Story of the CDO Market Meltdown' (n 32) 13.

88 Lewis, *The Big Short* (n 10) 74.

89 Quinn, 'The Failure of Private Ordering and the Financial Crisis of 2008' (n 75) 586.

90 Crouhy, Jarrow and Turnbull, 'The Subprime Credit Crisis of 07' (n 24) 16 (describing monoline insurers as counterparties of financial institutions selling to them surety wraps in the form of credit derivatives).

borrowing securitized tranches would be difficult.[91] An indirect option was to short companies that were exposed to the subprime mortgage market. Another option was more straightforward, easier to implement and a lot cheaper: buying CDS.[92] CDS were inexpensive because market sentiment was homogeneously favorable to the subprime mortgage market. At that point, only outsiders were willing to take this side of the bet. Wall Street banks were happy to find a few hedge funds willing to buy CDS. A market for side bets was able to develop alongside the subprime mortgage market.[93]

At a later stage, some market participants acknowledged the risk related to their high exposure to the subprime mortgage market. Especially in 2007, Wall Street banks preferred to buy CDS to decrease their risk exposure. Buying CDS could work as an insurance against the default of subprime borrowers.

In the Abacus case, Goldman Sachs was even accused by the SEC of structuring synthetic CDOs with the assistance of the hedge fund Paulson & Co, which bet against the subprime mortgage market.[94] Goldman Sachs' wrongdoing allegedly consisted of failing to disclose that Paulson & Co was not investing in the deal, but betting against it.[95] Goldman Sachs acted as a CDO arranger and allowed Paulson & Co to select the mortgage-related assets against which to bet. Accordingly, Paulson & Co could buy CDS of the assets that – in its opinion – would underperform. Goldman Sachs used these CDS to build the synthetic CDOs that it sold to investors such as IKB Deutsche Industriebank and ACA Capital Management. In July 2010 the SEC and Goldman Sachs settled the Abacus case.[96] By forcing Goldman Sachs to admit to some wrongdoing, the SEC signaled a more confrontational approach that would expose Wall Street to more investor lawsuits in the future.[97] Moreover, Goldman Sachs partly recognized being short on the mortgage-related securities when the subprime mortgage market collapsed. Goldman Sachs may

---

[91] Michael J Burry, 'A Primer on Scion Capital's Subprime Mortgage Short', November 7, 2006, 3.

[92] ibid.

[93] Partnoy, 'Overdependence on Credit Ratings was a Primary Cause of the Crisis' (n 86) 6.

[94] Susan Pulliam and Evan Perez, 'Criminal Probe Looks Into Goldman Trading' *The Wall Street Journal*, April 30, 2010.

[95] Frank Partnoy, 'Wall Street Beware: The Lawyers are Coming' *The Financial Times*, April 18, 2010.

[96] Jesse Westbrook and Joshua Gallu, 'SEC's Demand That Goldman Admit "Mistake" Could Spur Lawsuits' *Bloomberg*, July 21, 2010.

[97] ibid.

have engaged in proprietary trading in order to bet against the subprime mortgage market, ie by trading on its own account as well. In any case, litigation following the financial crisis will bring clarity to Goldman Sachs' dubious activities in the run-up to the subprime mortgage debacle.

Apart from the use of CDS in order to bet against the subprime market, hybrid CDOs were also created as a mixture of debt securities and synthetic assets. The debt securities consisted of the subprime mortgage assets. The synthetic assets were typically CDS. If these CDS were bought by the vehicle, they provided credit enhancement to the CDO structure. In this way they were able to partly hedge hybrid CDO investors against the credit risk exposure to the subprime mortgage assets. For this reason the buy-side was either composed of investors betting against the subprime mortgage market or investors willing to decrease their exposure to the subprime mortgage market.

7.4 REGULATORY INCENTIVES TO THE EXPANSION OF THE STRUCTURED FINANCE SEGMENT

Since the 1970s the regulatory environment has encouraged both the expansion of structured finance and the use of credit ratings. Furthermore, an environment of low interest rates encouraged investors to seek instruments that offered yield enhancement.[98]

As a result of a combination of OTC derivatives, risk-based capital requirements and favorable accounting rules, Wall Street banks were able to create a "de facto" assembly line for purchasing, packaging and selling unregistered securities, such as CDOs, to a wide range of institutional investors.[99] Regulators argued that the transfer of risk from bank balance sheets to a broad range of investors was a desirable spreading of credit risk.[100] To a great extent regulators encouraged the proliferation of off-exchange-traded derivatives and the use of off-balance-sheet entities.[101] However, in the light of the subprime mortgage crisis the size and concentration of risk proved to be destabilizing.[102]

---

98 Crouhy, Jarrow and Turnbull, 'The Subprime Credit Crisis of 07' (n 24) 4.

99 Whalen, 'The Subprime Crisis' (n 21) 5.

100 Alexander and others, 'Financial Supervision and Crisis Management in the EU' (n 19) 26.

101 Whalen, 'The Subprime Crisis' (n 21) 5.

102 Alexander and others, 'Financial Supervision and Crisis Management in the EU' (n 19) 22.

Two types of rating-based regulations artificially increased the importance of credit ratings. First, risk-based capital requirements may rely on CRAs to attribute risk weights to individual assets. Capital adequacy rules represent the most extensive incorporation of ratings in financial market regulations. Globally the BCBS establishes international standards relevant for national regulators and financial institutions such as international banks. The BCBS enacted the Basel II framework in 2004 to provide a solution to determine the riskiness of assets based on CRAs' assessments.[103] Hitherto, post-crisis reform measures taken in the Basel III framework have continued to rely extensively on ratings. The Standardized Approach of Basel II and III uses ratings to attribute different risk weights to assets.[104] Highly rated instruments have lower risk weights and badly rated instruments have higher risk weights. Because OTC assets like CDOs often carried investment-grade ratings, these less liquid assets carried lower risk-based capital requirements than other assets.[105] Banks were incentivized to design securities so as to get high ratings from the leading CRAs. Moreover, banks were incentivized to hold highly rated instruments on their balance sheets.

With the help of high ratings, a substantive number of mortgage-related securities benefited from lower risk weights than regular loans according to Basel II, which encouraged the securitization of loans.[106] Basel II ignored the systemic risks attached to concentrated positions in securities held by banks.[107]

Second, especially in the US, investment limitations required that certain types of investors only invest in investment-grade securities. These regulations forced a certain range of investors to take ratings into account while trading in the financial markets. Issuers needed high ratings in order to make their products available to a broader range of investors. If CRAs downgraded securities to speculative-grade ratings, charter-constrained investors had to sell off the downgraded securities. As noted above, the use of credit ratings in financial market regulations has a substantial effect on the behavior of market participants.

---

103 Weber and Darbellay, 'The Regulatory Use of Credit Ratings in Bank Capital Requirement Regulations' (n 34) 4.

104 *Basel II* (n 35) para 50.

105 Whalen, 'The Subprime Crisis' (n 21) 6.

106 George Soros, 'Do Not Ignore the Need for Financial Reform' *The Financial Times*, October 25, 2009.

107 ibid.

7.5 CRUCIAL ROLE PLAYED BY CREDIT RATING AGENCIES IN THE GROWTH OF STRUCTURED FINANCE

Rating agencies continue to create an even bigger monster – the CDO market. Let's hope we are all wealthy and retired by the time this house of cards falters.[108]

7.5.1 Credit Rating Agencies' Key Position in Structured Finance

The rapid expansion of structured products is closely associated with the issuance of structured finance ratings. The leading CRAs first issued credit ratings for MBS in the mid-1970s.[109] Relating to securitized assets they began rating cash CDOs in the late 1990s and synthetic CDOs in the early 2000s.[110]

In fact, the shift to a market-based financial system has raised new issues as regards the role of information intermediaries such as CRAs. Banks needed novel instruments to be rated by an independent and reputable third party, and the three leading CRAs offered this service.[111] CRAs have thus played a significant role in the functioning of the originate-and-distribute model of intermediation.[112] The objective of the study is to examine how CRAs helped the financial institutions that developed the complex financial instruments. They were an essential part of the chain. Without their involvement, structured finance could not have grown at such an extraordinary pace.

---

108 'Wall Street and the Financial Crisis' (n 6) Exhibit 27 (quoting a Standard & Poor's employee).

109 IOSCO, *Report of the Task Force on the Subprime Crisis* (Final Report, May 2008) 20. See also Claire A Hill, 'Why Did Rating Agencies Do Such a Bad Job Rating Subprime Securities?' (2010) 71 University of Pittsburgh Law Review 1, 5.

110 IOSCO, *The Role of Credit Rating Agencies in Structured Finance Markets* (Final Report, May 2008) 5.

111 Alexander and others, 'Financial Supervision and Crisis Management in the EU' (n 19) 18.

112 Douglas W Arner, 'The Global Credit Crisis of 2008: Causes and Consequences' (2009) Asian Institute of International Financial Law Working Paper No 3, 22 ‹http://www.law.hku.hk/aiifl/research/conference-papers.html› accessed January 10, 2013.

The favorable ratings of the leading CRAs were crucial for investor acceptance of the new financial instruments.[113] Investors relied on CRAs' assessments of the riskiness of securitization products because of their complexity and because the contents of the underlying asset pool were frequently not revealed.[114] Lack of transparency in the financial markets increased the importance of ratings.

The traditional rating scale was used by CRAs in the structured finance segment. CRAs argued that their credit ratings were consistent between traditional and novel instruments.[115] They were not willing to develop different rating methodologies for traditional products and structured products because investors were already familiar with corporate ratings, and were reassured by the comparison made possible between traditional and novel products.[116] Linking the risk of novel products to the traditional rating scale was therefore crucial to the growth of structured product markets.[117]

As a consequence of the evolving financial market structure, the leading CRAs may have acted as gatekeepers in the development of the structured finance market.[118] The dramatic growth of the structured finance segment would not have been possible without their involvement. In practice the leading CRAs' gatekeeper status seems unlikely to change in the near future.[119]

7.5.2 Credit Ratings as a Marketing Tool for Securitized Assets

The involvement of CRAs deserves particular attention in the securitization process. The key to a successful securitization is a high credit rating by one of the leading CRAs.[120] Without the sanction of the leading

---

[113] Hunt, 'Credit Rating Agencies and the "Worldwide Credit Crisis"' (n 26) 119.

[114] House of Lords, Select Committee on Economic Affairs, *Banking Supervision and Regulation* (June 2009) 40.

[115] Hunt, 'Credit Rating Agencies and the "Worldwide Credit Crisis"' (n 26) 161 (adding that, however, ratings on novel financial products behaved differently from corporate ratings during the recent financial crisis).

[116] Barnett-Hart, 'The Story of the CDO Market Meltdown' (n 32) 16.

[117] Hunt, 'Credit Rating Agencies and the "Worldwide Credit Crisis"' (n 26) 161.

[118] ibid 176.

[119] ibid 178.

[120] Flood, 'Rating, Dating, and the Informal Regulation and the Formal Ordering of Financial Transactions' (n 14) 154.

CRAs, most securitization would fail.[121] Therefore, the sale of most structured securities in the primary market was rating dependent.[122]

Issuers take advantage of high ratings to sell their products. Debt rated investment-grade tends to have more marketability, liquidity and a lower interest rate than otherwise identical debt that is not rated.[123] As a consequence, to obtain a high rating can become a motive for the creation and marketing of securities.[124] The best example in the subprime mortgage market was the pooling and repackaging of triple-B-rated tranches into a new CDO structure with a view to enhancing the overall rating of the asset pool. Securitization offered the opportunity to transform below-investment-grade assets into triple-B to triple-A assets, ie investment-grade assets.[125] The newly obtained triple-A-rated tranches could be sold off to a broad investor base eager to buy highly rated assets.

The reason is that triple-A assets with higher yields than other triple-A assets were especially appealing to investors. Indeed, the use of ratings permitted investors to buy triple-A-rated assets that paid 20 times the spread of other triple-A-rated instruments.[126]

To some extent, there is a regulatory explanation since a certain category of investors was restrained from buying speculative-grade assets. Accordingly, investment-grade ratings remained an important requirement in marketing structured finance products to a broader investor base.[127] Due to regulatory concerns, investment-grade ratings enhanced the marketability of the rated assets, thereby making them available to a broader investor base. CDOs allowed these investors to gain exposure to assets that, on their own, had been too risky.[128] Through the securitization process, issuers could make these investments available to a broader investor base.

---

[121] ibid 160–161.

[122] Rosner, 'Toward an Understanding' (n 8) 12.

[123] Claire A Hill, 'Regulating the Rating Agencies' (2004) 82 Washington University Law Quarterly 43, 53.

[124] 'Exclusion Zone, Regulators Promise a Belated Review of the Ratings Oligopoly' *The Economist*, February 8, 2003, 65–66.

[125] Crouhy, Jarrow and Turnbull, 'The Subprime Credit Crisis of 07' (n 24) 4.

[126] Frank Partnoy, 'Do Away With Rating-based Rules' *The Financial Times*, July 8, 2008.

[127] CGFS, *Ratings in Structured Finance* (n 56) 9.

[128] Barnett-Hart, 'The Story of the CDO Market Meltdown' (n 32) 7.

As a consequence, investors subject to regulatory investment limitations were particularly attracted to triple-A-rated structured credit products that had a higher yield than other safe assets.[129] For institutional investors in particular they seemed to constitute a great opportunity for gain as they were simultaneously considered safe.

7.5.3 Proliferation of Rating-driven Transactions

Some transactions are merely designed to capture high credit ratings.[130] To some extent, financial institutions learned how to take advantage of rating models and build structured products with the sole purpose of attracting higher ratings from the CRAs. CDO structures reflect the situation in the most illustrative way. Since the tranching could raise the rating of some parts, many of the subprime mortgages were included in structured finance products.[131] In some structured finance products, the sum of the parts could even be greater than the whole, which should not be possible in a competitive and efficient market.[132] This situation led banks to repackage triple-B CDOs and make a profit from the transaction. The CDO machine generated significant revenues partly thanks to generous ratings.

The rating process helped issuers get around the rating models.[133] Issuers first hired a CRA to rate the financial instruments. If not satisfied with the determination of the CRAs, issuers had the opportunity to adjust the structure to provide the requisite credit enhancement of the "senior" tranche in order to get the triple-A rating.[134] This endeavor is evidence that the transaction was rating driven. The added credit enhancement was merely provided in order to get a higher rating.

Last but not least, the investment-grade ratings allowed a market for side bets to develop alongside the subprime mortgage market. Depending on the way they were used, synthetic CDOs allowed market participants to place giant bets that had no other economic purpose than to bet against the subprime mortgage market. Synthetic CDOs replicated the cash flow structures of cash CDOs and significantly increased market exposure to

---

129 IMF, *Global Financial Stability Report, Containing Systemic Risks and Restoring Financial Soundness* (April 2008) 57.

130 Partnoy, 'The Siskel and Ebert of Financial Markets?' (n 25) 668–670.

131 IMF, *Global Financial Stability Report* (n 129) 57.

132 Partnoy, 'The Siskel and Ebert of Financial Markets?' (n 25) 667.

133 Morgenson and Story, 'Rating Agency Data Aided Wall Street in Deals' (n 1).

134 IOSCO, *Report of the Task Force on the Subprime Crisis* (n 109) 21.

the subprime mortgage market. High ratings allowed the market for synthetic CDOs to grow at an extraordinary pace. Without the labeling provided by leading CRAs, this market would never have reached such a significant proportion. Criticism has been voiced about the fact that synthetic CDOs did not add economic value to the financial system.[135] Only high ratings were able to make investors purchase securities without caring about the content of the assets. Hence synthetic CDOs were able to find investors as long as they were marketed as safe by the leading CRAs.

7.6 REGULATORY ARBITRAGE AND RATING ARBITRAGE

The opportunity for regulatory arbitrage deserves particular attention because it largely explains why investors craved for highly rated securities without caring about the quality of the underlying assets. Market behavior was partly caused by wrong regulatory incentives in the financial markets.

First, bank capital requirements allowed large banks to extend their balance sheets by applying low risk weights to their highly rated assets. Under such circumstances, buying triple-A-rated assets meant a relief of regulatory capital.[136] Two examples may highlight how these regulatory incentives played a structural role in the context of the subprime mortgage crisis. First, Citigroup was a big CDO arranger. Instead of selling off all the triple-A-rated securities, Citigroup took advantage of holding numerous assets with the lowest possible risk weight on its balance sheet.[137] Second, the Swiss bank UBS had very high exposure to the subprime market partly due to the same regulatory incentives. More precisely, with respect to UBS two aspects were combined allowing the investment bank part of UBS to massively invest in the subprime mortgage market. The first aspect was the low internal rates applied at the universal bank so that the investment bank part of UBS could borrow at low internal rates from the commercial bank part of UBS.[138] The

---

[135] See generally IMF, *Global Financial Stability Report* (n 129) 54.

[136] Christian Bluhm, *CDO Modeling: Techniques, Examples and Applications* (HypoVereinsbank 2003) 7.

[137] Whalen, 'The Subprime Crisis' (n 21) 15; Lewis, *The Big Short* (n 10) 86.

[138] 'Währungshüter halten Geld weiterhin billig, Aufwertungsdruck auf den Franken erhöht' *NZZ*, February 21, 2010 (quoting Thomas Jordan, former vice-president, Swiss National Bank (SNB)).

second aspect was the low risk weights applied to highly rated mortgage-related securities.[139] Indeed, UBS was able to buy a substantive amount of triple-A-rated "super senior" CDO tranches.[140] Before the subprime mortgage crisis, the UBS investment bank could mark a kind of arbitrage profit from investing in "super senior" with a slightly higher yield than the internal cost of capital. Just before the subprime mortgage crisis was triggered, UBS was declared highly capitalized.[141] UBS was still investing in triple-A-rated CDOs in July 2007.[142] Immediately after the massive rating downgrades, UBS capital ratio changed dramatically and showed a UBS that needed more capital to be considered safe. These two examples illustrate the regulatory incentives associated with bank capital requirement regulations.

Second, investors that were not allowed by regulations to engage in risky activities found a way to take risk with the consent of regulators thanks to the high ratings given to securitized assets. Because the same ratings were given to securities with greatly differing risks, charter-constrained investors were able to buy structured securities offering yields many times higher than equally rated corporate or municipal debt issues.[143] As a result, some financial institutions were able to engage in regulatory arbitrage and rating arbitrage on a large scale.[144]

Rating arbitrage involves finding a way of obtaining high credit ratings out of assets that are worth less, ie a sort of artificial transformation of debt quality. Wall Street investment banks were in a position to circumvent CRAs' models in order to obtain the highest rating possible.[145] For

---

139 Myret Zaki, *UBS, Les dessous d'un scandale, Comment l'empire aux trois clés a perdu son pari* (Editions Favre SA 2008) 125 (stating that UBS relied excessively on CRAs).

140 See further ibid 124 (adding that 75 percent of the total of "super senior" tranches on UBS bank balance sheet turned out to come from synthetic CDOs).

141 ibid 188 (stating that UBS could expand its balance sheet with the help of the risk-sensitive approach of the Basel II framework); FINMA, 'Finanzmarkt-krise und Finanzmarktaufsicht' (September 14, 2009) (also recognizing that regulators cannot content themselves with risk-sensitive capital ratios but have to take into account the expansion of bank balance sheets) 39–41.

142 Lewis, *The Big Short* (n 10) 216.

143 Rosner, 'Toward an Understanding' (n 8) 8.

144 Joe Nocera, 'Propping up a House of Cards' *The New York Times*, February 28, 2009.

145 Lewis, *The Big Short* (n 10) 101.

instance, CRAs used the average FICO scores[146] of pools of borrowers instead of looking at the list of FICO scores.[147] As a result, it was possible to include a borrower that had a very low FICO score and was virtually certain to default.[148] In order to offset the borrowers with low scores, the financial institutions had to find borrowers with high FICO scores. Again, it was possible for the banks to circumvent the system since CRAs did not discern between "thin-file" and "thick-file" FICO scores.[149] A "thin-file" FICO score depended on a short credit history, thereby allowing immigrants with a low income, for instance, to have a high "thin-file" FICO score.[150]

Because the pricing of CDOs depended extensively on credit ratings, CDO arrangers were able to engage in rating arbitrage, more particularly in spread arbitrage.[151] Investors would accept lower yields thanks to the high credit ratings. The issuing entity made a profit out of the difference between the payments that it got from the underlying assets and the lower yield that goes to its bond holders. Further, the temptation when CDO arrangers were manufacturing a structured security had been to put riskier assets from each rating class into the portfolio.[152] Traders were then able to arbitrage between assets carrying different risks but the same rating.[153] If high ratings attract the same regulatory privileges, and highly rated securities seem to be similar, financial institutions able to understand that not all triple-A securities bear the same risk could benefit from that knowledge.

---

[146] FICO is an acronym for the Fair Isaac Corporation, the creator of the FICO scores. FICO scores are credit reports that statistically calculate the creditworthiness of individuals.

[147] Lewis, *The Big Short* (n 10) 99–100.

[148] ibid.

[149] ibid 100.

[150] ibid.

[151] Bluhm, *CDO Modeling* (n 136) 6.

[152] 'Exclusion Zone' (n 124) 65–66.

[153] ibid.

8. Wrong incentives in the credit rating industry

8.1 CONFLICTS OF INTEREST

> The truth is [CRAs] are working for Wall Street, and they are going to give to Wall Street what Wall Street wants.[1]

8.1.1 Issuer-pays Business Model

CRAs' conflicts of interest are particularly acute in the structured finance segment. Since the 1970s the rating industry has shifted from an investor-pays business model to an issuer-pays business model.[2] CRAs could no longer count on investors to pay for credit ratings. This is partly based on the fact that information is a public good. Due to the public-good nature of ratings, it is hard to get any individual investor to pay for ratings.[3]

It is worth mentioning that communication technology has changed dramatically since the creation of the rating industry in 1909.[4] Above all, since the 1970s, low-cost photocopying explains why investors are not willing to pay for information that can easily be spread.[5] Information economics theory highlights the fact that ratings are hard to sell to

[1] Armen Keteyian, 'Ratings Agencies to Face Grilling on Goldman' *CBS News*, April 22, 2010 (quoting Senator Bernie Sanders).

[2] Text to n 76 in ch 2.

[3] Kern Alexander and others, 'Financial Supervision and Crisis Management in the EU' (2007) European Parliament, Policy Department, Economic and Scientific Policy, 52 ‹http://www.europarl.europa.eu/document/activities/cont/201108/20110818ATT25070/20110818ATT25070EN.pdf› accessed January 10, 2013.

[4] Urs Birchler and Monika Bütler, *Information Economics* (Routledge 2007) 106.

[5] Lawrence J White, 'A New Law for the Bond Rating Industry' [2007] Regulation 48, 49; SEC, 'Report on the Role and Function of Credit Rating Agencies in the Operation of the Securities Markets, As Required by Section 702(b) of the Sarbanes-Oxley Act of 2002' (January 2003) 41.

investors. The equilibrium selling price for rating information is zero.[6] In fact, each recipient of a rating could secretly sell the information to other investors for a somewhat lower price until the price for the rating information falls to zero.[7] From another perspective, less reliance on the CRAs to provide valuable information may partly have moved investors away from ratings.

In order to be profitable, CRAs had to rely on another source of revenue and they started being paid by the issuers. Accordingly, in modern financial markets one reason for CRAs' profitability is the issuers' strong demand for ratings.[8] Currently, conflicts of interest have been particularly acute since the vast majority of the leading CRAs' revenues are from issuers' fees.[9]

There is evidence that issuers did not hire CRAs because of the value of their credit ratings. Instead, they started to pay for the ratings because of the regulatory privileges they could get. Moreover, issuers might take advantage of high ratings in order to lower the cost of capital.[10] If investors are reassured about the quality of an investment, they tend to demand lower returns.[11] Further, high ratings make debt instruments marketable to a broader range of investors due to regulatory and behavioral reliance.

When CRAs depend to a large extent on issuers' fees, they lose their independence. CRAs automatically tend to concentrate on satisfying the needs and interests of their clients.[12] For instance, the rapid expansion of

---

[6] Birchler and Bütler, *Information Economics* (n 4) 105–106.

[7] ibid.

[8] ibid 106–107 (also stating that the industry's profits are less impressive when compared to the aggregate value of rated bonds).

[9] Frank Partnoy, 'How and Why Credit Rating Agencies Are Not Like Other Gatekeepers' (2006) University of San Diego Legal Studies Research Paper Series No 07-46, 68–69 (adding that approximately 90 percent of CRAs' revenues come from issuers' fees; however, the concern about conflicts of interest is more systemic than individualized since CRAs do not depend on any particular issuer).

[10] Nevertheless, this can have beneficial effects on the financial markets as long as it is deemed to address the principal-agent problem. Problems arise as soon as CRAs lose their independence, which is most likely to happen under the issuer-pays business model.

[11] IOSCO, *Report on the Activities of Credit Rating Agencies* (September 2003) 6.

[12] Timothy E Lynch, 'Deeply and Persistently Conflicted: Credit Rating Agencies in the Current Regulatory Environment' (2009) 59 Case Western Reserve Law Review 227, 246.

business opportunities creates a conflict of interest by encouraging corner-cutting to attract business from issuers.[13] In other words, CRAs focused more on raising revenue than on enhancing rating quality.[14] They did not allocate the necessary resources to improve their rating models. Furthermore, they are accused of inflating ratings in order to attract new deals or keep their market share. The competitive pressures gave rise to a "race to the bottom."[15] The leading CRAs increased or kept their market share by lowering their rating standards. Collecting fees and minimizing costs allowed them to maximize their profits.

The revenue model poses further problems as far as the ongoing monitoring of ratings is concerned. The ongoing fee payment structure created a second incentive problem among CRAs.[16] CRAs were reluctant to downgrade their ratings for fear of losing their market share.[17] The reliance on issuers' fees relating to the structured finance segment contributed to impair CRAs' independence.

8.1.2 Ancillary Services

The ancillary business contributed to a large part of CRAs' revenues in the structured finance segment. Nevertheless, the practice of offering ancillary services causes the most controversy. The risk arises that the integrity of the rating process may be damaged if ratings are used to generate lucrative additional business from issuers.[18] Doing ancillary

---

[13] House of Lords, Select Committee on Economic Affairs, *Banking Supervision and Regulation* (June 2009) 41–42.

[14] 'Credibility of Credit Ratings, the Investment Decisions Made Based on those Ratings, and the Financial Crisis, Hearings & Testimony Before the FCIC' (June 2, 2010) (testimony of Mark Froeba, former Moody's employee) 4.

[15] John C Coffee Jr, 'Ratings Reform: the Good, the Bad, and the Ugly' (2011) 1 Harvard Business Law Review 231, 234.

[16] Michel G Crouhy, Robert A Jarrow and Stuart M Turnbull, 'The Subprime Credit Crisis of 07' (2008) SSRN eLibrary, 9 ‹http:ssrn.com/abstract=1112467› accessed January 10, 2013.

[17] 'Wall Street and the Financial Crisis: The Role of Credit Rating Agencies, Hearing Before the Permanent Subcommittee on Investigations of the Senate Committee on Homeland Security and Governmental Affairs' (April 23, 2010) (written statement of Frank L Raiter, former Managing Director, Standard & Poor's) 2.

[18] Niamh Moloney, *EC Securities Regulation* (2nd edn, Oxford University Press 2008) 691.

business may generate conflicts of interest.[19] Concern has been raised about the influence of the purchase of ancillary services on the CRAs' rating decisions. Issuers may hope to get higher ratings if they purchase ancillary services or may conversely fear that their failure to do so could negatively impact on their rating.[20]

Further, ancillary services gave issuers the opportunity to work with CRAs on the composition of structured products. As far as CDOs were concerned, the selection and slicing were done in close association with CRAs, so that each tranche was awarded the appropriate credit rating.[21] The CRAs told the CDO arrangers the procedure it would use to rate the bonds such as the methods, historical default rates, prepayment rates and recovery rates.[22] The rating process was a fixed target: the CDO trust designed the liability structure to obtain a significant percentage of triple-A bonds.[23]

Therefore, issuers did not hire CRAs to take advantage of their expertise but rather to know how to create financial instruments in order to get a given rating.[24] CRAs' assistance did not help to enhance the quality of the structured product substantially. Instead, CRAs' advice was used to maximize the obtained rating. This process contrasts with the corporate rating process where issuers have far less opportunity to

---

19 See, eg, Claire A Hill, 'Regulating the Rating Agencies' (2004) 82 Washington University Law Quarterly 51; Rolf H Weber and Simone Baumann, 'Conflicts of Interest and Risk Management Practices in the CRA Industry' in Jan Kleineman and Lars Gorton (eds), *Credit Rating Agencies* (Stockholm Centre for Commercial Law, forthcoming 2013). See also Partnoy, 'How and Why Credit Rating Agencies Are Not Like Other Gatekeepers' (n 9) 68; Susan Emmenegger, 'Die Regulierung von Rating-Agenturen' [2006] Swiss Review of Business and Financial Market Law 32, 35–36.

20 IOSCO, *Report on the Activities of Credit Rating Agencies* (n 11) 11.

21 'Exclusion Zone, Regulators Promise a Belated Review of the Ratings Oligopoly' *The Economist*,February 8, 2003, 65–66.

22 Crouhy, Jarrow and Turnbull, 'The Subprime Credit Crisis of 07' (n 16) 9.

23 ibid.

24 But see Carol Ann Frost, 'Credit Rating Agencies in Capital Markets: A Review of Research Evidence on Selected Criticisms of the Agencies' (2007) 22 Journal of Accounting, Auditing & Finance 469, 480 (criticizing the practice of providing ancillary services, yet adding that documenting inappropriate behavior would be extremely difficult).

influence ratings.[25] This gives rise to concern about completely separating the formulation of ratings from the ancillary services offered to issuers on the engineering of complex financial products.[26]

8.1.3 Interferences between Credit Rating Agencies and Issuers

> I am getting serious pushback from Goldman on a deal that they want to go to market with today.[27]

The securitization process may have worked better if there had been greater independence in the creation of the CDO packages and their credit ratings.[28] CRAs saw drafts of the documentation during the structuring of the transaction, they could criticize it and exchange their ideas with issuers.[29] Issuers could accept these comments, or provide the requisite credit enhancement for the senior tranche to fulfill CRAs' expectations and obtain the desired triple-A rating.[30] They could also decide not to hire the CRA, in which case the issuer might or might not – depending on the engagement contract – have paid the CRA a "break-up fee."[31]

"Rating shopping" was possibly practiced as a result of interferences between issuers and CRAs. For instance, issuers frequently asked several CRAs to provide prospective assessments on CDO tranches before deciding which CRA to hire.[32] This process allowed issuers to shop around to insure they could get a triple-A rating for their products.[33] Under such circumstances, investment banks were able to put pressure on

---

[25] Alexander and others, 'Financial Supervision and Crisis Management in the EU' (n 3) 19.

[26] The High-Level Group on Financial Supervision in the EU, 'De Larosière Report' (2009) 19 ‹http://ec.europa.eu/internal_market/finances/docs/de_larosiere_report_en.pdf› accessed January 10, 2013.

[27] 'Wall Street and the Financial Crisis' (n 17) Exhibit 36, 156 (quoting a Moody's employee).

[28] Alexander and others, 'Financial Supervision and Crisis Management in the EU' (n 3) 18.

[29] John Flood, 'Rating, Dating, and the Informal Regulation and the Formal Ordering of Financial Transactions: Securitisations and Credit Rating Agencies' in Michael B Likosky (ed), *Privatising Development: Transnational Law, Infrastructure and Human Rights* (Martinus Nijhoff Publishers 2005) 154.

[30] ibid; IOSCO, *Report of the Task Force on the Subprime Crisis* (Final Report, May 2008) 21.

[31] ibid.

[32] ibid 28.

[33] De Larosière Report (n 26) 9.

CRAs. If CRAs did not give the highest ratings, investment banks would simply hire another CRA.

In addition, interferences between issuers and CRAs partly resulted from disclosure rules on CRAs in the US; in the spirit of transparency CRAs had to disclose computer application software that enabled issuers to input a CDO package and see what rating that package would acquire.[34] This helped issuers get around the rating system.[35] Investment banks worked backward and got involved in the practice of "reverse-engineering."[36] They could adjust their CDO packages to get the desired rating while minimizing the efforts made to improve the quality of the package.

Apart from that, CRAs used to hire out some of the CRA employees who had devised the ratings.[37] Former CRA analysts helped investment bankers construct the deals to be rated. They could easily get around rating models and get the highest ratings for investments that were riskier than the ratings suggested. These practices seriously jeopardized the independence of the issuers and CRAs.

Furthermore, Wall Street banks used to help CRAs create the rating models used to rate securitized assets. This endeavor was particularly striking as far as complex synthetic CDO structures were concerned. Initially CRAs did not have their own rating models to rate complex financial products, so banks sent their own models to the CRAs which

---

[34] Alexander and others, 'Financial Supervision and Crisis Management in the EU' (n 3) 18.

[35] Gretchen Morgenson and Louise Story, 'Rating Agency Data Aided Wall Street in Deals' *The New York Times*, April 23, 2010 (suggesting that because CRAs had to explain how they did things, investment banks could sometimes game it) (quoting Dan Rosen).

[36] ibid. ("Reverse-engineering" means gaming rating models in order to get the highest ratings possible even though the financial product did not always deserve them. By sharing their rating models, CRAs gave investment bankers the tools to tinker with their complicated mortgage deals until the models produced the desired ratings. Investment banks were able to engage in rating-driven transactions in order to get higher ratings while structuring the deal slightly differently without having to substantially enhance the quality of the underlying assets.)

[37] ibid. (For instance, Shin Yukawa, a former Fitch employee, joined Goldman Sachs in 2005 and helped create Abacus 2007-AC1. The most part of the Abacus deal obtained triple-A ratings that were not deserved.)

agreed to rate a large part of the newly securitized assets triple-A.[38] In this regard, investment banks improperly influenced the rating process.

Last but not least, interferences between issuers and CRAs were also common during the ongoing monitoring of the rated instruments. CRAs could threaten issuers with downgrading the debt instruments if issuers did not act in a certain way. As far as CDO structures were concerned, if substitutions were permitted the portfolio composition could be changed in order to maintain the desired rating.[39]

8.2 ABSENCE OF REPUTATIONAL CONSTRAINTS IN RATING STRUCTURED PRODUCTS

> We rate every deal. It could be structured by cows and we would rate it.[40]

Lack of competition in the credit rating industry meant that CRAs rated structured products recklessly even when they knew they were not able to provide accurate information. Reputational capital means that CRAs issue inaccurate ratings at their peril. The reputational capital view of CRAs works only if CRAs lose more in reputational capital from giving false ratings than they gain in increased fees.[41] However, in the structured finance segment reputational incentives failed to work. CRAs were not deterred from issuing low-quality ratings on novel products because the structured product markets were a great source of profit. The profit they could get was higher than the reputational constraints they faced. In other words, for that profit it was worth taking the risk of losing reputation in an uncertain future.

Evidence from the subprime mortgage crisis suggests that novel-product rating was lucrative enough to tempt CRAs to take the risk of

---

[38] Michael Lewis, *The Big Short, Inside the Doomsday Machine* (WW Norton & Company 2010) 76 (quoting a former CDO trader, Goldman Sachs).

[39] Alexander and others, 'Financial Supervision and Crisis Management in the EU' (n 3) 19.

[40] 'Wall Street and the Financial Crisis' (n 17) Exhibit 30a, 132 (quoting a Standard & Poor's employee).

[41] Frank Partnoy, 'The Siskel and Ebert of Financial Markets?: Two Thumbs Down for the Credit Rating Agencies' (1999) 77 Washington University Law Quarterly 619, 633.

reputational spillover.[42] If financial innovation continues to be important, CRAs will continue to face that temptation.[43]

The presence of conflicts of interest in the rating industry partly explains the wrong incentives that discouraged CRAs from acting independently. Issuers paid the leading CRAs to rate mortgage-related securities. CRAs had no incentive to refuse. If they were paid by investors, they would be subject to reputational constraints. It is not surprising that CRAs tended to satisfy the interests of the client that paid for the rating. Issuers were interested in low rating standards. Investors would have favored high-quality ratings. As far as competitive pressures in terms of rating quality are concerned, CRAs are subject to reputational constraints only under the investor-pays business model. Unlike the investor-pays business model, the issuer-pays business model creates competitive pressures in terms of a "race to the bottom" as regards the rating standards.

Overall, market participants did not seem to care about rating quality. To make matters worse, the market even penalized quality by awarding rating mandates based on the lowest credit enhancement needed for the highest rating.[44] In fact, the leading CRAs were facing a dilemma to maintain both market share and rating quality.[45] CRAs opted for market share in the sense that competitive pressures incentivized them to loosen their rating standards in order to guarantee issuers' fees. The CRA that required the lowest credit enhancement for the highest rating attracted the most business.[46] CRAs overreached themselves in order to capture higher fees from more complex deals, thereby compromising their standards.[47]

---

[42] John Patrick Hunt, 'Credit Rating Agencies and the "Worldwide Credit Crisis": The Limits of Reputation, the Insufficiency of Reform, and a Proposal for Improvement' [2009] Columbia Business Law Review 109, 172.

[43] ibid 173.

[44] 'Wall Street and the Financial Crisis' (n 17) Exhibit 24b, 115 (quoting Raymond W McDaniel, Chairman and Chief Executive Officer, Moody's).

[45] Karey Wutkowsky and Rachelle Younglai, 'Lawmakers, Former Execs Blast Credit Raters' *Reuters*, October 22, 2008 (quoting Raymond W McDaniel, Chairman and Chief Executive Officer, Moody's); 'Wall Street and the Financial Crisis' (n 17) Exhibit 24b, 116 (suggesting that bad ratings should be perceived to have worse consequences than market share slippage, which is not easy to implement) (quoting Raymond W McDaniel, Chairman and Chief Executive Officer, Moody's).

[46] Wutkowsky and Younglai, 'Lawmakers, Former Execs Blast Credit Raters' (n 45).

[47] CGFS, *Ratings in Structured Finance: What Went Wrong and What Can Be Done to Address Shortcomings* (BIS, CGFS Paper No 32, July 2008) 10.

Moreover, the leading CRAs had no incentive to allocate more resources in order to improve rating quality. Even if keeping pace with financial innovation would have required larger investment from the CRAs, it seems likely that a sufficient investment was not made.[48] As a consequence, there is a serious danger of rating inflation when CRAs lose the long-term value of their reputation due to the rapid expansion of business opportunities.[49]

In the critical area of rating novel credit instruments, such as those which may have contributed to the recent credit market meltdown, a well-functioning reputation mechanism is unlikely to produce ideal incentives for high rating quality.[50] CRAs are unlikely to be constrained from issuing a credit rating on a novel product for fear of depleting their reputational capital; if they have the opportunity to get high fees from rating a new and complex product, they will do it regardless of reputational constraints due to the fact that they have never rated the target product before.[51] Therefore, as long as financial innovation continues, CRAs will not be fixated on improving the reputation mechanism.[52]

Another reason is that a low-quality rating in a novel segment will not affect CRAs' reputations in traditional segments. Even though they cannot rate novel products satisfactorily, CRAs face no negative spillover in traditional segments such as the corporate segment.[53] Therefore, there is no reason not to issue a rating on novel products. CRAs can only benefit from rating novel instruments. Given that the expected benefits from rating novel products are high enough relative to the expected magnitude of negative spillover, CRAs will most likely risk any negative spillover effects.[54]

---

48 Hill, 'Regulating the Rating Agencies' (n 19) 81.

49 House of Lords, *Banking Supervision and Regulation Report* (n 13) 41–42.

50 Hunt, 'Credit Rating Agencies and the "Worldwide Credit Crisis"' (n 42) 112–115.

51 ibid 114, 172.

52 ibid 114.

53 ibid 169–172.

54 ibid 172.

8.3 OVER-RELIANCE ON QUANTITATIVE MODELS

8.3.1 Failure to Adapt Rating Models to New Market Trends

> It is only worth remarking at this point that economists, for example, frequently have to update forecasts made only three months ahead and those betting on houses, only seven minutes ahead.[55]

CRAs over-relied on quantitative models when rating structured products. Structured finance ratings are characterized by their heavy reliance on quantitative models while corporate debt ratings are more dependent on a long historical record and analyst judgment.[56] Models that are used to rate structured products are based on statistically derived assumptions while models that are used to rate corporate debt are based on a long history of empirical data.[57]

The failure to anticipate the subprime mortgage crisis was not primarily due to the scarcity of historic track records, but rather a failure to incorporate new information – such as increasing delinquency rates and falling house prices – in rating models.[58]

Available databases with histories of mortgage loans were not representative of new risk trends because the new mortgage loans typically had teaser rates, no principal payments in the beginning, different loan standards such as high loan-to-value ratios, and no documentation.[59] CRAs should have incorporated new market trends in the assumptions on which their rating models were based.[60]

---

[55] Philip R Wood QC, 'The Regulation of Credit Reference Agencies: A Wider View' in Jan Kleineman and Lars Gorton (eds), *Credit Rating Agencies* (Stockholm Centre for Commercial Law, forthcoming 2013).

[56] CGFS, *Ratings in Structured Finance* (n 47) 5. See also Adam B Ashcraft and Til Schuermann, 'Understanding the Securitization of Subprime Mortgage Credit' (2008) Federal Reserve Bank of New York Staff Reports, 44 ‹http://www.newyorkfed.org/research/staff_reports/sr318.pdf› accessed January 10, 2013.

[57] Joshua Rosner, 'Toward an Understanding: NRSRO Failings in Structured Ratings and Discreet Recommendations to Address Agency Conflicts' (2009) 14 (Issue 4) Journal of Structured Finance 7, 10.

[58] CGFS, *Ratings in Structured Finance* (n 47) 23 (arguing that the lack of comprehensive historical data is considered to have been an important source of model errors as revealed during the subprime mortgage crisis).

[59] Crouhy, Jarrow and Turnbull, 'The Subprime Credit Crisis of 07' (n 16) 16.

[60] Sewell Chan, 'Documents Show Internal Qualms at Rating Agencies' *The New York Times*, April 22, 2010 (reporting that the inquiry found that CRAs

In principle, historical data is used as an indicator to predict the future. Comprehensive historical data generally help to forecast market fluctuations. However, CRAs could not accurately base their models on historic track records because what was happening in the subprime mortgage market had not been experienced previously. In the past, mortgages tended to have high recovery rates, yet this was changing due to the declining underwriting standards in the subprime mortgage market, high debt-to-value ratios and falling house prices.[61] Historical data was almost useless because the past had only known an environment of low delinquency rates and rising house prices.

As a result, CRAs based their models on erroneous assumptions. As a consequence, their estimates of the probability of default and of the loss given default no longer reflected the reality.[62] The question arises whether CRAs could have seen what was happening in the subprime mortgage market earlier. In this regard, the lack of historical data was not the problem. Rather, the problem was the failure to perceive significant changes in the subprime mortgage market. CRAs should have focused more on understanding and interpreting the new circumstances that were impacting on the subprime mortgage market. If they had based their judgments on information reflecting market evolution, they should have seen that delinquency rates were rising and that house prices were about to fall.

Therefore, the problem was not that CRAs did not have historical data at their disposal, but that they kept using outdated models instead of taking into account new data.

8.3.2 Flaws in the Rating Models

It is worth recalling that the central assumptions at the core of CRA models in structured finance are default rates, recovery rates and correlations.[63] There were modeling inaccuracies that had to do with the

---

neglected to take mortgage fraud, lax underwriting and a declining housing market into account in their models).

[61] Crouhy, Jarrow and Turnbull, 'The Subprime Credit Crisis of 07' (n 16) 10.

[62] ibid.

[63] CGFS, *Ratings in Structured Finance* (n 47) 13. See further Ashcraft and Schuermann, 'Understanding the Securitization of Subprime Mortgage Credit' (n 56) 43 (stating that correlated losses must be taken into account in structured finance ratings since ABS structures represent claims on cash flows from a portfolio of underlying assets).

complexity of the CDO structures in the subprime mortgage market.[64] Above all, the conventional wisdom is that quantitative mistakes resulted from underestimating the cross-correlation of default.[65] Securitization theories fail to work if correlations are so high that asset diversification is not able to sufficiently reduce risk.[66] Moreover, to model the CDO collateral pool, CRAs needed to model the ABS bonds of the many different ABS trusts – approximately 100 – incorporated into the CDO structure.[67] ABS ratings, in turn, relied crucially on the ability of the CRA to predict how the level of losses for a particular loan pool would respond to different economic scenarios.[68] Furthermore, the modeling of the cash flows was almost impossible due to the scarcity of generally timely data on the collateral pool of specific ABS trusts.[69] Available data was incomplete with respect to the current state of the underlying mortgage loans.[70]

The modern portfolio theory developed by Harry Markowitz and extended by Robert Merton lies at the core of CRAs' statistical risk models.[71] Risk and return of instruments are distributions. Even though the resulting models have strong scientific support, market participants cannot rely on them exclusively.

---

[64] Alexander and others, 'Crisis Management, Burden Sharing and Solidarity Mechanisms in the EU' (2010) European Parliament, Policy Department, Economic and Scientific Policy, 8 ‹http://www.europarl.europa.eu/committees/en/cris/studiesdownload.html?languageDocument=EN&file=31711› accessed January 10, 2013 (stating that CRAs failed to use adequate risk-measurement methodologies to assess the underlying risks embedded in complex financial instruments).

[65] See generally Ashcraft and Schuermann, 'Understanding the Securitization of Subprime Mortgage Credit' (n 56) 43. Default was viewed as borrower-specific; however, correlated losses should have been taken into account.

[66] See generally Douglas J Lucas, Laurie S Goodman and Frank J Fabozzi, 'Collateralized Debt Obligations and Credit Risk Transfer' (2007) Yale ICF Working Paper No 07-06, 14 (stating that there is a higher correlation of default in the CRT market).

[67] Crouhy, Jarrow and Turnbull, 'The Subprime Credit Crisis of 07' (n 16) 16.

[68] CGFS, *Ratings in Structured Finance* (n 47) 5.

[69] Crouhy, Jarrow and Turnbull, 'The Subprime Credit Crisis of 07' (n 16) 16.

[70] ibid.

[71] Alexander and others, *Financial Supervision and Crisis Management in the EU* (n 3) 22.

Blind reliance on mathematical models can lead to an underestimation of the consequences should a low-probability event be realized.[72] What happened as regards the subprime mortgage crisis came from a low-probability economic event.[73] The market was over-confident because the highest tranches seemed to enjoy a low probability of default. However, due to the high risk correlation, even though the probability that the risk would materialize was low, if it did happen the whole market would collapse.

Furthermore, the subprime mortgage crisis has shed light on a shortcoming of equilibrium thinking, the tendency to underestimate the likelihood of sudden large events.[74] Financial fluctuations have fat tails, ie large fluctuations are more likely than normal distribution suggests.[75]

CRAs are reputed to do a better job at providing borrowers' or debt instruments' relative credit risk than their absolute credit risk.[76] In terms of relative credit risks, they gave higher ratings to higher tranches than lower tranches. Investors were convinced by the distinctions made between the various tranches. This gave the misleading impression that the highest tranches were protected from bad economic events.

However, CRAs and investors tended to forget systemic risk and human judgment.[77] Investors also relied on CRAs without sufficiently taking liquidity risk into account. Measuring and limiting liquidity risk cannot be achieved merely through quantitative criteria.[78] The originate-and-distribute banking model, ie the process of pooling and selling off loans, has introduced a new dimension of liquidity risk that should be taken into account by market participants.[79] For instance, certain financial instruments such as Structured Investment Vehicles (SIVs) depend to

---

72 See generally John M Griffin and Dragon Yongjun Tang, 'Did Subjectivity Play a Role in CDO Credit Ratings?' (2010) McCombs Research Paper Series No FIN-04-10, 28–29 (relating to rating inflation).

73 CGFS, *Ratings in Structured Finance* (n 47) 22.

74 Mark Buchanan, 'Crazy Money: How Can we Stop the Financial Markets Creating so Much Misery? Forget Textbook Economics, the Answer Lies Elsewhere' *New Scientist*, July 19, 2008.

75 ibid. See also Lewis, *The Big Short* (n 38) 218 (quoting John Mack).

76 Arturo Estrella and others, 'Credit Ratings and Complementary Sources of Credit Quality Information' (2000) BCBS Working Paper No 3, 131 ‹http://www.bis.org/publ/bcbs72a.pdf› accessed January 10, 2013.

77 Austin Murphy, 'An Analysis of the Financial Crisis of 2008: Causes and Solutions' (2008) SSRN eLibrary, 18 ‹http:ssrn.com/abstract=1295344› 6–7, accessed January 10, 2013 (mentioning human judgment).

78 De Larosière Report (n 26) 18.

79 ibid.

a large degree on short-term funding.[80] SIVs typically invest in long-term assets and rely on short-term debt to finance their activities. Further, CRAs ignored counterparty risk. For example, the highest rating could be obtained by purchasing a surety wrap from a triple-A-rated insurer.[81] This procedure failed to take into account the full picture of counterparty risk by over-relying on ratings to assess counterparty risk. In a nutshell, such rating flaws show that CRAs excessively depended on their models to assess liquidity or counterparty risk instead of exercising human judgment to measure qualitative criteria.

8.3.3 Dependence on Rating Models for Valuation Purposes

Moreover, credit ratings were crucial for pricing in structured finance.[82] Some investors – especially institutional investors – relied exclusively on ratings for valuation purposes.[83] As a result, ratings can explain a substantial proportion of variation in launch spreads as far as structured finance products are concerned.[84] The most striking example is the case of CDOs. The relationship between price and rating for each tranche is very close and consistent across all types of securitizations and considerably stronger than in the case of corporate bonds.[85] Investment bankers are able to sell to investors in the primary market at prices that depend only on ratings.[86]

In the subprime mortgage market, over-reliance on credit ratings led to a complete mispricing of credit risk. A good example is provided by the CDS market, ie the market for insuring securitized bonds. The valuation of mortgage-related CDS should logically have depended on new pieces of information relating to the mortgage market. Before the subprime mortgage crisis was triggered in July 2007, CDS prices of securitized assets should have been an early signal of a deteriorating market. Buying

---

80 ibid.

81 Crouhy, Jarrow and Turnbull, 'The Subprime Credit Crisis of 07' (n 16) 7.

82 Macij T Firla-Cuchra, 'Explaining Launch Spreads on Structured Bonds' (2005) Department of Economics Discussion Paper Series No 230, 16 ‹http://economics.ouls.ox.ac.uk/13375/1/Item.pdf› accessed January 10, 2013.

83 FSF, *Report of the Financial Stability Forum on Enhancing Market and Institutional Resilience* (April 2008) 37.

84 Firla-Cuchra, 'Explaining Launch Spreads on Structured Bonds' (n 82) 16.

85 ibid 24.

86 Michael J Brennan, Julia Hein and Ser-Huang Poon, 'Tranching and Rating' (2008) SSRN eLibrary, 1, 17, 23, 24 ‹http:ssrn.com/abstract=1108556› accessed January 10, 2013.

CDS should have become more expensive every time negative news hit the subprime mortgage market – at least since early 2007. Surprisingly however, CDS prices were falling just before the subprime mortgage crisis erupted.[87] If other factors played a role, one of the problems was undoubtedly that valuation depended on the ratings of the synthetic CDOs based on CDS. The triple-A-rated tranches of synthetic CDOs in particular were very valuable before the massive rating downgrades. As a consequence, market participants failed to incorporate market trends in CDS prices. The market for CDS was distorted.

Another example from the subprime mortgage crisis illustrates the over-reliance on rating models for valuation purposes. For instance, a Morgan Stanley hedge fund wanted to bet against the worst mortgage-related assets. The hedge fund selected triple-B-rated CDOs that it could short by purchasing CDS.[88] In order to pay the premium, the hedge fund invested in triple-A-rated CDOs.[89] Because the highly rated assets had a lower yield than the triple-B assets, the hedge fund had to purchase a significant amount of these triple-A assets.[90] The price of mortgage-related securities directly depended on their ratings. Because the hedge fund had to purchase many times more triple-A assets in order to finance its CDS bet, it suffered significant losses as soon as the subprime mortgage crisis hit the financial markets. Its great exposure to highly rated bonds resulted from an over-reliance on ratings with respect to the pricing of credit risk.

8.4 MARKET OVER-RELIANCE ON CREDIT RATINGS IN STRUCTURED FINANCE

In the run-up to the subprime mortgage crisis, investors over-relied on CRAs that were over-relying on quantitative models. There are several reasons that led to market over-reliance on CRAs in the structured finance segment.

First, information intermediaries such as CRAs have played an increasing role in monitoring CRT instruments. Indeed, the dispersion of credit risk through CRT instruments implies that holders of credit risk do not have a direct relationship with the borrowers.[91] Due to the breaking up of

---

87 Lewis, *The Big Short* (n 38) 95, 129.

88 ibid 95, 206.

89 ibid.

90 ibid.

91 CGFS, *Credit Risk Transfer* (BIS, January 2003) 23.

credit exposures into more diversified portfolios, risk-takers have less capacity themselves to monitor the creditworthiness of individual borrowers.[92] As a consequence, many market participants effectively outsourced their own valuations and risk analyses of mortgage-related securities to the leading CRAs.[93] In the first place it may have been considered a cheap and convenient solution to partly outsource credit risk management to CRAs.[94] Some institutional investors ended up relying too heavily on ratings in their investment guidelines and choices, in some cases fully substituting ratings for independent risk assessment and due diligence.[95]

Second, the dependence on credit ratings was particularly acute in structured finance due to the complexity of the rated products. Structured products are often considered to be less transparent and far more complicated than corporate debt instruments. Just before the subprime mortgage crisis was triggered, investors appeared to have relied heavily or solely on the CRA ratings as far as mortgage-related securities were concerned.[96] The complexity of financial instruments partly explains the over-reliance on ratings characterizing the structured finance segment. The analysis of the underlying assets and the estimate of correlations are quite challenging.[97] Investors in highly-rated products with low risk premia may lack expertise or be incentivized to avoid the costs of doing their own analysis.[98] Moreover, the absence of an active secondary market for these products and the lack of sufficient historical performance data make valuations of structured products even trickier.[99] These

---

[92] ibid.

[93] IOSCO, *The Role of Credit Rating Agencies in Structured Finance Markets* (Final Report, May 2008) 2.

[94] BCBS, *Consultative Document, Strengthening the Resilience of the Banking Sector* (BIS, December 2009) 55. However, when the subprime mortgage market collapsed, market participants ended up paying the high price; Lewis, *The Big Short* (n 38) 102 (suggesting that the subprime mortgage market had subcontracted its credit analysis to entities that were not even doing the credit analysis).

[95] FSF, *Report of the Financial Stability Forum on Enhancing Market and Institutional Resilience* (n 83) 37.

[96] IOSCO, *The Role of Credit Rating Agencies in Structured Finance Markets* (n 93) 7–8.

[97] FSF, *Report of the Financial Stability Forum on Enhancing Market and Institutional Resilience* (n 83) 37.

[98] ibid.

[99] ibid 37–38.

factors contributed to a situation where the investing community largely relied on CRAs to assess the risk of holding structured finance products.[100]

As a consequence, when the subprime mortgage crisis called rating quality into question, investors were left with no independent means of assessing the risk of mortgage-related securities.[101] In sum, a particular failure leading to the subprime mortgage crisis has been investor acceptance of structured finance ratings without understanding the basis on which those structured products were provided.[102] The financial turmoil emphasizes the importance for investors of exercising informed judgment.[103]

Third, the regulatory use of credit ratings creates and maintains an artificial demand for ratings and excessive reliance on CRAs.[104] Rating-based regulations are often considered to be the most important piece of the over-reliance puzzle. Basel II undoubtedly increased reliance on ratings by many buy-side firms.[105] Currently Basel III does not fully reverse this trend; the BCBS will likely focus more on reducing over-reliance on ratings in the future. Market participants tend to rely extensively on certified CRAs, which are referred to as ECAIs under the Basel II and III frameworks.[106] The use of ratings in financial market regulations should never eliminate the need for those taking investment decisions to exercise their own judgment.[107]

Fourth, to make matters worse, behavioral reliance on credit ratings has added to regulatory reliance.[108] This behavioral over-reliance probably derives from decades of regulatory dependence on ratings.[109] For instance, ratings help to determine at what cost a borrower can borrow

---

[100] ibid 38.

[101] ibid.

[102] De Larosière Report (n 26) 16.

[103] ibid 32.

[104] Jonathan R Macey, *Corporate Governance: Promises Kept, Promises Broken* (Princeton University Press 2008) 114. See also De Larosière Report (n 26) 9.

[105] De Larosière Report (n 26) 16.

[106] IOSCO, *Report of the Task Force on the Subprime Crisis* (n 30) 23.

[107] De Larosière Report (n 26) 16.

[108] Frank Partnoy, 'Overdependence on Credit Ratings was a Primary Cause of the Crisis' (2009) University of San Diego Legal Studies Research Paper Series No 09-015, 10.

[109] ibid.

money in the capital markets.[110] Another example is the extensive use of ratings in contracting. Rating downgrades or upgrades are widely used as a contractual signal of a borrower's creditworthiness.[111] "Rating triggers" can mean that payment obligations require the posting of collateral based upon a rating downgrade.[112] A downgrade can trigger a demand for a higher rate of interest on a loan or bond.[113] Contractual clauses can specify that counterparties are given the right to accelerate repayment of an outstanding loan if the rating falls below a certain level.[114] As a consequence, a rating downgrade can throw a company into default under the terms of its debt covenants.[115] Behavioral reliance on ratings enhances the effects of rating changes, thereby increasing market volatility.[116]

8.5 EXPLOITATION OF INFORMATION ASYMMETRY IN THE MARKET FOR SECURITIZED ASSETS

The over-reliance on CRAs that over-relied on quantitative models supported the creation of an opaque market for securitized assets. The securitization process generated information asymmetry in the financial markets. Investors in complex credit products had less information at their disposal to assess the underlying credit quality of the assets they held in their portfolios than the originators.[117] As information intermediaries, CRAs are supposed to alleviate information asymmetries in the financial markets. Third-party certifiers of quality should be able to reduce the "lemons problem"[118] in the financial markets.[119] In general,

---

[110] Ulrich Ackermann and Joachim Jäckle, 'Ratingverfahren aus Emittentensicht' (2006) 61 Betriebs-Berater 868, 878–879.

[111] 'Exclusion Zone' (n 21) 65–66.

[112] IOSCO, *Report on the Activities of Credit Rating Agencies* (n 11) 8.

[113] 'Exclusion Zone' (n 21) 65–66.

[114] IOSCO, *Report on the Activities of Credit Rating Agencies* (n 11) 8.

[115] 'Rating the Raters: Enron and the Credit Rating Agencies: Hearing Before the Senate Committee on Governmental Affairs' (2002) 107th Congress, S Hrg 107-471 (testimony of Jonathan R Macey, J DuPratt White Professor of Law, Cornell Law School) 44.

[116] Uwe Blaurock, 'Verantwortlichkeit von Ratingagenturen – Steuerung durch Privat- oder Aufsichtsrecht?' [2007] ZGR 603, 611.

[117] Crouhy, Jarrow and Turnbull, 'The Subprime Credit Crisis of 07' (n 16) 9.

[118] George A Akerlof, 'The Market for "Lemons": Quality Uncertainty and the Market Mechanism' (1970) 84 The Quarterly Journal of Economics 488, 490–491 (explaining the "lemons problem" in general).

the "lemons problem" refers to a situation in which the market value of an investment does not relate to its true value given informational inefficiencies.[120] In the subprime mortgage market CRAs could ideally have acted as private-sector certifiers of quality but they did not.[121] At any rate, end investors relied heavily on CRAs to assess the riskiness of the securitized assets. However, concern has been raised about CRAs' disinterest in providing investors with valuable information. They have no incentive to alleviate information asymmetry in the financial markets since they get paid even if their ratings are not accurate. Rather than helping investors to accurately value securitized assets, CRAs acted as a smokescreen and benefited from market opacity. Their ratings facilitated the development of "lemons markets" for securitized products instead of mitigating the problem.[122] When the subprime mortgage market confronted investors with serious inaccuracies in the rating models, the market for securitized assets suddenly dried up. The absence of an independent means of valuing assets in a liquidity crisis created a confidence crisis and increased uncertainty in the financial markets.[123] Accordingly, certification of quality by private parties such as CRAs cannot be expected to reduce the asymmetric-information problem.[124]

(i) The first aspect of the information asymmetry problem is that CRAs played a crucial role in helping issuers create a "lemons market" for securitized assets; in this respect, issuers favored informational inefficiencies, making the subprime mortgage market resemble a "market for lemons."[125] The originate-and-distribute model of intermediation implied that banks could sell off their exposure to the subprime mortgage market.

---

[119] Steven L Schwarcz, 'Disclosure's Failure in the Subprime Mortgage Crisis' [2008] Utah Law Review 1109, 1121.

[120] Lynne Dallas, 'Short-Termism, the Financial Crisis and Corporate Governance' (2011) University of San Diego Legal Studies Research Paper Series No 11-052, 37.

[121] ibid.

[122] Brian JM Quinn, 'The Failure of Private Ordering and the Financial Crisis of 2008' (2009) 5 NYU Journal of Law & Business 549, 553.

[123] FSF, *Report of the Financial Stability Forum on Enhancing Market and Institutional Resilience* (n 83) 37–38. See also IOSCO, *Report of the Task Force on the Subprime Crisis* (n 30) 23.

[124] Schwarcz, 'Disclosure's Failure in the Subprime Mortgage Crisis' (n 119) 1121. In the current state of the financial markets CRAs do not fulfill the requirements of an independent third-party certifier of quality. Conflicts of interest are too acute in the credit rating industry.

[125] Dallas, 'Short-Termism, the Financial Crisis and Corporate Governance' (n 120) 1.

CRT markets are particularly subject to the "lemons problem" because issuers have an incentive to transfer their low-quality assets. Banks could not have transferred credit risk as extensively without the help of the leading CRAs. Safe in the knowledge that they would receive triple-A ratings for the highest tranches of their securitized assets, banks permitted pools to become infected with low-quality assets.[126] CDO originators paid little attention to scrutinizing the quality of the underlying assets because the investment-grade ratings would help them sell off their product. They could get around rating models in such a way that the low quality of the underlying assets would not be reflected in the ratings.[127] CRAs did not reflect upon the pools' decreasing quality of assets in their ratings. Information failure on the CRAs' side implied that pools constituting assets of different quality would get similar ratings.

Nevertheless, investors relied on credit ratings for asset valuation purposes. Over-reliance on CRAs was an essential factor that contributed to developing an opaque market for securitizations.[128] CRAs ended up being the entities that priced the securitized assets. Indeed, the triple-A tranches all traded at one price, the triple-B tranches all traded at another, notwithstanding the important differences between one triple-B tranche and another.[129] Therefore, the most over-priced securitized assets were the ones that had been the most ineptly rated.[130] And the subprime mortgage meltdown showed that the most over-priced assets were generally the triple-A-rated assets. It is worth recalling that the defaults did not even need to eat into triple-A tranches to make them lose value; the mere fact that the cushion provided by the lowest tranches was eaten up made triple-A tranches lose value because they became more risky.

In this way the whole process generated a financial "lemons market."[131] CRAs facilitated the creation of a "lemons market" because they did not pay attention to reducing information asymmetry in the subprime mortgage market. They only performed the function of marketing issuers'

---

[126] Quinn, 'The Failure of Private Ordering and the Financial Crisis of 2008' (n 122) 579.

[127] ibid.

[128] ibid 582.

[129] Lewis, *The Big Short* (n 38) 101.

[130] ibid.

[131] Quinn, 'The Failure of Private Ordering and the Financial Crisis of 2008' (n 122) 579.

financial instruments. "Instead of acting as gatekeepers, they acted as guardians of information asymmetry."[132]

The adverse selection problem that led to the creation of a "lemons market" was especially striking in the CDS market. Arrangers of synthetic CDOs could select which subprime mortgages to include in the synthetic pool. CDS buyers were interested in insuring the worst mortgage-related securities. On the other side of the bet, investors merely relied on ratings to assess the riskiness of the novel product. CDO arrangers that hired the leading CRAs knew that they could get high ratings independently of the quality of the underlying assets. Therefore, CDO arrangers could accept the assistance of interested CDS buyers in the composition of the asset pool that would form a synthetic CDO, and sell off the resulting product thanks to the favorable ratings.

The Goldman Sachs case provides a good example of information asymmetry in the market for securitized assets. CDO arrangers such as Goldman Sachs did not fully rely on ratings.[133] Nevertheless, they could benefit from high ratings and were able to use information that was not reflected in ratings. In order to have CDS buyers, CDO originators would allow the interested hedge funds to select the subprime mortgages to include in the deal.[134] This endeavor gives rise to evidence of adverse selection in the composition of synthetic CDOs. In the Goldman Sachs case, the hedge fund Paulson & Co helped select the subprime mortgages included in the Abacus 2007-AC1 deal.[135] As a CDS buyer, Paulson & Co was interested in the worst CDO positions in order to bet against them. As a CDO arranger, Goldman Sachs agreed with the proceeding because it could get high ratings independently of the composition of the synthetic CDOs. The favorable ratings, in turn, allowed Goldman Sachs to sell off the product to investors. Therefore, informed market participants benefited from the high ratings and simultaneously took advantage

---

132 Aline Darbellay, 'Regulating Ratings, The Credit Rating Agency Oligopoly from a Regulatory Perspective' in Dieter Zobl, Mario Giovanoli and Rolf H Weber, *Schweizer Schriften zum Finanzmarktrecht, Band 102* (Schulthess 2011) 140.

133 Frank Partnoy, 'Wall Street Beware: The Lawyers are Coming' *The Financial Times*, April 18, 2010. See also Jesse Westbrook and Joshua Gallu, 'SEC's Demand That Goldman Admit "Mistake" Could Spur Lawsuits' *Bloomberg*, July 21, 2010.

134 Susan Pulliam and Evan Perez, 'Criminal Probe Looks Into Goldman Trading' *The Wall Street Journal*, April 30, 2010.

135 ibid.

of their knowledge of the subprime market in order to bet against the transaction.[136]

Furthermore, there was not only a problem of information asymmetry but also a problem of information failure on both sides.[137] To some extent, not even the CDO originators understood where the risks were. Some investment banks even considered the highest CDO tranches to be a safe asset to hold on their own books. For instance, Citigroup kept a significant amount of triple-A-rated CDO tranches on its balance sheet.[138]

(ii) The second aspect of the "lemons problem" is that when investors lost confidence in the asset valuation of mortgage-related securities, they completely moved away from the market. The market suddenly dried up. If securitized assets were overestimated before the crisis, market illiquidity drove asset valuations down to levels below their economic value. When investors in triple-A-rated assets realized that they actually owned junk bonds, a crisis of confidence destabilized the financial markets.[139] Unable to distinguish between good assets and bad assets, market participants stopped trading mortgage-related securities altogether.[140] The widespread gravity of the valuation troubles came to light in August 2007

---

[136] Andrew R Sorkin, 'What the Financial Crisis Commission should ask' *The New York Times Dealbook*, 11 January, 2010; Goldman is accused of misleading its clients because it sold the synthetic CDOs without saying that Paulson & Co. had composed the asset portfolio in order to bet against the securitized product. As market-maker or broker-dealer, investment banking activities usually imply no fiduciary duties, but disclosure requirements as regards informing their clients should be imposed on banks such as Goldman Sachs.

[137] Schwarcz, 'Disclosure's Failure in the Subprime Mortgage Crisis' (n 119) 1119.

[138] Christopher R Whalen, 'The Subprime Crisis, Cause, Effect and Consequences' (2008) Networks Financial Institute Policy Brief No 2008-PB-04, 15; Lewis, *The Big Short* (n 38) 86.

[139] Paul Krugman, 'A Catastrophe Foretold' *The New York Times*, October 26, 2007.

[140] As a result, the liquidity crisis became even deeper. Confidence was lost. There was a contagion to other market segments. Furthermore, market participants could not locate the losses. Financial institutions no longer trusted their counterparties. The interbank market was collapsing. See further IMF, *Global Financial Stability Report, Containing Systemic Risks and Restoring Financial Soundness* (April 2008) 55 ("The absence of liquid markets and the reliance on models for valuations meant that parties were unsure of the undisclosed losses on their own and others' balance sheets, as the interaction of credit and liquidity risk drove market valuations down to levels below theoretical assumptions").

when BNP Paribas froze three hedge funds, stating that it was impossible to value the securitized assets due to a lack of liquidity in the market.[141] Credit modeling tools proved completely ineffective in valuing CDO tranches in distressed market conditions.[142]

Market losses spilled over to the highest tranches. The tranches that were supposed to be the safest ones had the highest price and the lowest yield. They were the ones that lost the most in value, not least because they had much more value to lose than the lowest tranches. It is worth recalling that CDO tranches were primarily designed to inflate the value of the highest tranches. Therefore, the highest tranches were logically the ones that would lose the most value in an economic downturn.

Financial institutions had built up a "shadow banking system" in which there was little knowledge of the size and location of credit risk.[143] It became evident that CDO investors did not know the risk and therefore the value of their positions; to make matters worse, many CDO investors did not know whether they were exposed to the subprime mortgage market or even if they did know, they had little clue as to the quality of their positions.[144]

In an opaque market, investment decisions are based on artificial confidence. This confidence is elusive and slippery. Events such as sudden rating downgrades can easily trigger a loss of confidence in the market. A confidence crisis has wide repercussions on the behavior of market participants since they are left with no means to value their positions and the positions of their counterparties.[145] If they had blind faith in good times, they become risk-adverse and want to avoid riskier investments at any price in bad times, which partly explains the flight to quality.

There is a profound lack of transparency in the derivatives markets, especially with respect to OTC transactions. It is not disclosed who is on the other side of the bet. As a result bad economic events are able to

---

[141] Crouhy, Jarrow and Turnbull, 'The Subprime Credit Crisis of 07' (n 16) 21.

[142] Alexander and others, 'Financial Supervision and Crisis Management in the EU' (n 3) 29.

[143] De Larosière Report (n 26) 8.

[144] Alexander and others, 'Financial Supervision and Crisis Management in the EU' (n 3) 29.

[145] FSF, *Report of the Financial Stability Forum on Enhancing Market and Institutional Resilience* (n 83) 37–38; IOSCO, *Report of the Task Force on the Subprime Crisis* (n 30) 23.

trigger panic and result in a liquidity crisis because people do not know the size and location of the losses.

The market for "lemons" was characterized by the fact that liquidity in the market for securitized assets suddenly dried up. The entire market collapsed even though not all the securitized CDO tranches were about to default. All triple-A-rated tranches were revalued at much lower prices even where the underlying portfolio was of good quality.[146] Buyers could not distinguish between good and bad assets. Although a number of financial products still had a residual economic value, no buyers were interested in buying them. The reason was uncertainty. Because market participants failed to deal with asymmetric information, trade did not even take place at a discount.[147]

146 Alexander and others, 'Financial Supervision and Crisis Management in the EU' (n 3) 30.

147 Akerlof, 'The Market for "Lemons"' (n 118) 490–491.

9. Regulatory response to the problems of structured finance ratings

9.1 US AND EU REGULATORY REFORMS

In the aftermath of the financial crisis, both the US and the EU have partly overhauled the area of structured finance ratings. The key aspects of reform are symbology, disclosure requirements, conflicts of interest, qualifications and independence of rating analysts and supervisory sanctions.

9.1.1 Symbology

Regulators adopted symbology requirements to ensure that investors understand the difference between structured finance ratings and other rating sectors. They aim to solve the consistency problem that was observed during the subprime mortgage crisis.

In the US, CRAs are required to apply any symbol in a manner that is consistent for all types of securities for which the symbol is used.[1] This means that a triple-A rating in a given sector shall mean the same as a triple-A rating in another sector. If a triple-A rating in structured finance does not mean the same as a triple-A rating in the corporate or sovereign segments, CRAs shall adapt the given symbol to reflect the difference.[2]

In the EU, structured finance ratings are required to have an additional symbol to distinguish them from other rating classes.[3] In this sense, the EU regulators proceed from the assumption that a triple-A rating in

[1] Dodd-Frank Wall Street Reform and Consumer Protection Act of 2010, HR 4173, 111th Congress, 2nd Session (2010) (Dodd-Frank Act) Sec 938(a).

[2] Aline Darbellay and Frank Partnoy, 'Credit Rating Agencies and Regulatory Reform' in Claire A Hill and Brett H McDonnell (eds), *Research Handbook on the Economics of Corporate Law* (Edward Elgar 2012) 285.

[3] Regulation (EC) No 1060/2009 of 16 September 2009 on credit rating agencies [2009] OJ L302/1 (CRA Regulation) art 10 para 3; Siegfried Utzig, 'The Financial Crisis and the Regulation of Credit Rating Agencies: A European Banking Perspective' (2010) ADBI Working Paper No 188, 16 ‹http://www.

structured finance cannot mean the same as a triple-A rating in other segments. Thus, CRAs shall add an additional symbol so that investors are aware that structured finance ratings are different from other types of ratings. In sum, both reforms strive to bring consistency across rating classes.

9.1.2 Disclosure Requirements

More disclosure is necessary to allow investors to understand and compare ratings. Both the US and the EU reforms include transparency reports, transparency of rating performance and disclosure of rating methodologies. These reforms are expected to improve the information flow to investors in the opaque area of structured finance.

In the US, the Dodd-Frank Act of 2010 requires CRAs to report to the SEC and the public.[4] Both regulators and investors deserve to be better informed. The Act also focuses on the transparency of rating performance.[5] Accordingly, the SEC must implement provisions requiring that NRSROs disclose their rating performance.[6]

With respect to structured finance ratings, the SEC adopted a final rule in January 2011 aiming to implement one of the regulatory concerns. The SEC rule requires NRSROs to include information regarding the representations, warranties and enforcement mechanisms available to investors in an Asset-Backed Securities (ABS) offering in any report accompanying a rating issued in connection with such offering, including a preliminary rating.[7]

In addition, the Dodd-Frank Act focuses on the transparency of methodologies. Regulators require the disclosure of material changes to methodologies and of key assumptions having an impact on ratings.[8] An aspect relevant for structured finance ratings is that investors should be given access to information regarding the correlation of defaults.[9]

---

adbi.org/working-paper/2010/01/26/3446.credit.rating.agencies.european.banking› accessed November 15, 2012.

4 Dodd-Frank Act, Sec 932.

5 ibid Sec 932.

6 Aline Darbellay and Frank Partnoy, 'Credit Rating Agencies under the Dodd-Frank Act' (2011) 30 (Issue 12) Banking & Financial Services Policy Report 1, 5.

7 Securities Exchange Act of 1934, 17 CFR 240.17g-7.

8 Dodd-Frank Act, Sec 932.

9 Darbellay and Partnoy, 'Credit Rating Agencies and Regulatory Reform' (n 2) 285.

In the EU, transparency is also a key aspect of the CRA reform. The CRA Regulation of 2009 requires that CRAs publish annually a transparency report.[10] Among other things, CRAs shall make available detailed information on legal structure and ownership, internal control mechanisms and rating revenue.[11] Regarding the registration process with ESMA, technical standards mandate disclosure for each class. In particular, CRAs should disclose the number and volume of structured finance ratings.[12]

Moreover, CRAs shall submit information on historical performance to a central repository.[13] Regulators established technical standards to specify what information should be made available to the central repository operated by the ESMA. CRAs shall report data on structured finance ratings.[14] CRAs shall classify structured finance ratings within one of the following asset classes: Asset-Backed Securities (ABS), Residential Mortgage-Backed Securities (RMBS), Commercial Mortgage-Backed Securities (CMBS), Collateralized Debt Obligations (CDOs), Asset-Backed Commercial Papers (ABCP) or Other Structured Finance Instruments (OTH).[15] CRAs shall report "T" in cases where the rating scale is applicable to structured finance ratings.[16] Furthermore, the internal instrument identifier is a unique code to identify the instrument that is mandatory and used only for structured finance ratings.[17] The standard instrument identifier is an International Securities Identifying Number (ISIN) that is optional and applicable only for structured finance ratings.[18] Finally, the vintage year specifies the year of issuance of the rated instrument and is applicable for structured finance ratings.[19] These

---

[10] CRA Regulation, art 12.

[11] ibid Annex I Sec E(III).

[12] EU Commission Delegated Regulation (EU) No 449/2012 of 21 March 2012 supplementing Regulation (EC) No 1060/2009 with regard to regulatory technical standards on information for registration and certification of credit rating agencies [2012] OJ L140/32 Annex IX, art 23 para 2(d).

[13] CRA Regulation, art 11.

[14] EU Commission Delegated Regulation (EU) No 448/2012 of 21 March 2012 supplementing Regulation (EC) No 1060/2009 with regard to regulatory technical standards for the presentation of the information that credit rating agencies shall make available in a central repository established by the European Securities and Markets Authority [2012] OJ L140/17 art 3 para 5(b).

[15] ibid art 5 para 4 and Annex 2 Table 1 No 20.

[16] ibid Annex 1 Table 1 No 12 and Annex 2 Table 1 No 16.

[17] ibid Annex 2 Table 1 No 3.

[18] ibid Annex 2 Table 1 No 4.

[19] ibid Annex 2 Table 1 No 22.

technical standards show that regulators pay great attention to the problematic area of structured finance ratings.

With respect to the disclosure of rating methodologies, the EU has adopted mandatory rules since 2009. The CRA reform has incorporated the disclosure of methodologies, models and key rating assumptions, however not "sensitive business information."[20] Looking forward, the EU may even go a step further by introducing a process for the development and approval of rating methodologies.[21]

9.1.3 Conflicts of Interest

Conflicts of interest arise from the issuer-pays business model and ancillary services. In the run-up to the 2007–2009 financial crisis, they were especially acute in the structured finance segment. Regulators partly addressed them in the financial reforms.

In the US, NRSROs are required to establish, maintain and enforce written policies and procedures reasonably designed to address and manage conflicts of interest.[22] The Securities Exchange Act of 1934 was amended and makes a difference between conflicts of interest that have to be disclosed and conflicts of interest that are prohibited. On the one hand, Rule 17g-5(b) lists certain conflicts of interest that an NRSRO cannot have unless the conflict is disclosed and the NRSRO has and enforces policies and procedures to address and manage the conflict.[23] On the other hand, Rule 17g-5(c) lists certain other conflicts of interest that are prohibited.[24] To give an example of prohibited conflicts, an NRSRO cannot issue or maintain a rating that has been solicited by an entity that has provided 10 percent or greater of the NRSRO's total net revenue in the most recently ended fiscal year.[25] It is also prohibited to issue or maintain a rating to an entity – excluding sovereign nations –

---

20 CRA Regulation, preamble 25.

21 EU Commission, 'Proposal for a Regulation amending Regulation (EC) No 1060/2009 on credit rating agencies' COM (2011) 747 final ('Proposal for a CRA III Regulation') 5.

22 Securities Exchange Act of 1934, Sec 15E(h)(1).

23 ibid 17 CFR 240.17g-5(a) and (b).

24 ibid 17 CFR 240.17g-5(c). Staff of the SEC, '2012 Summary Report of Commission Staff's Examinations of Each Nationally Recognized Statistical Rating Organization, As Required by Section 15E(p)(3)(C) of the Securities Exchange Act of 1934' (November 2012).

25 Securities Exchange Act of 1934 17 CFR 240.17g-5(c)(1); Marilyn Blumberg Cane, Adam Shamir and Thomas Jodar, 'Below Investment Grade and Above the Law: A Past, Present and Future Look at the Accountability of Credit

where the NRSRO or any analysts who participated in determining the rating owns securities or other interests in the entity subject to the rating.[26]

Apart from that, the Dodd-Frank Act mandates a look-back requirement. CRAs should conduct a review to determine whether any conflicts of interest of the employee influenced the rating and take action to revise the rating if appropriate.[27] This rule strives to solve the problem of erroneous ratings due to interferences between rated entities and rating analysts. Further, the problem of conflicts of interest remains part of the regulatory debate as the Dodd-Frank asked the SEC to carry out studies with a view to proposing further reforms.[28]

In the EU, the CRA Regulation includes governance rules. Such conflict rules are mainly of a preventive nature.[29] For instance, CRAs shall establish internal policies to prevent, identify, eliminate or manage and disclose conflicts of interest.[30] Moreover, ancillary services are prohibited if this activity creates conflicts of interest with the issuing of ratings.[31] Looking forward, the public consultation on CRAs announced that dealing with conflicts of interest is one of the key aspects of step two of the CRA reform.[32] In November 2011 the EU issued a proposal for an amendment of the CRA Regulation that partly addresses the issue of conflicts of interest. Above all, a new provision would introduce a rotation mechanism for CRAs engaged by issuers.[33] The system is based on maximum durations of the contractual relationship between a CRA and an issuer. An issuer-paid CRA should not be hired for more than three years or for more than a year if it rates more than ten consecutive

Rating Agencies' (2012) 17 Fordham Journal of Corporate & Financial Law 1063, 1099.

26 Securities Exchange Act of 1934, 17 CFR 240.17g-5(c)(2); Cane, Shamir and Jodar, 'Below Investment Grade and Above the Law' (n 25) 1100.

27 Dodd-Frank Act, Sec 932.

28 Text to n 16 in ch 5.

29 Rolf H Weber and Simone Baumann, 'Conflicts of Interest and Risk Management Practices in the CRA Industry' in Jan Kleineman and Lars Gorton (eds), *Credit Rating Agencies* (Stockholm Centre for Commercial Law, forthcoming 2013).

30 CRA Regulation, preamble 26 and art 6.

31 ibid preamble 22.

32 EU Commission, 'Public consultation on credit rating agencies' (November 5, 2010).

33 'Proposal for a CRA III Regulation' (n 21) art 6b.

debt instruments of the same issuer.[34] This restriction lasts during a certain cooling-off period.

Here are also some key proposals of researchers that are partly incorporated into the CRA reforms: (i) to separate functions in a CRA in such a way that individual analysts would not have to fulfill conflicting duties, (ii) the income of analysts should not depend on fee generation, (iii) "Chinese walls" should be established in order to avoid exchanges of sensitive information between analysts working on conflicting mandates.[35] These aspects may also be considered as recent trends to overhaul the rating business. Therefore, the issue of conflicts of interest in the rating industry still presents an agenda for research.

9.1.4 Qualifications and Independence of Rating Analysts

In the run-up to the subprime mortgage crisis, there were serious flaws relating to the qualifications of rating analysts. Some of the analysts did not understand structured finance sufficiently to rate deals. Also, their lack of independence influenced them to give excessively high grades to novel financial products.

In the US, the Dodd-Frank Act of 2010 ensures that the qualifications of rating analysts fall under regulatory scrutiny.[36] The Act mandates the establishment of professional standards to train rating analysts.[37] These standards should ensure that rating analysts only agree to rate deals if they understand them, which is a potential issue in the case of complex deals such as in structured finance. With respect to the independence of employees, the US regulation forbids direct ownership interest in the rated entity; moreover, gifts in an aggregate value of more than 25 US dollars may not be accepted.[38]

In the EU, the CRA Regulation includes a short provision regarding the qualification of employees. The rule states that CRAs should ensure that rating analysts have appropriate knowledge and experience for the

---

34 ibid.

35 Weber and Baumann, 'Conflicts of Interest and Risk Management Practices in the CRA Industry' (n 29).

36 Darbellay and Partnoy, 'Credit Rating Agencies and Regulatory Reform' (n 2) 286.

37 Dodd-Frank Act, Sec 936.

38 Securities Exchange Act of 1934, 17 CFR 240.17g-5 (c)(7); Cane, Shamir and Jodar, 'Below Investment Grade and Above the Law: A Past, Present and Future Look at the Accountability of Credit Rating Agencies' (n 25) 1100–1101.

duties assigned.[39] As for the independence of employees, the CRA Regulation mandates that CRAs shall establish a rotation mechanism with regard to the rating analysts.[40] Accordingly, rating analysts may not be involved in the rating of the same entity for more than four or five years.[41] Compensation of rating employees shall not be contingent on the amount of revenue that the CRA derives from rated entities.[42]

9.1.5 Supervisory Sanctions

CRAs' interest in complying with the regulatory frameworks depends to a great extent on the efficacy of the enforcement mechanisms in place. In the US, the Dodd-Frank Act of 2010 created the Office of Credit Ratings (OCR), which conducts examinations of NRSROs to assess and promote compliance with regulatory requirements. The SEC has the authority to suspend or revoke the registration of NRSROs. Also, the SEC even has the ability to revoke the registration of an NRSRO with respect to a particular class of securities.[43] Furthermore, pursuant to the Securities Exchange Act of 1934 the SEC has the authority to impose a civil penalty in administrative proceedings against CRAs.[44] Among other things, this provision applies when CRAs have willfully violated any provision of the CRA regulation. The maximum amount of the penalty is 100,000 US dollars for a natural person or 500,000 US dollars for any other person.[45] Another sanction that can be imposed is a cease and desist order from committing other violations. Finally, the publication of the sanction is also a remedial measure.

For instance, the SEC charged Egan-Jones and its founder, Sean Egan, with willful and material misstatements and omissions when registering to become a NRSRO for ABS and government securities.[46] In January

---

39 CRA Regulation, art 7 para 1.

40 ibid art 7 para 4.

41 Weber and Baumann, 'Conflicts of Interest and Risk Management Practices in the CRA Industry' (n 29).

42 CRA Regulation, art 7 para 5.

43 Dodd-Frank Act, Sec 932(a)(3)(I).

44 Securities Exchange Act of 1934, Sec 21B.

45 ibid Sec 21B(b)(3).

46 SEC, Release No 68703, Administrative Proceeding, In the Matter of Egan-Jones Ratings Company and Sean Egan, Order Making Findings and Imposing Remedial Sanctions and Cease-and-Desist Orders Pursuant to Sections 15E(d) and 21C of the Securities Exchange Act of 1934 against Egan-Jones Ratings Company and Sean Egan (January 22, 2013); SEC, 'Egan-Jones and Founder Sean Egan Agree to 18-Month Bars from Rating Asset-Backed and

2013 Egan-Jones and Sean Egan agreed to settle the case with the SEC and be barred for at least 18 months from rating ABS and government securities.[47] It is worth mentioning that Egan-Jones is still allowed to identify such ratings as non-NRSRO ratings. Under the terms of this settlement, Egan-Jones agreed to pay a civil money penalty of 30,000 US dollars to the US Treasury.

In the EU, the CRA Regulation of 2009 established an enforcement process. The withdrawal of the registration is a remedial measure taken as a last resort, for instance if the CRA no longer meets the conditions or if the CRA has committed serious or repeated infringement of the regulation.[48] If CRAs commit an infringement of the CRA, the ESMA may also take supervisory measures and impose fines, issue a public notice, require the CRA to bring the infringement to an end, suspend the use of ratings for regulatory purposes or temporarily prohibit the CRA from issuing ratings in the EU.[49]

The EU framework goes very far as it can prevent CRAs from issuing ratings in the EU altogether. In contrast, the US framework merely prohibits the issuance of NRSRO ratings, ie certified ratings, but not the issuance of ratings in general. This illustrates the willingness of the EU to encompass every CRA in the regulatory oversight while the US leaves unregulated CRAs outside its oversight framework.

9.2 PRELIMINARY CONCLUSION

In modern financial markets structured finance is a crucial business segment for CRAs. Rating structured finance generates significant fees and has contributed to enhancing CRAs' profitability over the past decades. Moreover, CRAs have played a leading role in the growth of the structured finance segment as issuers needed high ratings to make their financial instruments marketable to a broad range of investors.

Government Securities Issuers as NRSRO' *Press Release* (January 22, 2013) ‹http://www.sec.gov/news/press/2013/2013-7.htm› accessed January 28, 2013.

[47] ibid.

[48] CRA Regulation, art 20 para 1.

[49] Regulation (EU) No 513/2011 of 11 May 2011 amending Regulation (EC) No 1060/2009 on credit rating agencies [1011] OJ L145/30 (CRA II Regulation) preamble (25); Felix Flinterman, 'ESMA: The European Supervisor of Credit Rating Agencies' in Jan Kleineman and Lars Gorton (eds), *Credit Rating Agencies* (Stockholm Centre for Commercial Law, forthcoming 2013).

However, rating flaws in the structured finance segment became apparent when the subprime mortgage crisis was triggered in July 2007. The practice of inflating ratings to generate issuers' fees was particularly acute in the years preceding the 2007–2009 financial crisis. Ill-advised competition between the leading CRAs allegedly resulted in "rating shopping," and caused a "race to the bottom."

Issuer-paid CRAs cannot rate independently of issuers who pay for credit ratings. Restoring competition in the rating industry requires establishing the independence of CRAs vis-à-vis the rated entities. Conflicts of interest need to be eliminated or mitigated in order to increase CRAs' incentives to provide investors with accurate ratings.

Although CRAs are supposed to resolve information asymmetries by providing investors with useful information, in the wake of the subprime mortgage crisis reliance on the leading CRAs resulted in the creation of an opaque market for securitized assets. As a consequence, investors moved away from the market when they lost confidence in rating assessments. Persistent information asymmetries exacerbated the collapse of the subprime mortgage market. Investors were not able to locate the losses as they were left with no independent means of assessing the value of mortgage-related securities.

CRA reforms post-crisis strive to address the causes of structured finance ratings' deficiencies leading to the subprime mortgage crisis. The key aspects of the US and EU reforms are symbology, transparency, conflicts of interest, qualifications of rating analysts and sanctions.

In a nutshell, the structured finance segment provides an illustrative example of how the leading CRAs' lack of independence jeopardizes competitive incentives in the rating industry. Market forces fail to play a disciplinary role when CRAs are not incentivized to improve rating quality. The CRA reforms post-crisis are expected to enhance transparency, integrity and consistency in the controversial segment of structured finance ratings.

PART 4

System-wide effects of credit rating downgrades

10. System-relevance of credit ratings

10.1 SYSTEMIC IMPORTANCE OF CREDIT RATINGS IN MODERN FINANCIAL MARKETS

> There are two superpowers in the world today in my opinion. There's the United States and there's Moody's Bond Rating Service. The United States can destroy you by dropping bombs, and Moody's can destroy you by downgrading your bonds. And believe me, it's not clear sometimes who's more powerful.[1]

The systemic relevance of credit ratings issued by the leading CRAs gives rise to increasing concerns in modern financial markets. On the one hand, stringent criticism has recently been raised about the rating industry in Europe, where politicians were livid at the downgrades of sovereign debt such as the Greek debt.[2] Leading CRAs were accused of exacerbating the financial turmoil in the EU by downgrading a number of sovereign bonds, thereby making bond refinancing more difficult.[3] On the other hand – with respect to legislation – the Dodd-Frank Act of 2010 expressly acknowledges the systemic importance of credit ratings.[4] This Act gives particular weight to the question by mentioning the systemic issue in the first sentence of its CRA reform. However, the agency reform embedded in the Dodd-Frank Act has not taken any direct measures

---

[1] Frank Partnoy, 'The Siskel and Ebert of Financial Markets?: Two Thumbs Down for the Credit Rating Agencies' (1999) 77 Washington University Law Quarterly 619, 620 (quoting 'The News Hour with Jim Lehrer: Interview with Thomas L Friedman' *PBS television broadcast* (February 13, 1996) (transcript on file with author)).

[2] 'The Other Vampires, Pressure Mounts on an Oligopoly' *The Economist*, May 15, 2010, 83–84; Jérôme Chartier, 'Rapport fait au nom de la commission des finances, de l'économie générale et du contrôle budgétaire sur le projet de loi de régulation bancaire et financière (No 2165)' (Assemblée nationale, May 25, 2010) 12.

[3] 'Debatte um "Schuld" der Rating-Agenturen, Schweizer Zurückhaltung bei anstehender Regulierung' *NZZ*, September 4, 2010, 35.

[4] Dodd-Frank Wall Street Reform and Consumer Protection Act of 2010, HR 4173, 111th Congress, 2nd Session (2010) (Dodd-Frank Act) Sec 931(1).

specifically designed to address systemic problems in the rating industry. Hitherto only a few research articles have focused on the systemic issue related to ratings.[5] On the global scale, the Financial Stability Board (FSB) released its Principles for Reducing Reliance on CRA Ratings in October 2010.[6] The fact that the FSB draws attention to the rating industry highlights the systemic relevance of CRAs as this international body is mandated to strengthen the financial system and deal with systemic risk. Therefore, the topic clearly presents an important agenda for research.

In the financial markets, it is inappropriate to give the same financial information to every market participant at the same time. More precisely, CRAs that have systemic relevance cannot reveal financial information of major importance without causing financial turmoil.

This part of the study analyzes the systemic importance of ratings in the light of rating downgrades. The lack of competition among leading CRAs manifests itself as a reluctance to downgrade ratings that are systemically relevant. Especially over the last decades, CRAs have without doubt performed poorly in anticipating major debacles. Investors have raised concern over how slow CRAs are to downgrade their ratings.[7] Leading CRAs tend not to lower their ratings until the evidence of poorer creditworthiness is overwhelmingly confirmed by external evidence.[8]

Relating to corporate ratings, in many cases leading CRAs have kept their high ratings until a few day before bankruptcies. In this respect, energy company Enron, telecommunications company WorldCom and investment bank Lehman Brothers are the most insightful examples.[9] The

---

[5] Hitherto there has been one prominent example among the very few articles focusing on the systemic importance of ratings: Amadou NR Sy, 'The Systemic Regulation of Credit Rating Agencies and Rated Markets' (2009) IMF Working Paper No 09/129 ‹http://www.imf.org/external/pubs/ft/wp/2009/wp09129.pdf› accessed January 10, 2013 (discussing the necessity of macro-prudential regulation in addressing the systemic risk inherent in ratings).

[6] FSB, *Principles for Reducing Reliance on CRA Ratings* (October 2010) 1–7.

[7] See, eg, David M Ellis, 'Different Sides of the Same Story: Investors' and Issuers' Views of Rating Agencies' (1998) 7 (Issue 4) The Journal of Fixed Income 35, 37. See also H Kent Baker and Sattar A Mansi, 'Assessing Credit Rating Agencies by Bond Issuers and Institutional Investors' (2002) 29 Journal of Business Finance & Accounting 1367, 1387 (analyzing the results of a survey asking investors and issuers about the timeliness of ratings).

[8] See, eg, Ellis, 'Different Sides of the Same Story' (n 7) 37.

[9] Claire A Hill, 'Regulating the Rating Agencies' (2004) 82 Washington University Law Quarterly 43, 78 (stating that "Enron is just one among a number

three leading CRAs lowered Enron's rating to a level below the investment grade just four days before Enron declared bankruptcy.[10] WorldCom retained its high rating until a few days prior to collapsing.[11] Lehman Brothers was downgraded to junk status on September 12, 2008 and filed for bankruptcy on September 15, 2008.[12] In each case CRAs proved unable to predict financial crises.

As far as structured finance ratings are concerned, the mortgage-related securities that caused the subprime mortgage crisis were all investment grade prior to triggering the 2007–2009 financial crisis. Empirical evidence suggests that the subprime mortgage crisis followed four years of inflated ratings.[13] The leading CRAs could have warned before July 2007 that the market was in danger of collapse but they were too slow. When they eventually downgraded the mortgage-related securities, they

---

of spectacular accounts of [CRAs'] lackluster performance in anticipating major debacles").

[10] 'Rating the Raters: Enron and the Credit Rating Agencies: Hearing Before the Senate Committee on Governmental Affairs' (2002) 107th Congress, S Hrg 107-471, 97. Enron was a big US energy company that was involved in extremely risky activities and went bankrupt after the fraud was discovered. See also Claire A Hill, 'Why Did Anyone Listen to the Rating Agencies after Enron?' (2009) 4 Journal of Business & Technology Law 283, 292.

[11] Gary Shorter and Michael V Seitzinger, 'Credit Rating Agencies and Their Regulation' (2009) Congressional Research Service, 3 ‹http://garrettforms.house.gov/uploadedfiles/credit_rating_agencies.pdf› accessed January 10, 2013.

[12] Beat Balzli and Frank Hornig, 'Exacerbating the Crisis, The Power of Rating Agencies' *Spiegel Online*, May 6, 2009 (translated from the German by Christopher Sultan); Lars Gorton and Aron Verständig, 'General Background of the Conference' in Jan Kleineman and Lars Gorton (eds), *Credit Rating Agencies* (Stockholm Centre for Commercial Law, forthcoming 2013).

[13] A number of empirical papers support this argument: John M Griffin and Dragon Yongjun Tang, 'Did Subjectivity Play a Role in CDO Credit Ratings?' (2010) McCombs Research Paper Series No FIN-04-10, 28–29; Jérôme Mathis, James McAndrews and Jean-Charles Rochet, 'Rating the Raters: Are Reputation Concerns Powerful Enough to Discipline Rating Agencies?' (2009) 56 Journal of Monetary Economics 657, 658–659; Christian C Opp, Marcus M Opp and Milton Harris, 'Rating Agencies in the Face of Regulation' (2012) SSRN eLibrary, 3–4 ‹http:ssrn.com/abstract=1540099› accessed January 10, 2013; Richard Stanton and Nancy Wallace, 'CMBS Subordination, Ratings Inflation, and the Crisis of 2007–2009' (2010) National Bureau of Economic Research (NBER) Working Paper No 16206, 39–40 ‹http://www.nber.org/papers/w16206› accessed January 10, 2013 (discussing rating inflation in the CMBS market due to over-optimistic subordination levels in the years preceding the subprime mortgage crisis).

did so massively.[14] The first explanation relates to conflicts of interest in the rating industry. CRAs have strong ties to the financial industry. With respect to the subprime mortgage market, the leading CRAs did not act independently since they were paid by the issuers they were rating. Accordingly, conflicts of interest partly explain why leading CRAs did not provide valuable information about deteriorating conditions in the subprime mortgage market. Another explanation relates to the impact of rating downgrades as regards the timing of the subprime mortgage meltdown. The financial crisis was triggered immediately after the leading CRAs downgraded mortgage-related securities to junk status. Indeed, leading CRAs started to downgrade mortgage-related securities massively in July 2007, ie when market participants were about to disclose significant losses in the subprime mortgage market. Hence, leading CRAs are necessarily slow to downgrade in a market environment where their rating announcements can trigger financial turmoil.

With respect to sovereign ratings, Moody's and Standard & Poor's rate the risk of lending to more than 100 sovereigns, the two CRAs together accounting for approximately 90 percent of the market for sovereign debt rating.[15] Sovereign ratings have especially gained prominence over the last decades due to the increased reliance of countries on bond financing. Greek debt was rated investment grade by the leading CRAs until the country got into financial troubles.[16] Standard & Poor's and Fitch downgraded Greek debt during the financial turmoil, thereby causing disruptions in the financial markets.[17] However, at the height of the Greek debt crisis, Moody's – the number one in the rating industry – had

---

[14] 'Testimony Concerning Oversight of Nationally Recognized Statistical Rating Organizations: Hearing Before the Senate Committee on Banking, Housing, and Urban Affairs' (2008) 110th Congress (statement of Christopher Cox, Chairman, SEC). (As of February 2008, Moody's had downgraded at least one tranche of 94.2 percent of the subprime RMBS rated in 2006. As of March 2008, Standard & Poor's had downgraded 44.3 percent of the subprime tranches rated between the first quarter of 2005 and the third quarter of 2007. As of December 2007, Fitch had downgraded almost 34 percent of the subprime tranches rated between 2006 and the first quarter of 2007.)

[15] Rawi Abdelal, *Capital Rules, The Construction of Global Finance* (Harvard University Press 2007) 162.

[16] Justin Carrigan, 'Greece May Have Rating Lowered to Junk, Moody's Says' *Bloomberg BusinessWeek*, May 10, 2010.

[17] 'The Other Vampires' (n 2) 83–84 (emphasizing that rating downgrades of Greece to junk status occurred just as officials were about to unveil a support plan).

not downgraded Greek debt to junk status.[18] During the Greek rescue, Moody's was aware of Greece's low competitiveness and high budget deficits, yet took no rating action.[19] Moody's only downgraded at a later stage. Evidence has shown that the leading CRAs are reluctant to downgrade borrowers and debt instruments when the repercussions of their decisions can be devastating to the financial markets.[20] If their initial ratings do not always give satisfaction, the ongoing monitoring of their ratings gives rise to even more alarming concerns. The situation is best explained by market over-reliance on leading CRAs and the systemic importance of ratings. When leading CRAs downgrade, there are direct effects on the financial markets. Moody's could likely not afford to downgrade Greek bonds at the same time as Standard & Poor's and Fitch.

After the flagrant rating flaws related to the recent financial debacles, market reliance on credit ratings would be expected to diminish. The subprime mortgage crisis in particular could have marked a transition given that the leading CRAs went beyond any limits in terms of rating inaccuracies. However, the Greek debt crisis highlights that market participants still depend on their ratings. Even though the subprime mortgage crisis shed light on the poor rating performance of the leading CRAs, market over-reliance on ratings seems to persist in the financial markets. Interest rates increased significantly immediately after the rating downgrades. Furthermore, when the European Central Bank (ECB) accepted junk bonds as collateral, the financial markets reacted negatively, perceiving this decision as a bad signal.[21]

Accordingly, in most of the recent financial crises, criticism has been raised about the fact that CRAs can harm the financial markets as a whole by the mere fact of massively downgrading debt issues. The paradox is that the more powerful CRAs are, the less valuable information they can give to the market. As a response to rating scandals, regulators have focused on providing an oversight of the rating industry

---

18 Carrigan, 'Greece May Have Rating Lowered to Junk' (n 16) (reporting that, in May 2010, Moody's was conducting a review of the Greek debt, but had not downgraded Greece).

19 See further ibid.

20 See, eg, Andrew Clark, 'Euro Falls as Spain Suffers Rating Downgrade' *The Guardian*, May 28, 2010 (reporting that on May 28, 2010, Fitch cut its sovereign rating for Spain by a single notch from triple-A to double-A+). See also Carrigan, 'Greece May Have Rating Lowered to Junk' (n 16).

21 Simon Kennedy and Lorenzo Totaro, 'ECB Comes to Greece's Aid by Waiving Collateral Rules' *Bloomberg BusinessWeek* , May 3, 2010.

in order to enhance CRAs' performance. Financial regulatory reforms in the aftermath of the subprime mortgage crisis have recognized the need to address conflicts of interest in the rating industry. Lawmakers and regulators believe that agency reforms will help create more adequate incentives in the industry. However, in the short term, the recent regulatory overhaul will not be able to solve the problems of market over-reliance on the leading CRAs and the systemic effects of rating downgrades.

10.2 FINANCIAL STABILITY AND SYSTEMIC RISK

> As investors began to perceive that defaults could spread beyond mortgages, the systematic risk premiums began to rise across all debt instruments, resulting in a fall in debt prices across the board. Systematically falling debt prices led to further increases in perceived systematic risk and further rises in systematic risk premiums in a cycle that brought us to the 2008 financial crisis.[22]

The stability of the financial system can be jeopardized by systemic risk. Systemic risk refers to the phenomenon whereby the misconduct of certain market participants is able to cause the collapse of the financial system as a whole.[23] Systemic risk is the risk that an entire system or market collapses – as opposed to one entity within that system.[24] If systemic linkages exist, a trigger event can cause a chain of bad economic consequences.[25] As a result, financial shocks can potentially lead to substantial, adverse effects on the real economy, for instance by causing a reduction in productive investment.[26] Regulators are responsible for ensuring the safety and soundness of the financial system and financial stability is one of the main objectives.[27]

---

22 Austin Murphy, 'An Analysis of the Financial Crisis of 2008: Causes and Solutions' (2008) SSRN eLibrary, 13 ‹http:ssrn.com/abstract=1295344› accessed January 10, 2013.

23 FINMA, 'Finanzmarktkrise und Finanzmarktaufsicht' (September 14, 2009) 69.

24 Kathleen A Scott, 'Addressing the Conditions Leading to "Systemic Risk" on a Global Basis' *New York Law Journal*, March 18, 2009.

25 Steven L Schwarcz, 'Systemic Risk' (2008) 97 Georgetown Law Journal 193, 198.

26 John Kambhu, Til Schuermann and Kevin J Stiroh, 'Hedge Funds, Financial Intermediation, and Systemic Risk' (2007) 13 (Issue 3) FRBNY (Federal Reserve Bank of New York) Economic Policy Review 1, 5.

27 Rolf H Weber and Douglas W Arner, 'Toward a New Design for International Financial Regulation' (2007) 29 University of Pennsylvania Journal

Regulators should focus on reducing systemic risk in the financial system. With respect to competition, particular attention has been paid to the "too big to fail" problem. The failure of system-relevant institutions disrupts the financial system. Regulators have to solve this problem because they cannot keep dealing with financial institutions that could bring down the economy by failing.[28]

Moreover, systemic risk is not only a question of financial institutions that are "too big to fail" but can also result from the failure of financial instruments that are linked to the financial system. In a market-based system, debt instruments are supposed to spread risk in the system.[29] A number of financial theorists plead for the diversification of credit risk. However, their theories fail to work if correlations are higher than estimated. With respect to complex financial instruments, not only are firm-specific risk characteristics to be taken into account, but also correlations between assets.[30]

Further, derivatives cause system-wide problems.[31] Linkages between counterparties can trigger serious systemic problems.[32] If large amounts of credit risk are concentrated in the hands of relatively few derivatives dealers, troubles can quickly infect their counterparties.[33] The use of credit derivatives makes it possible for market participants to multiply

---

of International Law 391, 392–393 (discussing financial stability with respect to international financial architecture).

28 Simon Johnson, 'The Quiet Coup' *The Atlantic*, May 2009, 10 (arguing that "too big to fail" is "too big to exist").

29 For instance, CRT instruments are used as a way of spreading credit risk and should be in the hands of market participants that are able to bear the risk, typically risk absorbers.

30 Adam B Ashcraft and Til Schuermann, 'Understanding the Securitization of Subprime Mortgage Credit' (2008) Federal Reserve Bank of New York Staff Reports, 43 ‹http://www.newyorkfed.org/research/staff_reports/sr318.pdf› accessed January 10, 2013 (explaining that corporate ratings are largely based on firm-specific risk characteristics; however, complex financial structures such as ABS structures represent claims on cash flows from a portfolio of underlying assets, implying that their ratings have to take into account systemic risk).

31 See, eg, Warren E Buffet, 'Berkshire Annual Report 2002' (2002) 15, ‹http://www.berkshirehathaway.com/2002ar/2002ar.pdf› accessed January 10, 2010 (suggesting – by way of illustrating the systemic dangers embedded in credit derivatives – that they are "financial weapons of mass destruction").

32 ibid 14 (arguing that some counterparties are linked in ways that could cause them to run into problems even because of a single event).

33 ibid.

their risk exposure.[34] With respect to the subprime mortgage crisis, credit derivatives such as CDS multiplied the effect of defaulting mortgage holders significantly beyond the original notional values, thereby increasing systemic risk.[35]

With respect to the subprime mortgage crisis triggered in 2007, financial institutions were confronted with the fact that asset securitization did not successfully move financial risk outside the financial system. One surprise of the financial crisis was indeed the substantial losses sustained by financial institutions. Even investment banks were excessively exposed to the subprime mortgage market.

In the insurance sector, concern has especially been raised about the "too interconnected to fail" problem.[36] Insurers and reinsurers are subject to systemic risk due to the fact that they conduct much of their business with others.[37] In the aftermath of the subprime mortgage debacle, the big insurance company AIG was the subject of a bailout due to its high exposure to the derivatives market, more precisely the CDS market.[38] As the market worsened, CDS buyers called for further collateral on companies selling the insurance – typically AIG.[39] The premiums charged on the CDS had not provided sufficient compensation for the higher default rates on mortgages.[40] As a consequence, companies such as AIG got into financial difficulties. If AIG collapsed, its counterparties

---

[34] Christopher R Whalen, 'The Subprime Crisis, Cause, Effect and Consequences' (2008) Networks Financial Institute Policy Brief No 2008-PB-04, 6 (explaining that – with respect to synthetic CDOs – market participants could sell almost unlimited amounts of CDS without margin requirements or reserves, making the potential to multiply the basis risk used to define a given transaction open-ended).

[35] Michel G Crouhy, Robert A Jarrow and Stuart M Turnbull, 'The Subprime Credit Crisis of 07' (2008) SSRN eLibrary, 17 ‹http:ssrn.com/abstract=1112467› accessed January 10, 2013.

[36] See generally Kern Alexander and others, 'Crisis Management, Burden Sharing and Solidarity Mechanisms in the EU' (2010) European Parliament, Policy Department, Economic and Scientific Policy, 8 ‹http://www.europarl.europa.eu/committees/en/cris/studiesdownload.html?languageDocument=EN&file=31711› accessed January 10, 2013 (stating that the excessive use of credit derivatives such as CDS has increased the complexity and interconnectedness of financial markets).

[37] Buffet, 'Berkshire Annual Report 2002' (n 31) 14.

[38] Joe Nocera, 'Propping up a House of Cards' *The New York Times*, February 28, 2009.

[39] Murphy, 'An Analysis of the Financial Crisis of 2008' (n 22) 13.

[40] ibid.

would have sustained significant losses. AIG was bailed out because of its systemic relevance.

To make matters worse, various other factors are able to exacerbate financial shocks in modern financial markets. All these factors cause procyclicality in modern financial markets. Even small market shocks can lead to contagious failures. In other words, market responses can be disproportionally large compared to the initial shock.[41] When there is a financial contagion following a downward change in asset prices, the shock may be accentuated by factors such as market-to-market accounting, bank capital requirement ratios or solvency constraints.[42] Regulatory requirements homogenize market behavior and have the potential to exacerbate market trends.

Moreover, in modern financial markets, market contagion is able to turn a financial shock into a liquidity crisis of systemic nature. A liquidity crisis emerges when market participants cease providing liquidity to the market, thereby aggravating the price declines.[43] The situation arises when more and more market participants sell, driving prices down.[44] As prices decline further, eventually no buyers step in.[45] Liquidity dries up and market gridlock takes hold.[46]

Therefore, typically in a market-based financial system, the disintermediation of financial activities implies the likelihood of an abrupt shift

---

41 Rodrigo Cifuentes, Gianluigi Ferrucci and Hyun Song Shin, 'Liquidity Risk and Contagion' (2005) Bank of England Working Paper Series No 264, 7 ‹http://www.bankofengland.co.uk/publications/Documents/workingpapers/wp264.pdf› accessed 10 January 2013.

42 ibid (stating that the combination of market-to-market accounting and solvency constraints has the potential to exacerbate market shocks). See also Alexander and others, 'Crisis Management, Burden Sharing and Solidarity Mechanisms in the EU' (n 36) 12 (stating that the major weakness of bank capital requirement regulations embedded in the Basel II Accord was their procyclicality. In an upturn, bank assets would appear safe and attract a lower capital charge; yet in a downturn, bank assets would appear riskier and attract a higher capital charge, thereby exacerbating a market shock).

43 Darryll Hendricks, John Kambhu and Patricia Mosser, 'Systemic Risk and the Financial System, Background Paper' (2006) NAS-FRBNY (Federal Reserve Bank of New York) Conference on the New Directions in Understanding Systemic Risk, 9 ‹https://www.newyorkfed.org/registration/research/risk/background.pdf› accessed January 10, 2013.

44 ibid.

45 ibid.

46 ibid.

from ample liquidity to liquidity shortage.[47] Liquidity can suddenly vanish.[48] Liquidity is an elusive, slippery concept.

It is worth mentioning that financial crises often cause problems to correlate.[49] Even previously uncorrelated assets may become correlated when market contagion takes place.[50] In fact, investors who share similar assets try to sell the same assets at the same time, thereby making volatility rise further.[51] Volatility spills over to other financial instruments, leading to a rise in correlations.[52] Under such circumstances, previous risk models immediately become erroneous with respect to their assessment of correlations. New risk measurements prompt investors to sell even further.

In addition, leading CRAs can play a crucial role in enabling and exacerbating financial crises. In the modern world, CRAs pose a systemic risk.[53] Credit ratings have spillover effects when market participants react to rating announcements so sharply that rating downgrades are able to trigger a financial crisis. Accordingly, the purpose of this part of the study is to analyze one of the factors that can trigger a systematic failure: massive rating downgrades by leading CRAs. The source of the problem arises out of the homogenizations of financial information and market

---

47 Laurent Clerc, 'A Primer on the Subprime Crisis' (2008) Banque de France, Occasional Paper No 4, 4 ‹http://www.banque-france.fr/fileadmin/user_upload/banque_de_france/La_Banque_de_France/pdf/Economie_et_Statistiques/primer_subprime_crisis.pdf› accessed January 10, 2013 (explaining this phenomenon by the prevailing uncertainty in the financial system).

48 See, eg, Avinash Persaud, 'Liquidity Black Holes, and Why Modern Financial Regulation in Developed Countries Is Making Short-Term Capital Flows to Developing Countries Even More Volatile' (2002) United Nations University World Institute for Development Economics Research (UNU/WIDER) Discussion Paper No 2002/31, 4 ‹http://archive.unu.edu/hq/library/Collection/PDF_files/WIDER/WIDERdp2002.31.pdf› accessed January 10, 2013 (defining episodes where liquidity suddenly disappears as "liquidity black holes").

49 Buffet, 'Berkshire Annual Report 2002' (n 31) 14.

50 Kern Alexander and others, 'Financial Supervision and Crisis Management in the EU' (2007) European Parliament, Policy Department, Economic and Scientific Policy, 6 ‹http://www.europarl.europa.eu/document/activities/cont/201108/20110818ATT25070/20110818ATT25070EN.pdf› accessed January 10, 2013.

51 ibid.

52 ibid.

53 Sy, 'The Systemic Regulation of Credit Rating Agencies and Rated Markets' (n 5) 3.

behavior.[54] Rating announcements have a direct impact on financial markets. Leading CRAs may significantly contribute to determining asset prices, resulting in the repricing of credit risk in the event of a downgrade. Such a situation may trigger further sales of assets leading to further asset depreciation leading to further sales.

Credit ratings are system-relevant if two criteria are fulfilled. The first depends on the importance of the CRA that issues the ratings. If the issuing CRA has enough market power, its ratings are likely to have a massive impact on the financial markets. Above all, the presence of a rating oligopoly makes rating announcements very powerful especially if the three leading CRAs – even coincidentally – coordinate their rating practices. The second criterion is the intensity of market reliance on ratings. Especially since the 1970s rating-based regulations have artificially increased reliance on ratings. Further, behavioral reliance has increased over the last decades and plays a significant role in modern financial markets. The combination of regulatory and behavioral reliance has driven to market over-dependence on ratings.

10.3 CREDIT RATING OLIGOPOLY

Three is no crowd.[55]

The question arises as to whether CRAs are in fact driven by private market forces. Regulatory concern has been raised about the lack of competition in the credit rating industry. The three leading CRAs – Moody's, Standard & Poor's and Fitch – have repeatedly been accused of abusing their market power. Their dominance of the rating market may have detrimental effects on the proper functioning of competitive forces in the rating industry. One specific issue is related to the potentially devastating effects of rating downgrades by the leading CRAs. Prior to analyzing this issue, attention is paid to describing concentration in the rating industry and the strong position of the Big Three.

---

[54] See, eg, Alexander and others, 'Financial Supervision and Crisis Management in the EU' (n 50) 19 (explaining the homogenization of reactions to rating downgrades in the subprime mortgage market).

[55] 'Three is No Crowd, Regulators Need a New Approach to an Entrenched Industry' *The Economist*, March 26, 2005, 15.

10.3.1 High Concentration in the Credit Rating Industry

The credit rating industry is without doubt heavily concentrated. As regards market structure, this industry is a 5 to 6 billion US dollar market.[56] As of December 31, 2011, Moody's, Standard & Poor's and Fitch accounted for 96 percent of all ratings in the US.[57] Moody's and Standard & Poor's controlled 83 percent of the rating market so that some talk about a duopoly of these two CRAs.[58] The third leading CRA, Fitch, is also very significant in the sense that the three are commonly referred to an oligopoly.[59] Overall, there are approximately 150 other smaller CRAs, which are regional or sectoral.[60] In any case, the three leading CRAs are the only relevant CRAs from the perspective of the international financial architecture.

---

[56] 'Credit Rating Agencies and the Financial Crisis: Hearing Before the House Committee on Oversight and Government Reform' (2008) 110th Congress 2nd Session, HR Serial No 110-155, 42 (statement of Sean J Egan, Managing Director, Egan-Jones Ratings).

[57] Staff of the SEC, '2012 Summary Report of Commission Staff's Examinations of Each Nationally Recognized Statistical Rating Organization, As Required by Section 15E(p)(3)(C) of the Securities Exchange Act of 1934' (November 2012) 7.

[58] ibid. See generally Credit Rating Agency Reform Act of 2006, S 3850, 109th Congress (2006) Sec 2(5) (stating that the two largest CRAs – Moody's and Standard & Poor's – serve the vast majority of the market). See, eg, 'Assessing the Current Oversight and Operation of Credit Rating Agencies: Hearing Before the Senate Committee on Banking, Housing and Urban Affairs' (2006) 109th Congress, S Hrg 109-997 (statement of Glenn L Reynolds, Chief Executive Officer, CreditSights) 8.

[59] Lawrence J White, 'Financial Regulation and the Current Crisis: A Guide for the Antitrust Community' (2009) SSRN eLibrary, 10 ‹http:ssrn.com/abstract=1426188› accessed January 10, 2013 (referring to Moody's and Standard & Poor's as the two largest CRAs and to Fitch as the third one). See also Balzli and Hornig, 'Exacerbating the Crisis' (n 12) (stating that Moody's, Standard & Poor's and Fitch are colloquially known as "The Big Three").

[60] See, eg, Arturo Estrella and others, 'Credit Ratings and Complementary Sources of Credit Quality Information' (2000) BCBS Working Papers No 3, 14 ‹http://www.bis.org/publ/bcbs_wp3.pdf› accessed November 10, 2012. See also Shorter and Seitzinger, 'Credit Rating Agencies and Their Regulation' (n 11) 1 (stating that there are approximately 100 CRAs); see further EU Commission, 'Staff Working Document, Impact Assessment, Accompanying document to the Proposal for a Regulation amending Regulation (EC) No 1060/2009 on credit rating agencies' COM (2010) 289 final, 7, 38 (stating that approximately 50 regional CRAs are established in the EU).

10.3.2 Barriers to Entering the Credit Rating Industry

Barriers to entering the rating industry can undermine competition. From a structural perspective, barriers to entry are the primary cause of the high concentration in the industry. Moreover, they reinforce the leading CRAs' market power. The presence of barriers to entry leads – in any case – to less vigorous competition than in a situation with fewer barriers and more players.[61] Potential competitors are able to exercise competitive pressure only if they are in a position to enter the rating market. Therefore, a key feature of a competitive market structure consists of keeping barriers to entry as low as possible.

CRAs face historical, natural, institutional and regulatory barriers to entry.[62] The historical barrier to entry results from trust based on the reputational capital that the leading CRAs have built up over many years.[63] Issuers tend to hire CRAs that are widely recognized among investors; new entrants – ie potential competitors – cannot present historic track records.[64] The natural barrier to entry is derived from the fact that the rating market may not be able to accommodate many general-purpose CRAs.[65] The presence of economies of scale suggests that the rating industry may necessarily be dominated by a few leading CRAs.[66]

The regulatory barrier to entry is created by regulators and does not exist "per se."[67] Rating-based regulations raise a regulatory barrier to entry.[68] In particular, the regulatory recognition of CRAs can potentially

---

[61] Hill, 'Regulating the Rating Agencies' (n 9) 63.

[62] ibid 84, 91.

[63] John Flood, 'Rating, Dating, and the Informal Regulation and the Formal Ordering of Financial Transactions: Securitisations and Credit Rating Agencies' in Michael B Likosky (ed), *Privatising Development: Transnational Law, Infrastructure and Human Rights* (Martinus Nijhoff Publishers 2005) 160.

[64] Uwe Blaurock, 'Verantwortlichkeit von Ratingagenturen – Steuerung durch Privat- oder Aufsichtsrecht?' [2007] ZGR 603, 607.

[65] Hill, 'Regulating the Rating Agencies' (n 9) 62 (adding that pre-NRSRO history provides some support for this argument).

[66] Steven L Schwarcz, 'Private Ordering of Public Markets: The Rating Agency Paradox' [2002] (Issue 2) University of Illinois Law Review 1, 12. Economies of scale exist if only large-scale entries are possible or if potential competitors suffer disadvantages when they try to conduct small-scale entries).

[67] See, eg, White, 'Financial Regulation and the Current Crisis' (n 59) 30.

[68] Arthur R Pinto, 'Control and Responsibility of Credit Rating Agencies in the United States' (2008) Brooklyn Law School Legal Studies Research Papers No 119, 9 (stating that the NRSRO status reduces competition in the rating

act as a barrier to entry for new market participants, ie potential competitors.[69] Hence the certification process reduces competition in the rating industry by limiting potential entrants.[70]

The combination of historical and regulatory barriers to entry has resulted in the widespread dominance of the leading CRAs.[71] As a consequence, eliminating the regulatory dependence on ratings is the best way to foster a competitive environment in the rating industry. If rating-based regulations are withdrawn, barriers to entry will probably not be fully eliminated but will at least be reduced significantly.

10.3.3 Collective Market Power of the Leading Credit Rating Agencies

High concentration in the credit rating industry and high barriers to entry resulted in the strong market dominance of the three leading CRAs. Indeed, the Big Three enjoy a certain privilege since market participants have little alternative to their ratings. Over the past decades, although rating scandals have repeatedly tarnished their reputation, the Big Three continue to flourish in the financial markets.[72] They have long dominated the rating market and continue to do so despite their failure to predict the subprime mortgage crisis.[73] The strong market power of the three leading CRAs significantly contributes to the lack of competition in the market for information. Leading CRAs dominate the rating market and – to some extent – even the market for information in a broader sense.

---

industry by limiting new entrants, ie potential competitors); Crouhy, Jarrow and Turnbull, 'The Subprime Credit Crisis of 07' (n 35) 9; Rolf H Weber and Aline Darbellay, 'The Regulatory Use of Credit Ratings in Bank Capital Requirement Regulations' (2008) 10 Journal of Banking Regulation 1, 6.

[69] FSF, *Report of the Financial Stability Forum on Enhancing Market and Institutional Resilience* (April 2008) 38. But see IOSCO, *Report on the Activities of Credit Rating Agencies* (September 2003) 9; IOSCO, *Report of the Task Force on the Subprime Crisis* (Final Report, May 2008) 27 (noting that the nature of the CRA market makes it difficult for new entrants to succeed regardless of any regulatory barriers to entry; moreover, regulatory recognition criteria are based on how extensively ratings are used by market participants, ie the reputation of CRAs in the market; in addition, market participants prefer to use ratings that regulators also use, implying that the cycle of discrimination is perpetual).

[70] Pinto, 'Control and Responsibility of Credit Rating Agencies in the United States' (n 68) 9 (referring to the NRSRO status in the US).

[71] Abdelal, *Capital Rules* (n 15) 173.

[72] See, eg, David Gillen, 'In Ratings Agencies, Investors Still Trust' *The New York Times*, June 5, 2009.

[73] Balzli and Hornig, 'Exacerbating the Crisis' (n 12).

Further, the fact that issuers and investors prefer to choose CRAs that enjoy the most market recognition reinforces the market power of the three leading CRAs. Concern has especially been raised about the issuer-pays business model. The issuer-pays business model is heavily criticized because it creates conflicts of interest in the rating process.[74] In this regard, the issuer-pays business model jeopardizes the independence of the CRAs. Moreover, as regards the market power of the Big Three there is another reason to be skeptical of the issuer-pays business model. Under the issuer-pays business model issuers prefer to hire CRAs that enjoy the greatest market reliance.[75] This means that CRAs that have the greatest market shares will automatically tend to be selected by issuers. Issuers are only willing to pay for ratings if the hired CRAs enjoy sufficient market recognition. This phenomenon contributes to strengthening the rating oligopoly even when the leading CRAs do not allocate more resources to the rating process. The more a specific CRA gains market share and obtains market reliance, the more issuers are interested in having their debt instruments rated by the targeted CRA. Therefore, leading CRAs tend to attract even more market power and be decreasingly subject to competitive pressures.

10.4 MARKET OVER-DEPENDENCE ON THE LEADING CREDIT RATING AGENCIES

> The stability and functioning of financial markets should not depend on the opinions of a small number of agencies.[76]

Over the past decades credit ratings have increasingly been used in the financial markets. On the one hand, regulators – especially since the 1970s – are partly responsible for this phenomenon. They have incorporated ratings into several types of financial market regulations. On the other hand, market participants have increasingly used ratings regardless of any regulatory mandates. Behavioral reliance has added to regulatory

---

[74] See, eg, Mathis, McAndrews and Rochet, 'Rating the Raters' (n 13) 669.

[75] IOSCO, *Report on the Activities of Credit Rating Agencies* (n 69) 9; IOSCO, *Report of the Task Force on the Subprime Crisis* (n 69) 27.

[76] The High-Level Group on Financial Supervision in the EU, 'De Larosière Report' (2009) 19 ‹http://ec.europa.eu/internal_market/finances/docs/de_larosiere_report_en.pdf› accessed January 10, 2013.

reliance.[77] The combination of regulatory and behavioral reliance on ratings has attributed a system-wide importance to CRAs. Accordingly, the ratings issued by the leading CRAs are deeply anchored in the financial markets.

10.4.1 Regulatory Reliance on Credit Ratings

Regulators are important users of credit ratings. They have created rating-based regulations, thereby forcing market participants to rely on ratings. Regulators also use ratings on their own behalf. For instance, central banks may rely on ratings when deciding which securities to accept as collateral.

10.4.1.1 Rating-based regulations

There are several mandates to use ratings in financial market regulations. Two types of regulatory intervention have system-wide impacts on the financial markets.

First, risk-sensitive measures of regulatory capital increase the importance of certified CRAs if their ratings are widely used to attribute the various risk weights to assets in the financial markets. The Basel II framework encouraged global implementation of risk-sensitive bank capital requirements, and the Basel III framework continues to do so. The use of external ratings in order to determine the appropriate risk weights is described under the Standardized Approach of Basel II and III.[78] The system-relevance of this method is derived from the use of ratings and its global acceptance. The fact that regulatory-prescribed risk models were widely adopted contributed to homogenizing market participants' behavior.[79] Before the subprime mortgage crisis, banks were able to report relatively high risk-weighted capital ratios.[80] Basically, banks could benefit from risk-sensitive capital requirements. They were holding triple-A-rated assets on their balance sheets. The contrast between the

---

77 Frank Partnoy, 'Overdependence on Credit Ratings was a Primary Cause of the Crisis' (2009) University of San Diego Legal Studies Research Paper Series No 09-015, 10.

78 BCBS, *International Convergence of Capital Measurement and Capital Standards, A Revised Framework (Basel II)* (BIS, June 2004) para 50.

79 Alexander and others, 'Financial Supervision and Crisis Management in the EU' (n 50) 20.

80 ibid (arguing that at the end of 2006, the ratio of regulatory capital to risk-weighted assets was 13 percent in the US, 12.9 percent in the UK, 12.2 percent in Germany, 10.7 percent in Italy – significantly above the 8 percent minimum).

risky activities that banks were increasingly associated with and the increasingly healthy ratio of their regulatory capital was striking.[81] As long as bank assets were highly rated, banks could extend their balance sheets and enjoy high leverage ratios with the consent of regulators.[82] However, troubles became visible along with massive rating downgrades in July 2007. In the subprime mortgage crisis triple-A-rated assets were downgraded to junk status in an extremely short space of time. This phenomenon had negative impacts on the capital ratios of banks using ratings to define the risk weights of their assets. Bank capital ratios deteriorated instantly after the downgrades so that affected banks had to raise new capital or dispose of assets.[83] Therefore, the use of ratings in bank capital market regulations exacerbates market trends if widely adopted by regulators and market participants. In this respect, a significant improvement of the Basel III reform measures is the idea of countercyclical capital buffers to mitigate the procyclical effects of the risk-weighted capital requirements.[84]

Second, investment limitations imposed on charter-constrained investors can – under certain regulations – depend on ratings.[85] Financial market regulations using ratings to design permitted investments have essentially been developed in the US for the pension funds and insurance sectors. Highly regulated entities are subject to portfolio restrictions in view of investor protection.[86] As a consequence, market participants may be forced to sell their holdings for regulatory reasons.[87]

---

81 ibid.

82 BCBS, *Consultative Document, Strengthening the Resilience of the Banking Sector* (BIS, December 2009) 60 (recognizing that the Basel II framework allowed banks to build up excessive leverage while still reporting strong risk-based capital ratios).

83 'De Larosière Report' (n 76) 12.

84 BCBS, *Consultative Document, Countercyclical Capital Buffer Proposal* (BIS, June 2010) 1.

85 The Joint Forum, *Stocktaking on the Use of Credit Ratings* (BIS, June 2009) 7.

86 See further ibid 8 (explaining that, for instance in Italy, ratings are required by regulation only when securities are sold to non-professional investors; in this regard, regulatory intervention aims at protecting unsophisticated investors).

87 Kathleen Casey and Frank Partnoy, 'Downgrade the Ratings Agencies' *The New York Times*, June 4, 2010.

Such rating-based regulations can have unintended and counter-productive effects. At any rate, they contribute to increasing the importance attributed to the ratings of certified CRAs.[88] Especially massive rating downgrades may have negative impacts on the financial markets. Before the subprime mortgage crisis, charter-constrained investors were allowed to buy mortgage-related securities as long as they were rated investment grade by the certified CRAs. As a direct consequence of the massive rating downgrades in July 2007, charter-constrained investors were forced to sell the assets downgraded to a level below the investment grade.[89] They had to sell at the worst moment since the repricing of credit risk implied a repricing of asset prices at lower levels. Moreover, the fact that market participants were homogeneously selling dropped asset prices even further.[90] Therefore, regulations forcing market participants to rely on ratings caused exacerbated market reactions to rating downgrades. The purpose of investor protection was not achieved when highly regulated market participants had to sell at the worst time.

The two aforementioned examples highlight the serious repercussions of rating-based regulations on the behavior of market participants. When designing financial market regulations, regulators should take into account the unintended effects of their regulatory activities. A macroprudential approach to financial market regulations is required in order to assess the side effects of the regulatory frameworks.[91]

10.4.1.2 Collateral policy of central banks

Regulators can also use credit ratings for their own purposes. More particularly, the use of ratings by central banks plays a crucial role in modern financial markets and partly contributes to over-reliance on ratings.[92] Central banks have, to a considerable extent, incorporated ratings into their lending rules in order to determine eligible collateral for loans. In other words, certified CRAs play a crucial role in helping

---

[88] Abdelal, *Capital Rules* (n 15) 171 (stating that the dangers of using ratings in regulations to limit investors' exposure to risky securities became clear very quickly).

[89] Casey and Partnoy, 'Downgrade the Ratings Agencies' (n 87) (arguing that – due to investment restrictions requiring so many funds to hold highly rated assets – a rating downgrade can set off a financial collapse by forcing investors to sell).

[90] Alexander and others, 'Financial Supervision and Crisis Management in the EU' (n 50) 25.

[91] Sy, 'The Systemic Regulation of Credit Rating Agencies and Rated Markets' (n 5) 3.

[92] FSB, *Principles for Reducing Reliance on CRA Ratings* (n 6) 3.

central banks decide what assets can be used as a guarantee for central bank loans.

Central banks' collateral rules gain prominence in times of crisis. During a financial crisis, central banks extensively intervene as providers of liquidity since financial institutions no longer perform this function adequately. Generally, central banks agree to lend money if borrowers provide investment-grade securities as a guarantee. Ratings are typically used in central bank policies due to their convenience. Although CRAs proved to be unreliable in the subprime mortgage market, central banks continued to use ratings to determine eligible collateral at the height of the financial crisis.[93]

In the US, the Fed's 1 trillion US dollar TALF plan – a colossal program to encourage lending – mandated that only securities rated by at least two major NRSROs were eligible for aid.[94] Borrowers could only use triple-A rated assets as collateral.[95] In other words, regulatory reliance on ratings still persisted in the aftermath of the subprime mortgage crisis. Critics questioned the use of ratings in the Fed's collateral rules, yet central banks seemed to have difficulty finding a practical alternative.[96]

In Europe, the ECB experienced the downside of using ratings to determine eligible collateral with respect to the Greek rescue package. The ECB took steps to accept below-investment-grade bonds as collateral for ECB loans, which was not welcomed by the financial markets.[97] Investors interpreted this decision as a bad signal. They believed that the situation had deteriorated to such a considerable extent that the ECB was willing to accept junk bonds as collateral.

It is worth mentioning how central banks address global liquidity squeeze in times of crisis. They mainly intervene in financial markets through market operations. Above all, they lend money to banks and lower interest rates to increase money supply as part of their ordinary

---

93 'The Big Barofsky, Someone in Washington is Standing up for Taxpayers' *The Wall Street Journal*, April 29, 2009 (quoting Neil Barofsky, Special Inspector General, Troubled Asset Relief Program (TARP)).

94 Aline Darbellay and Frank Partnoy, 'Credit Rating Agencies and Regulatory Reform' in Claire A Hill and Brett H McDonnell (eds), *Research Handbook on the Economics of Corporate Law* (Edward Elgar 2012) 278.

95 Casey and Partnoy, 'Downgrade the Ratings Agencies' (n 87).

96 See, eg, 'The Big Barofsky' (n 93) (quoting Neil Barofsky, Special Inspector General, TARP).

97 Kennedy and Totaro, 'ECB Comes to Greece's Aid by Waiving Collateral Rules' (n 21).

operations. In addition, they also use quantitative easing and qualitative easing when their conventional monetary policies are insufficient to address liquidity problems. Quantitative easing refers to a massive provision of liquidity, for instance by outright purchases of securities or other financial instruments. Qualitative easing refers to the acceptance of securities of lower quality with a view to extending facilities even further. This includes central banks' policy to accept below-investment-grade bonds as collateral.[98] In this respect, market participants may consider that the ECB implemented qualitative easing when it accepted junk bonds as collateral.

Nevertheless, another interpretation is more likely to explain the new trends in the financial markets: central banks no longer want to depend on certified CRAs. The trend toward decreasing reliance on ratings has been initiated. In this regard, the decision of the ECB to accept below-investment-grade bonds not only amounts to qualitative easing but also reflects the fact that central banks are willing to cease relying excessively on ratings in their collateral policies.[99] It is indeed better that central banks reach their own credit judgements on the financial instruments they accept as collateral.[100]

10.4.2 Behavioral Reliance on Credit Ratings

Apart from the regulatory use of credit ratings, financial markets have incorporated ratings into many investment decisions. Over-reliance on ratings probably derives from decades of rating-based regulations, yet it has become a more widespread, behavioral phenomenon.[101] Ratings have become hard-wired into the financial infrastructure because of their importance not only in regulations but also in private contracts.[102] This results in mechanistic reliance on ratings by market participants.[103]

---

[98] ibid (stating that the ECB joined the international rescue of Greece by accepting the country's debt as collateral for a central bank loan regardless of its rating).

[99] 'The Other Vampires' (n 2) 83–84 (reporting that while deciding what asset constitutes eligible collateral, the ECB will no longer be strictly guided by leading CRAs' ratings).

[100] FSB, *Principles for Reducing Reliance on CRA Ratings* (n 6) 3.

[101] Partnoy, 'Overdependence on Credit Ratings was a Primary Cause of the Crisis' (n 77) 10.

[102] John Patrick Hunt, 'Credit Rating Agencies and the "Worldwide Credit Crisis": The Limits of Reputation, the Insufficiency of Reform, and a Proposal for Improvement' [2009] Columbia Business Law Review 109, 151.

[103] FSB, *Principles for Reducing Reliance on CRA Ratings* (n 6) 1–2.

10.4.2.1 "Rating triggers" in contracting

Many private agreements include "rating triggers," under which a rating downgrade below a specified level has contractual effects.[104] There are two main types of "rating triggers." First, companies may have "rating triggers" in their financing documents.[105] In this case, investors will be able to take action against such companies if their debt ratings fall below a specified level.[106] Potential action may include acceleration of debt, calling a technical default or raising the debt's interest rate.[107] These types of "rating triggers" can appear for instance in the form of OTC swap agreements including rating-based termination provisions.[108] Investors tend to include these types of "rating triggers" in debt covenants with a view to mitigating counterparty risk. If their counterparty is downgraded, they are interested in relinquishing their engagements. Their objective is to act before the company's failure. They trust ratings as an early signal of a deteriorating financial situation. However, the problem posed by these "rating triggers" is derived from the homogeneous behavior of market participants in the aftermath of a rating announcement. Market participants will suddenly move away from the company. As a consequence, a rating downgrade will cause the financial situation of the company to deteriorate, which may cause a further downgrade, which may cause a further deterioration.[109] This, in turn, may eventually drive the company into bankruptcy. Therefore, if market reliance on ratings is excessive, rating downgrades may easily trigger downward financial spirals.[110]

Second, companies may be subject to internal "rating triggers." Their internal investment restrictions or policies may force them to hold securities above a specified rating grade.[111] If the securities in their portfolios are downgraded below the prescribed line, charter-constrained companies have to sell the downgraded securities. Investors tend to

---

104 ibid.

105 Hill, 'Regulating the Rating Agencies' (n 9) 67.

106 ibid 67–68.

107 Richard Routier, 'De nouvelles pistes pour la gouvernance?' [2003] Bulletin Joly Sociétés 611, 611ff; Hill, 'Regulating the Rating Agencies' (n 9) 68. See also Niamh Moloney, *EC Securities Regulation* (2nd edn, Oxford University Press 2008) 690.

108 'Assessing the Current Oversight and Operation of Credit Rating Agencies' (statement of Glenn L Reynolds, Chief Executive Officer, CreditSights) (n 58) 38.

109 Hill, 'Regulating the Rating Agencies' (n 9) 68.

110 ibid.

111 IOSCO, *Report on the Activities of Credit Rating Agencies* (n 69) 7.

include these types of "rating triggers" if they are concerned about how money managers deal with their funds. They cannot control every investment decision, yet they can internally impose investment restrictions on money managers. However, such types of "rating triggers" may have unintended effects. They may force investment funds to liquidate assets at the worst possible time.[112] A rating downgrade by a leading CRA causes asset prices to fall. If funds are required to sell assets, asset prices will fall further. Market participants have a tendency to sell homogeneously after a downgrade due to their reliance on the ratings of the few leading CRAs. The market suddenly becomes illiquid.

Overall, "rating triggers" are usually not publicly disclosed since they are private agreements. Therefore, it is challenging to assess what impact rating downgrades have on financial markets. It is also difficult to determine to what extent market reactions to rating downgrades can be attributed to "rating triggers." What is certain is that if the existence of a "rating trigger" is not publicly known, financial crises can be more sudden and unexpected.[113] "Rating triggers" are sharply criticized for their cascading effects.[114] Following Enron's bankruptcy, voices have been heard to the effect that CRAs should take into account how a company can survive a rating downgrade prior to taking their decision to downgrade.[115] Because of the presence of "rating triggers," leading CRAs may become more reluctant to downgrade and hence partly lose independent judgment.

10.4.2.2 Rating-dependent "collateral triggers" in contracting

Market participants may require their counterparty to post more or less collateral depending on the credit rating of the borrower or of the purchased debt instrument. For instance, they may request sellers of CDS

---

[112] See further Crouhy, Jarrow and Turnbull, 'The Subprime Credit Crisis of 07' (n 35) 24 (giving another reason why money market funds sell their holdings when they are downgraded: in order to retain their triple-A ratings, money market funds are restricted from investing in low-rated securities).

[113] 'Exclusion Zone, Regulators Promise a Belated Review of the Ratings Oligopoly' *The Economist*, February 8, 2003, 65–66.

[114] Timothy E Lynch, 'Deeply and Persistently Conflicted: Credit Rating Agencies in the Current Regulatory Environment' (2009) 59 Case Western Reserve Law Review 227, 246.

[115] Tim Reason, 'Not Trigger Happy, Credit-rating Firms are Taking a Closer Look at How Corporate Credit Agreements Employ Rating Triggers' *CFO Magazine*, February 21, 2002.

to post more collateral in order to mitigate counterparty risk.[116] When engaging in financial transactions, market participants may require collateral only to the extent that they are concerned about counterparty risk. Further, "downgrade triggers" may contractually require the downgraded counterparty to post more collateral.[117] In fact, the market did not require collateral when buying CDS from triple-A-rated insurance companies such as AIG. The market considered highly rated companies to be creditworthy, thereby making collateral requirements unnecessary. In this sense, AIG's high rating became the only security against counterparty risk.[118] In the case of AIG, collateral calls were triggered by the reduction in the fair value of the underlying CDOs and the rating downgrades of AIG.[119] Therefore, the use of ratings to assess counterparty risk causes instability in the financial system.

Further, creditors may require investment-grade securities as collateral. Ratings play a role in determining the quality of the posted collateral. Borrowers may have to post more or less collateral of a certain quality. If the quality of the posted collateral decreases, for instance when CRAs downgrade the collateral in question, borrowers may have to post additional collateral as guarantees. In distress times, borrowers are generally required to tie up more capital or other assets as collateral.

In the AIG case, the aforementioned elements simultaneously played a role in aggravating the insurance company's financial troubles at the height of the financial crisis. Before the subprime mortgage debacle, AIG could sell CDS – ie credit protection – to investors without collateral or margin requirements by reason of its high rating. As the subprime mortgage market collapsed, AIG became subject to the downside effects of "collateral triggers."[120] When AIG's CDS positions were downgraded by the leading CRAs, CDS buyers could ask for collateral because the value of AIG's assets had dropped significantly. Moreover, AIG was about to be dramatically downgraded, which would have enhanced

---

116 Brian JM Quinn, 'The Failure of Private Ordering and the Financial Crisis of 2008' (2009) 5 NYU Journal of Law & Business 549, 585.

117 BCBS, *Consultative Document, International Framework for Liquidity Risk Measurement, Standards and Monitoring* (BIS, December 2009) 15 (discussing how financial institutions can mitigate liquidity risk with respect to these "downgrade triggers").

118 Quinn, 'The Failure of Private Ordering and the Financial Crisis of 2008' (n 116) 585.

119 Michael Corkery, 'Joe Cassano's Testimony: AIG CDS Worked Just Fine' *The Wall Street Journal Blogs*, June 30, 2010 (quoting Joe Cassano).

120 Nocera, 'Propping up a House of Cards' (n 38) (quoting Seamus P McMahon, banking expert, Booz & Company).

counterparty risk from the point of view of CDS buyers. If AIG had been downgraded to a level below the investment grade, AIG's swap counterparties would have asked for more collateral because of the insurance company's declining creditworthiness. AIG's bailout was necessary to avoid this chain of events driving the insurance company into a death spiral. Moreover, AIG was "too interconnected to fail" and its failure would have produced a "domino effect," thereby endangering other financial institutions.[121] A bailout of AIG – being a systemically relevant insurance company – was actually a bailout of its trading partners.[122]

---

121 ibid (quoting Seamus P McMahon, banking expert, Booz & Company).
122 ibid.

11. Market reactions to credit rating downgrades and their consequences

11.1 HOMOGENIZATION OF INFORMATION IN THE FINANCIAL MARKETS

Due to the over-reliance on a concentrated credit rating market, participants tend to react homogeneously to rating announcements. This homogenization of market behavior is especially acute in the face of extreme events. Massive rating downgrades often occur as a cause or as an immediate trigger of financial turmoil.

First, market participants tend to rely on ratings as a homogeneous source of financial information. Various factors have homogenized the market for credit information: CRAs have become a preferred source of credit information as opposed to other gatekeepers. The high concentration in the rating industry gives a privilege to information stemming from the leading CRAs as compared with smaller CRAs. The three leading CRAs issue a significant percentage of the totality of the ratings.[1] The issuer-pays business model incentivizes the leading CRAs to attribute investment-grade ratings to most debt instruments. Under an issuer-pays business model, information is further made easily available to a wide range of investors.

Second, the very fact that a rating downgrade has occurred not only reflects information but is autonomous information.[2] Even when no additional information about the present financial situation of the company is conveyed, investors will react to the rating announcement.[3] Many market participants react to rating downgrades not because they think that the downgrades convey new information, but because they know that the financial markets will react negatively to them.

---

[1] Gary Shorter and Michael V Seitzinger, 'Credit Rating Agencies and Their Regulation' (2009) Congressional Research Service, 3 ‹http://garrettforms.house.gov/uploadedfiles/credit_rating_agencies.pdf› accessed January 10, 2013.

[2] Claire A Hill, 'Regulating the Rating Agencies' (2004) 82 Washington University Law Quarterly 4, 68.

[3] ibid.

Third, as a consequence, homogeneous information and the signaling effects of rating downgrades tend to homogenize market behavior. Market participants pay attention to rating announcements even when they are skeptical of the function of CRAs as information intermediaries. Market participants are – to some extent – forced to adapt their investment strategies to rating changes. These findings illustrate the prevailing market over-reliance on leading CRAs.

11.1.1 Amount of Available Information and Selection of Relevant Information

> We have all had the sensation of drowning in a sea of information – the challenge we face is to learn to swim in that sea, rather than drown in it.[4]

There is no doubt that information is very powerful in modern financial markets. We most definitely live in the Information Age.[5] The well-functioning of financial markets depends on the collection and the diffusion of an optimal amount of information. Market participants access different sources of information and take investment decisions accordingly. To a certain extent they may even be overwhelmed by the amount of information at their disposal.[6] Since the modern world is surrounded by an unprecedented amount of information, the most successful market participants are those who can capture and select valuable

---

[4] Peter Lyman and Hal R Varian, 'How Big Is the Information Explosion?' *iMP Magazine*,November 22, 2000.

[5] Urs Birchler and Monika Bütler, *Information Economics* (Routledge 2007) 1 (quoting Hal R Varian). To some extent, we may even have reached the Over-Information Age.

[6] See generally John Foley, 'New Tools Can Help Tame an Ocean of Data' *InformationWeek*, October 30, 1995 (statement of Paul Saffo, Institute for the Future) (stating, however, that information overload is not a function of the volume of information; rather, it is a gap between the volume of information and the tools we have to turn that information into useful knowledge). See also Rolf H Weber, 'Kassandra oder Wissensbroker – Dilemma im "Global Village"' in Jürgen Becker, Reto M Hilty, Jean-Fritz Stöckli and Thomas Würtenberger (eds), *Recht im Wandel seines sozialen und technologischen Umfeldes, Festschrift für Manfred Rehbinder* (CH Beck 2002) 407; Bettina J Cassad, 'Confirmation Bias' in Roy F Baumeister and Kathleen D Vohs (eds), *Encyclopedia of Social Psychology* (SAGE 2007) 162 ("Humans are bombarded with information [...] and cannot possibly take the time to carefully process each piece of information to form an unbiased conclusion"); Claire A Hill, 'Why Did Anyone Listen to the Rating Agencies after Enron?' (2009) 4 Journal of Business & Technology Law 283, 287–288 (quoting Bettina J Cassad).

information, manage and process information, diffuse information and reach targeted people, or keep the information and act upon it.

With respect to the credit rating industry, CRAs are important producers of financial market information.[7] As information intermediaries, their role has significantly evolved since their inception. First, their main task – at the beginning of the twentieth century – was to gather and distribute a sufficient amount of information. If CRAs were created to provide investors with information, today access to information is no longer the most challenging issue. Rather, new problems are faced in modern financial markets due to the quantity of information at the disposal of market participants. CRAs are used to screen valuable information and distill the complexity of the financial world into simple rankings;[8] in selecting, analyzing and summarizing information CRAs play their most crucial role in the modern world.

11.1.2 Credit Ratings of the Leading Credit Rating Agencies as a Homogenizing Factor

> [W]hile structured finance initially offered the potential of tailored and diverse solutions, the rating process just described, developed in the name of transparency and standardisation is an important force of homogenisation in the selection and valuation of portfolios.[9]

The credit ratings of the leading CRAs tend to homogenize the financial information that market participants use to take their decisions despite the complexity of the modern world. Ideally, the market for financial information reflects a wide range of perspectives. In particular, the rating market is competitive if it is characterized by the presence of various CRAs issuing a great variety of ratings. Financial markets should reflect a diversity of opinions that enable market participants to trade according to their individual perceptions.[10] However, concern has been raised about the homogenization of financial information in the rating industry. This

---

[7] Birchler and Bütler, *Information Economics* (n 5) 105.

[8] John C Coffee Jr, *Gatekeepers: The Professions and Corporate Governance* (Oxford University Press 2006) 283.

[9] Kern Alexander and others, 'Financial Supervision and Crisis Management in the EU' (2007) European Parliament, Policy Department, Economic and Scientific Policy, 18 ‹http://www.europarl.europa.eu/document/activities/cont/201108/20110818ATT25070/20110818ATT25070EN.pdf› accessed 10 January 2013.

[10] ibid 4 (stating that to some extent investors behave differently due to their access to different financial information).

problem arises out of the wide diffusion of ratings issued by a heavily concentrated industry. Three factors contribute to this phenomenon:

(i) First, credit ratings represent a privileged source of financial information. There are many sources of financial information other than ratings in the financial markets. For instance, financial analysts are, under certain circumstances, in direct competition with CRAs as providers of financial information.[11] Nevertheless, ratings enjoy a specific status among the investing community. CRAs take advantage of their favored status as opposed to other information providers.

Above all, CRAs often have access to information that other market participants such as gatekeepers and investors do not have. For instance if CRAs are hired by issuers, issuers provide them with valuable information. Broadly speaking, the lack of transparency in the financial markets may increase the importance of ratings when investors have no alternatives to assess the value of debt instruments. In this sense, information asymmetry can explain the emergence of systemic crises.[12] This was the case in the subprime mortgage crisis when investors realized that the ratings went wrong, and that they were left with no other independent means of valuing the complex securities they were buying.[13]

(ii) Second, a too concentrated rating industry enjoying excessive market reliance can lead to a homogenization of opinions in the financial markets. Due to rating-based regulations, certified CRAs are privileged compared to non-certified CRAs. Moreover, the leading CRAs have advantages over smaller CRAs. Market recognition makes sure that the most powerful CRAs easily reach investors through their rating announcements. The situation results in market over-reliance on the Big Three. Such a concentrated rating industry provides an increasingly homogenized source of information to market participants.

(iii) Third, a factor that tends to homogenize information is derived from the public availability of credit ratings. The wide and rapid diffusion of ratings implies that financial information reaches a wide

---

[11] Above all, sophisticated investors have their own financial analysts who undertake research on their behalf.

[12] Christoph Kuhner, 'Financial Rating Agencies: Are They Credible? – Insights into the Reporting Incentives of Rating Agencies in Times of Enhanced Systemic Risk' (2001) 53 Schmalenbach Business Review 2, 5.

[13] FSF, *Report of the Financial Stability Forum on Enhancing Market and Institutional Resilience* (April 2008) 37–38; See also IOSCO, *Report of the Task Force on the Subprime Crisis* (Final Report, May 2008) 23.

range of market participants at the same time.[14] Broad rating disclosures contribute to homogenizing financial information. Under the issuer-pays business model, ratings are typically made publicly available.[15] This differs from the investor-pays business model where supposedly only the subscribers have access to the ratings.[16] Apart from that, there were also regulatory requirements to publicly disclose ratings in prospectuses or regulatory filings.[17] These requirements significantly enhanced the availability and importance of ratings.

11.1.3 Signaling Effects of Credit Rating Downgrades

In modern financial markets, rating announcements do not only reflect available information but also convey autonomous information to market participants. For instance, the very fact of a rating downgrade has an effect in the financial markets.[18] Even where no additional information about the present financial situation of the company is conveyed, investors will react to the rating announcement.[19] Disclosing information sends a signal to the financial markets. Investors interpret a rating downgrade as a negative signal of the company's creditworthiness; even if they do not rely on ratings, they pay attention to the downgrade because they consider that other market participants may react negatively

---

14 The mere fact that rumors circulate may cause disruption to financial markets. Consequently, it is not surprising that rating downgrades have tremendous impact on financial markets when they rapidly reach a wide range of investors.

15 Edward I Altman, Sabri Oncu, Anjolein Schmeits and Lawrence J White, 'What Should Be Done about the Credit Rating Agencies?' *New York University (NYU) Stern Regulating Wall Street Blog*, April 6, 2010 ‹http://w4.stern.nyu.edu/blogs/regulatingwallstreet/2010/04/what-should-be-done-about-the.html#more› accessed January 10, 2013 (mentioning the public availability of ratings as an advantage of the issuer-pays business model as opposed to the investor-pays business model).

16 Carol Ann Frost, 'Credit Rating Agencies in Capital Markets: A Review of Research Evidence on Selected Criticisms of the Agencies' (2007) 22 Journal of Accounting, Auditing & Finance 469, 473 (also referring to investor-paid ratings as undisclosed or confidential ratings).

17 IOSCO, *Report on the Activities of Credit Rating Agencies* (September 2003) 9.

18 Hill, 'Regulating the Rating Agencies' (n 2) 68.

19 ibid.

to the downgrade. Investors will react to the rating downgrade independently of any additional information reflected in the ratings. As a result, a rating downgrade will automatically worsen the company's financial situation.[20]

The financial markets have assimilated the fact that the leading CRAs are slow to downgrade. Rating downgrades are typically disclosed when it is too late. Moreover, belated rating action amplifies the effects of rating downgrades since an extremely negative signal is sent out. Market participants tend to interpret downgrades as revealing the default of borrowers or debt instruments, especially as regards downgrades to a level below the investment grade.

In fact, leading CRAs have acquired a reputation for downgrading big companies only a few days before those companies filed for bankruptcy. Some famous examples are WorldCom, Enron and Lehman Brothers.[21] Market participants have heavily criticized the leading CRAs because their downgrades were not timely. They have also reproached the leading CRAs for precipitating the collapse of distressed companies because of the devastating effects of rating downgrades in financial markets. The important lesson is that the financial markets have – in the aftermath of these big bankruptcies – learned that rating downgrades by the leading CRAs only occur at a late stage. As a consequence, common interpretation of a rating downgrade in the financial markets is that it is too late to rescue the company. If the leading CRAs believe that a distressed company may return to financial health, they would refrain from downgrading the company in the first place.[22]

11.1.4 Homogenization of Market Behavior

> Because so many funds are required to hold highly rated assets, a downgrade can set off a financial collapse by forcing investors to sell.[23]

Leading CRAs contribute to the phenomenon of homogeneous market behavior to a great extent. The danger is that due to over-reliance on

---

[20] ibid.

[21] Shorter and Seitzinger, 'Credit Rating Agencies and Their Regulation' (n 1) 3 (reporting that firms such as the energy company Enron and the telecommunications company WorldCom retained their high ratings until a few days prior to filing for bankruptcy).

[22] Hill, 'Regulating the Rating Agencies' (n 2) 69.

[23] Kathleen Casey and Frank Partnoy, 'Downgrade the Ratings Agencies' *The New York Times*, June 4, 2010 (referring to rating-based regulations as a cause of the homogenization of market behavior).

credit ratings, market behavior is homogenized so that a confidence crisis in ratings or massive rating downgrades may totally destabilize the financial markets. Rating changes literally move markets, particularly if a certified CRA downgrades a security from above investment grade to below investment grade, thereby prompting a sell-off by institutional investors.[24] With respect to the subprime mortgage crisis, there is evidence that the homogenization of market participants' behavior worsened the 2007–2009 financial crisis.[25]

Rating downgrades by leading CRAs have extremely negative impacts on a company's access to capital markets. When a company is downgraded by a system-relevant CRA it will be unable to attract the credit needed to finance its operations, and may even collapse; therefore, leading CRAs are extremely reluctant to downgrade a company's debt.[26]

Given the comprehensive effects of rating downgrades, not only market participants that directly rely on ratings will keep up to date with rating announcements. Even other market participants have an interest in paying close attention to ratings. Many market participants react to rating downgrades not because they think the downgrades convey new information, but because they know that the financial markets will react negatively to those downgrades.[27] Expectations about the actions of other market participants imply strong market reactions. Investment decisions by market participants may thus be influenced by the market reactions of other market participants.[28] If there is a tendency toward strong market reliance on ratings, even market participants that do not personally trust CRAs have no other choice but to care about rating announcements. Therefore, these issues tend to homogenize market behavior even more.

---

[24] Rawi Abdelal, *Capital Rules, The Construction of Global Finance* (Harvard University Press 2007) 171.

[25] See generally Alexander and others, 'Financial Supervision and Crisis Management in the EU' (n 9) 20.

[26] Jonathan R Macey, 'Efficient Capital Markets, Corporate Disclosure, and Enron' (2004) 89 Cornell Law Review 394, 406.

[27] Aline Darbellay, 'Regulating Ratings, The Credit Rating Agency Oligopoly from a Regulatory Perspective' in Dieter Zobl, Mario Giovanoli and Rolf H Weber, *Schweizer Schriften zum Finanzmarktrecht, Band 102* (Schulthess 2011) 166.

[28] See further Alexander and others, 'Financial Supervision and Crisis Management in the EU' (n 9) 19 (stating that – in the market for securitized assets – many investors do similar things at the same time with the same set of assets as a result of the homogenizing effect of ratings).

11.2 PROCYCLICALITY

> Once credit rating agencies started to revise their credit ratings for CDOs downwards, banks were required to adjust their risk-weighted capital requirements upwards.[29]

Procyclicality refers to the exacerbation of market trends in financial markets. Credit ratings are often criticized as being procyclical, ie they are able to aggravate the negative consequences of a financial crisis.[30] In fact, CRAs tend to upgrade borrowers and debt instruments in good times and to downgrade them in bad times.[31] In this regard, over-reliance on ratings may heighten the impact of rating announcements by leading CRAs. According to the FSB, rating downgrades can amplify procyclicality and cause systemic disruption through "cliff effects" such as experienced in the 2007–2009 financial crisis.[32]

All episodes of financial distress of a systemic nature – with potentially significant implications for the real economy – have at their root an expansion of risk-taking and an overextension of bank balance sheets in good

---

[29] The High-Level Group on Financial Supervision in the EU, 'De Larosière Report' (2009) 12 ‹http://ec.europa.eu/internal_market/finances/docs/de_larosiere_report_en.pdf› accessed January 10, 2013.

[30] See, eg, Amadou N R Sy, 'The Systemic Regulation of Credit Rating Agencies and Rated Markets' (2009) IMF Working Paper No 09/129, 3 ‹http://www.imf.org/external/pubs/ft/wp/2009/wp09129.pdf› accessed January 10, 2013. See also Adrian Blundell-Wignall and Paul Atkinson, 'Thinking Beyond Basel III: Necessary Solutions for Capital and Liquidity' [2010] (Issue 1) OECD Journal: Financial Market Trends 1, 5–6 ‹http://www.oecd.org/finance/financialmarkets/45314422.pdf› accessed January 10, 2013.

[31] Howell E Jackson, 'The Role of Credit Rating Agencies in the Establishment of Capital Standards for Financial Institutions in a Global Economy' in Eilís Ferran and Charles AE Goodhart (eds), *Regulating Financial Services and Markets in the 21st Century* (Hart Publishing 2001) 317 (relating to good times); Richard Sylla, 'An Historical Primer on the Business of Credit Rating' in Richard M Levich, Giovanni Majnoni and Carmen Reinhart (eds), *Ratings, Rating Agencies and the Global Financial System* (Kluwer Academic Publishers 2002) 29 (relating to good times); Claudio Borio, 'The Financial Turmoil of 2007–?: A Preliminary Assessment and Some Policy Considerations' (2008) BIS Working Papers No 251, 16 ‹http://www.bis.org/publ/work251.pdf› accessed January 10, 2013 (relating to good times); Kuhner, 'Financial Rating Agencies' (n 12) 4, 20 (relating to bad times).

[32] FSB, *Principles for Reducing Reliance on CRA Ratings* (October 2010) 1.

times.[33] With respect to the recent financial crisis, two structural factors in particular contributed to enhancing procyclicality in the financial markets.

First, modern bank capital requirement regulations lead market participants to use procyclical risk models.[34] On the global scale, Basel II has procyclical tendencies, reinforcing market trends rather than counterbalancing them.[35] The most frequent criticism of the Basel II framework is that it increases procyclicality with negative consequences for firms' financing since credit is scarce in economic slowdown phases.[36] Indeed, the regulatory use of ratings to measure bank capital ratios accentuated the recent financial crisis. Broadly speaking, it is inevitable that a regulatory system based on risk-sensitivity has – to some extent – procyclical effects.[37] Nevertheless, macroprudential measures can be taken to mitigate the procyclical effects of risk-based capital requirements.[38] For instance, Basel III reform measures include a proposal for countercyclical capital buffers.[39]

Second, another aspect that contributes to enhancing procyclicality in the financial markets is fair value accounting. It is a widespread view that international standards on fair value accounting exacerbated the subprime mortgage crisis.[40] Mark-to-market valuation of assets meant that when credit prices fell sharply and asset values were written down, banks were

---

33 Borio, 'The Financial Turmoil of 2007–?' (n 31) 12. See also BCBS, *Consultative Document, Countercyclical Capital Buffer Proposal* (BIS, June 2010) 2.

34 Alexander and others, 'Financial Supervision and Crisis Management in the EU' (n 9) 25.

35 See, eg, Rolf H Weber and Aline Darbellay, 'The Regulatory Use of Credit Ratings in Bank Capital Requirement Regulations' (2008) 10 Journal of Banking Regulation 1, 9.

36 Marie-Florence Lamy, 'The Treatment of Credit Risk in the Basel Accord and Financial Stability' (2006) 11 International Journal of Business 159, 162.

37 'De Larosière Report' (n 29) 17.

38 Kern Alexander, 'Bank Capital Management and Macro-Prudential Regulation – A Law and Finance Perspective' [2012] Journal of Banking Law and Banking 331, 341.

39 BCBS, *Countercyclical Capital Buffer Proposal* (n 33) 1.

40 See, eg, 'De Larosière Report' (n 29) 17 (stating that the procyclical effects of the regulatory framework stem in particular from the interaction of risk-sensitive capital requirements and the application of the mark-to-market principle in distressed market conditions). But see George Mundstock, 'The Trouble with FASB' (2003) 28 North Carolina Journal of International Law & Commercial Regulation 813; George Mundstock, 'GAAP Did Their Job During the Economic Meltdown' (2009) 4 Florida International University Law Review 463.

forced to sell assets and pull back credit lines to raise capital, which lowered asset prices further, causing more write-downs and more capital losses. Fair value accounting enhanced the procyclical behavior of financial institutions, forcing them to sell assets at the worst moment and accelerating the falls in prices.

With respect to ratings, procyclicality refers to rating inflation in good times and massive rating downgrades when financial turmoil is triggered. On the one hand, CRAs tend to upgrade borrowers and debt instruments while the economy is rising. In the years preceding the subprime mortgage crisis, the tendency of leading CRAs to inflate ratings was actually primarily caused by conflicts of interest in the rating industry. The issuer-pays business model has widely been recognized as creating wrong incentives in the rating industry. The leading CRAs did not compete on rating quality but rather on lowering their standards in order to gain market share.

On the other hand, CRAs tend to downgrade their ratings in bad times. Massive downgrades can even trigger a financial crisis. In July 2007 the fact that the housing bubble burst could partly be attributed to sudden and massive downgrades by the leading CRAs. To a great extent, the wide and rapid distribution of information relating to rating changes contributes to homogenizing market reactions. Rating downgrades have devastating effects when the financial markets receive the same signal simultaneously. Further, rating-based regulations typically have procyclical effects that exacerbate market reactions to rating announcements.[41] The subprime mortgage debacle illustrated this trend. Due to the use of ratings in bank capital requirements, once certified CRAs started to revise their ratings for mortgage-related assets downwards, banks were required to adjust their risk-weighted capital requirements upwards.[42]

In addition, rating-based investment restrictions force a wide range of investors to follow rating changes, and because so many funds are required to hold highly rated assets, a rating downgrade can rapidly trigger financial collapse by forcing those investors to sell.[43]

At any rate, financial market regulations have a role to play as far as procyclicality is concerned.[44] Macroprudential regulations should reduce

---

[41] See, eg, 'De Larosière Report' (n 29) 17 (referring to ratings used in risk-sensitive bank capital requirements).

[42] ibid 12.

[43] Casey and Partnoy, 'Downgrade the Ratings Agencies' (n 23).

[44] BCBS, *Countercyclical Capital Buffer Proposal* (n 33) 2 (discussing a countercyclical capital buffer proposal that is a consistent instrument in the suite of macroprudential tools at the disposal of national regulators).

the potential procyclicality and systemic risk stemming from CRAs.[45] Financial market regulations are ill designed if they encourage risk-taking at the height of the boom and discourage lending when the bubble bursts.[46] Regulatory intervention should break the cycle instead of accentuating market trends. Indeed, regulatory frameworks should give the right incentives to financial institutions with a view to accumulating the necessary reserves during economic booms in order to be able to overcome financial crises.[47] Procyclical risk models enhance systemic risk by generating systemic selling or buying instead of tempering market behavior.[48] Procyclicality reinforces market instability hence regulators should focus on financial stability and macroprudential regulations.

11.3 SPILLOVER EFFECTS OF CREDIT RATING DOWNGRADES BY THE LEADING CREDIT RATING AGENCIES

We were preparing for a rainstorm and it was a tsunami.[49]

Leading CRAs' announcements may have cascading effects. Credit rating downgrades can imply a downward spiral of asset prices that may – in turn – imply further downgrades.[50] Broadly speaking, even a relatively

---

45 Sy, 'The Systemic Regulation of Credit Rating Agencies and Rated Markets' (n 30) 3.

46 Alexander and others, 'Financial Supervision and Crisis Management in the EU' (n 9) 25 (discussing the negative effects of placing procyclical risk models at the heart of capital adequacy requirements).

47 Edward I Altman and Anthony Saunders, 'An Analysis and Critique of the BIS Proposal on Capital Adequacy and Ratings' (2001) 25 Journal of Banking & Finance 25, 25ff (explaining that a well-designed regulatory system should see capital rising during periods of high profitability and falling during recessions as unexpected losses are written off against capital); Weber and Darbellay, 'The Regulatory Use of Credit Ratings in Bank Capital Requirement Regulations' (n 35) 9 (referring to the procyclicality concern with respect to bank capital requirement regulations).

48 Alexander and others, 'Financial Supervision and Crisis Management in the EU' (n 9) 25.

49 Sam Jones, 'When Junk Was Gold' *The Financial Times*, October 17, 2008 (quoting Brian Clarkson, former President and Chief Operating Officer, Moody's) (suggesting that CRAs were aware of the market repercussions of their rating downgrades; however, they did not expect such a devastating turmoil).

50 H Kent Baker and Sattar A Mansi, 'Assessing Credit Rating Agencies by Bond Issuers and Institutional Investors' (2002) 29 Journal of Business Finance

small event can trigger a rush for liquidity and produce a market gridlock in very large markets.[51] Downgraded companies that initially have a liquidity problem may end up having a solvency problem due to the spillover effects caused by the downgrades.[52]

The system-wide effects of rating downgrades depend on two components. First, the CRA that announces the downgrade has to have a certain importance in the financial markets: it has to be a system-relevant CRA. The three leading CRAs typically fulfill this criterion. Second, system-wide effects can arise only if the rating downgrade attains a certain magnitude. The importance of the downgraded borrower or debt instrument plays a crucial role.

With respect to the subprime mortgage crisis, massive rating downgrades by the leading CRAs in July 2007 immediately triggered the financial meltdown.[53] The leading CRAs caused a downward spiral of asset price falls, thereby exacerbating market trends. The valuation of securitized assets was closely linked to ratings. As leading CRAs downgraded massively, asset prices fell sharply. More sellers in the subprime mortgage market implied further falls in asset prices that implied further downgrades. And downgrades depressed prices even further.

Even financial institutions such as investment banks were surprised by the fact that the entire market collapsed so suddenly. In particular, not only the lowest securitized tranches were downgraded but also the "safest" tranches. Asset securitization failed to spread credit risk among investors even though it was its driving purpose. Credit risk ended up being concentrated in the hands of financial institutions and market participants that were unable to bear the risk. Moreover, diversification theories failed to account for the high correlations between different CDO tranches.[54] Investors had mistakenly sought a diversification of

---

& Accounting 1367, 1388 (stating that the magnitude of downgrading effects increases dramatically as the rating moves from a level above the investment grade to a level below the investment grade).

51 Alexander and others, 'Financial Supervision and Crisis Management in the EU' (n 9) 2.

52 'De Larosière Report' (n 29) 12.

53 Claire A Hill, 'Why Did Rating Agencies Do Such a Bad Job Rating Subprime Securities?' (2010) 71 University of Pittsburgh Law Review 1, 1 (stating that the leading CRAs downgraded a significant portion of the subprime mortgage-related securities that were rated too generously in the years preceding the financial meltdown).

54 See generally Adam B Ashcraft and Til Schuermann, 'Understanding the Securitization of Subprime Mortgage Credit' (2008) Federal Reserve Bank of

their portfolios by buying different securitized assets. Yet securitization could not meet the purpose of diversification when the market collapsed as a whole. Furthermore, the collapse of the subprime mortgage market had been widely considered to be a low-probability event. Under such circumstances, financial markets were predisposed to underestimate the likelihood of dramatic change.[55] These shortcomings were partly attributable to the excessive reliance on ratings in structured finance. Market participants were dependent on ratings as a quasi unique source of information. And given that the rating market was in the hands of a concentrated industry, market participants were relying on a very homogeneous source of information.

In addition, the ratings related to insurers can play a systemic role in the financial markets. Concern has been raised about counterparty risk and its systemic repercussions. The declining creditworthiness of insurers poses systemic risk. For instance, if AIG was downgraded, the assets that it has insured must be downgraded as well. This market contagion accentuates the effects of rating downgrades. Another example derives from the linkage between the rating of a monoline insurer and the rating of the structured finance products it has wrapped.[56] If leading CRAs downgrade a monoline insurer, there are further declines in the interconnected markets. From a systemic point of view, the issue is that when a monoline insurer is downgraded, all the debt instruments it has insured must be downgraded too.[57]

11.4 LEADING CREDIT RATING AGENCIES' RELUCTANCE TO DOWNGRADE

> A rating agency can't ignore how markets will react to the ratings change itself, and not just to the information that the rating change is intended to reflect.[58]

New York Staff Reports, 43 ‹http://www.newyorkfed.org/research/staff_reports/sr318.pdf› accessed January 10, 2013.

55 Michael Lewis, *The Big Short, Inside the Doomsday Machine* (WW Norton & Company 2010) 108.

56 CGFS, *Ratings in Structured Finance: What Went Wrong and What Can Be Done to Address Shortcomings* (BIS, CGFS Paper No 32, July 2008) 6. Monoline insurers are financial guarantors.

57 Michel G Crouhy, Robert A Jarrow and Stuart M Turnbull, 'The Subprime Credit Crisis of 07' (2008) SSRN eLibrary, 15 ‹http:ssrn.com/abstract=1112467› accessed January 10, 2013.

58 Hill, 'Regulating the Rating Agencies' (n 2) 70.

CRAs lack independence in their decisions to downgrade. The system-relevance of the leading CRAs partly explains why leading CRAs are slow to downgrade. Sudden and massive rating downgrades jeopardize the efforts made by central banks, regulators and governments to contain a financial crisis. As a result, leading CRAs tend to be slow to downgrade.

Indeed, a macroeconomic explanation of belated actions to downgrade results from the system-wide effects of rating announcements. Downgrades cause financial deteriorations that may drive a distressed company or a distressed country into bankruptcy. Under such circumstances, CRAs cannot predict financial shocks. They are automatically slow to downgrade, because they downgrade only when it is too late to rescue the borrower. Market over-reliance on ratings prevents the leading CRAs from being timely in their rating downgrades.

Upon downgrading, leading CRAs effectively restrict companies' and countries' access to capital markets. Rating downgrades have direct impacts on the financial markets due to market reactions to rating announcements. With respect to corporate ratings, leading CRAs are reluctant to downgrade companies if the targeted company cannot survive a downgrade. For instance, the leading CRAs had been aware of problems at Enron a relatively long time prior to downgrading its debt to junk status. Nevertheless, they did not downgrade Enron's debt timely as compared with other smaller CRAs such as Egan-Jones.[59] Leading CRAs had incentives to believe that the financial deterioration was only short term, and that if they did not downgrade, Enron would return to financial health.[60] The issue was that a timely downgrade would have automatically driven Enron into bankruptcy even if a climb back up had potentially been possible.[61]

---

[59] See further Richard Johnson, 'An Examination of Rating Agencies' Actions Around the Investment-Grade Boundary' (2003) Research Division Federal Reserve Bank of Kansas City, RWP 03-01, 3 ‹http://www.kc.frb.org/publicat/reswkpap/pdf/rwp03-01.pdf› accessed January 10, 2013 (showing empirical evidence that Egan-Jones systemically downgraded companies 21 to 70 days before its competitor Standard & Poor's).

[60] Hill, 'Regulating the Rating Agencies' (n 2) 70.

[61] Ibid 69 ("On November 8, 2001, Moody's was asked not to downgrade Enron's debt below investment grade because Enron would go bankrupt and markets would be disrupted").

11.4.1 Rating Stability

> From a regulatory perspective, rating stability is desirable to prevent procyclicality effects.[62]

Leading CRAs are aware that their rating downgrades have – under specific circumstances – systemic effects, and they are consequently reluctant to downgrade. They aim to avoid jeopardizing financial stability. Accordingly, they adopt prudent and conservative behavior.[63] Their tardiness in downgrading securities reflects this trend. Belated decisions to downgrade are frequent among the leading CRAs.

Technically, rating stability is, for instance, achieved by "through-the-cycle" methodologies and by CRAs' migration policies. First, "through-the-cycle" methodologies are defined as opposed to "point-in-time" perspectives.[64] CRAs strive to suppress the influence of short-term fluctuations in credit quality.[65] The rationale is that leading CRAs may also think that the deterioration is only short term, and that if they do not downgrade immediately, the issuer will return to financial health.[66] CRAs typically prefer to incorporate only changes with long-term implications into their ratings.[67] Second, CRAs' migration policy implies delay and

---

62 Edward I Altman and Herbert A Rijken, 'The Effects of Rating Through the Cycle on Rating Stability, Rating Timeliness and Default Prediction Performance' (2004) NYU Working Paper No FIN-04-032, 3 ‹http://archive.nyu.edu/bitstream/2451/26559/2/FIN-04-032.pdf› accessed January 10, 2013.

63 See further Frost, 'Credit Rating Agencies in Capital Markets' (n 16) 475 (arguing that rating stability is needed given the use of ratings in regulation and contracting).

64 Edward I Altman and Herbert A Rijken, 'How Rating Agencies Achieve Rating Stability' (2004) 28 Journal of Banking & Finance 2679, 2681–2682; Frost, 'Credit Rating Agencies in Capital Markets' (n 16) 475.

65 Altman and Rijken, 'How Rating Agencies Achieve Rating Stability' (n 64) 2681.

66 Hill, 'Regulating the Rating Agencies' (n 2) 69 (adding that if the leading CRAs downgrade, the downgraded company may be thrown into bankruptcy even when the deterioration would have only been short term; this happens due to the spillover effects of rating downgrades).

67 Baker and Mansi, 'Assessing Credit Rating Agencies by Bond Issuers and Institutional Investors' (n 50) 1388 (analyzing the results of a survey asking investors and issuers about rating accuracy. The survey found that a majority of investors and issuers prefer up-to-date ratings in contradistinction to CRAs which prefer conservative ratings).

spread over time with respect to the necessary changes.[68] For instance, Moody's came to the conclusion that investors want rating stability but do not favor aggressive ratings.[69]

Above all, the combination of regulatory and behavioral reliance on ratings has prevented the leading CRAs from being accurate. Instead of providing timely information, the leading CRAs are conservative in the sense that they are slow to downgrade. This phenomenon is due to the system-wide effects of rating downgrades. Indeed, rating-based regulations imply the need for stability more than timeliness.[70] As a result, leading CRAs automatically fail to provide an early warning signal of declining creditworthiness.

At any rate, the leading CRAs are aware of the devastating effects of their downgrades. As a result, they are reluctant to downgrade borrowers and debt instruments. After Enron's bankruptcy, they asserted that prior to downgrading they always have to assess whether the targeted company can survive a downgrade.[71]

The finding is that as soon as CRAs become system-relevant, they no longer have predictive power. This fact is not necessarily derived from conflicts of interest in the rating industry but simply from market over-reliance on the leading CRAs. If too many regulators and market participants rely on the same CRAs, rating downgrades by these system-relevant CRAs will have spillover effects in the financial markets.

11.4.2 "Too Big to Downgrade"

The main reason for the leading CRAs to be reluctant to downgrade may be their systemic relevance. If their rating downgrades cause disruptions to the financial markets, CRAs may refrain from downgrading in a timely fashion. They are aware of the devastating impacts their downgrades can have. Even when there is serious reason to doubt the financial strength of a borrower or a debt instrument, they have to assess the potential effect of a downgrade on the financial system prior to taking their decision.[72]

---

[68] Altman and Rijken, 'How Rating Agencies Achieve Rating Stability' (n 64) 2682.

[69] ibid.

[70] Altman and Rijken, 'The Effects of Rating Through the Cycle on Rating Stability, Rating Timeliness and Default Prediction Performance' (n 62) 3.

[71] Tim Reason, 'Not Trigger Happy, Credit-rating Firms Are Taking a Closer Look at How Corporate Credit Agreements Employ Rating Triggers' *CFO Magazine*, February 21, 2002.

[72] ibid.

Evidence shows that only smaller CRAs can afford to be more timely in their rating downgrades. For instance, smaller CRAs such as Egan-Jones Ratings Co, Kroll Bond Rating Agency Inc and Morningstar Credit Ratings LLC have gained some market share as numerous investors consider them to be more accurate than the leading CRAs.[73] Egan-Jones downgraded Lehman Brothers about six months before it went bankrupt while the three leading CRAs maintained their high ratings until a few days prior to the collapse.[74] Egan-Jones and other small competitors were also more accurate than the three leading CRAs with respect to other companies that experienced financial problems, such as AIG.[75] This trend may be explained by the fact that smaller CRAs – as opposed to systemic-relevant CRAs – can afford timely downgrades; smaller CRAs are never accused of disrupting the financial markets. In other words, the leading CRAs are "too big to downgrade." Therefore, it is not surprising that system-relevant CRAs downgrade borrowers and debt instruments only when it is too late.

Further, the recent Greek debt crisis illustrates the systemic relevance of the leading CRAs. At the height of the Greek debt crisis, Moody's contented itself with conducting a review of Greece.[76] At the time of the Greek rescue, Moody's did not downgrade Greek bonds.[77] Moody's was not able to act independently of the repercussions of its rating downgrades on the European debt crisis.

In a time of crisis, financial market regulators need to reassure investors in order to prevent the problem from escalating. It does not take much to stir up the financial markets.[78] The mere threat of downgrading coming from a leading CRA may put financial markets under intense

---

[73] See, eg, Shorter and Seitzinger, 'Credit Rating Agencies and Their Regulation' (n 1) 2; Janet Morrissey, 'Disillusioned Advisers Eye Smaller Rating Firms; Interest in Subscriber-Based Raters Grows at the Expense of the Big Three Agencies' *Investment News*, February 15, 2009; Al Yoon and Jeannette Neumann, 'S&P Moves to Revamp Its CMBS Rating System' *Wall Street Journal*, June 4, 2012.

[74] Beat Balzli and Frank Hornig, 'Exacerbating the Crisis, The Power of Rating Agencies' *Spiegel Online*, May 6, 2009 (translated from the German by Christopher Sultan).

[75] Balzli and Hornig, 'Exacerbating the Crisis' (n 74).

[76] Justin Carrigan, 'Greece May Have Rating Lowered to Junk, Moody's Says' *Bloomberg BusinessWeek*, May 10, 2010 (reporting that, in May 2010, Moody's was conducting a review of Greek debt, but had not yet downgraded it).

[77] ibid.

[78] Michael Kröger, 'Rampant Skepticism, Aid for Greece Hasn't Stopped Euro's Slide' *Spiegel Online*, June 5, 2010.

pressure. For this reason, the three leading CRAs may sometimes refrain from downgrading so that they do not jeopardize the stability of the financial markets.

12. Regulatory response to the systemic issue

12.1 US AND EU REGULATORY REFORMS

12.1.1 Reducing Over-reliance on Credit Ratings

The systemic importance of credit ratings results from over-reliance on the ratings of the Big Three. The key objective of reforms consists of moving away from regulatory references to ratings and behavioral reliance.

From a regulatory perspective, the main problem of pre-crisis regulations is that they primarily focused on individual market participants rather than the financial system as a whole. In particular, Basel II embodied the failure of regulators to incorporate systemic risks into bank capital requirements.[1] Financial reforms post-crisis tend to shift to macroprudential regulation.[2] Accordingly, Basel III introduced countercyclical capital buffers but it has not yet proposed a new model to withdraw the regulatory use of ratings from capital requirement regulations.

With respect to CRA reforms, the trend to eliminate the use of ratings for regulatory purposes has been initiated. In the US, the Dodd-Frank Act of 2010 has acknowledged that rating-based regulations are inconsistent with the proper functioning of market forces in the rating industry. The Act removed regulatory references to ratings from financial market regulations.[3] This step is a substantial measure designed to reduce over-reliance on ratings.

Another regulatory trend consists of increasing the number of certified CRAs. The Credit Rating Agency Reform Act of 2006 aimed to improve rating quality by fostering accountability, transparency and competition

---

[1] Kern Alexander, 'Bank Capital Management and Macro-Prudential Regulation – A Law and Finance Perspective' [2012] Journal of Banking Law and Banking 331, 336.

[2] ibid 331.

[3] Dodd-Frank Wall Street Reform and Consumer Protection Act of 2010, HR 4173, 111th Congress, 2nd Session (2010) (Dodd-Frank Act) Sec 939–939A.

in the rating industry.[4] The Securities and Exchange Commission (SEC) designated more NRSROs in order to enhance competition among them. The rating industry went up to ten registered NRSROs as of December 2012.[5] Although the Dodd-Frank Act of 2010 introduced the most sweeping changes to the rating industry, it no longer seems to pursue this direction. From 2010 onwards, the US has not shown any regulatory will to continue to increase the number of NRSROs apart from granting the registration of HR de México SA de CV in November 2012. The lessons drawn from the Credit Rating Agency Reform Act of 2006 best explain why competition in the rating industry was an unpopular target post-crisis. In the run-up to the subprime mortgage crisis, CRAs competed more on gaining market share by lowering rating standards rather than enhancing rating quality. "Rating shopping" and "rating inflation" became serious problems. As a consequence, the Dodd-Frank Act does not state competition as an objective and the number of NRSROs will be unlikely to explode in the near future.

The EU experience also deserves particular attention. Step two of the CRA Regulation aims to address topics that were not included in the Regulation of 2009, such as over-reliance on credit ratings and lack of competition.[6] With respect to the regulatory use of ratings, EU policy-makers have been slower to react than US policymakers, but the EU definitely shares US concern against rating-based regulations.

Competition is a clear target in the EU.[7] The argument that is probably the most successful in the EU is that increasing the number of CRAs would reduce the significant market power of Moody's and Standard & Poor's. The reason why competition in the rating industry is such a popular topic is that the EU experienced the downside of being subject to the market power of the Big Three in the wake of the euro debt crisis.

---

4 Credit Rating Agency Reform Act of 2006, S 3850, 109th Congress (2006) preamble and Sec 2(5).

5 See further Staff of the SEC, '2012 Summary Report of Commission Staff's Examinations of Each Nationally Recognized Statistical Rating Organization, As Required by Section 15E(p)(3)(C) of the Securities Exchange Act of 1934' (November 2012) 4.

6 EU Commission, 'Public consultation on credit rating agencies' (November 5, 2010) 1–28.

7 John Ryan, 'The Negative Impact of Credit Rating Agencies and Proposals for Better Regulation' (2012) SWP Working Paper FG 1, 2012/No 1, 17 ‹http://www.swp-berlin.org/fileadmin/contents/products/arbeitspapiere/The_Negative_Impact_of_Credit_Rating_Agencies_KS.pdf› accessed January 10, 2013.

The problems identified were high concentration in the rating market, high barriers to entry and lack of comparability of ratings.[8]

Enhancing competition is a key objective of the regulatory proposal of November 2011. Related topics are the proposed amendments with respect to comparability of ratings and transparency. The level of competition in the rating industry will benefit from several proposals as follows. CRAs shall submit rating information to ESMA, which will publish ratings on a European Rating Index.[9] This would allow investors to compare ratings. In addition, ESMA is empowered to establish a harmonized rating scale.[10] This proposed amendment would also enhance competition among CRAs by facilitating the comparability of ratings. Further, fees charged by CRAs should be non-discriminatory and not based on any form of contingency.[11] Such a change would prevent CRAs from succumbing to issuer pressures in order to maximize market share and revenue. Last, CRAs should annually disclose a list of fees and their pricing policy to ESMA.[12] This proposal would improve transparency.

Apart from that, the EU wishes to explore and assess the feasibility of the establishment of an independent European CRA.[13] As of December 2012 there are 19 registered CRAs and one certified CRA in the EU.[14] With a view to anticipating potential attempts to undermine competition, the EU has already expressed concerns about the likelihood of future consolidation in the CRA market.[15] If the Big Three try to merge with smaller CRAs, they might jeopardize European efforts to encourage the presence of more players.

12.1.2 Regulating Sovereign Debt Ratings

The segment of sovereign debt ratings has recently given rise to concern due to downgrades related to the euro debt crisis especially.

---

[8] EU Commission, 'Proposal for a Regulation amending Regulation (EC) No 1060/2009 on credit rating agencies' COM (2011) 747 final ('Proposal for a CRA III Regulation') explanatory memorandum.

[9] ibid art 11a.

[10] ibid art 21(4a).

[11] ibid Annex I, Sec B, point 3a.

[12] ibid Annex 1, Sec 2, Part II, points 2(a) and 2(aa).

[13] ibid explanatory memorandum.

[14] Felix Flinterman, 'ESMA: The European Supervisor of Credit Rating Agencies' in Jan Kleineman and Lars Gorton (eds), *Credit Rating Agencies* (Stockholm Centre for Commercial Law, forthcoming 2013).

[15] 'Proposal for a CRA III' (n 8) preamble (17).

In the US, sovereign ratings have not been subject to stringent criticism. US Treasury bonds are highly rated. In the history of the US, hitherto one single event has destabilized the everlasting era of triple-A ratings. This occurred in August 2011 when Standard & Poor's downgraded the US debt from AAA to AA+. The financial markets momentarily oscillated, but market participants discredited the rating announcement and Treasury bonds' interest rates did not skyrocket.[16] Not surprisingly, the US reform has not paid significant attention to the segment of sovereign debt ratings.

In the EU, the regulation of sovereign debt ratings is part of step two of the CRA reform.[17] In a non-legislative resolution, the EU Parliament acknowledged that the downgrade of sovereign ratings may produce a systemic impact.[18] The Parliament also noted that recent developments in the euro crisis highlight the significant role of sovereign ratings and the problem of procyclicality in the use of ratings for regulatory purposes.[19] Moreover, the Parliament asked the rating industry to clarify which methodology and judgments are used to calibrate sovereign debt ratings.[20] Information on sovereigns should be more easily available in the public domain so that certain market players are able to rely on their own judgment to assess sovereign credit risk.[21] However, the November 2011 proposal for an amendment of the CRA Regulation does not substantially reform the segment of sovereign ratings in particular. This proposal merely refers to sovereign ratings in the part related to the results of consultation and impact assessments, stating that CRAs should disclose specific information on certain types of ratings including sovereign ratings.[22] Therefore, the reform of sovereign ratings is a regulatory project of the EU but has not yet moved forward. Such a reform would definitely consider the systemic importance of the ratings of the Big Three. Nevertheless, in January 2013 the EU Parliament approved new rules on when and how CRAs may rate state debts. CRAs will have to set

---

[16] Aline Darbellay and Frank Partnoy, 'Agences de notation et conflits d'intérêts' (2012) 105 Revue d'économie financière 309, 310, 313.

[17] EU Commission, 'Public consultation on credit rating agencies' (n 6) 1–28.

[18] European Parliament, 'Resolution of 8 June 2011 on credit rating agencies: future perspectives' (2010/2302(INI)) para 40.

[19] ibid preamble (K).

[20] ibid para 35.

[21] ibid para 38.

[22] 'Proposal for a CRA III' (n 8) 4.

up a calendar indicating when they will rate Member States.[23] To avoid market disruption, these ratings will only be published after the close of business and at least one hour before the opening of trading venues in the EU.[24] These new rules illustrate the willingness of the EU to deeply regulate rating activities.

12.1.3 Comparing the US and EU Approaches

The US and the EU experienced the over-reliance on credit ratings in different ways. While the three leading CRAs are based in the US, the EU was helpless in monitoring them in the run-up to the 2007–2009 financial crisis. The EU reacted in adopting a sweeping reform. The US reform does not seem to be as comprehensive at first sight, but its effects on CRAs are likely substantial.[25]

This study argues that the two regulatory responses have a great deal of similarities. In terms of rating-based regulations, both the US and EU regulators agree that it is crucial to reduce the regulatory reliance on CRAs. The US goes even further than the EU by removing regulatory references to ratings without mentioning alternatives. In so doing, the US took a bold step in order to restore market forces in the rating industry. This study argues that moving away from the regulatory use of ratings is a very efficient way to encourage competition and decrease the excessive market power of the Big Three.

As far as the number of certified CRAs is concerned, the two frameworks have chosen a different approach. In the US, there are ten NRSROs as of December 2012 and there is no regulatory willingness to increase this number. In the EU, there are 19 registered CRAs and one certified CRA as of December 2012. With respect to competition, this illustrates the EU desire that newly established CRAs compete with the Big Three. However, the number of CRAs does not mean that they automatically take market share from the Big Three. Moreover, even if new entrants issue numerous ratings, it does not imply that they are able to generate a significant part of rating revenue. Last, it would be

---

23 EU Commission, 'Memo, Statement by Commissioner Michel Barnier following the vote in the European Parliament on new European rules to regulate credit rating agencies' (Brussels, January 16, 2013).

24 ibid.

25 Aline Darbellay, 'Competition and Credit Rating Agencies' in Jan Kleineman and Lars Gorton (eds), *Credit Rating Agencies* (Stockholm Centre for Commercial Law, forthcoming 2013).

important for the EU to draw lessons from the US experience arising from the designation of more NRSROs.

With respect to sovereign ratings, this specific segment is a regulatory concern in the EU but not in the US. This fact is best explained by the negative effects of rating downgrades on the euro debt crisis. EU countries were downgraded several times to a significant extent by the leading CRAs. However, the US did not experience devastating repercussions in the aftermath of the slight downgrade of its Treasury bonds by Standard & Poor's.

In a nutshell, the financial reforms are expected to decrease the importance of the Big Three. If they achieve their goal, the ratings of the Big Three will likely lose their systemic relevance in the future. Fewer market participants would follow the announcements of the same CRAs and market reactions to significant events would be more diverse. Such a trend would be beneficial to the stability of the financial markets.

12.2 PRELIMINARY CONCLUSION

Over-reliance on credit ratings results in spillover effects following rating downgrades. For instance, the systemic relevance of the leading CRAs caused adverse consequences in relation to the European debt crisis.

The devastating effects of rating downgrades jeopardize the independence of system-relevant CRAs as financial information providers. Prior to downgrading, CRAs have no choice but to assess the repercussions of a downgrade on the financial markets. Accordingly, the leading CRAs tend to be reluctant to downgrade. This situation is detrimental to the rating market because financial information cannot be released freely. In other words, the systemic importance of ratings is a source of disruption in the market for financial information.

In order to understand the root of the problem, it is worth recalling the factors contributing to the systemic relevance of CRAs. First and foremost, regulatory and behavioral reliance on credit ratings have increased the importance of the leading CRAs. Furthermore, high concentration in the rating industry ensures that only a few leading CRAs enjoy significant market power. Last, the public availability of ratings allows rating announcements to spread rapidly among market participants. In the aftermath of rating announcements, market behavior tends to be homogeneous. Market participants generally react to rating information following the same pattern. This phenomenon is regrettable because financial markets should rather reflect a diversity of opinions and approaches rather than homogeneous reactions.

It is therefore not surprising that the ongoing monitoring of ratings gives rise to the most significant concerns in the industry. CRAs are not in a position to provide investors with valuable information if they have to consider the effects of their rating actions prior to downgrading. If initial ratings are not subject to these issues, the timeliness and the accuracy of rating reviews are seriously affected by the systemic effects of rating announcements.

As a consequence, ratings are procyclical and are able to exacerbate a financial crisis. This situation is particularly threatening when regulatory requirements are based on ratings. Moreover, the leading CRAs are reluctant to downgrade and do not provide investors with valuable information. For instance, the leading CRAs may be regarded as "too big to downgrade" when they do not act given the systemic repercussions that their downgrades would have on the financial markets.

Finally, more competition in the rating industry is expected to improve the current situation. Both the US and EU reforms are following this path even though the US reform did not specifically state competition as an objective. Above all, moving away from regulatory reliance on ratings is a priority both in the US and in the EU. This process may restore competitive incentives in the rating industry. Excessive market power of the leading CRAs should be reduced in proportion to the informational value of their ratings. Smaller CRAs and alternatives to ratings should be able to compete with the leading CRAs so that the market for information reflects the diversity of opinions in financial markets. The systemic importance of ratings would not be an issue if market forces worked properly in the rating industry. Therefore, it is positive that the US and EU regulatory reforms acknowledged the interplay between market forces and regulatory intervention.

PART 5

Trends and outlook

13. Restoring competition in the credit rating industry

13.1 CONCERNS ABOUT THE LEVEL OF COMPETITION

13.1.1 Distortions of Competition among Leading Credit Rating Agencies

> We are meeting with your group this week to discuss adjusting criteria for rating CDOs of real estate assets this week because of the ongoing threat of losing deals. […] Lose the CDO and lose the base business – a self reinforcing loop.[1]

Concerns have been raised about the level of competition among CRAs. Some scholars and market participants contend that competition still exists despite the oligopoly of the Big Three.[2] Other scholars argue that there is insufficient competition since well-established CRAs keep their market shares despite their poor rating performance.[3] Some refer to an absence of competition in the rating industry.[4] Others suggest that the

---

[1] Sewell Chan, 'Documents Show Internal Qualms at Rating Agencies' *The New York Times*, April 22, 2010 (quoting Professor Lawrence J White, NYU Stern School of Business). See also Staff of the SEC, 'Summary Report of Issues Identified in the Commission Staff's Examinations of Select Credit Rating Agencies' (July 2008) 26 (quoting a Standard & Poor's employee).

[2] They mainly argue that CRAs compete on prices.

[3] Aline Darbellay, 'Competition and Credit Rating Agencies' in Jan Kleineman and Lars Gorton (eds), *Credit Rating Agencies* (Stockholm Centre for Commercial Law, forthcoming 2013).

[4] See, eg, 'Assessing the Current Oversight and Operation of Credit Rating Agencies: Hearing Before the Senate Committee on Banking, Housing and Urban Affairs' (2006) 109th Congress, S Hrg 109997 (statement of Glenn L Reynolds, Chief Executive Officer, CreditSights) 8 (specifically referring to the Moody's and Standard & Poor's duopoly).

impact of increased competition would be problematic.[5] Few assert that there is competition, yet competition affects ratings and should not be a regulatory target.[6] Disparate opinions exist concerning the level of and need for competition, and researchers have recently shown an increased interest in the topic. This academic work focuses on the causes and consequences of the competitive concerns in the rating industry.

13.1.1.1 Oligopolistic market structure

CRAs operate in an oligopolistic market that offers limited incentives to compete on quality ratings.[7] Since the first CRA was founded at the beginning of the twentieth century, the same three leaders – Moody's, Standard & Poor's and Fitch – have dominated the industry.

The question arises as to whether CRAs are driven by private market forces. As regards market structure, there is no doubt that the rating industry is heavily concentrated. Of the Big Three, the most dominant CRAs are Moody's and Standard & Poor's since they controlled 83 percent of the US rating market as of December 31, 2011.[8] Some speak of a duopoly of these two CRAs.[9] The third leading CRA Fitch is also significant, hence reference to an oligopoly.[10] As of December 31, 2011,

---

[5] John C Coffee Jr, 'Ratings Reform: the Good, the Bad, and the Ugly' (2011) 1 Harvard Business Law Review 231, 234.

[6] Bo Becker and Todd Milbourn, 'How Did Increased Competition Affect Credit Ratings?' (2011) 101 Journal of Financial Economics 493, 493–514. See also Nelson Camanho, Pragyan Deb and Zijun Liu, 'Credit Rating and Competition' (2012) SSRN eLibrary, 30 ‹http:ssrn.com/abstract=1573035› accessed January 10, 2013 (arguing that competition in the rating industry tends to amplify CRAs' lax behavior and reduce total welfare).

[7] EU Commission, 'Proposal for a Regulation on Credit Rating Agencies' COM (2008) 704 final, explanatory memorandum.

[8] Staff of the SEC, '2012 Summary Report of Commission Staff's Examinations of Each Nationally Recognized Statistical Rating Organization, As Required by Section 15E(p)(3)(C) of the Securities Exchange Act of 1934' (November 2012) 7.

[9] See generally Credit Rating Agency Reform Act of 2006, S 3850, 109th Congress (2006) Sec 2(5) (stating that the two largest CRAs – Moody's and Standard & Poor's – serve the vast majority of the market). See, eg, 'Assessing the Current Oversight and Operation of Credit Rating Agencies' (statement of Glenn L Reynolds, Chief Executive Officer, CreditSights) (n 4) 8.

[10] John Flood, 'Rating, Dating, and the Informal Regulation and the Formal Ordering of Financial Transactions: Securitisations and Credit Rating Agencies' in Michael B Likosky (ed), *Privatising Development: Transnational Law, Infrastructure and Human Rights* (Martinus Nijhoff Publishers 2005) 161 (describing the three leading CRAs as the only CRAs of global reach); Carol Ann Frost,

Moody's, Standard & Poor's and Fitch accounted for 96 percent of all outstanding ratings in the US.[11] The situation of high concentration has barely evolved post-crisis since the number reported in 2010 was 97 percent of all ratings for the Big Three, ie only 1 percent higher than a year later.[12] Further, there are only five global CRAs if we add AM Best and DBRS to the three leading CRAs.

Nevertheless, the high level of concentration in the rating industry is not sufficient to state that CRAs are immune to competitive forces. It is also important to highlight the impact of high concentration on the market behavior of the leading CRAs. Above all, regulations created high barriers to entering the industry, thereby shielding CRAs from competition. The leading CRAs became more powerful and gained market dominance due to regulatory reasons. Certified CRAs may, as a result, have little incentive to be responsive to investors' needs because they can take advantage of an oligopolistic market structure.[13]

Relevant with respect to competition is the price of credit ratings in comparison to their informational value. Some researchers contend that the rating industry is competitive because rating prices are low in proportion to the value of the markets in which they operate. However, CRAs are excessively profitable compared to the value of the financial information that they provide to the markets. Therefore, competition is not about the level of rating prices in absolute terms, but about the level of rating prices as compared with the value of information. In a competitive market, information of little value should not be sold even at a discount. Absence of competition would imply that CRAs could sell their ratings even if they do not provide valuable information.

In addition, as a signal of anticompetitive practices it is worth mentioning that CRA profit margins are very high.[14] Profit margins at the

---

'Credit Rating Agencies in Capital Markets: A Review of Research Evidence on Selected Criticisms of the Agencies' (2007) 22 Journal of Accounting, Auditing & Finance 469, 471 (referring to the three leading CRAs as the most influential in the financial markets).

[11] Staff of the SEC, 'Summary Report 2012' (n 8) 7.

[12] ibid.

[13] William H Beaver, Catherine Shakespeare and Mark T Soliman, 'Differential Properties in the Ratings of Certified Versus Non-certified Bond-rating Agencies' (2006) 42 Journal of Accounting and Economics 303, 305 (adding that Moody's unresponsiveness to investors' needs could simply be due to the lack of competition in the rating industry).

[14] Frank Partnoy, 'The Siskel and Ebert of Financial Markets?: Two Thumbs Down for the Credit Rating Agencies' (1999) 77 Washington University Law Quarterly 619, 655; David Gillen, 'In Ratings Agencies, Investors Still Trust' *The*

leading CRAs climbed as structured finance revenues rose. Leading up to the subprime mortgage crisis, Moody's enjoyed profit margins far outpacing those of the mightiest companies including Microsoft and Exxon.[15] From 2000 to 2007, Moody's documents revealed operating margins averaging 53 percent, whereas in 2007 Microsoft and Exxon had margins of 36 and 17 percent respectively.[16]

13.1.1.2 Credit rating agencies in the run-up to the subprime mortgage crisis

> The focus of Moody's shifted from protecting investors to being a marketing-driven organization. [...] Management's focus increasingly turned to maximizing revenues.[17]

Distortions of competition in the credit rating industry were particularly striking during the years preceding the subprime mortgage crisis. From 2000 through 2007, Moody's effectively behaved as a triple-A factory; in this period of time, the number one in the industry effectively attributed its triple-A rating to 42,625 RMBS.[18] In 2006, 869 billion US dollars' worth of mortgage-related securities were rated triple-A by Moody's,

---

New York Times, June 5, 2009 (quoting David Einhorn, hedge fund manager, Greenlight Capital: "As a classic oligopolist, Moody's earns exceedingly high margins while paying only the needed lip service to product quality").

[15] Gretchen Morgenson, 'Debt Watchdogs: Tamed or Caught Napping?' *The New York Times*, December 7, 2008.

[16] ibid. See also 'Wall Street and the Financial Crisis: The Role of Credit Rating Agencies, Hearing Before the Permanent Subcommittee on Investigations of the Senate Committee on Homeland Security and Governmental Affairs' (April 23, 2010) (memorandum of Senator Carl Levin, Subcommittee Chairman and Senator Tom Coburn, Ranking Member) Exhibit 1a.

[17] Morgenson, 'Debt Watchdogs' (n 15) (quoting Jerome S Fons, former Managing Director, Moody's).

[18] 'Credibility of Credit Ratings, the Investment Decisions Made Based on those Ratings, and the Financial Crisis, Hearings & Testimony Before the FCIC' (June 2, 2010) (opening remarks of Phil Angelides, Chairman, FCIC) 1 (adding that in 2006, Moody's put the triple-A label on 9,029 MBS, ie more than 30 a day). See also Beat Balzli and Frank Hornig, 'Exacerbating the Crisis, The Power of Rating Agencies' *Spiegel Online*, May 6, 2009 (translated from the German by Christopher Sultan) (describing the leading CRAs in the years preceding the subprime mortgage crisis as "profit machines").

83 percent of which went on to be downgraded within six months.[19] Under no circumstances could such unprecedented rating activity – followed by such massive rating downgrades – be consistent with a competitive market in financial information.

The rating industry experienced the downside of the use of ratings in a great number of financial market regulations. The poor performance of structured finance ratings was primarily the consequence of focusing on maintaining and increasing revenue and market share instead of competing on rating quality.[20] There had been a complete culture change at the leading CRAs.[21] Before Moody's' "obsession" with gaining market share, a rating analyst's worst fear was to contribute to a wrong rating assessment and damage Moody's' reputation; in the aftermath of the culture change at Moody's an analyst's worst fear was to jeopardize Moody's' market share, impair Moody's revenue and be fired.[22] In the run-up to the financial crisis, CRAs were overwhelmed by the significant number of transactions to rate.[23] They were not concerned with allocating sufficient resources to rate deals properly.[24] They were attracted by significant issuers' fees and hence had no incentive to refuse to rate any deals.

Pressure to inflate ratings was exerted at two levels. The leading CRAs were under pressure from their clients, ie bankers and issuers, and junior CRA employees from their seniors.[25] On the one hand, "rating shopping"

---

[19] 'Credibility of Credit Ratings' (n 18) (opening remarks of Phil Angelides, Chairman, FCIC) 1. See also Gretchen Morgenson and Louise Story, 'Rating Agency Data Aided Wall Street in Deals' *The New York Times*, April 23, 2010.

[20] 'Credibility of Credit Ratings' (n 18) (testimony of Eric Kolchinsky, former Managing Director, Moody's) 3.

[21] Sam Jones, 'When Junk Was Gold' *The Financial Times*, October 17, 2008 (arguing that the culture change at Moody's occurred when the company went public in 2000).

[22] 'Credibility of Credit Ratings' (n 18) (testimony of Mark Froeba, former Moody's employee) 4.

[23] Morgenson and Story, 'Rating Agency Data Aided Wall Street in Deals' (n 19) (quoting a former Moody's employee).

[24] 'Credibility of Credit Ratings' (n 18) (testimony of Eric Kolchinsky, former Managing Director, Moody's) 4 (stating that despite the increasing number of deals and their increasing complexity, Moody's group involved in rating synthetic CDOs did not receive adequate resources).

[25] Staff of the SEC, 'Summary Report 2008' (n 1) 12. See also Claire A Hill, 'Who Were the Villains in the Subprime Crisis, and Why it Matters' (2010) 4 Entrepreneurial Business Law Journal 323, 339; 'Credibility of Credit Ratings' (n 18) (testimony of Mark Froeba, former Moody's employee) 7 ("[Moody's senior management] used intimidation to create a docile population of analysts

implied that if a CRA said no to a transaction investment bankers could easily take their business to another CRA and obtain the desired triple-A rating.[26] Given the threat of losing business to a competitor, CRA unwillingness to say no to transactions grew.[27] On the other hand, CRA employees had to explain and defend every missed deal to their superiors.[28] Although no explicit directives dictated lower rating standards, employees felt pressured to issue high ratings.[29] The "cultural revolution" that senior managements imposed on rating analysts corrupted the rating analysis.[30] Rating quality decreased insofar as rating models were adapted to inflate ratings.[31]

13.1.1.3 Deformation of incentives in the credit rating industry

> Now, it was a slippery slope, what happened in 2004 and 2005 with respect to subordinated tranches is that our competition, Fitch and S&P, went nuts. Everything was investment grade. It didn't really matter. We tried to alert the market. We said we're not rating it. This stuff isn't investment grade. No one cared because the machine just kept going.[32]

The lack of competition in the credit rating industry is associated with misaligned incentives. In modern financial markets, rating quality may not be as high as would be the case if the rating industry were more

---

afraid to upset investment bankers and ready to cooperate to the maximum extent possible").

[26] ibid (testimony of Eric Kolchinsky, former Managing Director, Moody's) 3 (explaining that he only said no to one questionable deal, and that did not stop the transaction since the banker enlisted two other CRAs and obtained two triple-A ratings).

[27] ibid (testimony of Richard Michalek, former Moody's employee) 2.

[28] ibid (testimony of Eric Kolchinsky, former Managing Director, Moody's) 3.

[29] ibid.

[30] ibid (testimony of Mark Froeba, former Moody's employee) 18.

[31] ibid (adding that it would be interesting to observe correlations between material methodological changes and revenue and market share pressures; in his opinion, Moody's responded to revenue and market share pressures by initiating major methodological changes).

[32] 'Credit Rating Agencies and the Financial Crisis: Hearing Before the House Committee on Oversight and Government Reform' (2008) 110th Congress 2nd Session, HR Serial No 110-155, 161 (quoting Raymond W McDaniel, Chairman and Chief Executive Officer, Moody's).

competitive.[33] With respect to the subprime mortgage market, inaccuracies were observed in the form of inflated ratings. For instance, an extreme example was the case of Moody's: Moody's was eager to find a way for the novel instruments to be rated triple-A; when Moody's discovered flaws in its rating models, it adjusted the models so that the instruments could maintain their high ratings.[34] Moody's would not have maintained inflated ratings if its behavior had been driven by competitive market forces. CRAs should face reputational costs when rating so that they are incentivized to generate accurate and timely information.

The US Federal Crisis Inquiry Commission (FCIC) referred to the behavior of Moody's and Standard & Poor's in the years preceding the subprime mortgage crisis as the consequence of competitive pressures.[35] Critics contend that CRAs inevitably compete for a share in the market, either on price or by lowering their rating standards to attract their clients.[36] However, the problem did not result from competition in general but from ill-conceived competition. Competitive pressures can be counterproductive if they create wrong incentives.

One source of a lack of competition among leading CRAs comes from the payment structure. Since the 1970s, the leading CRAs have increasingly been paid by issuers and not investors. The resulting conflicts of interest jeopardize rating quality. CRAs have less need to be responsible to investors. Issuer-paid CRAs tend to rate as high as possible to generate issuers' fees but in so doing disregard investors' interests.

The most important aspect to address is that regulation can distort competition. Rating-based regulations prevent reputational constraints from playing their disciplining role in the rating industry. Regulatory reliance on credit ratings artificially gives recognition to a few certified CRAs. This situation is best explained by the fact that rating-based regulations create incentives for CRAs to compete to lower rating standards in order to issue higher ratings instead of maximizing rating

---

[33] Claire A Hill, 'Regulating the Rating Agencies' (2004) 82 Washington University Law Quarterly 43, 44 (proposing to address the problem with regulation).

[34] Claire A Hill, 'Why Did Rating Agencies Do Such a Bad Job Rating Subprime Securities?' (2010) 71 University of Pittsburgh Law Review 1, 9.

[35] 'Wall Street and the Financial Crisis' (n 16) Exhibits, 1–4.

[36] Aline Van Duyn, 'Reform of Rating Agencies Poses Dilemma' *The Financial Times*, June 10, 2010 (quoting Warren E Buffet, Chairman and Chief Executive Officer, Berkshire Hathaway Inc, who adds that a monopoly might be the best answer since one CRA would not need to compete).

quality. CRAs sell "regulatory licenses."[37] Over the past decades certified CRAs have played a hybrid gatekeeper role, an unusual cross between government and private providers of rating services.[38] As long as credit ratings are used in regulations, competition has counterproductive effects. It is thus not surprising that the Credit Rating Agency Reform Act of 2006 created wrong incentives in the rating industry even though its primary objective was to enhance competition among CRAs.[39] Recognizing too many CRAs to use them for regulatory purposes can lead to a "race to the bottom" in the sense that certified CRAs compete amongst themselves to lower rating standards instead of focusing on rating quality. As a consequence, rating-based regulations and competition are not compatible.

As noted above, post-crisis financial reforms have taken a significant step toward removing rating-based regulations. CRAs will – in the future – lose their quasi-governmental status and remain basically private actors. The scope of the functions performed by CRAs will be newly defined by market participants. Therefore, competition issues will arise from a different angle in the rating industry. The need for a competitive environment should now become a clear target. Market forces will have to play their disciplining role with respect to rating services. The essential questions are not whether competition is required but what competition means with respect to CRAs, and what kind of competition will meet investors' needs.

13.1.2 Concept of Competition with Respect to Credit Rating Agencies

> The real problem is not that the market underweights rating quality but rather that in some sectors it actually penalizes rating quality. It turns out that rating quality has surprisingly few friends: issuers want high ratings; investors don't want rating downgrades; short-sighted bankers labor short-sightedly to game the rating agencies.[40]

---

[37] Partnoy, 'The Siskel and Ebert of Financial Markets?' (n 14) 623. See further FSF, *Report of the Financial Stability Forum on Enhancing Market and Institutional Resilience* (April 2008) 39 (describing certified ratings as "official seals of approval").

[38] David Segal, 'Debt Raters Avoid Overhaul After Crisis' *New York Times*, December 8, 2009 (describing CRAs as "one of capitalism's strangest hybrids: profit-making companies that perform what is essentially a regulatory role").

[39] Credit Rating Agency Reform Act, preamble and Sec 2(5).

[40] 'Credit Rating Agencies and the Financial Crisis' (n 32) 2 (quoting Raymond W McDaniel, Chairman and Chief Executive Officer, Moody's).

Competition is incentive driven. Ideally its presence creates incentives for market participants to lower prices, to innovate or to provide services of high quality. Competitive markets are generally deemed to yield economic benefits such as economic welfare, economic freedom or economic efficiency.[41] Overall, competition is associated with the proper functioning of private market forces. In the absence of competition, CRAs would have no incentive to provide accurate credit ratings.

There are three levels relevant to competition in the rating industry. First, competition in the market for information takes CRAs into account in contradistinction to other gatekeepers. Second, competition in the market for ratings accounts for certified CRAs as compared with non-certified CRAs, and the leading CRAs as compared with smaller CRAs. Third, competition in the market for certified ratings takes into account the counterproductive effects of competition among certified CRAs; competing for increasing market share and revenue may lead to a "race to the bottom" in the presence of rating-based regulations.

Broadly speaking, the rating industry is highly concentrated. In general, oligopolistic structures give incumbents the power to charge monopoly prices and get higher profits.[42] Some economists contend that there is enough competition in the rating industry because CRAs do not charge monopoly prices despite the presence of an oligopoly. Competition was traditionally understood in the narrow meaning of price competition. However, in the modern world, competition among CRAs does not only relate to price fixing.[43] Over the last few decades the scope of competition has expanded beyond its initial meaning for it is crucial that CRAs compete on rating quality. Therefore, it is important to define competition in terms of not only price but also quality competition.[44]

In the rating industry the negative impacts of the oligopoly are derived from rating inaccuracies in the sense that leading CRAs have no incentive to predict financial debacles. Competition pressures are counterproductive if CRAs engage in a "race to the bottom." Further,

---

41 Giorgio Monti, *EC Competition Law* (Cambridge University Press 2007) 23–25, 44–45.

42 See further Lawrence J White, 'The Growing Influence of Economics and Economists on Antitrust: An Extended Discussion' (2008) NYU Center for Law and Economics Working Paper No 08-07, 14.

43 Thomas E Kauper, 'Oligopoly: Facilitating Practices and Plus Factors' in Barry E Hawk (ed), *Annual Proceedings of the Fordham Competition Law Institute, International Antitrust Law & Policy* (Juris Publishing, Inc 2008) 751–756.

44 See further Coffee Jr, 'Ratings Reform' (n 5) 235.

conflicts of interest impair the independence of the leading CRAs. The lack of competitive incentives is especially striking in the issuer-pays business model. "Rating shopping" jeopardizes the issuance of independent ratings. To make matters worse, the ratings of leading CRAs have such a substantial effect on the financial markets that they cannot afford to downgrade on a timely basis. This trend is referred to as the systemic relevance of the leading CRAs. CRAs cannot rate independently of the repercussions of their rating downgrades on the financial system.

In addition, a competitive rating market requires as few barriers to entry as possible, as well as no "barriers to exit" in the sense that CRAs not providing valuable information should not survive.[45]

Competition also means that market participants purchase ratings because of their additional value, ie, if the expected benefit of the rating minus the actual cost of the rating is positive as well as greater than the expected benefit of an independent investigation minus the actual cost of such an investigation.[46] Nevertheless, given the nature of information as a public good it is challenging to extract investors' fees.[47]

Moreover, a competitive rating market signifies that there are divergent opinions, and that CRAs do not act in a homogeneous way. Financial information should be available to market participants on a competitive basis.

Last but not least, reputational constraints are at the core of a competitive rating market. The "reputational capital" view of ratings is indeed consistent with the need for competition in the rating industry.[48] Competition means that CRAs' reputational capital is at stake in the sense that CRAs would lose more from giving inaccurate ratings than they would gain in receiving higher fees.[49] The reputational motivation should be sufficient to create incentives for CRAs to provide accurate ratings.[50] The dominant view of rating quality is that a well-functioning reputation mechanism will give CRAs optimum incentives for producing

---

45 Partnoy, 'The Siskel and Ebert of Financial Markets?' (n 14) 639.

46 ibid 629.

47 Stéphane Rousseau, 'Regulating Credit Rating Agencies after the Financial Crisis: The Long and Winding Road Toward Accountability' (2009) SSRN eLibrary, 45 ‹http:ssrn.com/abstract=1456708› accessed January 10 2013 (discussing the difficulties of limiting the accessibility of information by excluding investors who have not paid for it).

48 Partnoy, 'The Siskel and Ebert of Financial Markets?' (n 14) 627.

49 ibid 633.

50 Steven L Schwarcz, 'Private Ordering of Public Markets: The Rating Agency Paradox' [2002] (Issue 2) University of Illinois Law Review 1, 26 (suggesting that the profitability of CRAs is directly tied to reputation).

high-quality ratings.[51] In other words, if competition incentives work adequately in the rating industry, CRAs have an overriding incentive to maintain a reputation for high-quality, accurate ratings.[52] Therefore, a competitive rating market is one which is based on reputation-driven business.[53]

13.2 THEORETICAL APPROACH TO COMPETITION IN THE CREDIT RATING INDUSTRY

13.2.1 General Competition Law and Sector-specific Regulation

Conventional wisdom reads that competitive markets lead to welfare maximization.[54] General competition law pursues this objective. In the case of externalities, however, competitive markets fail to deliver expected benefits, and sector-specific regulation is used to correct the faulty market mechanism.[55] In such cases, regulators have a role to play beside competition authorities. Therefore, competition principles have to coexist with other government policies "designed to correct market

---

[51] John Patrick Hunt, 'Credit Rating Agencies and the "Worldwide Credit Crisis": The Limits of Reputation, the Insufficiency of Reform, and a Proposal for Improvement' [2009] Columbia Business Law Review 109, 112–114, 127–128 (adding, however, that the author does not agree with this dominant view, especially not in relation to structured finance ratings).

[52] Richard Cantor and Frank Packer, 'The Credit Rating Industry' [1994] FRBNY Quarterly Review 1, 4.

[53] Howell E Jackson, 'The Role of Credit Rating Agencies in the Establishment of Capital Standards for Financial Institutions in a Global Economy' in Eilís Ferran and Charles AE Goodhart (eds), *Regulating Financial Services and Markets in the 21st Century* (Hart Publishing 2001) 312 (arguing that to preserve the value of their ratings in this market CRAs need to maintain a good reputation for accurate ratings, and that this desire to maintain their reputation enhances the credibility of their ratings).

[54] Frederick Jenny, 'The "Coming Out" of Abuse of Superior Bargaining Power in the Antitrust World' in Barry E Hawk (ed), *Annual Proceedings of the Fordham Competition Law Institute, International Antitrust Law & Policy* (Juris Publishing 2009) 561. See further G Monti, 'EC Competition Law: The Dominance of Economic Analysis?' in Roger Zäch, Andreas Heinemann and Andreas Kellerhals (eds), *The Development of Competition Law, Global Perspectives* (Edward Elgar 2010) 6–7.

[55] Jenny, 'The "Coming Out" of Abuse of Superior Bargaining Power in the Antitrust World' (n 54) 562.

failure, to respond to externalities and to deal with the issue of asymmetric information" in the marketplace.[56]

The terms competition law and competition policy do not have identical meanings.[57] General competition law is a set of legal provisions that aim to protect the process of competition.[58] It is a remedy to market failure. Competition policy has a wider scope than competition law, and there are various types of public policies that amount to competition policy.[59] Typically, public policies can affect the process of competition in the marketplace. Sector-specific regulation may fall within the scope of competition policy when regulatory intervention seeks a competitive objective.

It is worth describing general competition law and sector-specific regulation in more detail. With respect to general competition law, legal frameworks contain three typical pillars as follows.

13.2.1.1 Anticompetitive agreements

Combating anticompetitive practices comprises prohibiting collusion between firms.[60] The most serious breaches of competition law are horizontal agreements and practices or conspiracies between firms such as price-fixing, market-sharing and output limitation.[61]

13.2.1.2 Abuse of dominant position

Firms can also harm competition when acting unilaterally.[62] An essential criterion to measure market dominance is market power.[63] When firms acquire market power, they can be tempted to take advantage of their privileged position in the marketplace. What is prohibited is not the

---

[56] Rainer Geiger, 'The Development of the World Economy and Competition Law' in Roger Zäch, Andreas Heinemann and Andreas Kellerhals (eds), *The Development of Competition Law, Global Perspectives* (Edward Elgar 2010) 238.

[57] Maher M Dabbah, *International and Comparative Competition Law* (Cambridge University Press 2010) 12.

[58] ibid.

[59] ibid 61.

[60] ibid 32–33.

[61] ibid. See also Geiger, 'The Development of the World Economy and Competition Law' (n 56) 246 (describing agreements on price-fixing and market-sharing as universally condemned).

[62] Dabbah, *International and Comparative Competition Law* (n 57) 34.

[63] Daniel Mainguy, Jean-Louis Respaud and Malo Depincé, *Droit de la concurrence* (Litec 2010) 284.

achieving of market power but the abuse of dominant position, whereby discerning between legitimate behavior and illegal behavior is the central question.[64]

13.2.1.3 Merger control

Mergers – also referred to as concentrations – may occur through amalgamation, acquisition of control or joint ventures.[65] Some firms may merge to become more efficient. Some other mergers may have anti-competitive effects, for instance if they decrease the number of competitors to cause adverse effects on the market.[66] As a consequence, legal frameworks may be designed to control mergers and acquisitions *ex ante*.

With respect to sector-specific regulation, it is important to highlight that some industries tend to be more significantly regulated than others, as is increasingly the trend in the rating industry. Sector-specific regulation can derogate from general competition law. Nevertheless, some sector-specific rules fall within the scope of competition policy by seeking to promote or preserve competition.[67] At any rate, sector-specific regulation constitutes a massive intervention in the market process and requires well-founded justification.[68] For instance, competition policy objectives can justify sector-specific regulatory intervention in cases of market power.[69]

Regulatory activity is indeed necessary with a view to disciplining market power in specific sectors.[70] For instance, the telecommunications sector furnishes a good example of which mechanisms can be used to regulate competition in a regulated marketplace.[71] In some countries, this sector offers a case study on the benefits of competition, the necessity of regulation and how to balance these two components.[72]

---

64 ibid 285–291.

65 Dabbah, *International and Comparative Competition Law* (n 57) 35.

66 ibid.

67 Damien Gerardin and Michel Kerf, *Controlling Market Power in Telecommunications, Antitrust vs. Sector-Specific Regulation* (Oxford University Press 2003) 1–3.

68 Günter Knieps, 'Sector-Specific Market Power Regulation versus General Competition Law: Criteria for Judging Competitive versus Regulated Markets' in Fereidoon P Sioshansi and Wolfgang Pfaffenberger (eds), *Electricity Market Reform: An International Perspective* (Elsevier Ltd 2006) 49.

69 ibid.

70 ibid.

71 Dabbah, *International and Comparative Competition Law* (n 57) 339.

72 ibid.

Clearly, the rating industry is being increasingly regulated and subjected to competitive concerns. Despite a cumbersome degree of regulatory control, market forces should play their disciplinary role. In this sense, competitive objectives should be a clear focus of regulatory intervention. In sum, sector-specific regulation may be used to respond to competitive concerns in the rating industry.

13.2.2 Antitrust Laws as a Response to Market Failure

General competition laws intervene to remedy market failure. If private market forces do not work properly, antitrust laws are enacted to rectify the situation. However, antitrust lawsuits against CRAs have not gone forward.[73] Even though the rating industry is highly concentrated and not subject to an adequate level of competition, the idea of implementing antitrust laws in the rating industry has rarely been explored by lawmakers and regulators.[74]

Traditionally, antitrust laws served the key purpose of preventing price fixing. Especially since the 1970s, economics thinking has influenced the interpretation of antitrust policies and broadened their scope.[75] This study strives to analyze the rating industry pursuant to a modern view of antitrust legislation. Broadly speaking, there is a need to overhaul antitrust legislation to take into account the evolving structure of the financial system. If antitrust laws created more than a century ago were designed to combat industrial monopolies that could influence prices, in modern financial markets antitrust laws should serve to reduce systemic risks in the financial system.[76] Due to the fact that antitrust laws are currently rarely enforced in the rating industry, the question arises as to whether they could play an increasing role in the future.

---

[73] Frank Partnoy, 'The Paradox of Credit Ratings' in Richard M Levich, Giovanni Majnoni and Carmen M Reinhart (eds), *Ratings, Rating Agencies and the Global Financial System* (Kluwer Academic Publishers 2002) 79; Frost, 'Credit Rating Agencies in Capital Markets' (n 10) 480–482.

[74] Partnoy, 'The Paradox of Credit Ratings' (n 73) 79.

[75] See further White, 'The Growing Influence of Economics and Economists on Antitrust' (n 42) 21.

[76] Simon Johnson, 'The Quiet Coup' *The Atlantic*, May 2009, 10 (discussing systemic risks with respect to the "too big to fail" problem: "too big to fail" is "too big to exist" in the sense that financial markets cannot tolerate the presence of firms that could bring down the economy if they failed).

The author of an award-winning study argues that there is a possible economic case for antitrust intervention against CRAs.[77] According to his view, credit ratings are information goods subject to reputational constraints.[78] Forecast accuracy and reputation drive competition in the rating industry.[79] Yet in an industry subject to significant market power, the benefits of competition are broken.[80] Such a phenomenon results in poor rating quality. As a consequence, the study of this professor suggests that antitrust scrutiny is the best solution to the problem.[81]

In my opinion, there are two pillars of competition law that may be taken into account. First, the interdiction of vertical agreements could be extended to cases in which issuers and CRAs excessively interfere with each other. CRAs can be accused of accepting loss of their independence in favor of issuers' fees. As a result, they harm investors by issuing ratings that are inflated and misleading. Antitrust laws may force CRAs to preserve their independence. Second, the European model of competition law gives particular weight to the question of the abuse of dominant position. The leading CRAs may misuse their market power and take advantage of their strong position in the financial markets. In this regard, proposals for new antitrust laws could be based on the EU approach to competition law.

However, there is no evidence that the leading CRAs adopt colluding practices to gain unfair advantages. Moreover, it is difficult to prove that CRAs are abusing their dominant market position. Although high barriers ensure that the leading CRAs have a privileged position, there is no evidence to prove that they abuse their market dominance. Apart from that, mergers are currently not a relevant issue in the rating industry so merger control cannot help discipline the industry. Hitherto general competition law has not offered a satisfactory response to competitive problems in the rating industry.

The reasoning behind the very limited scope for antitrust enforcement in the rating industry may be that the concentrated market structure results from economies of scale and rating-based regulations, not primarily from CRAs' anticompetitive behavior. As the interpretation of antitrust laws has evolved, emphasis has increasingly been put on the context. The regulatory context plays such a crucial role that lack of

[77] Nicolas Petit, 'Credit Rating Agencies, the Sovereign Debt Crisis and Competition Law' (2011) 7 European Competition Journal 587, 588.

[78] ibid 594–596.

[79] ibid 596.

[80] ibid 597.

[81] ibid 588.

competition in the industry cannot solely be attributed to the CRAs' market conduct. In an antitrust case it would be extremely difficult to prove that the lack of competition was a result of CRAs' anticompetitive practices.[82] The two areas where general competition policies can play a role are (i) unsolicited ratings and (ii) notching.[83] Last but not least, rating scandals have highlighted the fact that the rating market suffers from market failures that are probably not self-correcting.[84]

In sum, little can be expected from antitrust liability in order to reform the rating industry as a whole; rather, structural change should be initiated by redesigning financial market regulations. As long as ratings are used in financial market regulations, competition may not be enhanced successfully in the rating industry. Given the fact that antitrust laws offer a limited response to rating failures, lawmakers should focus on sector-specific regulation.

13.2.3 Revisited Incentive-based Financial Market Regulations as a Response to Regulatory Failure

A competition framework for CRAs may be established through regulatory intervention. This research is based on the conviction that incentive-based regulations are needed to ensure that market forces operate fairly. The key to a successful overhaul of the credit rating industry is to remove structural impediments to competition.[85] Financial market regulations have to be established in the light of economic principles. They should be designed to create appropriate incentives among market participants.

Not only individual firms but the regulatory framework as a whole had negative effects on the competitive environment in the rating industry. The presence of an excessively concentrated industry may be due to a failure of the regulatory system more than the behavior of individual firms. For instance, there is a need to scrutinize systemic risk with respect to the global use of ratings. Macroprudential regulations can play

---

[82] Frost, 'Credit Rating Agencies in Capital Markets' (n 10) 480–481 (stating that providing empirical evidence of unfair practices would be extremely difficult).

[83] ibid 481–482.

[84] Harry McVea, 'Credit Rating Agencies, the Subprime Mortgage Debacle and Global Governance: the EU Strikes Back' (2010) 59 International and Comparative Law Quarterly 701, 715.

[85] Aline Darbellay, 'Regulating Ratings, The Credit Rating Agency Oligopoly from a Regulatory Perspective' in Dieter Zobl, Mario Giovanoli and Rolf H Weber, *Schweizer Schriften zum Finanzmarktrecht, Band 102* (Schulthess 2011) 200.

a role in identifying and controlling risks across the financial system.[86] To move away from market over-reliance on ratings is a regulatory concern. Regulators have to take into account the place of the leading CRAs in the international financial architecture.

Focus is put on determining which regulatory interventions are beneficial to competition. Under certain circumstances, necessary amendments may mean the withdrawal of regulations such as rating-based regulations. In other cases, regulatory reforms are needed and must be analyzed with respect to their effect on competitive issues. Indeed, competitive concerns imply that regulators should not only sanction CRAs' anticompetitive practices but also judge their own financial market regulations with regard to their effect on competition. The absence of competition in the rating industry can partially result from a regulatory failure. Therefore, while redesigning regulations, regulators should anticipate the impact new regulations would have on competition in the rating industry.

Over the last three decades we have lived in an era of deregulation – especially in the US.[87] The level of financial market regulations has decreased. However, the subprime mortgage crisis may have marked a turning point in the history of the financial markets, thereby probably triggering an era of re-regulation. In this process, regulators must always be aware of the incentives that they create in the financial system. For this purpose, they have to measure the repercussions of their frameworks on the financial system as a whole. They cannot concentrate their efforts on a single institution without considering the effects on other institutions.

Restoring competition requires the alignment of incentives. If policymakers design incentive-based regulations, market participants would adapt their behavior and adopt competitive practices. For instance, with a view to restoring the independence of CRAs, regulatory intervention could create an incentive to move away from the issuer-pays business model and shift to the investor-pays business model.[88] Such proceedings would address conflicts of interest in the rating industry more efficiently than governance rules merely requiring that CRAs avoid conflicts of

---

[86] Kern Alexander, 'Bank Capital Management and Macro-Prudential Regulation – A Law and Finance Perspective' [2012] Journal of Banking Law and Banking 331, 331.

[87] According to the conclusions drawn by the Chicago school, antitrust laws have barely been enforced in the US during this period.

[88] House of Lords, Select Committee on Economic Affairs, *Banking Supervision and Regulation* (June 2009) 41 (suggesting a legally imposed change from an issuer-pays to an investor-pays business model).

interest by implementing a code of conduct. Furthermore, if regulators are concerned about enhancing rating quality, they cannot content themselves with inviting CRAs to allocate more resources to improve their ratings; however, structural change has to occur with respect to restoring reputational constraints in the rating industry. As regards concentration in the rating industry, regulators should try not to raise barriers to entry in a way that is inconsistent with a competitive market for credit ratings.

The objective of the Dodd-Frank Act of 2010 is to remove certified CRAs' quasi-governmental function and to reconsider them as exclusively private-sector entities. Although it does not explicitly state competition as an objective, a core aim of the Act is to affirm that the credit rating market should be a competitive market. Market forces should play their disciplinary role with respect to the leading CRAs. Efforts on the part of legislators to reduce the power of the rating oligopoly could give alternative solutions more of a chance.[89] The role of the leading CRAs in the financial system will be newly defined pursuant to the implementation of CRA reforms.

In sum, financial market regulations are responsible for structural change in the financial industry, and enhancing the level of competition in the rating industry requires structural change. Indeed, CRAs' market conduct is primarily considered as a consequence of the regulatory environment, and behavioral change at the leading CRAs will only occur in the aftermath of the new financial regulatory reforms.

13.3 ROAD AHEAD FOR A COMPETITIVE RATING MARKET

The presence of a rating oligopoly implies that the Big Three have been able to gain and maintain their market power. Unfortunately CRAs have issued inaccurate credit ratings that have harmed the financial markets. CRAs generally respond to criticism by downplaying the importance of the ratings they issue, pretending that they are merely opinions.[90] Yet CRAs will – in the future – be liable for their misconduct. Now the question arises as to whether regulators and market participants will eventually downplay the importance of credit ratings. In the aftermath of

---

[89] Van Duyn, 'Reform of Rating Agencies Poses Dilemma' (n 36) (quoting Jules Kroll).

[90] David M Ellis, 'Different Sides of the Same Story: Investors' and Issuers' Views of Rating Agencies' (1998) 7 (Issue 4) The Journal of Fixed Income 35, 37.

the subprime mortgage crisis, a trend has been initiated toward decreasing reliance on ratings. Some facts suggest that market sentiment has partly moved away from the leading CRAs.[91] Nevertheless, regulators and market participants seem to be in a difficult situation as regards finding substitutes for ratings. Other findings suggest that the market continues to rely on ratings despite the leading CRAs' recent poor performance.[92] Specialists have to help regulators and market participants eliminate the rating trap.

First and foremost, the removal of regulatory references to credit ratings is necessary due to the incompatibility of competition and rating-based regulations.[93] If ratings are widely used in financial market regulations, competition among certified CRAs is automatically counterproductive. In fact, rating-based regulations create wrong incentives such as the "race to the bottom" and "rating shopping." The Dodd-Frank Act of 2010 requires regulators to move away from regulatory reliance on ratings.[94] Regulatory changes should seek to encourage new entrants and also smaller CRAs to expand their market share.[95] Yet implementation of the CRA reform will be a very challenging task. The question arises as to what will happen when rating-based regulations are completely removed from legal and regulatory frameworks. The most appropriate solution would be to replace the certification process for CRAs by mere registration.

Second, a competitive rating market requires CRAs to be accountable for their credit ratings. The regulatory structure must impose on CRAs a cost for issuing wrong ratings. In this regard, the Dodd-Frank Act has established a liability regime for CRAs.[96] Other countries have also adopted special liability regimes against CRA post-crisis or will use the

---

[91] See, eg, 'Oberwasser für "Rating-Rebellen", Unternehmen profitieren von der derzeitigen Beliebtheit der "Corporate Bonds"' *NZZ*, August 30, 2010, 21 (stating that investors increasingly tend to disregard ratings and mentioning a trend toward "rating-rebellion").

[92] See, eg, Heinz Zimmermann and Wolfgang Hafner, 'Trotz Kritik kein Verzicht auf Rating-Agenturen, Ungebrochene Nachfrage nach Bonitätsbewertungen in unsicheren Zeiten' *NZZ*, August 19, 2010, 26.

[93] Text to n 80 in ch 4.

[94] Dodd-Frank Wall Street Reform and Consumer Protection Act of 2010, HR 4173, 111th Congress, 2nd Session (2010) (Dodd-Frank Act) Sec 939–939A.

[95] Van Duyn, 'Reform of Rating Agencies Poses Dilemma' (n 36) (also quoting Daniel Curry of the Toronto-based CRA DBRS, who suggests that investors' enhanced interest in looking for other opinions gives to smaller CRAs a chance to sell themselves).

[96] Dodd-Frank Act, Sec 933 and Sec 939G. Text to n 93 in ch 5.

general civil liability rules they already had pre-crisis. The presence of litigation costs is deemed to encourage CRAs to provide more accurate ratings. Litigation following the financial crisis will without doubt bring clarity with respect to the new CRA liability rules. In any case, in the US, CRA liability will be limited to cases in which CRAs knowingly or recklessly failed to conduct a reasonable investigation or to obtain reasonable verification of factual elements relied upon by their methodology.[97] For instance, cases in which synthetic CDOs were involved may have the most chance of success before the courts. In these cases, evidence can most likely be shown that CRAs deliberately inflated their ratings.[98] In November 2012 a Federal Court in Australia found against Standard & Poor's in a case involving structured finance products that collapsed during the subprime mortgage crisis.[99] The Federal Court found that Standard & Poor's triple-A rating was misleading and deceptive.[100] The judgment described the novel instruments as "grotesquely complicated."[101] Standard & Poor's said it will appeal against the decision. At any rate, these new developments are important steps of the litigation post-crisis.

Third, a series of measures also helps regulators and market participants move away from over-reliance on ratings. These measures consist of incentivizing investors' own due diligence, enhancing disclosure requirements, finding substitutes for ratings and decreasing the systemic importance of ratings.

13.3.1 Incentivizing Investors' Own Due Diligence

Investors' own due diligence plays a key role in combating market over-reliance on credit ratings. With respect to the subprime mortgage crisis, the problem partly arose out of market participants' lack of due diligence.[102]

---

97 Dodd-Frank Act Sec 933(b)(2).

98 See, eg, John M Griffin and Dragon Yongjun Tang, 'Did Subjectivity Play a Role in CDO Credit Ratings?' (2010) McCombs Research Paper Series No FIN-04-10, 28–29.

99 Glenda Korporaal, 'The Music Stops for Mega Ratings Agencies' *The Australian*, November 10, 2012.

100 ibid.

101 ibid.

102 Gert Wehinger, 'Lessons from the Financial Market Turmoil: Challenges ahead for the Financial Industry and Policy Makers' [2008] OECD Journal: Financial Market Trends 1 ‹http://www.oecd.org/finance/financialmarkets/41942918.pdf› accessed January 10, 2013. 5.

Even when ratings are available, it is still vital for every market participant to understand the risks and make independent credit judgments.[103] Ratings can be used to guide investment decisions, yet they should never be considered as a sufficient basis for decision-making.

Above all, rating-based regulations are said to discourage investors from performing their own due diligence.[104] The removal of rating-based regulations is a key element of the agency reform puzzle.[105] Moreover, the lack of investors' own due diligence contributed to enhancing behavioral reliance on ratings. This, in turn, exacerbated market over-reliance on ratings. Further, an aspect key to enabling investors to perform their own due diligence relates to the disclosure of relevant information. Broad disclosure allows investors to conduct their own analyses more easily.[106] The reputational constraint can be effective in disciplining CRAs only if investors perform their own due diligence. In a competitive and transparent market for ratings, CRAs make money because investors value the ratings' information content.[107] According to the reputational model, CRAs that inflate ratings to satisfy issuers will – eventually – lose investor confidence.[108]

More concretely, the necessary changes in risk management are not limited to relatively unsophisticated investors but also include relatively sophisticated risk managers.[109] Banks are legally not entitled to outsource their risk management to CRAs and they should by no means try to

---

103 CRMPG III, *Containing Systemic Risk: The Road to Reform* (August 2008) 53.

104 FSF, *Report of the Financial Stability Forum on Enhancing Market and Institutional Resilience* (n 37) 37–38. See also IOSCO, *Report of the Task Force on the Subprime Crisis* (Final Report, May 2008) 39.

105 Text to n 82 in ch 4.

106 Rousseau, 'Regulating Credit Rating Agencies after the Financial Crisis' (n 47) 33.

107 Hunt, 'Credit Rating Agencies and the "Worldwide Credit Crisis"' (n 51) 155.

108 ibid 155–156 (adding, however, that even a well-functioning reputation mechanism is unlikely to constrain CRAs from issuing ratings on novel financial instruments they do not know how to rate; therefore, financial innovation – ie structured finance in particular – deserves specific treatment).

109 CGFS, *Ratings in Structured Finance: What Went Wrong and What Can Be Done to Address Shortcomings* (BIS, CGFS Paper No 32, July 2008) 11.

escape from their legal obligations. The subprime mortgage crisis revealed the weaknesses of partly outsourcing risk management to CRAs.[110]

13.3.2 Appropriate Disclosure Requirements of Financial Information

> Warning: this rating was paid for by the issuer of this security.[111]

The availability of financial information has a direct impact on the competitive environment in the rating industry. Lawmakers and regulators should aim to require the optimal level of disclosure.

Market participants are able to sanction CRAs that issue inaccurate credit ratings only if they have access to relevant information.[112] In this regard, transparency enhances competition in the rating industry.[113] This aspect relates to disclosure in the light of investor protection. For instance, prior to the financial turmoil, investors based their decisions – with respect to complex financial instruments – almost entirely on ratings; they did not even ask for more disclosure.[114] Therefore, excessive reliance on ratings contributed to lack of transparency especially in structured finance. The level of information available to investors must be sufficient so that investors are not forced to rely blindly on CRAs.

Appropriate disclosure requirements include measures to enhance transparency in the market for financial information. A key point relates to full disclosure as regards past performance. The reputational view of ratings implies that market participants must be in a position to judge CRAs' performances. CRAs should disclose rating track records. A functioning reputation mechanism presumes that market participants are able to engage in *ex post* monitoring of rating quality.[115] Investors should be informed about the performance of the rated instruments over time to

---

[110] IOSCO, *The Role of Credit Rating Agencies in Structured Finance Markets* (Final Report, May 2008) 2 (stating that financial institutions effectively outsourced their risk management to CRAs).

[111] Balzli and Hornig, 'Exacerbating the Crisis' (n 18) (adding that critics of the issuer-pays business model call for full disclosure or would even prefer to see the establishment of a new business model for the leading CRAs).

[112] Piero Cinquegrana, 'The Reform of the Credit Rating Agencies: A Comparative Perspective' (2009) ECMI Policy Brief No 12, 3.

[113] ibid.

[114] CGFS, *Ratings in Structured Finance* (n 109) 28.

[115] Hunt, 'Credit Rating Agencies and the "Worldwide Credit Crisis"' (n 51) 114.

assess whether or not ratings were of high quality.[116] For instance, the standardization of performance reports would support the monitoring of CRAs.[117] Disclosure requirements as regards rating performance must be designed in a way that facilitates comparison between CRAs, ie between competitors.

Apart from that, disclosing rating methodologies and critical assumptions underlying credit ratings allows investors to check whether ratings are accurate.[118] Moreover, rating scales should enable investors to distinguish between plain vanilla corporate bonds and structured finance products.[119] If the rating scales are the same, it may easily mislead certain groups of investors, especially unsophisticated investors. Further, for the sake of transparency, it would make sense to compel CRAs to disclose who paid how much for which ratings.

In particular, disclosure requirements are a crucial issue in structured finance. Reform initiatives to enhance competition in the rating industry seek to address the relative absence of information on complex securities.[120]

In the past, the problem was that CRAs depended to a great extent on information that the issuers disclosed to them and had to get financial information from issuers in order to be able to rate novel instruments. The leading CRAs used to engage in a dialogue with issuers to gain access to certain non-public information.[121] Investor-paid CRAs had an information disadvantage as compared with issuer-paid CRAs. Moreover, there was no gatekeeper in structured finance because unsolicited rating was quite impossible in this field.[122] From a competitive point of view, it is problematic if the issuer-pays model is the only one possible given the lack of publicly available information in structured finance. Nevertheless, the question arises as to how this situation will evolve in the aftermath of the financial reforms. At any rate, general disclosure requirements should be enhanced – particularly relating to OTC-derivatives. Issuers' ongoing

---

116 ibid 138, 141–142.

117 CGFS, *Ratings in Structured Finance* (n 109) 13.

118 Cinquegrana, 'The Reform of the Credit Rating Agencies' (n 112) 3.

119 CGFS, *Ratings in Structured Finance* (n 109) 14.

120 Rousseau, 'Regulating Credit Rating Agencies after the Financial Crisis' (n 47) 33.

121 IOSCO, *Report on the Activities of Credit Rating Agencies* (September 2003) 12.

122 IOSCO, *The Role of Credit Rating Agencies in Structured Finance Markets* (n 110) 8.

disclosure obligations become crucial to the rating process.[123] This trend reflects the importance of not excluding investor-paid CRAs and CRAs that seek to provide unsolicited ratings. Issuers of structured finance products should disclose relevant information in a format which CRAs and sufficiently sophisticated investors can analyze.[124]

It is worth mentioning that there is a difference between public offerings and private offerings. Generally, regulators have disclosure requirements for public offerings of structured finance products.[125] By contrast, in private offerings the degree of disclosure is individually negotiated by investors and originators and issuers because of the contractual basis of the transaction.[126] To create incentives for market participants to trade on exchanges may be the best way to enhance transparency in structured finance markets.[127] Accordingly, concern has been raised about developing a secondary market trade reporting system in the market for structured finance products.[128] Such a system would provide buyers and sellers with more information regarding the frequency with which a given security trades and the most recent bid and ask prices.[129] Such a system could also be designed to capture secondary market structured finance transactions even if the transactions are entirely private.[130]

Further, the key issue is to enhance transparency and give investors the information that they need to assess risk and calculate where the losses may be.[131] CRAs should present information in a way that facilitates comparisons of risk within and across classes of different structured finance products.[132] For instance, users have to know whether the characteristics of underlying assets have changed significantly.[133] Users

---

123 IOSCO, *Report on the Activities of Credit Rating Agencies* (n 121) 12.

124 IOSCO, *Report of the Task Force on the Subprime Crisis* (n 104) 11.

125 ibid 7.

126 ibid.

127 Joshua Rosner, 'Toward an Understanding: NRSRO Failings in Structured Ratings and Discreet Recommendations to Address Agency Conflicts' (2009) 14 (Issue 4) Journal of Structured Finance 7, 13.

128 IOSCO *Report of the Task Force on the Subprime Crisis* (n 104) 10.

129 ibid.

130 ibid.

131 Christopher R Whalen, 'No True Sale: Interview with Joseph Mason', *The Institutional Risk Analyst*, March 3, 2008 (quoting Joseph Mason).

132 CGFS, *Ratings in Structured Finance* (n 109) 13 (also arguing that "CRAs should document the sensitivity of SF tranche ratings to changes in their central assumptions regarding default rates, recovery rates and correlations").

133 ibid.

should be able to analyze the ratings and assess whether or not they should trust CRAs. In this regard, critics suggest that CRAs should regularly disclose to investors the economic assumptions underlying their structured finance ratings, and document the type of scenario which could lead to a severe impairment of a tranche.[134] Accordingly, a more user-friendly access to CRA structured finance models should be in the hands of market participants.[135] However, if disclosure requirements are too extensive, issuers will be able to circumvent rating models. Therefore, it is worth mentioning that the main purpose of broader disclosure requirements is to help investors understand the ratings, but not to provide issuers with information allowing them to game rating models in order to obtain higher ratings.

13.3.3 Finding Substitutes for Credit Ratings

In the aftermath of the withdrawal of rating-based regulations, the most challenging task of regulators and market participants consists of finding alternatives to the use of credit ratings. Decreasing market over-reliance on ratings is automatically associated with finding substitutes for ratings. Above all, the withdrawal of rating-based regulations implies that regulators need alternatives to ratings in their financial market regulations.

Credit ratings are so deeply anchored in the financial markets that finding substitutes will take time.[136] The Dodd-Frank Act of 2010 has merely taken the lead by imposing the removal of regulatory reliance on regulators and market participants. Replacing the rating requirement with "meet[ing] standards of creditworthiness as established by the [SEC]" leaves an open-ended standard in need of definition.[137]

---

134 ibid 14.

135 ibid 13.

136 Aline Darbellay and Frank Partnoy, 'Credit Rating Agencies and Regulatory Reform' in Claire A Hill and Brett H McDonnell (eds), *Research Handbook on the Economics of Corporate Law* (Edward Elgar 2012) 294. See further The High-Level Group on Financial Supervision in the EU, 'De Larosière Report' (2009) 20 ‹http://ec.europa.eu/internal_market/finances/docs/de_larosiere_report_en.pdf› accessed January 10, 2013 (recognizing the negative effects of rating-based regulations, yet stating that the regulatory use of ratings is unavoidable at this stage given the lack of alternatives).

137 Dodd-Frank Act, Sec 939; Marilyn Blumberg Cane, Adam Shamir and Thomas Jodar, 'Below Investment Grade and Above the Law: A Past, Present and Future Look at the Accountability of Credit Rating Agencies' (2012) 17 Fordham Journal of Corporate & Financial Law 1063, 1118.

At any rate, it makes sense for regulators and market participants to adopt a variety of solutions rather than homogeneous practices. The systemic relevance of ratings was partly caused by the homogenization of market behavior as a consequence of regulatory reliance on ratings.[138] The key point is that regulators and market participants will have to find an alternative to ratings that best suits their own needs.

The question arises as to what mechanisms could potentially be used as substitutes for credit ratings.[139] The Dodd-Frank Act leaves the door open to market-based measures, which seems to be the most popular solution among scholars. For instance, critics of rating-based regulations already proposed the use of credit spreads as a substitute for ratings a long time before the adoption of the Dodd-Frank Act.[140]

Moreover, scholars have recently turned to market-based measures such as CDS as a viable alternative to ratings.[141] However, some scholars are skeptical of the use of CDS and contend that they could have greater shortcomings than ratings; according to them, the risk of mispricing credit risk would remain.[142] In my opinion, alternatives represent a danger if they are designed in such a way that they can be manipulated by market participants. For instance, the IRB approach may be used extensively only if regulators find a way to monitor financial entities so that they are not able to take advantage of the approach to extend their balance sheets. Market-based measures such as credit spreads and CDS spreads are also problematic if regulated entities find a way to manipulate them. At any rate, finding alternatives to ratings presents a very challenging agenda for future research.

---

138 Text to n 23 in ch 11.

139 SEC, 'Report on the Role and Function of Credit Rating Agencies in the Operation of the Securities Markets, As Required by Section 702(b) of the Sarbanes-Oxley Act of 2002' (January 2003) 15.

140 Partnoy, 'The Siskel and Ebert of Financial Markets?' (n 14) 705; Edward I Altman and Anthony Saunders, 'An Analysis and Critique of the BIS Proposal on Capital Adequacy and Ratings' (2001) 25 Journal of Banking & Finance 25, 25ff (referring to credit spreads as a commonly used barometer of risk in financial systems and for economic cycles by both the government and banks).

141 Mark J Flannery, Joel F Houston and Frank Partnoy, 'Credit Default Swap Spreads As Viable Substitutes for Credit Ratings' (2010) 158 University of Pennsylvania Law Review 2085.

142 Rosner, 'Toward an Understanding' (n 127) 12.

13.3.4 Reducing the Systemic Importance of Credit Ratings

Lawmakers and regulators around the world have acknowledged the major problems arising from the systemic risks posed by credit ratings, yet they have not directly taken regulatory measures to address the problem.[143] In the EU, policymakers and regulators heavily criticized the leading CRAs' decisions to downgrade Greek bonds at the height of the debt crisis.[144] To some extent, they were referring to the system-relevance of the three leading CRAs. Major market disruptions are caused by the devastating effects of rating downgrades of system-relevant CRAs. Accordingly, the EU suggests that a home-grown CRA should be created in Europe as a counterweight to the US trio.[145] In this regard, the EU recognizes the necessity of enhancing competition in the rating industry in order to decrease the market dominance of the three leading CRAs. The recent market turmoil has highlighted that regulators should increasingly deal with the systemic risks generated by market over-reliance on the leading CRAs.

From a regulatory perspective, the systemic relevance of ratings highlights the importance of macroprudential supervision in the rating industry.[146] The 2007–2009 financial crisis has demonstrated that the changing nature of financial markets and systemic risks necessitates broader macroprudential controls and oversight of the financial system.[147] As macroprudential regulators, the FSB and the new European Systemic Risk Board (ESRB) have broad mandates to strengthen the financial system. Both bodies are designed to operate without legally binding powers.[148] Within the scope of their broad mandates they could take into account the systemic risks posed by the use of ratings. Both the FSB and ESRB could help national regulators coordinate their

---

143 See, eg, Dodd-Frank Act, Sec 931(1).

144 'The Other Vampires, Pressure Mounts on an Oligopoly' *The Economist*, May 15, 2010, 83–84 (emphasizing that rating downgrades of Greek bonds to junk status occurred just as officials were about to unveil a support plan).

145 ibid.

146 See, eg, Amadou N R Sy, 'The Systemic Regulation of Credit Rating Agencies and Rated Markets' (2009) IMF Working Paper No 09/129, 3 ‹http://www.imf.org/external/pubs/ft/wp/2009/wp09129.pdf› accessed January 10, 2013, 8.

147 Eilís Ferran and Kern Alexander, 'Can Soft Law Bodies Be Effective? Soft Systemic Risk Oversight Bodies and the Special Case of the European Systemic Risk Board' (2011) University of Cambridge Faculty of Law Research Paper No 36/2011, 3.

148 ibid.

approaches to combat the systemic use of ratings. Because CRAs have become part of the international financial architecture, it makes sense to incorporate the systemic risks posed by ratings into the mandates of the FSB and the ESRB.

Accordingly, the FSB took a step in the right direction when it published its Principles for Reducing Reliance on Credit Ratings in October 2010.[149] The FSB suggested that systemic reliance on ratings has its roots in regulatory and behavioral reliance.[150] Reducing over-reliance on ratings necessarily comes along with moving away from ratings in regulations.[151] Market participants are also required to exercise their own due diligence when making investment decisions.[152]

Further, it is worth mentioning that several measures potentially taken to combat the systemic use of ratings do not directly target CRAs, but have an indirect influence on the use of ratings by market participants. For instance, the most important measure taken by regulators to prevent banks from expanding their balance sheets was the introduction of a leverage ratio. Leading up to the subprime mortgage crisis, the rating-based approach of Basel II allowed banks to build up excessive leverage while still reporting strong risk-based capital ratios.[153] It is widely recognized that the primary cause was its Standardized Approach, ie the regulatory reliance on ratings. Therefore, under the Basel III reform measures the BCBS recommends introducing a leverage ratio as a supplement to the risk-weighted ratio.[154] The introduction of a leverage

---

[149] FSB, *Principles for Reducing Reliance on CRA Ratings* (October 2010) 1–7.

[150] ibid.

[151] ibid 1.

[152] ibid 5–6.

[153] BCBS, *Consultative Document, Strengthening the Resilience of the Banking Sector* (BIS, December 2009) 60.

[154] ibid; Adrian Blundell-Wignall and Paul Atkinson, 'Thinking Beyond Basel III: Necessary Solutions for Capital and Liquidity' [2010] (Issue 1) OECD Journal: Financial Market Trends 1, 9 ‹http://www.oecd.org/finance/financial markets/45314422.pdf› accessed January 10, 2013; Nout Wellink, 'The New Framework for Banking Supervision' *Basel Committee Speeches, Remarks at the FSI High Level Meeting on "The Emerging Framework to Strengthen Banking Regulation and Financial Stability" for Africa* (Cape Town, January 27, 2011) 2 ‹http://www.bis.org/speeches/sp110127.pdf› accessed January 10, 2013. See also Peter Nobel, *Schweizerisches Finanzmarktrecht und internationale Standards* (3rd edn, Stämpfli 2010) 207.

ratio is likely to be the single most important regulatory reform to combat the causes of the financial crisis.[155]

Accordingly, Switzerland introduced a leverage ratio during the financial crisis as a supplement to the risk-weighted capital ratio under Basel II.[156] This action was one of the core measures that Swiss regulators took in the aftermath of the subprime mortgage debacle. The major cause of the regulatory concerns was that the Swiss universal bank UBS was highly leveraged as a result of the implementation of the risk-sensitive approach of Basel II.[157] UBS obviously took advantage of the rating-based approach of the Basel II framework.[158] The high leverage in the years preceding the subprime mortgage crisis partly explains how UBS became so excessively exposed to the US subprime mortgage market. Therefore, the introduction of a leverage ratio was the most efficient measure to take to prevent UBS from expanding its balance sheet.

A further example of regulatory measures indirectly playing a role against the systemic use of credit ratings relates to the trading of individual assets. Collateral and margin requirements in the financing of trading positions contribute to a move away from over-reliance on ratings. Instead of contenting themselves with the ratings of the leading CRAs, regulators and market participants have to make sure that counterparty risk is properly mitigated through collateral and margin requirements. Such a measure contributes to deterring the over-leveraging of assets in the financial markets.

---

155 Blundell-Wignall and Paul Atkinson, 'Thinking Beyond Basel III' (n 154) 10.

156 FINMA, 'Finanzmarktkrise und Finanzmarktaufsicht' (September 14, 2009) 39; Myret Zaki, *UBS, Les dessous d'un scandale, Comment l'empire aux trois clés a perdu son pari* (Editions Favre SA 2008) 187–190. See also Christine Kaufmann and Patrick Götze, 'Geld- und Währungsordnung' in Andreas Lienhard (ed), *Finanzrecht, Schweizerisches Bundesverwaltungsrecht (SBVR), Band 10* (Helbing & Lichtenhahn 2011) 118.

157 Blundell-Wignall and Paul Atkinson, 'Thinking Beyond Basel III' (n 154) 16 (arguing that UBS had a leverage of 64 in 2007, which portrays the Swiss banks as one of the most leveraged banks worldwide in the run-up to the subprime mortgage crisis). See also Zaki, *UBS* (n 156) 187.

158 It is worth mentioning that UBS had already partly implemented Basel II on a voluntary basis before the Swiss Capital Adequacy Ordinance of 2006 came into force.

14. Concluding remarks

Apart from the Big Three – Moody's, Standard & Poor's and Fitch – no other leading CRA has appeared as profitable since the emergence of the credit rating industry at the beginning of the twentieth century. Before the 1970s, the rating industry was still subject to private market forces. CRAs were neither significantly used in financial market regulations nor regulated. From the 1970s onwards, regulators increasingly incorporated regulatory references to ratings in their financial market regulations. Yet the rating industry itself remained unregulated. Recently, 2010 has marked a turning point in the rating industry. Regulators have been removing the rating-based regulations they developed over the last four decades. Moreover, lawmakers have decided to regulate CRAs similarly to other financial gatekeepers such as securities analysts and auditors. While tending to reduce over-reliance on certified ratings, lawmakers and regulators have nevertheless acknowledged the crucial role played by the leading CRAs in modern financial markets.

After a century of existence, the rating industry has currently faced its most significant regulatory overhaul. The role of the leading CRAs in modern financial markets is a fascinating and challenging topic given their relevance on the global stage. With regard to the adoption of the US Dodd-Frank Act of 2010 and the EU CRA Regulation of 2009, a new era has begun where CRAs will be highly regulated in keeping with the crucial role they play in the financial system.

Over the twentieth century, the use of ratings has significantly expanded given the regulatory environment in which they operate. From the 1970s onwards, the leading CRAs have acted as gatekeepers in the growth of novel financial instruments. The shift from the investor-pays business model to the issuer-pays business model is primarily attributed to regulatory incentives. Private market forces would have never placed CRAs at the core of the international financial architecture if regulatory intervention had not artificially increased the role of certified CRAs.

It is undoubtedly impossible to return to the system prevailing before the 1970s given the structural changes in modern financial markets – especially financial innovation. Regulators have no other choice but to supervise the rating industry, thereby taking into account its importance in the financial system as a whole. However, criticism has been voiced about the new regulatory and supervisory framework for CRAs. If regulators inadvertently elevated CRAs to a crucial position by using their ratings in financial market regulations, regulators will now keep CRAs at the center of the international financial architecture by regulating them similarly to other important market participants. The regulatory barrier arising out of the regulatory recognition of certified CRAs may be replaced by a new regulatory barrier based on the costs of compliance with enhanced CRA oversight.

At any rate, lawmakers and regulators are responsible for creating the appropriate incentives in the rating industry. Competition should eventually be restored in order to discipline the three leading CRAs. Although competition relating to CRAs is unpopular in the US in the aftermath of the subprime mortgage crisis, competition among CRAs is needed and should gain prominence in the future. This study finds that competition among CRAs can only be effectively enhanced if regulators remove rating-based regulations from their financial market regulations. As long as ratings are excessively used for regulatory purposes, competitive pressures have detrimental effects on the financial markets.

Therefore, competition will gain prominence as soon as regulators successfully remove the excessive regulatory reliance on credit ratings. In this regard, the first step toward the creation of appropriate incentives in the rating industry consists of lessening over-reliance on the leading CRAs. Moreover, CRAs will be forced to innovate as soon as they can no longer count on regulatory-driven services. A key objective of an appropriate market structure in the rating industry lies in the creation of incentive-based competition. Appropriate incentives are created if CRAs compete on improving the quality of their ratings. Performance should count above all in the rating industry, even if it means that CRAs will eventually be less profitable than they were in the 2000s.

Bibliography

BOOKS AND PERIODICAL MATERIALS

'Debatte um "Schuld" der Rating-Agenturen, Schweizer Zurückhaltung bei anstehender Regulierung' *NZZ*, September 4, 2010, 35.

'Exclusion Zone, Regulators Promise a Belated Review of the Ratings Oligopoly' *The Economist*, February 8, 2003, 65–66.

'Negative Outlook, Europe Misfires in its Attack on the Rating Agencies' *The Economist*, November 15, 2008, 91.

'Oberwasser für "Rating-Rebellen", Unternehmen profitieren von der derzeitigen Beliebtheit der "Corporate Bonds"', August 30, 2010, 21.

'Taming the Beast, How Far Should Finance Be Re-regulated?' *The Economist*, October 11, 2008, 6–16.

'The Big Barofsky, Someone in Washington is Standing up for Taxpayers' *The Wall Street Journal*, April 29, 2009.

'The Other Vampires, Pressure Mounts on an Oligopoly' *The Economist*, May 15, 2010, 83–84.

'Three is No Crowd, Regulators Need a New Approach to an Entrenched Industry' *The Economist*, March 26, 2005, 15.

'Währungshüter halten Geld weiterhin billig, Aufwertungsdruck auf den Franken erhöht' *NZZ*, February 21, 2010.

Abdelal R, *Capital Rules, The Construction of Global Finance* (Harvard University Press 2007).

Ackermann U and Jäckle J, 'Ratingverfahren aus Emittentensicht' (2006) 61 Betriebs-Berater 868.

Akerlof GA, 'The Market for "Lemons": Quality Uncertainty and the Market Mechanism' (1970) 84 The Quarterly Journal of Economics 488.

Alexander K, 'Bank Capital Management and Macro-Prudential Regulation – A Law and Finance Perspective' [2012] Journal of Banking Law and Banking 331.

– 'Bank Capital Regulation and the Role of External Ratings: Unresolved Issues' in J Kleineman and L Gorton (eds), *Credit Rating Agencies* (Stockholm Centre for Commercial Law, forthcoming 2013).

Alexander K and others, 'Financial Supervision and Crisis Management in the EU' (2007) European Parliament, Policy Department, Economic and Scientific Policy ‹http://www.europarl.europa.eu/document/activities/cont/201108/20110818ATT25070/20110818ATT25070EN.pdf›.

– 'Crisis Management, Burden Sharing and Solidarity Mechanisms in the EU' (2010) European Parliament, Policy Department, Economic and Scientific Policy ‹http://www.europarl.europa.eu/committees/en/cris/studiesdownload.html?languageDocument=EN&file=31711›.

Altman EI, Oncu S, Schmeits A and White LJ, 'What Should Be Done About the Credit Rating Agencies?' *New York University (NYU) Stern Regulating Wall Street Blog* (New York, April 6, 2010) ‹http://w4.stern.nyu.edu/blogs/regulatingwallstreet/2010/04/what-should-be-done-about-the.html#more›.

Altman EI and Rijken HA, 'How Rating Agencies Achieve Rating Stability' (2004) 28 Journal of Banking & Finance 2679.

– 'The Effects of Rating Through the Cycle on Rating Stability, Rating Timeliness and Default Prediction Performance' (2004) NYU Working Paper No FIN-04-032 ‹http://archive.nyu.edu/bitstream/2451/26559/2/FIN-04-032.pdf›.

Altman EI and Saunders A, 'An Analysis and Critique of the BIS Proposal on Capital Adequacy and Ratings' (2001) 25 Journal of Banking & Finance 25.

Andrieu P, *Ratingagenturen in der Krise, Über die Einführung von Qualitätsstandards für Ratings durch die Europäische Union* (Peter Lang 2010).

Arner DW, 'The Global Credit Crisis of 2008: Causes and Consequences' (2009) Asian Institute of International Financial Law Working Paper No 3 ‹http://www.law.hku.hk/aiifl/research/conference-papers.html›.

Ashcraft AB and Schuermann T, 'Understanding the Securitization of Subprime Mortgage Credit' (2008) Federal Reserve Bank of New York Staff Reports, 40 ‹http://www.newyorkfed.org/research/staff_reports/sr318.pdf›.

Baker HK and Mansi SA, 'Assessing Credit Rating Agencies by Bond Issuers and Institutional Investors' (2002) 29 Journal of Business Finance & Accounting 1367.

Balzli B and Hornig F, 'Exacerbating the Crisis, The Power of Rating Agencies' *Spiegel Online* (Hamburg, May 6, 2009) (translated from the German by Christopher Sultan).

Barnett-Hart AK, 'The Story of the CDO Market Meltdown: An Empirical Analysis' (BA thesis, Harvard College 2009) 7 ‹http://www.hks.harvard.edu/m-rcbg/students/dunlop/2009-CDOmeltdown.pdf›.

Beaver WH, Shakespeare C and Soliman MT, 'Differential Properties in the Ratings of Certified Versus Non-certified Bond-rating Agencies' (2006) 42 Journal of Accounting and Economics 303.

Becker B and Milbourn T, 'How Did Increased Competition Affect Credit Ratings?' (2011) 101 Journal of Financial Economics 493.
Beckman TN, *Credits and Collections in Theory and Practice* (McGraw-Hill Company 1930).
Birchler U and Bütler M, *Information Economics* (Routledge 2007).
Blaurock U, 'Control and Responsibility of Credit Rating Agencies' (2007) 11 Electronic Journal of Comparative Law 1.
– 'Verantwortlichkeit von Ratingagenturen – Steuerung durch Privat- oder Aufsichtsrecht?' [2007] ZGR 603.
Bluhm C, *CDO Modeling: Techniques, Examples and Applications* (HypoVereinsbank 2003).
Blundell-Wignall A and Atkinson P, 'Thinking Beyond Basel III: Necessary Solutions for Capital and Liquidity' [2010] (Issue 1) OECD Journal: Financial Market Trends 1 ‹http://www.oecd.org/finance/financialmarkets/45314422.pdf›.
Borio C, 'The Financial Turmoil of 2007–?: A Preliminary Assessment and Some Policy Considerations' (2008) BIS Working Papers No 251 ‹http://www.bis.org/publ/work251.pdf›.
Brennan MJ, Hein J and Poon S-H, 'Tranching and Rating' (2008) SSRN eLibrary ‹http:ssrn.com/abstract=1108556›.
Buchanan M, 'Crazy Money: How Can We Stop the Financial Markets Creating So Much Misery? Forget Textbook Economics, the Answer Lies Elsewhere' *New Scientist*, July 19, 2008.
Buffet WE, 'Berkshire Annual Report 2002' (2002) ‹http://www.berkshirehathaway.com/2002ar/2002ar.pdf›.
Burry MJ, 'A Primer on Scion Capital's Subprime Mortgage Short' (November 7, 2006).
– 'I Saw the Crisis Coming. Why Didn't the Fed?' *The New York Times*, April 4, 2010.
Camanho N, Deb P and Liu Z, 'Credit Rating and Competition' (2012) SSRN eLibrary ‹http:ssrn.com/abstract=1573035›.
Cane MB, Shamir A and Jodar T, 'Below Investment Grade and Above the Law: A Past, Present and Future Look at the Accountability of Credit Rating Agencies' (2012) 17 Fordham Journal of Corporate & Financial Law 1063.
Cantor R and Packer F, 'The Credit Rating Industry' [1994] FRBNY Quarterly Review 1.
Carrigan J, 'Greece May Have Rating Lowered to Junk, Moody's Says' *Bloomberg BusinessWeek*, May 10, 2010.
Casey K and Partnoy F, 'Downgrade the Ratings Agencies' *The New York Times*, June 4, 2010.
Cassad BJ, 'Confirmation Bias' in RF Baumeister and KD Vohs (eds), *Encyclopedia of Social Psychology* (SAGE 2007).

Chandler AD, *Henry Varnum Poor: Business Editor, Analyst and Reformer* (Harvard University Press 1956).

Chan S, 'Documents Show Internal Qualms at Rating Agencies' *The New York Times*, April 22, 2010.

Chartier J, 'Rapport fait au nom de la commission des finances, de l'économie générale et du contrôle budgétaire sur le projet de loi de régulation bancaire et financière (No 2165)' (Assemblée nationale, May 25, 2010).

Chorafas DN, *Economic Capital Allocation with Basel II, Cost, Benefit and Implementation Procedures* (Elsevier Butterworth-Heinemann 2004).

Cifuentes R, Ferrucci G and Shin HS, 'Liquidity Risk and Contagion' (2005) Bank of England Working Paper Series No 264 ‹http://www.bankofengland.co.uk/publications/Documents/workingpapers/wp264.pdf›.

Cinquegrana P, 'The Reform of the Credit Rating Agencies: A Comparative Perspective' (2009) ECMI Policy Brief No 12.

Clark A, 'Euro Falls as Spain Suffers Rating Downgrade' *The Guardian*, May 28, 2010.

Clerc L, 'A Primer on the Subprime Crisis' (2008) Banque de France, Occasional Paper No 4 ‹http://www.banque-france.fr/fileadmin/user_upload/banque_de_france/La_Banque_de_France/pdf/Economie_et_Statistiques/primer_subprime_crisis.pdf›.

Coffee Jr JC, *Gatekeepers: The Professions and Corporate Governance* (Oxford University Press 2006).

– 'Ratings Reform: the Good, the Bad, and the Ugly' (2011) 1 Harvard Business Law Review 231.

Corkery M, 'Joe Cassano's Testimony: AIG CDS Worked Just Fine' *The Wall Street Journal Blogs*, June 30, 2010.

Coval JD, Jurek J and Stafford E, 'The Economics of Structured Finance' (2008) Harvard Business School Finance Working Paper No 09-060.

Crouhy MG, Jarrow RA and Turnbull SM, 'The Subprime Credit Crisis of 07' (2008) SSRN eLibrary ‹http:ssrn.com/abstract=1112467›.

Dabbah MM, *International and Comparative Competition Law* (Cambridge University Press 2010).

Dallas L, 'Short-Termism, the Financial Crisis and Corporate Governance' (2011) University of San Diego Legal Studies Research Paper Series No 11-052.

Darbellay A, 'Regulating Ratings, The Credit Rating Agency Oligopoly from a Regulatory Perspective' in D Zobl, M Giovanoli and RH Weber, *Schweizer Schriften zum Finanzmarktrecht, Band 102* (Schulthess 2011).

– 'Competition and Credit Rating Agencies' in J Kleineman and L Gorton (eds), *Credit Rating Agencies* (Stockholm Centre for Commercial Law, forthcoming 2013).

Darbellay A and Partnoy F, 'Credit Rating Agencies under the Dodd-Frank Act' (2011) 30 (Issue 12) Banking & Financial Services Policy Report 1.

– 'Credit Rating Agencies and Regulatory Reform' in CA Hill and BH McDonnell (eds), *Research Handbook on the Economics of Corporate Law* (Edward Elgar 2012).

– 'Agences de notation et conflits d'intérêts' (2012) 105 Revue d'économie financière 309.

De Haan J and Amtenbrink F, 'Credit Rating Agencies' (2011) De Nederlandsche Bank (DNB) Working Paper No 278.

Earling PR, *Whom to Trust: A Practical Treatise on Mercantile Credits* (Rand, McNally & Co 1890).

Ellis DM, 'Different Sides of the Same Story: Investors' and Issuers' Views of Rating Agencies' (1998) 7 (Issue 4) The Journal of Fixed Income 35.

Emmenegger S, 'Die Regulierung von Rating-Agenturen' [2006] Swiss Review of Business and Financial Market Law 32.

– 'Rating und Haftung' in W Wiegand (ed), *Basel II – die rechtlichen Konsequenzen* (Stämpfli Verlag 2006).

Estrella A and others, 'Credit Ratings and Complementary Sources of Credit Quality Information' (2000) BCBS Working Papers No 3 ‹http://www.bis.org/publ/bcbs_wp3.pdf›.

Ferran E and Alexander K, 'Can Soft Law Bodies Be Effective? Soft Systemic Risk Oversight Bodies and the Special Case of the European Systemic Risk Board' (2011) University of Cambridge Faculty of Law Research Paper No 36/2011.

Fight A, *The Ratings Game* (John Wiley & Sons Ltd 2001).

Firla-Cuchra MT, 'Explaining Launch Spreads on Structured Bonds' (2005) Department of Economics Discussion Paper Series No 230.

Flannery MJ, Houston JF and Partnoy F, 'Credit Default Swap Spreads As Viable Substitutes for Credit Ratings' (2010) 158 University of Pennsylvania Law Review 2085.

Flinterman F, 'ESMA: The European Supervisor of Credit Rating Agencies' in J Kleineman and L Gorton (eds), *Credit Rating Agencies* (Stockholm Centre for Commercial Law, forthcoming 2013).

Flood J, 'Rating, Dating, and the Informal Regulation and the Formal Ordering of Financial Transactions: Securitisations and Credit Rating Agencies' in MB Likosky (ed), *Privatising Development: Transnational Law, Infrastructure and Human Rights* (Martinus Nijhoff Publishers 2005).

Foley J, 'New Tools Can Help Tame an Ocean of Data' *InformationWeek*, October 30, 1995.

Frost CA, 'Credit Rating Agencies in Capital Markets: A Review of Research Evidence on Selected Criticisms of the Agencies' (2007) 22 Journal of Accounting, Auditing & Finance 469.

Geiger R, 'The Development of the World Economy and Competition Law' in R Zäch, A Heinemann and A Kellerhals (eds), *The Development of Competition Law, Global Perspectives* (Edward Elgar 2010).

Gerardin D and Kerf M, *Controlling Market Power in Telecommunications, Antitrust vs. Sector-Specific Regulation* (Oxford University Press 2003).

Gillen D, 'In Ratings Agencies, Investors Still Trust' *The New York Times*, June 5, 2009.

Gorton L and Verständig A, 'General Background of the Conference' in J Kleineman and L Gorton (eds), *Credit Rating Agencies* (Stockholm Centre for Commercial Law, forthcoming 2013).

Granier T, 'Éclairage. Le règlement communautaire sur les agences de notation: un début de régulation de l'activité?' [2010] Bulletin Joly Bourse 8.

Griffin JM and Tang DY, 'Did Subjectivity Play a Role in CDO Credit Ratings?' (2010) McCombs Research Paper Series No FIN-04-10.

Harold G, *Bond Ratings as an Investment Guide, An Appraisal of their Effectiveness* (The Ronald Press Company 1938).

Hendricks D, Kambhu J and Mosser P, 'Systemic Risk and the Financial System, Background Paper' (2006) NAS-FRBNY (Federal Reserve Bank of New York) Conference on New Directions in Understanding Systemic Risk ‹https://www.newyorkfed.org/registration/research/risk/background.pdf›.

Hill CA, 'Regulating the Rating Agencies' (2004) 82 Washington University Law Quarterly 43.

– 'Why Did Anyone Listen to the Rating Agencies after Enron?' (2009) 4 Journal of Business & Technology Law 283.

– 'Who Were the Villains in the Subprime Crisis, and Why it Matters' (2010) 4 Entrepreneurial Business Law Journal 323.

– 'Why Did Rating Agencies Do Such a Bad Job Rating Subprime Securities?' (2010) 71 University of Pittsburgh Law Review 1.

– 'Limits of Dodd-Frank's Rating Agency Reform' (2011) 15 Chapman Law Review 133.

Hirsch C and Bannier C, 'The Economic Function of Credit Rating Agencies – What Does the Watchlist Tell Us?' (2009) SSRN eLibrary ‹http:ssrn.com/abstract=1343421›.

Hunt JP, 'Credit Rating Agencies and the "Worldwide Credit Crisis": The Limits of Reputation, the Insufficiency of Reform, and a Proposal for Improvement' [2009] Columbia Business Law Review 109.
Ishmael S-M, 'What's the SEC To Do About 436(g)? Call a Time Out' *FT Alphaville*, July 22, 2010.
Jackson HE, 'The Role of Credit Rating Agencies in the Establishment of Capital Standards for Financial Institutions in a Global Economy' in E Ferran and CAE Goodhart (eds), *Regulating Financial Services and Markets in the 21st Century* (Hart Publishing 2001).
Jenny F, 'The "Coming Out" of Abuse of Superior Bargaining Power in the Antitrust World' in BE Hawk (ed), *Annual Proceedings of the Fordham Competition Law Institute, International Antitrust Law & Policy* (Juris Publishing 2009).
Johnson R, 'An Examination of Rating Agencies' Actions Around the Investment-Grade Boundary' (2003) Research Division Federal Reserve Bank of Kansas City, RWP 03-01 ‹http://www.kc.frb.org/publicat/reswkpap/pdf/rwp03-01.pdf›.
Johnson S, 'The Quiet Coup' *The Atlantic*, May 2009.
Jones S, 'When Junk Was Gold' *The Financial Times*, October 17, 2008.
Kambhu J, Schuermann T and Stiroh KJ, 'Hedge Funds, Financial Intermediation, and Systemic Risk' (2007) 13 (Issue 3) FRBNY (Federal Reserve Bank of New York) Economic Policy Review 1.
Kaufmann C and Götze P, 'Geld- und Währungsordnung' in A Lienhard (ed), *Finanzrecht, Schweizerisches Bundesverwaltungsrecht (SBVR), Band 10* (Helbing & Lichtenhahn 2011).
Kaufmann C and Weber RH, 'The Role of Transparency in Financial Regulation' (2010) 13 Journal of International Economic Law 779.
Kauper TE, 'Oligopoly: Facilitating Practices and Plus Factors' in BE Hawk (ed), *Annual Proceedings of the Fordham Competition Law Institute, International Antitrust Law & Policy* (Juris Publishing, Inc 2008).
Kennedy S and Totaro L, 'ECB Comes to Greece's Aid by Waiving Collateral Rules' *Bloomberg BusinessWeek*, May 3, 2010.
Keteyian A, 'Ratings Agencies to Face Grilling on Goldman' *CBS News*, 22 April 2010.
Knieps G, 'Sector-Specific Market Power Regulation versus General Competition Law: Criteria for Judging Competitive versus Regulated Markets' in FP Sioshansi and W Pfaffenberger (eds), *Electricity Market Reform: An International Perspective* (Elsevier Ltd 2006).
Korporaal G, 'The Music Stops for Mega Ratings Agencies' *The Australian*, November 10, 2012.

Korth P, 'Dritthaftung von Ratingagenturen' in G Teubner and others (eds), *Internationale Studien zur Privatrechtstheorie, Band 10* (Nomos 2009).

Kröger M, 'Rampant Skepticism, Aid for Greece Hasn't Stopped Euro's Slide' *Spiegel Online* June 5, 2010.

Krugman P, 'A Catastrophe Foretold' *The New York Times*, October 26, 2007.

Kuhner C, 'Financial Rating Agencies: Are They Credible? – Insights into the Reporting Incentives of Rating Agencies in Times of Enhanced Systemic Risk' (2001) 53 Schmalenbach Business Review 2.

Lamy M-F, 'The Treatment of Credit Risk in the Basel Accord and Financial Stability' (2006) 11 International Journal of Business 159.

Lewis M, *The Big Short, Inside the Doomsday Machine* (WW Norton & Company 2010).

Lombardini C, *Droit bancaire suisse* (2nd edn, Schulthess 2008).

Lowenstein R, 'Triple-A Failure, The Ratings Game' *The New York Times*, April 27, 2008.

Lucas DJ, Goodman LS and Fabozi FJ, *Collateralized Debt Obligations, Structures & Analysis* (2nd edn, John Wiley & Sons, Inc 2006).

– 'Collateralized Debt Obligations and Credit Risk Transfer' (2007) Yale ICF Working Paper No 07-06.

Lumpkin S, 'Resolutions of Weak Institutions: Lessons Learned from Previous Crises' [2008] OECD Journal: Financial Market Trends 1 ‹http://www.oecd.org/finance/financialmarkets/41942943.pdf›.

Lyman P and Varian HR, 'How Big Is the Information Explosion?' *iMP Magazine*, November 22, 2000.

Lynch TE, 'Deeply and Persistently Conflicted: Credit Rating Agencies in the Current Regulatory Environment' (2009) 59 Case Western Reserve Law Review 227.

Macey JR, 'Efficient Capital Markets, Corporate Disclosure, and Enron' (2004) 89 Cornell Law Review 394.

– *Corporate Governance: Promises Kept, Promises Broken* (Princeton University Press 2008).

Madison JH, 'The Evolution of Commercial Credit Reporting Agencies in Nineteenth-Century America' (1974) 48 The Business History Review 164.

Mainguy D, Respaud J-L and Depincé M, *Droit de la concurrence* (Litec 2010).

Manns J, 'Rating Risk After the Subprime Mortgage Crisis: A User Fee Approach for Rating Agency Accountability' (2009) 87 North Carolina Law Review 1012.

Marini P, 'Rapport No 703 (2009–2010) fait au nom de la commission des finances' (Sénat, September 14, 2010).

Mathis J, McAndrews J and Rochet J-C, 'Rating the Raters: Are Reputation Concerns Powerful Enough to Discipline Rating Agencies?' (2009) 56 Journal of Monetary Economics 657.

McVea H, 'Credit Rating Agencies, the Subprime Mortgage Debacle and Global Governance: the EU Strikes Back' (2010) 59 International and Comparative Law Quarterly 701.

Meier H, 'Regulierung von Ratingagenturen, Auswirkungen auf die Schweiz' [2009] Der Schweizer Treuhänder 945.

Moloney N, *EC Securities Regulation* (2nd edn, Oxford University Press 2008).

Monti G, *EC Competition Law* (Cambridge University Press 2007).

– 'EC Competition Law: The Dominance of Economic Analysis?' in R Zäch, A Heinemann and A Kellerhals (eds), *The Development of Competition Law, Global Perspectives* (Edward Elgar 2010).

Morgenson G, 'Debt Watchdogs: Tamed or Caught Napping?' *The New York Times*, December 7, 2008.

Morgenson G and Story L, 'Rating Agency Data Aided Wall Street in Deals' *The New York Times*, April 23, 2010.

Morrissey J, 'Disillusioned Advisers Eye Smaller Rating Firms; Interest in Subscriber-Based Raters Grows at the Expense of the Big Three Agencies' *Investment News*, February 15, 2009.

Mundstock G, 'The Trouble with FASB' (2003) 28 North Carolina Journal of International Law & Commercial Regulation 813.

– 'GAAP Did Their Job During the Economic Meltdown' (2009) 4 Florida International University Law Review 463.

Murphy A, 'An Analysis of the Financial Crisis of 2008: Causes and Solutions' (2008) SSRN eLibrary ‹http:ssrn.com/abstract=1295344›.

Nobel P, *Schweizerisches Finanzmarktrecht und internationale Standards* (3rd edn, Stämpfli 2010).

Nocera J, 'Propping up a House of Cards' *The New York Times*, February 28, 2009.

Opp CC, Opp MM and Harris M, 'Rating Agencies in the Face of Regulation' (2012) SSRN eLibrary ‹http:ssrn.com/abstract=1540099›.

Partnoy F, 'The Siskel and Ebert of Financial Markets?: Two Thumbs Down for the Credit Rating Agencies' (1999) 77 Washington University Law Quarterly 619.

– 'The Paradox of Credit Ratings' in RM Levich, G Majnoni and CM Reinhart (eds), *Ratings, Rating Agencies and the Global Financial System* (Kluwer Academic Publishers 2002).

– 'How and Why Credit Rating Agencies Are Not Like Other Gatekeepers' (2006) University of San Diego Legal Studies Research Paper Series No 07-46.

– 'Do Away with Rating-based Rules', *The Financial Times*, July 8, 2008.
– 'Overdependence on Credit Ratings was a Primary Cause of the Crisis' (2009) University of San Diego Legal Studies Research Paper Series No 09-015.
– 'Wall Street Beware: The Lawyers are Coming' *The Financial Times*, April 18, 2010.
Partnoy F and Eisinger J, 'What's Inside America's Banks?' *The Atlantic*, January/February, 2013.
Partnoy F and Turner LE, 'Bring Transparency to Off-Balance Sheet Accounting' (2010) Roosevelt Institute ‹http://www.rooseveltinstitute.org/sites/all/files/Off-Balance%20Sheet%20Transactions.pdf›.
Persaud A, 'Liquidity Black Holes, and Why Modern Financial Regulation in Developed Countries Is Making Short-Term Capital Flows to Developing Countries Even More Volatile' (2002) United Nations University World Institute for Development Economics Research (UNU/WIDER) Discussion Paper No 2002/31 ‹http://archive.unu.edu/hq/library/Collection/PDF_files/WIDER/WIDERdp2002.31.pdf›.
Petit N, 'Credit Rating Agencies, the Sovereign Debt Crisis and Competition Law' (2011) 7 European Competition Journal 587.
Pinches GE and Singleton JC, 'The Adjustment of Stock Prices to Bond Rating Changes' (1978) 33 The Journal of Finance 29.
Pinto AR, 'Control and Responsibility of Credit Rating Agencies in the United States' (2008) Brooklyn Law School Legal Studies Research Papers No 119.
Pulliam S and Perez E, 'Criminal Probe Looks into Goldman Trading' *The Wall Street Journal*, April 30, 2010.
Quinn BJM, 'The Failure of Private Ordering and the Financial Crisis of 2008' (2009) 5 NYU Journal of Law & Business 549.
Reason T, 'Not Trigger Happy, Credit-rating Firms Are Taking a Closer Look at How Corporate Credit Agreements Employ Rating Triggers' *CFO Magazine*, February 21, 2002.
Rosner J, 'Toward an Understanding: NRSRO Failings in Structured Ratings and Discreet Recommendations to Address Agency Conflicts' (2009) 14 (Issue 4) Journal of Structured Finance 7.
Rousseau S, 'Regulating Credit Rating Agencies after the Financial Crisis: The Long and Winding Road Toward Accountability' (2009) SSRN eLibrary ‹http:ssrn.com/abstract=1456708›.
Routier R, 'De nouvelles pistes pour la gouvernance?' [2003] Bulletin Joly Sociétés 611.
Ryan J, 'The Negative Impact of Credit Rating Agencies and Proposals for Better Regulation' (2012) SWP Working Paper FG 1, 2012/No 1

‹http://www.swp-berlin.org/fileadmin/contents/products/arbeitspapiere/The_Negative_Impact_of_Credit_Rating_Agencies_KS.pdf›.

Schwarcz SL, 'The Role of Rating Agencies in Global Market Regulation' in E Ferran and CAE Goodhart (eds), *Regulating Financial Services and Markets in the 21st Century* (Hart Publishing 2001).

– 'Enron and the Use and Abuse of Special Purpose Entities in Corporate Structures' (2002) 70 University of Cincinnati Law Review 1309.

– 'Private Ordering of Public Markets: The Rating Agency Paradox' [2002] (Issue 2) University of Illinois Law Review 1.

– 'Systemic Risk' (2008) 97 Georgetown Law Journal 193.

– 'Disclosure's Failure in the Subprime Mortgage Crisis' [2008] Utah Law Review 1109.

– 'Keynote Address: Understanding the Subprime Financial Crisis' (2009) 60 South Carolina Law Review 549.

Scott KA, 'Addressing the Conditions Leading to "Systemic Risk" on a Global Basis' *New York Law Journal*, March 18, 2009.

Segal D, 'Debt Raters Avoid Overhaul After Crisis' *New York Times*, December 8, 2009.

Shorter G and Seitzinger MV, 'Credit Rating Agencies and Their Regulation' (2009) Congressional Research Service ‹http://garrettforms.house.gov/uploadedfiles/credit_rating_agencies.pdf›.

Sinclair TJ, *The New Masters of Capital, American Bond Rating Agencies and the Politics of Creditworthiness* (Cornell University Press 2005).

Sorkin AR, 'Citi Chief on Buyouts: "We're Still Dancing"' *The New York Times*, July 10, 2007.

– 'What the Financial Crisis Commission Should Ask' *The New York Times Dealbook*, January 11, 2010.

– 'A Hand in a House of Cards' *The New York Times DealBook*, February 16, 2010.

– 'Congress Drops Changes for Credit-Rating Agencies' *The New York Times DealBook*, June 16, 2010.

Soros G, 'Do Not Ignore the Need for Financial Reform' *The Financial Times*, October 25, 2009.

Stanton R and Wallace N, 'CMBS Subordination, Ratings Inflation, and the Crisis of 2007–2009' (2010) National Bureau of Economic Research (NBER) Working Paper No 16206 ‹http://www.nber.org/papers/w16206›.

Sy ANR, 'The Systemic Regulation of Credit Rating Agencies and Rated Markets' (2009) IMF Working Paper No 09/129 ‹http://www.imf.org/external/pubs/ft/wp/2009/wp09129.pdf›.

Sylla R, 'An Historical Primer on the Business of Credit Rating' in RM Levich, G Majnoni and C Reinhart (eds), *Ratings, Rating Agencies and the Global Financial System* (Kluwer Academic Publishers 2002).

Tchotourian I, 'Agences de notation: encadrement et responsabilité' [2011] Bulletin Joly Bourse 119.

Thépot C, 'L'encadrement légal de l'activité des agences de notation par la loi de régulation bancaire et financière' (2010) 250 Petites Affiches 26.

– 'L'encadrement des agences de notation: "trop de loi tue la loi"' (2011) (on file with author).

Utzig S, 'The Financial Crisis and the Regulation of Credit Rating Agencies: A European Banking Perspective' (2010) ADBI Working Paper No 188 ‹http://www.adbi.org/working-paper/2010/01/26/3446.credit.rating.agencies.european.banking›.

Van Duyn A, 'Reform of Rating Agencies Poses Dilemma' *The Financial Times*, June 10, 2010.

Vasella D, 'Die Haftung von Ratingagenturen, Ein Beitrag zur Expertenhaftung' in K Alexander and others (eds), *Zürcher Studien zum Privatrecht, Band 236* (Schulthess 2011).

Wakeman LM, 'The Real Function of Bond Rating Agencies' in MC Jensen and CW Smith, Jr (eds), *The Modern Theory of Corporate Finance* (McGraw-Hill Book Company 1984).

Weber RH, 'Kassandra oder Wissensbroker – Dilemma im "Global Village"' in J Becker, RM Hilty, J-F Stöckli and T Würtenberger (eds), *Recht im Wandel seines sozialen und technologischen Umfeldes, Festschrift für Manfred Rehbinder* (CH Beck 2002).

– 'Mapping and Structuring International Financial Regulation – A Theoretical Approach' (2009) 20 European Business Law Review 651.

Weber RH and Arner DW, 'Toward a New Design for International Financial Regulation' (2007) 29 University of Pennsylvania Journal of International Law 391.

Weber RH and Baumann S, 'Conflicts of Interest and Risk Management Practices in the CRA Industry' in J Kleineman and L Gorton (eds), *Credit Rating Agencies* (Stockholm Centre for Commercial Law, forthcoming 2013).

Weber RH and Darbellay A, 'The Regulatory Use of Credit Ratings in Bank Capital Requirement Regulations' (2008) 10 Journal of Banking Regulation 1.

Wehinger G, 'Lessons from the Financial Market Turmoil: Challenges Ahead for the Financial Industry and Policy Makers' [2008] OECD Journal: Financial Market Trends 1 ‹http://www.oecd.org/finance/financialmarkets/41942918.pdf›.

Wellink N, 'The New Framework for Banking Supervision' *Basel Committee Speeches, Remarks at the FSI High Level Meeting on "The Emerging Framework to Strengthen Banking Regulation and Financial Stability" for Africa* (Cape Town, 27 January 2011) ‹http://www.bis.org/speeches/sp110127.pdf›.

West RR, 'Bond Ratings, Bond Yields and Financial Regulation: Some Findings' (1973) 16 Journal of Law and Economics 159.

Westbrook J and Gallu J, 'SEC's Demand That Goldman Admit "Mistake" Could Spur Lawsuits' *Bloomberg*, July 21, 2010.

Whalen CR, 'The Subprime Crisis, Cause, Effect and Consequences' (2008) Networks Financial Institute Policy Brief No 2008-PB-04.

– 'No True Sale: Interview with Joseph Mason' *The Institutional Risk Analyst*, March 3, 2008.

White LJ, 'A New Law for the Bond Rating Industry' [2007] Regulation 48.

– 'The Growing Influence of Economics and Economists on Antitrust: An Extended Discussion' (2008) NYU Center for Law and Economics Working Paper No 08-07.

– 'Financial Regulation and the Current Crisis: A Guide for the Antitrust Community' (2009) SSRN eLibrary ‹http:ssrn.com/abstract=1426188›.

Wood PR, 'The Regulation of Credit Reference Agencies: A Wider View' in J Kleineman and L Gorton (eds), *Credit Rating Agencies* (Stockholm Centre for Commercial Law, forthcoming 2013).

Wutkowsky K and Younglai R, 'Lawmakers, Former Execs Blast Credit Raters' *Reuters*, October 22, 2008.

Yoon A and Neumann J, 'S&P Moves to Revamp Its CMBS Rating System' *Wall Street Journal*, June 4, 2012.

Zaki M, *UBS, Les dessous d'un scandale, Comment l'empire aux trois clés a perdu son pari* (Editions Favre SA 2008).

Zimmermann H and Hafner W, 'Trotz Kritik kein Verzicht auf Rating-Agenturen, Ungebrochene Nachfrage nach Bonitätsbewertungen in unsicheren Zeiten' *NZZ*, August 19, 2010, 26.

INSTITUTIONAL MATERIALS

'Assessing the Current Oversight and Operation of Credit Rating Agencies: Hearing Before the Senate Committee on Banking, Housing and Urban Affairs' (2006) 109th Congress, S Hrg 109-997.

'Credibility of Credit Ratings, the Investment Decisions Made Based on Those Ratings, and the Financial Crisis, Hearings & Testimony Before the FCIC' (June 2, 2010).

'Credit Rating Agencies and the Financial Crisis: Hearing Before the House Committee on Oversight and Government Reform' (2008) 110th Congress 2nd Session, HR Serial No 110-155.

'Rating the Raters: Enron and the Credit Rating Agencies: Hearing Before the Senate Committee on Governmental Affairs' (2002) 107th Congress, S Hrg 107-471.

'Testimony Concerning Oversight of Nationally Recognized Statistical Rating Organizations: Hearing Before the Senate Committee on Banking, Housing, and Urban Affairs' (2008) 110th Congress.

'Wall Street and the Financial Crisis: The Role of Credit Rating Agencies, Hearing Before the Permanent Subcommittee on Investigations of the Senate Committee on Homeland Security and Governmental Affairs' (April 23, 2010).

AMF, 'Response to the European Commission Consultation on Future Measures to be Taken on Credit Rating Agencies' (January 6, 2011).

BCBS, *International Convergence of Capital Measurement and Capital Standards, A Revised Framework (Basel II)* (BIS, June 2004).

– *Consultative Document, International Framework for Liquidity Risk Measurement, Standards and Monitoring* (BIS, December 2009).

– *Consultative Document, Strengthening the Resilience of the Banking Sector* (BIS, December 2009).

– *Consultative Document, Countercyclical Capital Buffer Proposal* (BIS, June 2010).

– *Basel III: A Global Regulatory Framework for More Resilient Banks and Banking Systems* (BIS, December 2010).

CESR, *Report on Compliance of EU Based Credit Rating Agencies with the 2008 IOSCO Code of Conduct* (May 2009).

CGFS, *Credit Risk Transfer* (BIS, January 2003).

– *Ratings in Structured Finance: What Went Wrong and What Can Be Done to Address Shortcomings* (BIS, CGFS Paper No 32, July 2008).

CRMPG III, *Containing Systemic Risk: The Road to Reform* (August 2008).

ESMA, 'Guidelines on the Application of the Endorsement Regime under Article 4(3) of the Credit Rating Regulation 1060/2009, Consultation Paper' (18 March 2011).

EU Commission, 'Proposal for a Regulation on credit rating agencies' COM (2008) 704 final.

– 'Staff Working Document accompanying the Proposal for a Regulation on credit rating agencies, Impact Assessment' COM (2008) 704.

– 'Proposal for a Regulation on amending Regulation (EC) No 1060/2009 on credit rating agencies' COM (2010) 289 final ('Proposal for a CRA II Regulation').

– 'Staff Working Document, Impact Assessment, Accompanying document to the Proposal for a Regulation amending Regulation (EC) No 1060/2009 on credit rating agencies' COM (2010) 289 final.
– 'Public consultation on credit rating agencies' (November 5, 2010).
– 'Proposal for a Directive amending Directive 2009/65/EC on the coordination of laws, regulations and administrative provisions relating to undertakings of collective investment in transferable securities (UCITS) and Directive 2011/61/EU on alternative investment funds managers in respect of the excessive reliance on credit ratings' COM (2011) 746 final.
– 'Proposal for a Regulation amending Regulation (EC) No 1060/2009 on credit rating agencies' COM (2011) 747 final ('Proposal for a CRA III Regulation').
– 'Memo, Statement by Commissioner Michel Barnier following the vote in the European Parliament on new European rules to regulate credit rating agencies' (Brussels, January 16, 2013).

European Parliament, 'Resolution of 8 June 2011 on credit rating agencies: future perspectives' (2010/2302(INI)).

'Final Report of the Commission of Experts for Limiting the Economic Risks Posed by Large Companies' (Swiss TBTF Report) (September 30, 2010).

FINMA, 'Finanzmarktkrise und Finanzmarktaufsicht' (September 14, 2009).

FSB, *Principles for Reducing Reliance on CRA Ratings* (October 2010).

FSF, *Report of the Financial Stability Forum on Enhancing Market and Institutional Resilience* (April 2008).

House of Lords, Select Committee on Economic Affairs, *Banking Supervision and Regulation* (June 2009).

IMF, *Global Financial Stability Report, Containing Systemic Risks and Restoring Financial Soundness* (April 2008).

IOSCO, *Report on the Activities of Credit Rating Agencies* (September 2003).
– *Code of Conduct Fundamentals for Credit Rating Agencies* (Revised May 2008).
– *Report of the Task Force on the Subprime Crisis* (Final Report, May 2008).
– *The Role of Credit Rating Agencies in Structured Finance Markets* (Final Report, May 2008).
– *Regulatory Implementation of the Statement of Principles Regarding the Activities of Credit Rating Agencies* (Consultation Report, May 2010).

SEC, 'Report on the Role and Function of Credit Rating Agencies in the Operation of the Securities Markets, As Required by Section 702(b) of the Sarbanes-Oxley Act of 2002' (January 2003).

– 'Egan-Jones and Founder Sean Egan Agree to 18-Month Bars from Rating Asset-Backed and Government Securities Issuers as NRSRO' *Press Release* (January 22, 2013) ‹http://www.sec.gov/news/press/2013/2013-7.htm›.

Staff of Senate Committee on Governmental Affairs, 'Financial Oversight of Enron: The SEC and Private-Sector Watchdogs' (2002) 107th Congress, 2nd Session, S Prt 107-75.

Staff of the SEC, 'Summary Report of Issues Identified in the Commission Staff's Examinations of Select Credit Rating Agencies' (July 2008).

Staff of the SEC, '2012 Summary Report of Commission Staff's Examinations of Each Nationally Recognized Statistical Rating Organization, As Required by Section 15E(p)(3)(C) of the Securities Exchange Act of 1934' (November 2012).

Staff of the SEC, 'Report to Congress on Assigned Credit Ratings, As Required by Section 939F of the Dodd-Frank Wall Street Reform and Consumer Protection Act' (December 2012).

The High-Level Group on Financial Supervision in the EU, 'De Larosière Report' (2009) ‹http://ec.europa.eu/internal_market/finances/docs/de_larosiere_report_en.pdf›.

The Joint Forum, *Stocktaking on the Use of Credit Ratings* (BIS, June 2009).

The United Kingdom Authorities 'Response to the European Commission Internal Market and Services Consultation Document on Credit Rating Agencies' (January 31, 2011).

Index

Abacus 2007-AC1 deal 110, 125, 140
ABCP (Asset-Backed Commercial Papers) 146
Abdelal, Rawi 5, 6, 10, 32, 96, 185
  history of credit rating agencies 21, 23, 26
  rating-based regulations 46, 53
  system-relevance of credit ratings 158, 168, 172
ABS (Asset-Backed Securities) *see* Asset-Backed Securities (ABS)
abuse of dominant position 165, 218–19, 221
ACA Capital Management 110
Ackermann, Ulrich 38, 137
AIG (American International Group, Inc) 107, 162–3, 177–8, 191
Akerlof, George A 8, 137
Alexander, Kern 10, 39, 164, 165, 223, 233
  downgrades of credit ratings, reactions to 181, 185, 187, 189
  incentives, wrong (in rating industry) 120, 124, 125, 131
  rating-based regulations 46, 48, 54, 62
  structured finance segment 98, 100, 101, 103, 106, 111, 113
  system-relevance of credit ratings 162, 170, 172
Alt-A loans 105–6
Alternative Investment Funds Managers (AIFMs), Directive on 63
Altman, Edward I 3, 93, 189, 193, 194
American International Group, Inc (AIG) 107, 162–3, 177–8, 191
Amtenbrink, Fabian 65, 66
ancillary business services 32–3, 122–4
announcements, rating 165, 179, 189
anticompetitive practices/agreements 209, 218
antitrust laws, and market failure 220–2
arbitrage, regulatory 57, 117–19
Arner, Douglas W. 54, 113, 160
Ashcraft, Adam B 107, 129, 130, 131, 161
Asset-Backed Commercial Papers (ABCP) 146
Asset-Backed Securities (ABS) 31, 71, 131, 145, 146
  structured finance segment, growth 106, 109
assets 110, 112
  mark-to-market asset valuation 187–8
  securitized *see* securitizations/securitized assets
Atkinson, Paul 58, 186, 235

bailouts 177
Baker, H Kent 156, 189, 193
Balzli, Beat 157, 168, 195, 228
banks 47, 60–1
  balance sheet, complexity 99
  bank-based financial system, transfer to market-based 96–8
  capital requirement regulations 48–9
  certificates of deposit 31
  financial disintermediation 96–7, 103
  and financial engineering 99–100
  high risk-weighted capital ratios prior to subprime mortgage crisis 54, 112, 170, 171
  leverage, increasing 99–101, 102, 171
  risk-sensitive capital requirements 170–1
  shadow banking system 142

Wall Street 109–10, 111, 125–6
see also central banks; financial institutions; investment banks
Bannier, Christina 37, 42
Barnett-Hart, Anna Katherine 100, 105, 106, 109, 115
Basel Capital Framework
Basel II 10, 30, 39, 136, 235
Internal Ratings-Based Approach 61
procyclicality 187
rating-based regulations 46, 47, 48, 49, 53, 55, 56, 57, 61
risk-based approach 57–8
Standardized Approach 53, 100–1, 112, 170, 234
Basel III 10, 112, 136
and credit ratings as regulatory tools 39–40
rating-based regulations 46, 47, 48, 49, 55, 60
reform measures 171, 197, 234
Standardized Approach 112, 170, 234
Basel Committee on Banking Supervision (BCBS) 112
bank capital requirement regulations 48–9
Basel III: A Global Regulatory Framework for More Resilient Banks and Banking Systems 40
and certified credit rating agencies 46–7
Countercyclical Capital Buffer Proposal 171, 187
International Convergence of Capital Measurement and Capital Standards 30, 47, 170
leverage ratio, recommendation for 234–5
Strengthening the Resilience of the Banking Sector 55, 56, 58, 171
Baumann, Simone 123, 148, 149, 150
Baumeister, Roy F 180
Beaver, William H. 37, 38, 41, 209
Becker, Bo 208
Beckman, Theodore N 15
behavioral reliance on credit ratings 165, 174–8
and regulatory reliance 136–7, 194
Big Three *see* leading credit rating agencies (Big Three)
Birchler, Urs 25, 37, 120, 121, 180, 181
Blaurock, Uwe 52, 65, 81, 137, 167
credit rating industry 30, 34, 37, 38, 40
Bluhm, Christian 117, 119
Blum, Mike 105
Blumberg Cane, Marilyn 72
Blundell-Wignall, Adrian 58, 186, 235
bonds, corporate 31
covered bond offerings 50
plain vanilla corporate bonds vs. structured finance products 229
tranches of 104, 106–7, 108, 110, 116, 118
triple-B rated 21
Borio, Claudio 97, 102, 103, 187
Bradstreet Agency 16
break-up fees 36, 124
Brennan, Michael J 133
Bretton Woods system, collapse (1970s) 23
Buchanan, Mark 132
Buffet, Warren E 99, 161, 164, 213
Burry, Michael J 106, 110
Bütler, Monika 25, 37, 120, 121, 180, 181

Cantor, Richard 21, 24, 217
capital adequacy rules 112
Cark, Andrew 159
Carrigan, Justin 158, 159, 195
Casey, Kathleen 3–4, 93, 171, 172, 173, 184
rating-based regulations 55, 59, 60, 62
CDOs (Collateral Debt Obligations) *see* Collateral Debt Obligations (CDOs)
CDS (Credit Default Swap) contracts *see* Credit Default Swap (CDS) contracts
central banks, collateral policy 172–4

certificates of deposit, bank 31
certified credit rating agencies 46–7, 51, 170
  collateral policy of central banks 172–3, 174
  and competition 209, 215
  privileged position of 182
  "rating shopping" and inflated ratings 58–9
CESR *see* Committee of European Securities Regulators (CESR)
CGFS *see* Committee on the Global Financial System (CGFS)
Chan, Sewell 87, 129
Chandler, Alfred D 16
charter-constrained investors 172
Chartier, Jérôme 80
Chicago School 223
Chorafas, Dimitris N 61
Cifuentes, Rodrigo 163
Cinquegrana, Piero 49
Citigroup 117, 141
civil liability regime for credit rating agencies
  "commercial speech" 77
  confidence, liability based on 82
  contractual liability 81–2
  in European Union
    national liability regimes 79–83
    special EU liability regime 83–4
  expert liability 82
  privileged treatment of credit rating industry *see* privileged treatment of credit rating industry
  prospectus liability 82
  quasi-contractual liability 81, 82
  tort, liability in 81, 82, 83
  in United States 77–9
Clay Singleton, J 22
Clerc, Laurent 105, 164
CMBS (Commercial Mortgage-Backed Securities) 146
Code of Conduct (IOSCO) 64–5, 67, 72
  "comply or explain" principle 65, 66
Coffee, John C, Jr 29, 122, 181, 208, 215
Collateral Debt Obligations (CDOs) 7, 32, 95
  ancillary business services 123
  cash 109, 113
  "CDO squared" structures 108
  dependence on rating models for valuation purposes 133
  hybrid 110
  "lemons problem" 140
  regulatory response to problems of structured finance ratings 146
  and subprime mortgage crisis 102, 104, 106–7, 108, 109
  synthetic *see* synthetic CDOs
  tranches of bonds 104, 106–7, 108, 110, 116, 118
"collateral triggers," in contracting 176–8
Commercial Mortgage-Backed Securities (CMBS) 146
commercial paper 31
"commercial speech" 77
Committee of European Securities Regulators (CESR), *Report on Compliance of EU Based Credit Rating Agencies with the 2008 IOSCO Code of Conduct* 65
Committee on the Global Financial System (CGFS)
  Credit Risk Transfer 134
  Ratings in Structured Finance (CGFS) 30, 129, 130, 131, 132, 191, 227, 229
community technology 120–1
competition in credit rating industry
  abuse of dominant position 218–19, 221
  anticompetitive agreements 218
  antitrust laws as response to market failure 220–2
  and certified credit rating agencies 209, 215
  competition law vs. competition policy 218
  competitive advantage of credit rating agencies 76
  concept of competition with respect of credit rating agencies 214–17
  determination of regulatory interventions beneficial to 223

distortions
among leading credit rating agencies 207–14
deformation of incentives 212–14
market over-reliance on credit ratings 54–7
oligopolistic market structure 208–10
rating-based regulations, with respect to 51–9
rating-driven market behavior 57–9
regulatory barriers to entering credit rating industry 51–4
subprime mortgage crisis, run-up to 210–12
incentivizing investors' due diligence 226–8
Nationally Recognized Statistical Rating Organizations 68
oligopolistic market structure 208–10
and payment structure 213
as reform target 198–9
restoring 207–35
disclosure requirements, appropriate 228–31
road ahead 5, 224–35
substitutions for credit ratings, finding 231–2
theoretical approach 217–24
abuse of dominant position 218–19, 221
anticompetitive agreements 218
general competition law and sector-specific regulation 217–20
merger control 219–20
competition in credit rating industry, restoring, concerns regarding level of competition 207–17
comply or explain principle, IOSCO Code of Conduct 65, 66
concentrations *see* merger control
confidence crisis 138, 142, 185
conflicts of interest 69, 127, 158, 188
ancillary services 122–4
interferences between credit rating agencies and issuers 124–6
issuer-pays business model 120–2
in structured finance segment 103, 147–9
Constitution of United States, First Amendment 77–8, 94
contagion, market 163, 191
contracting
contracting tools, credit ratings as 40–1
"rating triggers" in 40, 175–6
rating-dependent "collateral triggers" in 176–8
contractual liability 81–2
Corkery, Michael 177
corporate ratings 31, 71
Coval, Joshua D 25, 94
covered bond offerings 50
CRA Regulation of 2009 on credit rating agencies 4–5, 236
over-reliance on credit ratings industry, reducing 198
practical importance of credit rating agency reforms 85, 88, 198, 200
regulatory treatment of credit rating agencies 73, 75, 80, 83
structured finance segment 146, 148–50, 151
see also European Union (EU)
Credit Default Swap (CDS) contracts 100, 107, 110
see also derivatives, credit
credit derivatives *see* derivatives, credit
credit enhancement 107, 111, 127
credit rating agencies (CRAs)
background 3–5
certified *see* certified credit rating agencies
Codes of Conduct 65
competition, concept of with respect to 214–17
core activities 29–33
ancillary business, counseling issuer in doing 32–3
external credit ratings, providing investors with 29–32
evolution 6–9
fees of issuers, dependence on 121–2

gatekeeper role 69, 76, 86, 103, 114, 140
general-purpose 52
and growth of structured finance 113–17
independent European CRA 199
as information intermediaries 37–8, 96, 181
and issuers 124–6
leading *see* leading credit rating agencies (Big Three)
migration policy 193–4
profit margins 209–10, 236
quasi-governmental function 8, 45–6, 214, 224
reforms, practical importance 85–90
reputational capital, building 19–20
reputational constraints 22–3
research scope and perspectives 9–11
and subprime mortgage crisis *see* subprime mortgage crisis
trust, position of 81, 82
US model for regulation and supervision 68–72
US-based, widespread importance 10–11
see also criticism of credit rating agencies
credit rating industry
barriers to entering 51–4, 167–8
core activities of credit rating agencies
counseling issuers in doing ancillary business 32–3
providing investors with external credit ratings 29–32
deformation of incentives 212–14
main uses of ratings in modern financial markets
credit ratings as contracting tools 40–1
credit ratings as monitoring tools 41–2
credit ratings as regulatory tools 39–40
financial information provision 37–9
oligopoly in *see* oligopoly, in credit rating industry
origins 17–20
over-reliance on *see* over-reliance on credit ratings
oversight of 64–75
strengthening 68–75
privileged treatment *see* privileged treatment of credit rating industry
rating process
providing initial credit ratings 34–6
reviewing credit ratings 36–7
reforms *see* reforms, regulatory
regulatory barrier to entering 51–4
self-regulation in 64–5
wrong incentives in *see* incentives, wrong (in rating industry)
see also credit rating agencies (CRAs); credit ratings
credit ratings 54–7
announcements 165, 179, 189
attitude of investors to 18–19
as contracting tools 40–1
corporate 31
definition of a credit rating 29–31
dependence on rating models for valuation purposes 133–4
financial information provision 31–2, 37–9
finding substitutes for 231–2
high ratings to "senior" tranches 132
initial, provision of 34–6
internal vs. external 30
issuers' demand for 121
main uses in modern financial markets 37–42
as marketing tool 114–16
as monitoring tools 41–2
over-reliance on *see* over-reliance on credit ratings
paradox of 7–9
public availability of 182–3
"race to the bottom" regarding standards 59, 68, 122, 127, 152, 214, 215, 225
reducing systemic importance of 233–5

as regulatory tools 39–40
reliance of investors on 94
review of 36–7
sovereign 31, 32, 71, 199–201
structured finance 31–2, 93–6
system-relevance *see* system-relevance of credit ratings
trend to reduce regulatory dependence on 59–61
use in financial market regulations 8–9
see also credit rating agencies (CRAs); credit rating industry
Credit Risk Transfer (CRT) instruments 97, 161
expansion 98–9
creditworthiness of borrowers and debt instruments, assessing 29, 38–9
see also uncreditworthy borrowers
criticism of credit rating agencies 7–8
doubts over accuracy and decline of investor confidence (between 1930s and 1970s) 21–3
prior to 1907 16–17
see also incentives, wrong (in rating industry)
Crouhy, Michel G
downgrades of credit ratings, reactions to 191
and incentives, wrong (in rating industry) 122, 123, 129, 130, 133, 137
structured finance growth 52, 99, 102, 103, 105, 107, 109, 111
system-relevance of credit ratings 162, 176
CRTs *see* Credit Risk Transfer (CRT) instruments

Dabbah, Maher M 218, 219
Dallas, Lynne 138
Darbellay, Aline 85, 140, 173, 185, 187, 222
rating-based regulations 48, 60
regulatory response to problems of structured finance ratings 145
regulatory treatment of credit rating agencies 71, 76, 79
structured finance segment, growth 100, 112
systemic issue, regulatory responses 201
De Haan, Jakob 65, 66
De Larosière Report 102, 103, 124, 132, 136, 187
debt securities, in hybrid CDOs 110
default rates 32, 103–4
high-risk, low probability economic events 132
and rating downgrades 137
see also subprime mortgage crisis
Depincé, Malo 218
deregulation 223
derivatives, credit 108, 109, 142–3, 229
system-wide problems caused by 161–2
see also Credit Default Swap (CDS) contracts
disappointment of confidence, notion of 82
disclosure requirements
financial information 228–31
oversight of credit rating industry 69, 71
disintermediation, financial 96–7, 103, 163–4
diversification theories 189–90
Dodd-Frank Wall Street Reform and Consumer Protection Act, 2010 4, 9, 236
agency regulation and supervision model 69–72
and France 80–1
liability regime 78–9
over-reliance on credit ratings industry, reducing 197, 198
practical importance of credit rating agency reforms 85–6
structured finance segment 93, 145, 148, 149, 150
substitutes for credit ratings, finding 231–2
systemic importance of credit ratings 155–6

withdrawal of rating-based regulations 11, 61–2
see also United States (US)
downgrades of credit ratings and impacts of 3–4, 102, 142, 172, 179–96, 202
amount of available information and selection of relevant information 180–1
confidence crisis 142
and contracting 40–1
default risk 137
financial crises, triggering 188
homogenization of information in financial markets 179–85
credit rating of leading agencies as homogenizing factors 181–3
procyclicality 163, 186–9
rating of stability 193–4
reluctance of leading agencies to downgrade 122, 159, 184, 191–6
signaling effects 183–4
spillover effects by leading agencies 128, 189–91
and subprime mortgage crisis *see* subprime mortgage crisis
system-wide effects 194
due diligence of investors, incentivizing 226–8
Dun Agency 16

Earling, Peter R 16
ECAIs (External Credit Assessment Institutions) 47, 136
ECB (European Central Bank) 159, 173
Egan, Sean 151
Egan-Jones Ratings Co (small CRA) 151, 192, 195
Eisinger, Jesse 100
Ellis, David M 156, 224
Emmenegger, Susan 8, 11, 45, 64, 82
Enron, collapse and bankruptcy 77–8, 156, 157, 176, 184, 192, 194
equilibrium thinking, shortcomings 132
equity tranche, CDOs 108
ESMA (European Securities and Markets Authority) 62–3, 73, 146, 199
ESRB (European Systemic Risk Board) 233
Estrella, Arturo 17, 31, 35, 38, 132, 165
euro debt crisis, liability of credit rating agencies 3–4
European Central Bank (ECB) 159, 173
European Rating Index 199
European Securities and Markets Authority (ESMA) 62–3, 73, 146, 199
European Systemic Risk Board (ESRB) 233
European Union (EU)
agency regulation and supervision model 72–5
Capital Requirement Directive, 2006 49
CRA Regulation of 2009 *see* CRA Regulation of 2009 on credit rating agencies
credit ratings issued outside the EU 74–5
insurance and reinsurance directives 50
liability regime for credit rating agencies
EU special liability regime 83–4
national liability regimes 79–83
regulatory reforms 4, 144–51, 197–202
withdrawal of rating-based regulations 62–3
evolution of credit rating industry
analyzing 26–8
evolving role of agencies in modern financial markets 6–9
origins 17–20
expert liability 82
External Credit Assessment Institutions (ECAIs) 47
external vs. internal credit ratings 30
Exxon 210

Fabozzi, Frank J 98, 105, 106, 107, 109, 131
Fair Isaac Corporation (FICO) 119
fair value accounting 187–8
FCIC (Federal Crisis Inquiry Commission) 213
Federal Crisis Inquiry Commission (FCIC) 213
Federal Register, US 60
Federal Reserve (Fed) 21
fees, shift from subscribers' to issuers' 24–5
Ferran, Eilís 233
Ferrucci, Gianluigi 163
FICO (Fair Isaac Corporation) 119
Fight, Andrew 23, 25
financial crises 13, 15, 26, 48, 189
  downgrades triggering 188
  and leading credit rating agencies (Big Three) 164–5
  system-relevance of credit ratings 157, 159, 164–5, 176
  see also financial crisis, 1837; global financial crisis (2007–2009); subprime mortgage crisis
financial disintermediation 96–7, 103, 163–4
financial engineering 99–100
financial information
  disclosure requirements 228–31
  embedded within credit ratings 31–2
  provided by credit ratings 37–9
financial institutions
  increasing leverage of 99–101, 102, 171
  losses sustained by 162
  and systemic risk 161
  see also banks
financial instruments
  complexity 28, 103, 135
  Credit Risk Transfer instruments, expansion 98–9
  novel, rating of *see* novel financial instruments
  Structured Investment Vehicles (SIVs) 100, 132–3
  and subprime mortgage crisis 105–11
  subprime mortgage crisis, at heart of 105–11
    see also subprime mortgage crisis
Financial Market Supervisory Authority (FINMA) 47, 49
Financial Stability Board (FSB), *Principles for Reducing Reliance on CRA Ratings, 2010* 156, 172, 174, 186, 234
Financial Stability Forum (FSF), *Report on Enhancing Market and Institutional Resilience* 52, 53, 56, 59, 135, 138
FINMA (Financial Market Supervisory Authority) 47, 49
Firla-Cuchra, Macij T 133
Fitch (leading credit rating agency) 3, 11, 29, 158
  dominance of 165, 166, 208, 209
  regulation and supervision 73, 74, 75
Fitch Publishing Company 18
Flannery, Mark J 232
Flinterman, Felix 73, 199
Flood, John 41, 42, 52, 97, 99, 124, 167, 208
fluctuations, financial 132
Foley, John 180
foreclosures 104
France, and Dodd-Frank Act, 2010 80–1
Franken, Senator Al/Franken amendment 88
fraud 78
free-rider problem 24
Froeba, Mark 212
Frost, Carol Ann 123, 183, 193, 222
FSF *see* Financial Stability Forum (FSF)

Gallu, Joshua 110
gatekeeper role of credit rating agencies 69, 76, 86, 103, 114
  failure in acting as gamekeepers 140
Geiger, Rainer 218
general-purpose credit rating agencies 52
Germany 81, 82

Gillen, David 8
global financial crisis (2007–2009) 102
ancillary business services 33
and background of credit rating industry 3, 5
Basel II Accord 10
"cliff effects" 186
conflicts of interest 147
housing bubble, bursting of in 2007 7–8
procyclicality 186, 187
regulation and supervision of credit rating agencies 66–7
self-regulation, merits and weaknesses 66
see also subprime mortgage crisis
Goldman Sachs 110–11, 125, 140
Goodman, Laurie S 98, 105, 106, 107, 109, 131
Gorton, Lars 66, 81, 123, 129, 148, 201
Granier, Thierry 88
Great Depression 69
Greek debt crisis 155, 173
and Moody's 158–9, 195
gridlock, market 163
Griffin, John M 35, 93, 132, 157, 226

Hafner, Wolfgang 26
Harold, Gilbert 15, 17, 18, 19, 20, 22
Harris, Milton 59
hedge funds 110, 134
Hein, Julia 133
Hendricks, Darryll 97, 98, 163
high ratings, effect 38, 57–9
High-Level Group on Financial Supervision, EU 33, 55, 102, 124, 169, 186
highly regulated entities 53
Hill, Claire A 7, 123
competition in credit rating industry 213
credit rating industry 33, 36
downgrades of credit ratings, reactions to 179, 183, 189–90
history of credit rating agencies 21, 26
rating-based regulations 51, 52, 62
structured finance segment, growth 95, 115
system-relevance of credit ratings 156, 157, 167, 175
Hirsch, Christian 37, 42
history of credit rating agencies
analyzing evolution of credit rating industry 26–8
between 1909 and 1930s
attitude of investors to credit ratings 18–19
emergence of first agencies 17–18
reputational capital, building 19–20
decreasing interest in credit rating agencies between 1930s and 1970s 20–3
doubts over accuracy and decline of investor confidence 21–3
enhanced profitability since the 1970s
expanding use of credit ratings in regulation 23–4
fees, shift from subscribers' to issuers' 24–5
rating of novel financial instruments 25–6
prior to 1907
dominance of informal channels and increasing need for credit information 13–14
mercantile agencies, creation 15–17
relevance to financial crises 13
home equity loans (HEL) 106
homogenization
credit rating of leading agencies as homogenizing factors 181–3
of information in financial markets 179–85
of market behavior 184–5
Hornig, Frank 157, 168, 195, 228
housing bubble, bursting of in 2007 7–8
Houston, Joel F 232
Hunt, John Patrick 6, 7, 60, 99, 114, 127, 174, 217, 227
credit rating industry 30, 31, 32

history of credit rating agencies 25, 26
hybrid CDOs 111

IKB Deutsche Industriebank 110
immunity from prosecution 78
inaccurate ratings 7–8
incentives, wrong (in rating industry) 45, 120–43, 214
absence of reputational constraints in rating structured products 126–8
alignment of incentives, need for 223–4
conflicts of interest
ancillary services 122–4
interferences between credit rating agencies and issuers 124–6
issuer-pays business model 120–2
deformation of incentives in credit rating industry 212–14
expansion of structured finance market 111–12
inflated ratings 58–9, 69, 128
lack of academic consensus 5
quantitative models, over-reliance on 129–34
regulation failure, revisiting incentive-based financial market regulations as response to 222–4
independence of CRAs, effect of loss 121, 124
industrialization, nineteenth century 14
inflated ratings 58–9, 69, 128, 188
information
access to 182
available, amount of 180–1
failure of 141
homogenization of in financial markets 179–85
as a public good 120
relevant, selection of 28, 180–1
see also information asymmetries
Information Age 180
information asymmetries 7, 15
exploitation of in market for securitized assets 137–43
financial information provision 37–8
information economics theory 120–1
information intermediaries, CRAs as 37–8, 96, 181
innovation, financial 105
insurance sector 18, 21
"too interconnected to fail" problem 162–3, 177
interest rates, and subprime mortgage crisis 102, 103
interest-only mortgages 106
Internal Ratings-Based (IRB) Approach 61
internal vs. external credit ratings 30
International Monetary Fund (IMF), *Global Financial Stability Report* 116
International Organization of Securities Commissions (IOSCO)
Code of Conduct 63–4, 66, 67, 72
Report of the Task Force on the Subprime Crisis 32, 47, 53, 113, 116, 136, 168
Report on the Activities of Credit Rating Agencies 29, 33, 34, 35, 36, 41, 47, 53, 56, 113, 123, 137, 168, 169, 175, 183
Role of Credit Rating Agencies in Structured Finance Markets 135, 228
International Securities Identifying Number (ISIN) 146
investigation costs, savings in 19
investment banks 141, 162, 190
and arbitrage 118–19
conflicts of interest 124–5, 126
see also banks; financial institutions
investment limitations 50
investment restrictions, regulatory 47, 49–51
investment-grade ratings 21, 30, 50, 68, 115
below-investment-grade bonds, accepting as collateral 173, 174
securities as collateral 177
and structured finance growth 112, 115, 116
see also speculative-grade ratings

investor-pays model 27, 120, 183, 223, 229, 230
  see also issuer-pays business model
IOSCO *see* International Organization of Securities Commissions (IOSCO)
IRB (Internal Ratings-Based) Approach 61
Ishmael, Stacy-Marie 79
ISIN (International Securities Identifying Number) 146
issuer-pays business model 81, 152, 169, 213
  conflicts of interest 120–2
  vs. investor-pays business model 27, 120, 183, 223, 229
issuers' fees, shift to 24–5

Jäckle, Joachim 38, 137
Jackson, Howell E 186, 217
Jarrow, Robert A
  downgrades of credit ratings, reactions to 191
  incentives, wrong (in rating industry) 122, 123, 129, 130, 133, 137
  and structured finance growth 52, 99, 102, 103, 105, 107, 109, 111
  system-relevance of credit ratings 162, 176
Jenny, Frederick 217
Jodar, Thomas 72
Johnson, Richard 192
Johnson, Simon 220
Jones, Sam 189, 211
"junior" tranches, CDOs 106, 107, 108
junk status 108, 159
  downgrading to 157–8, 171
Jurek, Jakob 94

Kambhu, John 97, 98, 160, 163
Kaufmann, Christine 49
Kauper, Thomas E 215
Kennedy, Simon 159, 173
Keteyian, Armen 120
Kleineman, Jan 123, 129, 148, 201
Knieps, Günter 219
Kolchinsky, Eric 58, 95, 212
Korporaal, Glenda 226
Kröger, Michael 195
Kroll Bond Rating Agency Inc 195
Krugman, Paul 141
Kuhner, Christoph 182

Lamy, Marie-Florence 187
leading credit rating agencies (Big Three)
  absence of reputational constraints in rating structured products 128
  abuse of dominant position, accusations of 165
  collective market power of 168–9
  competition distortions 207–14
  credit ratings of as homogenizing factor 181–3
  domination of rating industry 26, 165, 166, 198, 208, 218–19
  duopoly of Moody's and Standard & Poor's 75
  exacerbation of financial crises 164–5
  favorable ratings of 114
  high concentration in credit rating industry 166
  homogenization of market behavior 184–5
  inflated ratings of *see* inflated ratings
  issuer-pays business model 122
  market behavior 209
  market over-dependence on 169–78
  over-reliance on 169–78, 180
  profit margins 209–10, 236
  reforms, effect on 202
  reluctance to downgrade 122, 159, 184, 191–6
  vs. smaller agencies 179
  spillover effects of downgrades by 189–91, 202
  and structured finance growth 94–5, 113
  and subprime mortgage crisis 3, 101–2, 103, 157–8
  surveillance teams 37
  as "too big to downgrade" 195
  worldwide operation 6

see also credit rating agencies (CRAs); Fitch (leading credit rating agency); Moody's (leading credit rating agency); oligopoly, in credit rating industry; Standard & Poor's (leading credit rating agency)
Lehman Brothers, bankruptcy of 156, 157, 184, 195
"lemons problem," in financial markets 137–8, 139, 140, 141, 143
leverage of financial institutions, increasing 99–101, 102, 171
leverage ratio, recommendation for 234–5
Levich, Richard M 8
Levin, Carl 94
Lewis, Michael 95, 106, 109, 118, 119, 126, 132, 134, 191
liability regime for credit rating agencies *see* civil liability regime for credit rating agencies, burden of proof 84
"licenses, regulatory" 27, 39, 86, 214
Lieberman, Joseph I 8
Likosky, Michael B 124
liquidity 132
crises 138, 141, 163, 173–4
as elusive and slippery concept 104, 164
and subprime mortgage crisis 102, 103, 104
Lombardini, Carlo 47
Lowenstein, Roger 94
Lucas, Douglas J. 98, 105, 106, 107, 109, 131
Lumpkin, Stephen 97, 99
Lyman, Peter 180
Lynch, Timothy E 15, 121, 176

MacDonald Wakeman, Lee 13
Macey, Jonathan R 27, 41, 51, 59, 137, 185
macroprudential approach, requirement for 172, 187, 188–9, 222–3
Madison, James H 14, 15, 16
Mainguy, Daniel 218
Majnoni, Giovanni 13
Manns, Jeffrey 52
Mansi, Sattar A 156, 189, 193
Marini, Philippe 81
market failure, antitrust laws as response to 220–2
market-based financial system
financial disintermediation 163–4
prominence of credit rating agencies in 39
transfer from bank-based 96–8
markets, financial
failure to adapt rating models to new market trends 129–30
homogenization of market behavior 184–5
"lemons problem" 137–8, 139, 140, 143
over-reliance on credit ratings industry 54–7, 134–7, 169–78
procyclicality 186–9
rating-driven behavior 57–9
securitized assets 137–43
mark-to-market asset valuation 187
mathematical models 35
Mathis, Jérôme 3, 58, 169
MBS *see* Mortgage-Backed Securities (MBS)
McAndrews, James 3, 58, 169
McVea, Harry 65, 73, 102, 222
medium-term note programs 31
Meier, Heinz 11, 49
mercantile agencies, creation 15–17
Mercantile Agency 15
merger control 219–20
"mezzanine" tranches, CDOs 106, 107, 108
Michalek, Richard 212
Microsoft 210
migration policy, credit reference agencies 193–4
Milbourn, Todd 208
Moloney, Niamh 65, 122
monitoring tools, credit ratings as 41–2
Monte Carlo simulation 35
Monti, Giorgio 215
Moody, John 17, 21

Moody's (leading credit rating agency) 3, 11, 26, 29, 68, 155, 158
dominance of 165, 166, 198, 208, 209
and emergence of first credit rating agencies 17–18
and Greek debt crisis 158–9, 195
profit margins 210
regulation and supervision 74, 75
and subprime mortgage crisis 104
subsidiaries of 73
triple-A ratings of 210–11, 213
"Watchlist" 42
Morgan Stanley 134
Morgenson, Gretchen 3, 20, 33, 116, 125, 210, 211
Morningstar Credit Ratings LLC 195
Mortgage-Backed Securities (MBS) 103, 113
see also Residential Mortgage-Backed Securities (RMBS); subprime mortgage crisis
mortgage-related securities 3, 7, 110, 127, 135, 136, 152, 172
ceasing to trade in 141–2
downgrades to junk status 157–8, 171
incorrect rating of 42, 93, 94, 190
and subprime mortgage crisis 157–8
see also Asset-Backed Securities (ABS); Mortgage-Backed Securities (MBS); Residential Mortgage-Backed Securities (RMBS); subprime mortgage crisis
Mosser, Patricia 97, 98, 163
municipal bonds 31
Murphy, Austin 100, 132, 160, 162

national liability regimes, EU 79–83
Nationally Recognized Statistical Rating Organizations (NRSROs) 23, 71, 89, 173, 198, 201
conflicts of interest 147
decreased reliance on 60, 61
disclosure requirements 145
examinations of 150
rating-based regulations 46, 59, 60
registration and qualification process 68
new business segments, bank reliance on 97
New Century (subprime lender) 104
New York, CRAs in (prior to 1907) 15
Nocera, Joe 118, 162, 177
novel financial instruments 95, 102, 128
historical aspects 25–6
and subprime mortgage crisis 104–5, 126–7
NRSROs (Nationally Recognized Statistical Rating Organizations) *see* Nationally Recognized Statistical Rating Organizations (NRSROs)

Obama, Barack 61
OCR (Office of Credit Ratings), SEC 70
off-balance sheet activities 100, 111
Office of Credit Ratings (OCR), SEC 70, 89, 150
Office of the Comptroller of the Currency 20, 21
oligopoly, in credit rating industry 166, 215, 224
barriers to entering credit rating industry 167–8
collective market power of leading agencies 168–9
of leading credit rating agencies (Big Three) 165, 166, 198, 207, 218–19
market structure 208–10
system-relevance of credit ratings 165–9
see also competition in credit rating industry; leading credit rating agencies (Big Three)
Oncu, Sabri 3
opaque market
securitized assets 96, 137, 139, 142, 145, 152
see also transparency, lack of
opinions, homogenization of 182
Opp, Christian C 58
Opp, Marcus M 58

"originate-and-distribute" financial intermediation model 102, 132, 138–9
Other Structured Finance Instruments (OTH) 146
overcollateralization, credit enhancement 107
over-reliance on credit ratings industry 4, 8, 94
AIFMs Directive, amendment proposals 63
behavioral reliance 136–7, 165, 174–8
collateral policy of central banks 172–4
"collateral triggers" in contracting, rating-dependent 176–8
competition distortions, rating-based regulations 54–7
Credit Rating Agency Reform Act, 2006 197–8
dependence on rating models for valuation purposes 133–4
market over-reliance 54–7, 134–7, 169–78
quantitative models 129–34
"rating triggers" in contracting 40, 175–6
rating-based regulations 55–6, 57, 170–2
reducing 197–9, 237
see also Principles for Reducing Reliance on CRA Ratings, 2010 (FSB)
regulatory reliance 56–7, 136–7, 170–4
in structured finance segment 134–7
trend to reduce regulatory dependence on credit ratings 59–61
triple-A ratings 54–5
UCITS Directive, amendment proposals 63

Packer, Frank 21, 24, 217
Parliament, EU 200
Partnoy, Frank 3–4, 8, 9, 71, 172, 184
competition in credit rating industry 209, 214, 216, 220, 232
credit rating industry 39, 40
history of credit rating agencies 17, 18, 19, 22, 24, 27
incentives, wrong (in rating industry) 121, 123, 126, 136, 140
rating-based regulations 45, 46, 51, 55, 59, 60, 62
regulatory response to problems of structured finance ratings 145
regulatory treatment of credit rating agencies 76, 78, 79
structured finance segment 93, 99–100, 110, 115, 116
system-relevance of credit ratings 155, 171, 173
Paulson & Co (hedge fund) 110, 140
Penn Cental, default of 24
pension funds 21
Perez, Evan 110, 140
Persaud, Avinash 164
Petit, Nicolas 221
Pinches, George E 22
Pinto, Arthur R. 24, 53, 167, 168
"point-in-time" perspectives 193
Poon, Ser-Huang 133
Poor, Henry Varnum 16
Publishing Company 18
see also Standard & Poor's (leading credit rating agency)
preferred stock 31
preliminary ratings 71
price fixing 215, 218, 220
see also inflated ratings
prices, quasi-monopoly 53
Prince, Charles O 101
principal-agent problem, issuer-pays business model 121
Principles for Reducing Reliance on CRA Ratings, 2010 (FSB) 172, 174, 186, 234
private offerings, vs. public offerings 230
private placements 31
privileged treatment of credit rating industry 23, 45, 56, 76, 182

historically privileged position, in US 77–8
procyclicality 163, 186–9
profit margins 209–10, 236
prospectus liability 82
public offerings, vs. private offerings 230
public sector, sovereign ratings attributed to entries in 32
Pulliam, Susan 110, 140

qualitative easing 174
quality, CRAs not acting as certifiers of 138
quantitative easing 174
quantitative models, over-reliance on 129–34
dependence on rating models for valuation purposes 133–4
failure to adapt rating models to new market trends 129–30
flaws in rating models 130–3
quasi-contractual liability 81, 82
quasi-governmental function of credit rating agencies 8, 45–6, 214, 224
Quinn, Brian JM 107, 109, 138, 139, 177

"race to the bottom," rating standards 59, 68, 122, 127, 152
competition in credit rating industry 214, 215, 225
railroad corporations, US 14, 16
Raiter, Frank L 122
rating analysts, qualifications and independence 71, 149–50
rating announcements 165, 179, 189
rating arbitrage, and regulatory arbitrage 117–19
rating committees 34
rating methodologies 71
rating process
initial credit ratings, providing 34–6
reviewing credit ratings 36–7
rating scales 30, 114
"rating shopping" 57, 58–9, 124–5, 216, 225
in run-up to subprime mortgage crisis 211–12
"rating triggers," in contracting 40, 175–6
rating-based regulations *see* regulations, rating-based
rating-driven behavior
competition distortions, rating-based regulations 57–9
structured finance, proliferation of transactions 116–17
Ratings in Structured Finance (CGFS) 30, 129, 130, 131, 132, 191, 227, 229
Reason, Tim 176, 194
reforms, regulatory 144–51, 197–202
as catalyst for change in rating industry 4–5
comparing US and EU approaches 201–2
conflicts of interest 147–9
disclosure requirements 145–7
qualifications and independence of rating analysts 149–50
reducing over-reliance on credit ratings 197–9
road ahead 5, 224–35
sovereign debt ratings, regulating 199–201
supervisory sanctions 150–1
symbology 144–5
regulation
credit ratings as regulatory tools 39–40
expanding use of credit ratings in 23–4
failure of 222–4
first uses of credit ratings in 20–1
sector-specific 12, 52, 217–20, 222
self-regulation 64–6
sovereign ratings 199–201
and supervision 66–7
in European Union 72–5
in United States 68–72
see also regulatory treatment of credit rating agencies
regulations, rating-based 8–9, 45–63, 194, 197, 224, 227

bank capital requirement 48–9
certified credit ratings, depending on 46–51
competition distortions 51–9
EU model for regulation and supervision 73
over-reliance on credit ratings industry 55–6
procyclicality 188–9
regulatory investment restrictions 49–51
regulatory reliance on credit ratings 170–2
slow evolution prior to 1970s 21
subscribers' fees, shift to issuers' 24–5
system-relevance of credit ratings 170, 171
withdrawal 86, 90
Dodd-Frank Wall Street Reform and Consumer Protection Act, 2010 11, 61–2
EU proposals 62–3
rating-driven behavior 58
reduction of regulatory dependence on credit ratings 59–61
regulatory advantage of credit rating agencies 45
regulatory arbitrage 57, 117–19
"regulatory licenses" 27, 39, 86, 214
regulatory reliance on credit ratings 56–7
and behavioral reliance 136–7, 194
collateral policy of central banks 172–4
rating-based regulations 170–2
regulatory treatment of credit rating agencies 64–84
EU model for regulation and supervision 72–5
liability regimes 76–84
oversight of credit rating industry 64–75
strengthening 68–75
privileged treatment of credit rating industry *see* privileged treatment of credit rating industry
self-regulation 64–6
US liability regime for credit rating agencies 77–9
Dodd-Frank Wall Street Reform and Consumer Protection Act, 2010 78–9
historically privileged position of credit rating agencies 77–8
US model for regulation and supervision
Credit Rating Agency Reform Act, 2006 68–9
Dodd-Frank Wall Street Reform and Consumer Protection Act, 2010 69–72
regulatory trends 85–90
practical importance of credit rating agency reforms 85–90
Reinhart, Carmen 13
Report of the Task Force on the Subprime Crisis (IOSCO) 32, 47, 53, 113, 116, 136, 168
Report on Enhancing Market and Institutional Resilience (FSF) 52, 53, 56, 59, 135, 138
Report on the Activities of Credit Rating Agencies (IOSCO) 29, 33, 34, 35, 36, 41, 47, 53, 56, 113, 123, 137, 168, 169, 175, 183
reputational capital 216
building 19–20
defined 126
reputational constraints, absence of in rating structured products 126–8
Residential Mortgage-Backed Securities (RMBS) 7, 102, 158
see also Mortgage-Backed Securities (MBS); mortgage-related securities
Respaud, Jean-Louis 218
"reverse-engineering" 125
review of credit ratings 36–7
Reynolds, Glenn L 175
Rijken, Herbert A 193, 194
risks
concentration of 190
liquidity 132
in market-based financial system 98

regulatory capital, risk-sensitive measures 47, 60–1, 170–1
risk-weighted capital ratios of banks, prior to subprime mortgage crisis 54, 112, 170, 171
spreading of 161
systemic 112, 132, 160–5
"too big to fail" problem 161
see also Credit Risk Transfer (CRT) instruments
risk-sensitive capital requirements 47, 170–1
abandoning measurement of 60–1
RMBS (Residential Mortgage-Backed Securities) *see* Residential Mortgage-Backed Securities (RMBS)
Rochet, Jean-Charles 3, 58, 169
Rosner, Joshua 34, 36, 59, 69, 78, 95, 115, 118, 129, 232
Rousseau, Stéphane 67, 216, 227, 229
Routier, Richard 175
rumors, disrupting effects of 183
Ryan, John 198

sanctions, supervisory 150–1
Saunders, Anthony 189
scandals, corporate 8, 156–7
Schuermann, Til 107, 129, 130, 131, 161
Schwarcz, Steven L 6, 67
competition in credit rating industry 216
credit rating industry 37, 38
incentives, wrong (in rating industry) 138, 141
rating-based regulations 47, 53
structured finance segment 96, 101, 102
system-relevance of credit ratings 160, 167
Scott, Kathleen A 160
sector-specific regulation 12, 52, 222
and competition 217–20
Securities and Exchange Commission (SEC) 69, 110
and Nationally Recognized Statistical Rating Organizations 23, 60, 68, 71, 145, 198
Office of Credit Ratings 70, 89, 150
securities fraud 78
securitizations/securitized assets
credit ratings as marketing tool for 114–16
definition of securitizations 50
dependence on rating models for valuation purposes 133–4
downgrading of 104
and expansion of Credit Risk Transfer instruments 98–9
exploitation of information asymmetry in market for 137–43
lower-quality mortgage loans 105
opaque market 96, 137, 139, 142, 145, 152
and structured finance growth 114–16
and subprime mortgage crisis 98–9, 102, 104, 105–6, 189
Segal, David 87, 214
Seitzinger, Michael V 157, 179, 184, 195
self-regulation
in credit rating industry 64–5
merits and weaknesses 65–6
"senior" tranches, CDOs 106, 107, 108, 116, 132
biggest losses from 104, 132, 142
"super senior" 118
shadow banking system 142
Shakespeare, Catherine 37, 38, 41, 209
Shamir, Adam 72
shelf registrations 31
Shin, Hyun Song 163
shocks, financial 160, 163, 192
Shorter, Gary 157, 179, 184, 195
signaling effects, credit rating downgrades 183–4
Sinclair, Timothy J 21, 30, 35, 36, 37, 38, 42, 86
SIVs (Structured Investment Vehicles) 100, 132–3
Soliman, Mark T 37, 38, 41, 209
Sorkin, Andrew R 88, 101, 141

sovereign ratings 31, 32, 71
regulation 199–201
and systemic importance of credit ratings 158–9
special liability regime, EU 83–4
Special Purpose Vehicle (SPV) 108
speculative-grade ratings 21, 30, 50
and structured finance growth 112, 115
see also investment-grade ratings
spillover effects by leading agencies 128, 189–91, 202
spread, excess 107
SPV (Special Purpose Vehicle) 108
stability, financial
rating of stability 193–4
and systemic risk 160–5
see also Financial Stability Board (FSB); Financial Stability Forum (FSF)
Stafford, Erik 94
Standard & Poor's (leading credit rating agency) 3, 11, 26, 29, 68, 158
court action against 226
"CreditWatch" 42
dominance of 166, 198, 208, 209
downgrades by 200, 202
formation, 1941 18
rating scale 30
regulation and supervision 73, 74, 75
and subprime mortgage crisis 104
Standard Statistics Company 18
Standardized Approach, Basel framework 53, 100–1, 112, 170, 234
Story, Louise 33, 116, 125, 211
structured finance segment
absence of reputational constraints in rating structured products 126–8
arbitrage, regulatory and rating 117–19
conflicts of interest in 103, 147–9
credit rating agencies, key position 113–14
credit ratings as marketing tool for securitized assets 114–16
dependence on rating models in 135
estimate of recovery rates 32
financial institutions, increasing leverage of 99–101, 102
financial market context
from bank-based to market-based financial system 96–8
expansion of Credit Risk Transfer instruments 98–9
increasing leverage of financial institutions 99–101, 102, 171
growth 93–119
crucial role played by credit rating agencies 113–17
over-reliance on credit ratings in 134–7
plain vanilla corporate bonds vs. structured finance products 229
qualifications and independence of rating analysts 71, 149–50
rating flaws 152
rating-driven transactions, proliferation 116–17
regulatory incentives to expansion of 111–12
regulatory response to problems 144–52
conflicts of interest 147–9
disclosure requirements 145–7
preliminary conclusions 151–2
qualifications and independence of rating analysts 71, 149–50
supervisory sanctions 150–1
structured finance ratings 31–2, 93–6
subprime mortgage crisis *see* subprime mortgage crisis
symbology 144–5
triple-A ratings 71
Structured Investment Vehicles (SIVs) 100, 132–3
subordination, credit enhancement 107
subprime mortgage crisis 42, 98, 101, 132, 136, 158, 162, 191
Alt-A loans 105–6
and Collateral Debt Obligations 102, 104
credit rating agencies in run-up to 210–12
default rates 103–4

events at core of meltdown 101–5, 128, 189
failure to anticipate 129, 130
financial instruments at heart of 105–11
high risk-weighted capital ratios of banks, prior to 54, 112, 170, 171
housing bubble, bursting of in 2007 7–8
and interest rates 102, 103
and leading credit rating agencies (Big Three) 3, 101–2, 103, 157–8
and liquidity 102, 103, 104
and mortgage-related securities 157–8
and novel financial instruments 104–5, 126–7
and securitizations 98–9, 102, 104, 105–6, 189
subprime loans 105–6
uncreditworthy borrowers 103, 106
see also Asset-Backed Securities (ABS); global financial crisis (2007–2009); mortgage-related securities; Residential Mortgage-Backed Securities (RMBS)
subscribers' fees, shift to issuers' 24–5
Supreme Court, United States 77
surveillance teams, leading CRAs 37
Switzerland
Capital Adequacy Ordinance, 2006 49, 235
credit rating regulation in 10–11, 47
Sy, Amadou NR 156, 172, 186, 189
Sylla, Richard 13, 14, 15
synthetic CDOs 95, 125, 140, 141, 162, 211, 226
credit rating agencies, role in growth of structured finance 113, 116, 117
and structured finance growth 116–17, 117, 118
and subprime mortgage crisis 108–9, 110, 111
triple-A ratings 134
see also Collateral Debt Obligations (CDOs)
systemic issue, regulatory responses 197–203
comparing US and EU approaches 201–2
preliminary conclusions 202–3
reducing over-reliance on credit ratings 197–9, 233–5
sovereign ratings, regulating 199–201
US and EU regulatory reforms 197–202
systemic risk, and financial stability 160–5
system-relevance of credit ratings 155–78
credit rating oligopoly 165–9
barriers to entering credit rating industry 167–8
collective market power of leading agencies 168–9
high concentration in credit rating industry 166
financial stability and systemic risk 160–5
regulatory reliance on credit ratings 170–4
collateral policy of central banks 172–4
rating-based regulations 170–2
regulatory response to 197–203
systemic importance of ratings in modern financial markets 155–60

TALF (Term Auction Lending Facility) plan 60, 173
Tang, Dragon Yongjun 35, 93, 132, 157, 226
Tappan, Lewis 15
Tchotourian, Ivan 80
Term Auction Lending Facility (TALF) plan 60, 173
Thépot, Cécile 80
"through-the-cycle" methodologies 193
tort, liability in 81, 82, 83

Totaro, Lorenzo 159, 173
transparency
disclosure requirements 145, 146
lack of 96, 114, 142, 182, 228
reform proposals 199
see also opaque market
triple-A ratings 30, 58, 71
and arbitrage 117, 118
incentives, wrong (in rating industry) 124–5, 126
market over-reliance on ratings 54–5
of Moody's 210–11, 213
and over-priced assets 139
rating-based regulations 170
of Standard & Poor's 225
and structured finance growth 115, 116
symbology 144–5
of synthetic CDOs 134
triple-B ratings 21
trust, credit rating agencies' position of 81, 83
Turnbull, Stuart M
downgrades of credit ratings, reactions to 191
and incentives, wrong (in rating industry) 111, 122, 123, 129, 130, 133, 137
and structured finance growth 52, 99, 102, 103, 105, 107, 109
system-relevance of credit ratings 162, 176
Turner, Lynn E 100

UBS (Swiss bank) 117, 118, 235
UCITS (Undertakings for Collective Investment in Transferable Securities) Directive *see* Undertakings for Collective Investment in Transferable Securities (UCITs) Directive
uncreditworthy borrowers 191, 103, 106
Undertakings for Collective Investment in Transferable Securities (UCITs) Directive, amendment proposals 63
underwriting standards 104
United Kingdom (UK) 83
United States (US)
agency regulation and supervision model
Credit Rating Agency Reform Act, 2006 68–9
Dodd-Frank Wall Street Reform and Consumer Protection Act, 2010 69–72
Constitution, First Amendment 77–8
deregulation in 223
Dodd-Frank Wall Street Reform and Consumer Protection Act, 2010 *see* Dodd-Frank Wall Street Reform and Consumer Protection Act, 2010
liability regime for credit rating agencies
Dodd-Frank Wall Street Reform and Consumer Protection Act, 2010 78–9
historically privileged position of credit rating agencies 77–8
Nationally Recognized Statistical Rating Organizations *see* Nationally Recognized Statistical Rating Organization (NRSROs)
regulatory reforms 4, 144–51, 197–202
US-based agencies, widespread importance 10–11
withdrawal of rating-based regulations 11, 61–2

valuation, dependence on rating models for purposes of 133–4
Van Duyn, Aline 213, 224
Varian, Hal R 180
Vasella, David 81
Verständig, Aron 66, 81
Vohs, Kathleen D 180
volatility 164

Wall Street banks 109–10, 111, 125–6

Weber, Rolf H 48, 49, 65, 67, 100, 112, 123, 148, 149, 150, 160, 180, 187
Wehinger, Gert 226
Wellink, Nout 48, 55, 58, 60
West, Richard R 18, 21
Westbrook, Jesse 110
Whalen, Christopher R 98, 111, 117, 141, 162, 230
White, J DuPratt 137
White, Lawrence J 3, 20, 87, 120, 165, 215
  credit rating industry 30, 40
  rating-based regulations 46, 53, 59
Wood, Philip R 129
WorldCom, collapse and bankruptcy 156, 157, 184
Wutkowsky, Karey 127

Younglai, Rachelle 127
Yukawa, Shin 125

Zaki, Myret 118
Zimmermann, Heinz 26